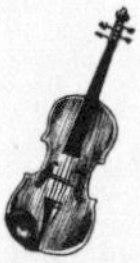

Your Lie in April

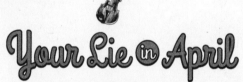

I met the girl
under full-bloomed cherry blossoms,
and my fate has begun to change.

6

Naoshi Arakawa

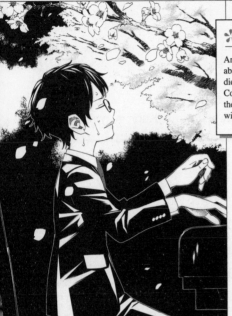

Kōsei Arima

An ex-piano prodigy who lost his ability to play when his mother died. He played in the Maihō Music Competition but was eliminated after the first round. He will be performing with Kaori again in a gala concert!

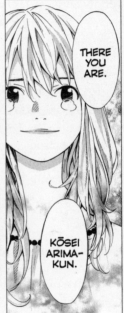

THERE YOU ARE.
KŌSEI ARIMA-KUN.

Kaori Miyazono

A violinist who is overwhelmingly unique. She was invited to play in the Tōwa Hall gala concert at the recommendation of the sponsor.

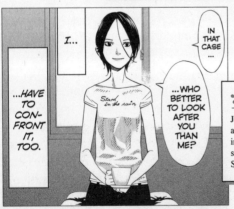

Hiroko Seto

Japan's leading pianist. She agreed to be Kōsei's piano instructor. She went to music school with Kōsei's mother, Saki Arima.

IN THAT CASE...
...WHO BETTER TO LOOK AFTER YOU THAN ME?
I...
...HAVE TO CONFRONT IT, TOO.
Stand in the rain

✤ STORY & CHARACTERS ✤

When his mother died in the autumn of his twelfth year, piano prodigy Kōsei Arima lost his ability to play. He lost his purpose, and his days lost all color, continuing on in a drab monotone. But then, in the spring when he was fourteen, he met the quirky violinist Kaori Miyazono.

As the boy spent time with the sharp-tongued but very talented girl, his gray days began to fill with color.

Then came the Tōwa Music Competition, where he performed as Kaori's accompanist. Kōsei overcame his inability to hear the music and gave a masterful performance, after which the audience showered them with applause.

Little by little, Kōsei's feelings for music grew within him. Kaori seemed to sense this and told him to participate in the Maihō Music Competition. This was his first competition in three years, and his former rivals, having improved their own skills, awaited him eagerly.

Takeshi Aiza delivered a powerful yet sensitive performance, and Emi Igawa entrusted her intense emotions fully to the music. With his rivals playing at the highest level, Kōsei's turn drew near. Although he played his prelude precisely, when his mother's ghost appeared, Kōsei sank into a soundless darkness.

However, from the bottom of the gloom, the boy saw a light. "I know. I'll play for you." With Kaori on his mind, Kōsei's fingers started moving again. His music was transformed, and his bewildered listeners were captivated...

Kōsei was eliminated from the competition after the first round. With the pain of defeat in his heart, the boy resolved to face the piano again. He apprenticed himself to his mother's friend Hiroko Seto. Kōsei joined forces with Kaori and began to practice for the Tōwa Music Competition's commemorative gala concert!

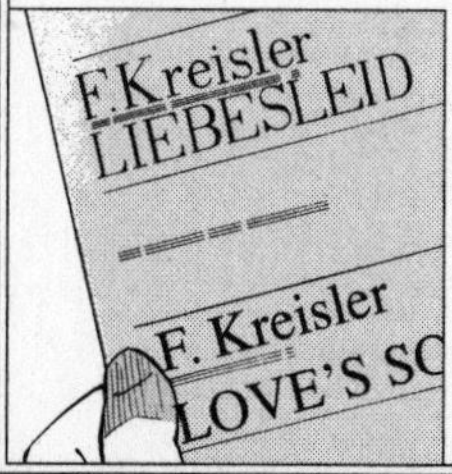

contents

Chapter 21: Candied Apple

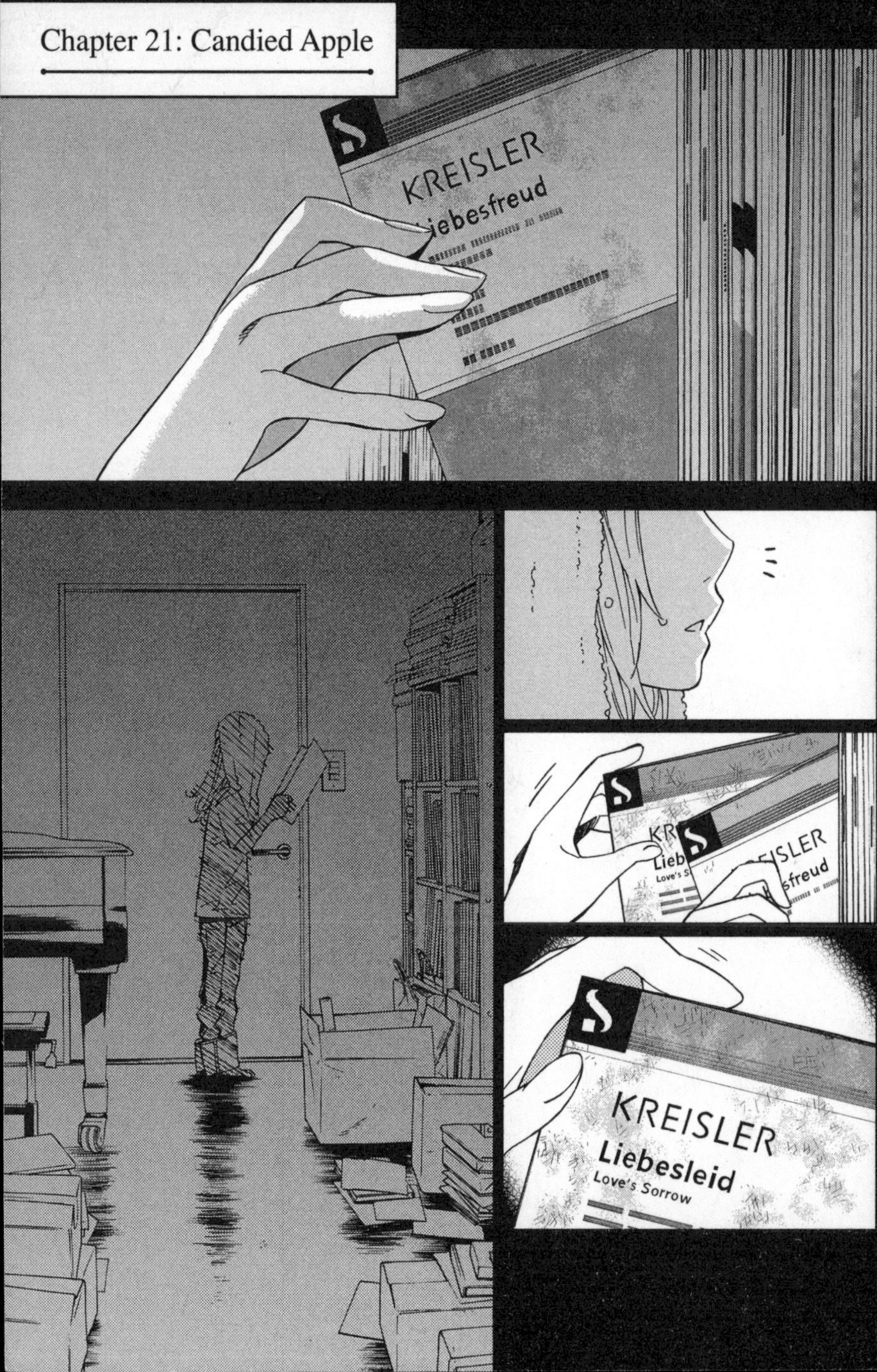
KREISLER
Liebesfreud
KREISLER
Liebesleid
Love's Sorrow

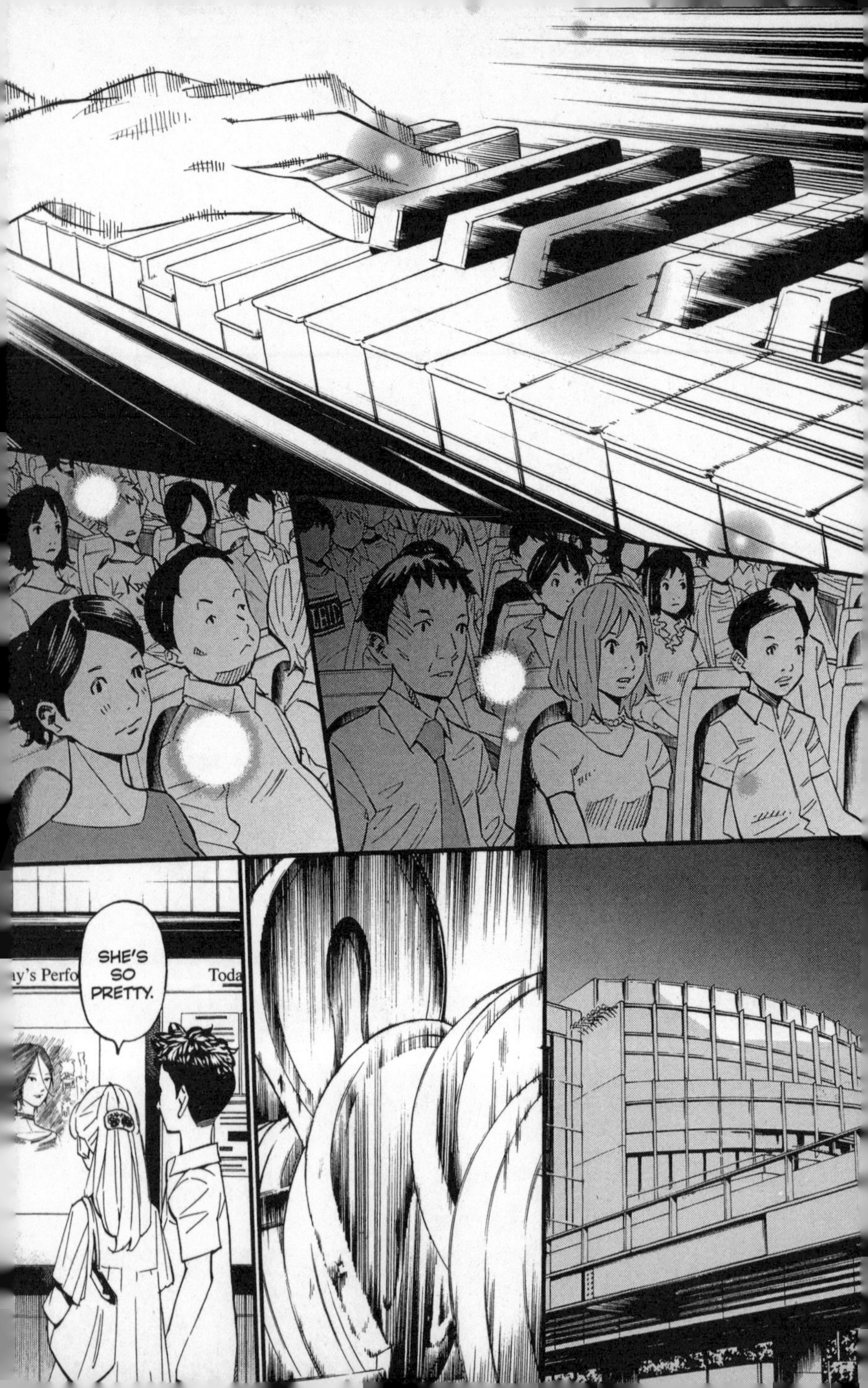
Toda
SHE'S SO PRETTY.
ay's Perfo

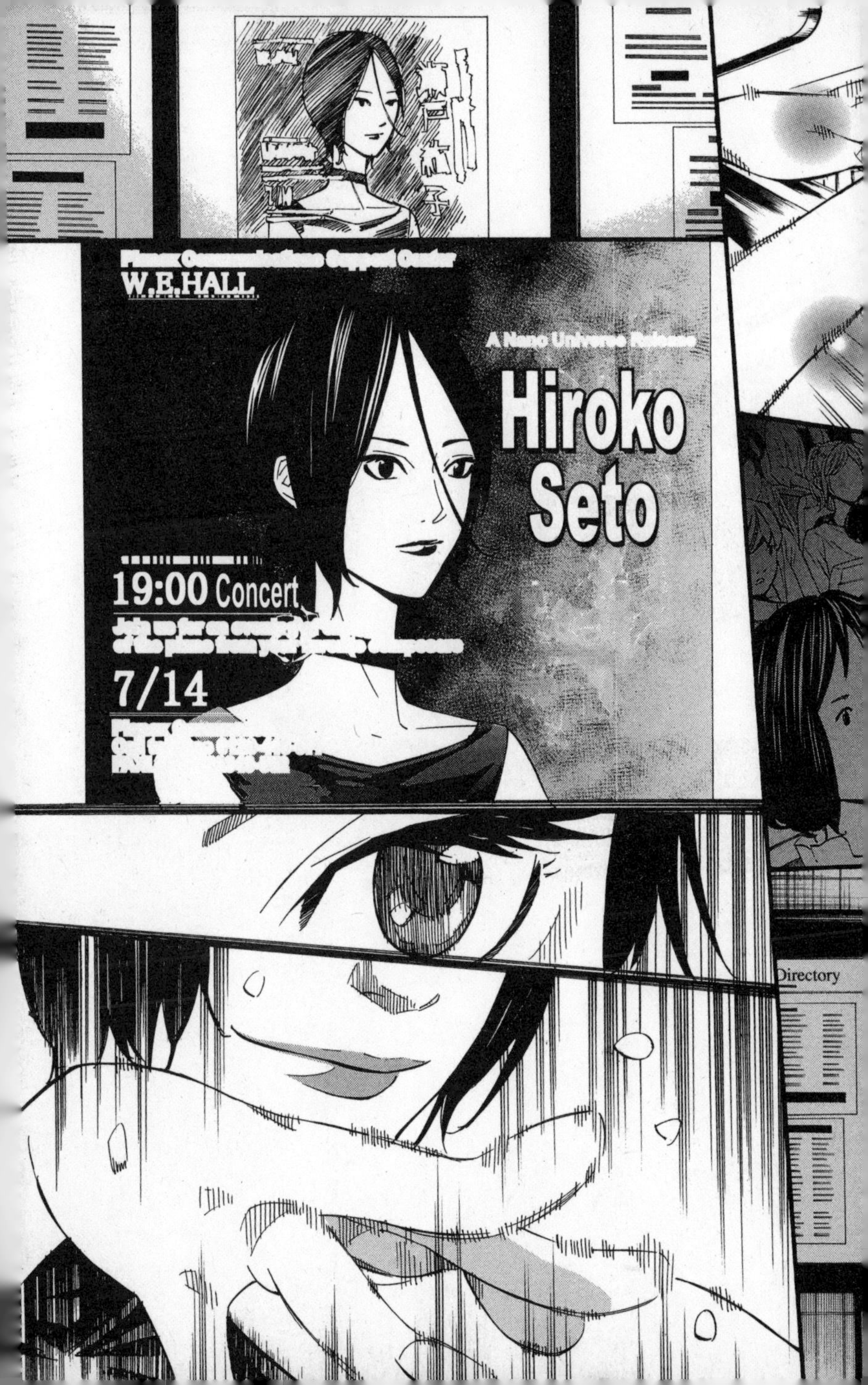
W.E.HALL
A Nano Universe Release
Hiroko Seto
19:00 Concert
7/14
Directory

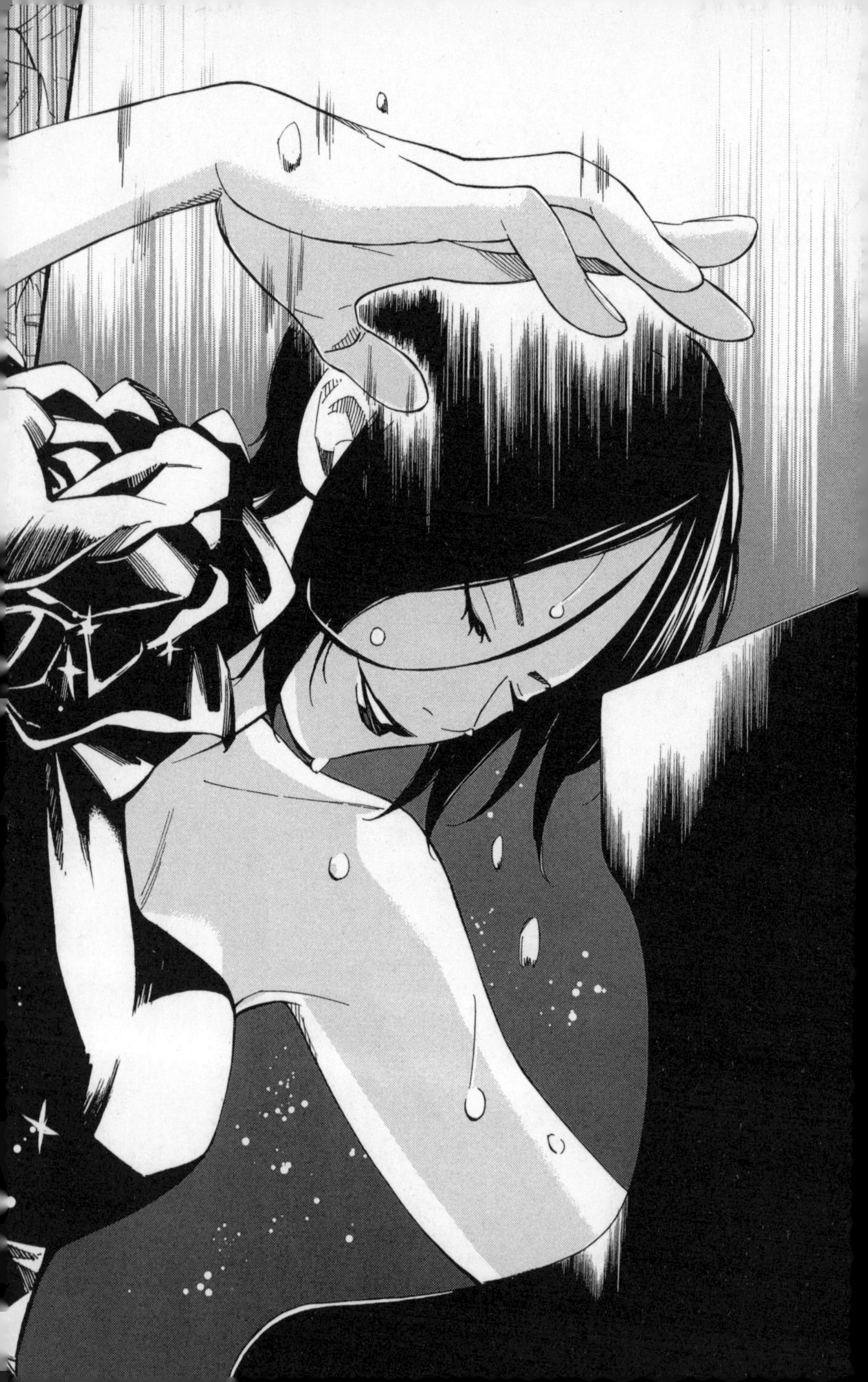

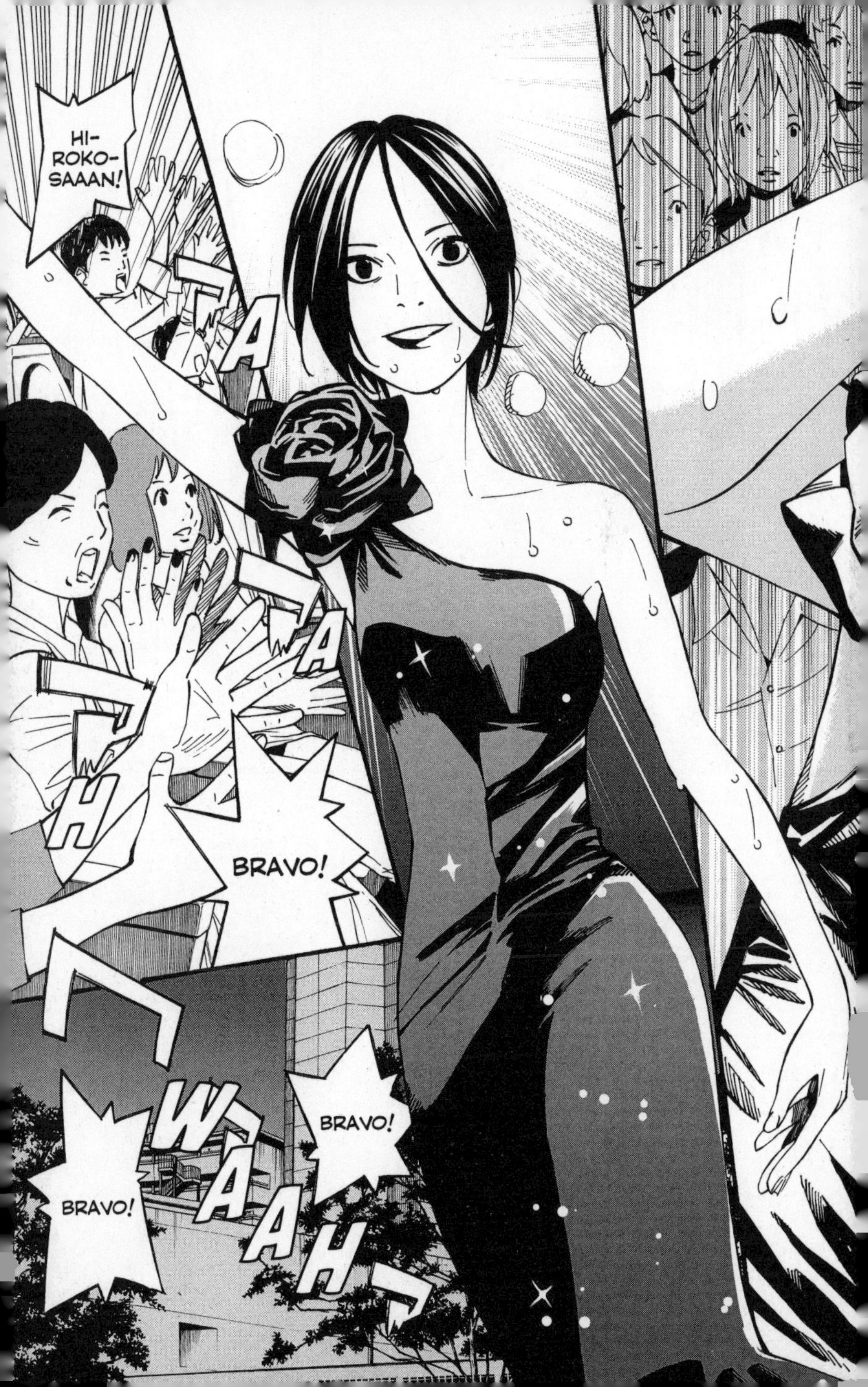
HI-ROKO-SAAAN!
BRAVO!
BRAVO!
BRAVO!
WAAAH

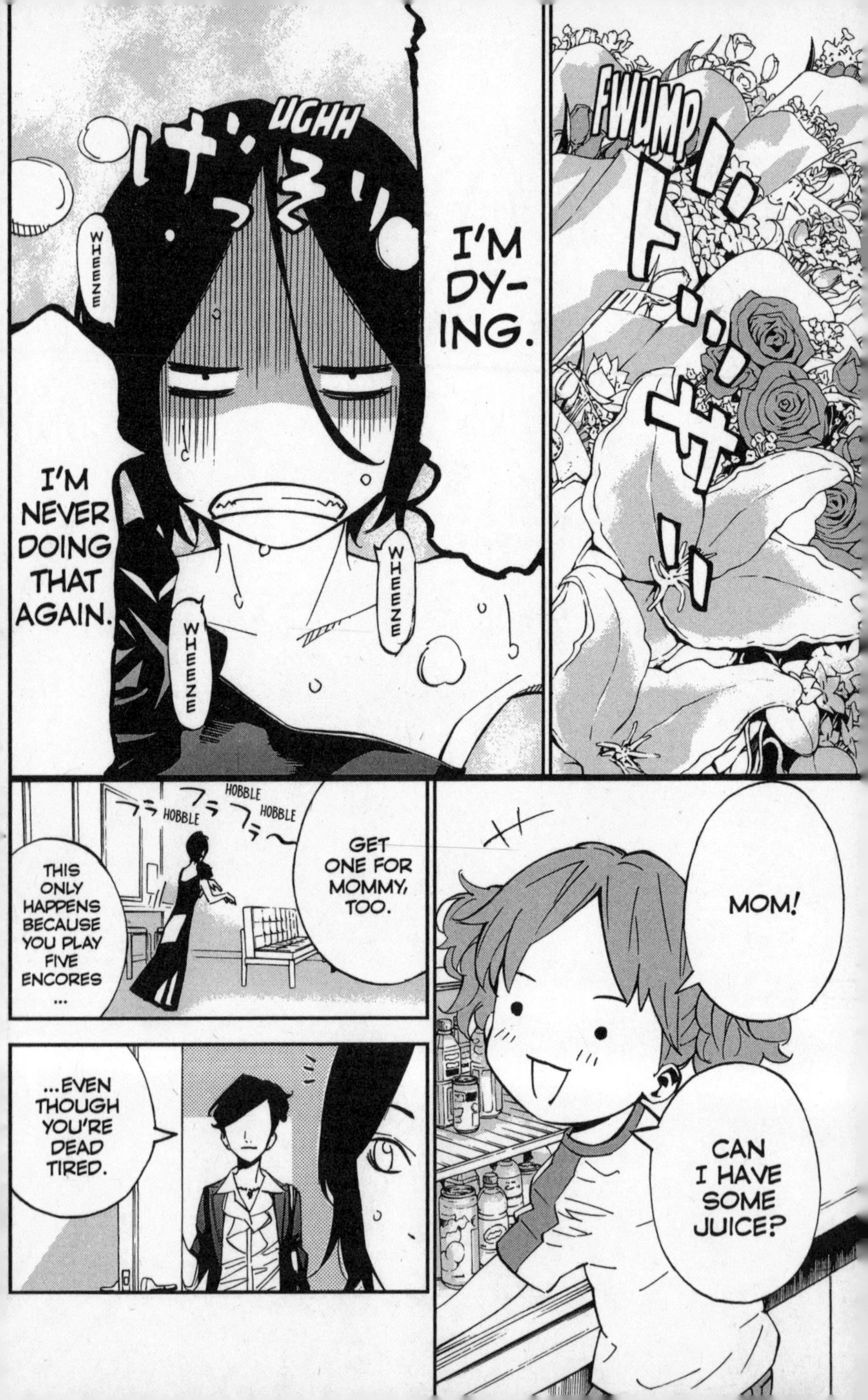
FWUMP
UGHH
WHEEZE
I'M DY-ING.
WHEEZE
WHEEZE
I'M NEVER DOING THAT AGAIN.
MOM!
CAN I HAVE SOME JUICE?
GET ONE FOR MOMMY, TOO.
HOBBLE HOBBLE HOBBLE
THIS ONLY HAPPENS BECAUSE YOU PLAY FIVE ENCORES ...
...EVEN THOUGH YOU'RE DEAD TIRED.

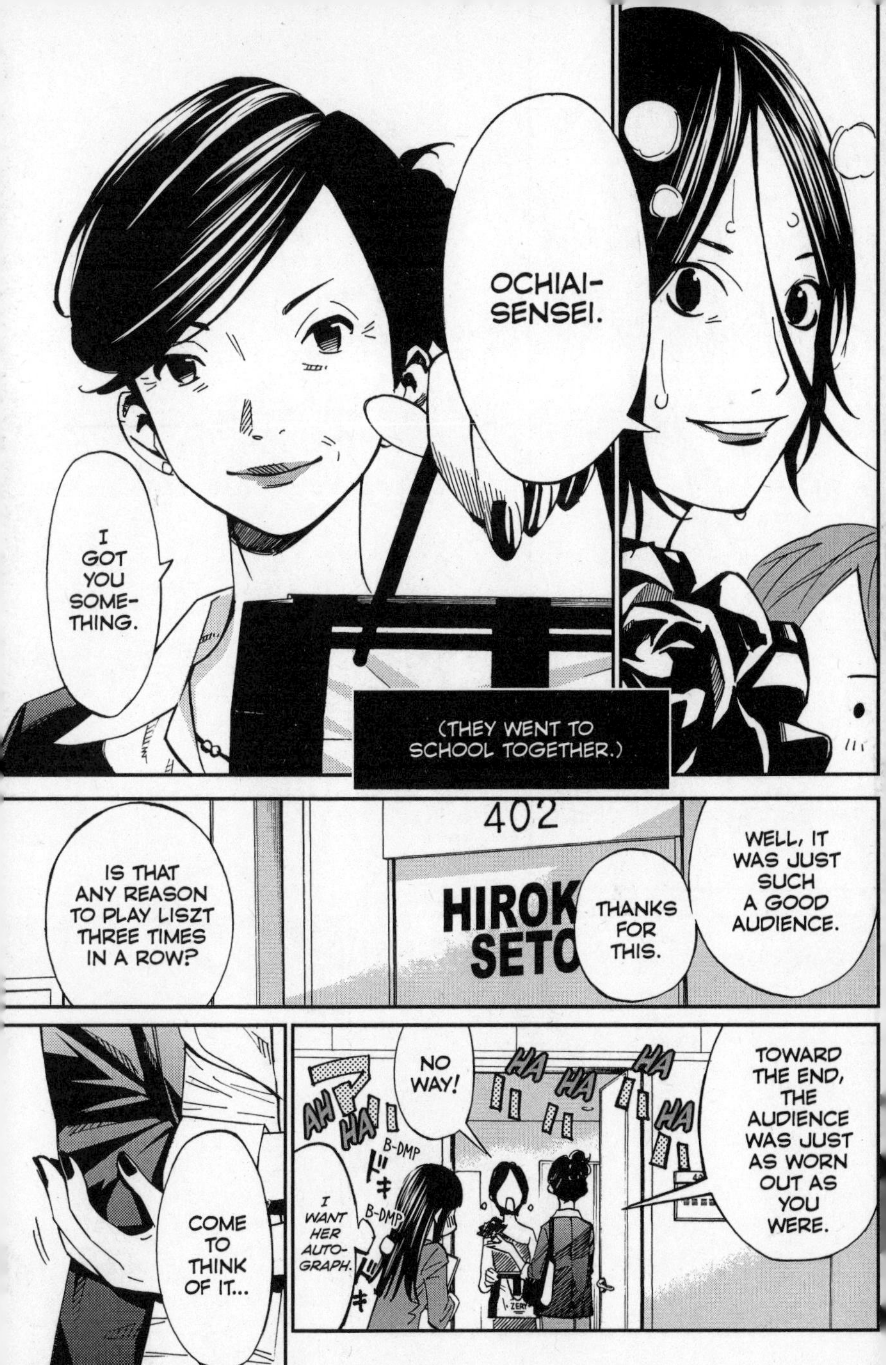
OCHIAI-SENSEI.
I GOT YOU SOMETHING.
(THEY WENT TO SCHOOL TOGETHER.)
402
WELL, IT WAS JUST SUCH A GOOD AUDIENCE.
THANKS FOR THIS.
HIROK
SETO
IS THAT ANY REASON TO PLAY LISZT THREE TIMES IN A ROW?
TOWARD THE END, THE AUDIENCE WAS JUST AS WORN OUT AS YOU WERE.
HA HA HA HA
NO WAY!
AH HA HA
B-DMP ドキ
B-DMP ドキ
I WANT HER AUTOGRAPH.
COME TO THINK OF IT...

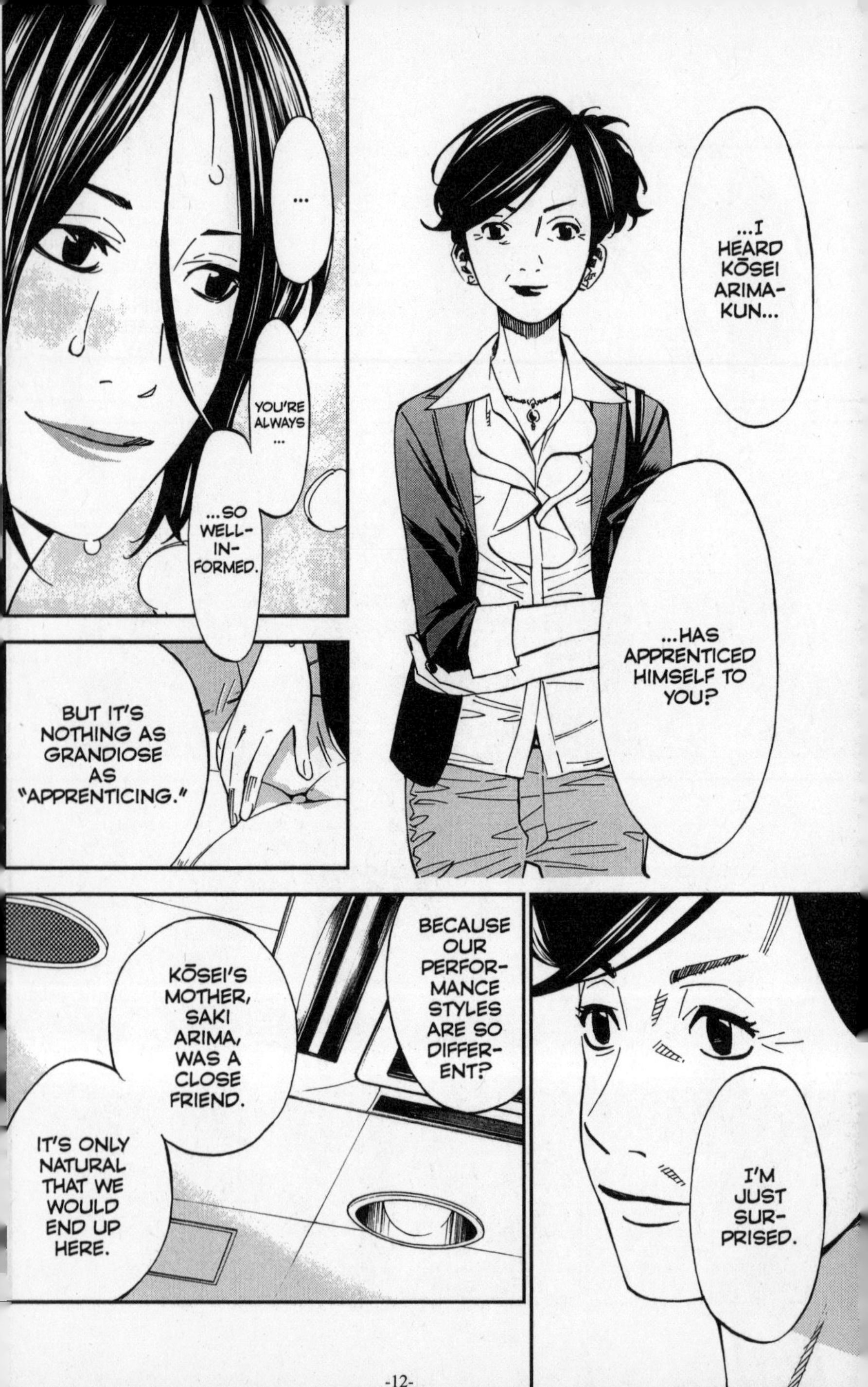
...I HEARD KŌSEI ARIMA-KUN...
...HAS APPRENTICED HIMSELF TO YOU?
...
YOU'RE ALWAYS ...
...SO WELL-INFORMED.
BUT IT'S NOTHING AS GRANDIOSE AS "APPRENTICING."
I'M JUST SURPRISED.
BECAUSE OUR PERFORMANCE STYLES ARE SO DIFFERENT?
KŌSEI'S MOTHER, SAKI ARIMA, WAS A CLOSE FRIEND.
IT'S ONLY NATURAL THAT WE WOULD END UP HERE.

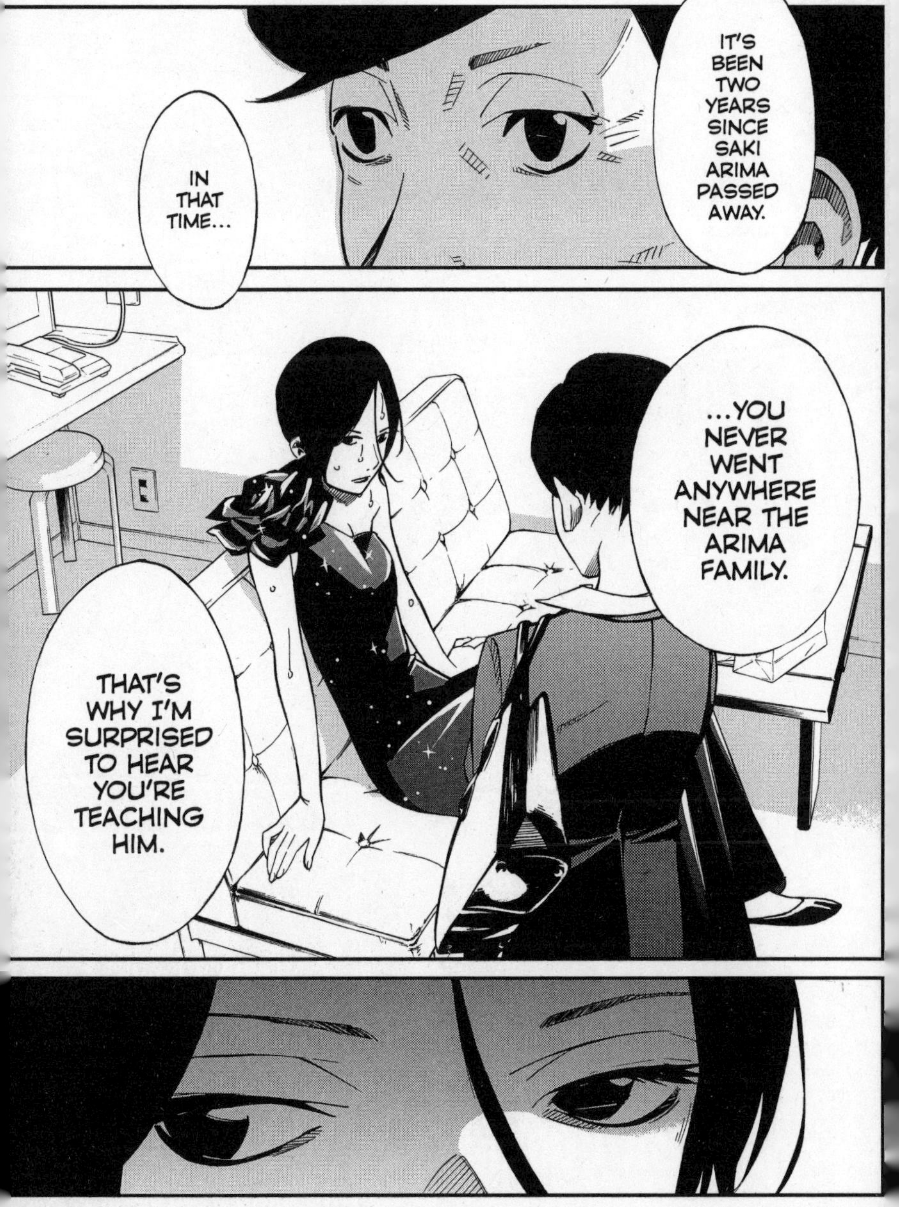
IT'S BEEN TWO YEARS SINCE SAKI ARIMA PASSED AWAY.
IN THAT TIME...
...YOU NEVER WENT ANYWHERE NEAR THE ARIMA FAMILY.
THAT'S WHY I'M SURPRISED TO HEAR YOU'RE TEACHING HIM.

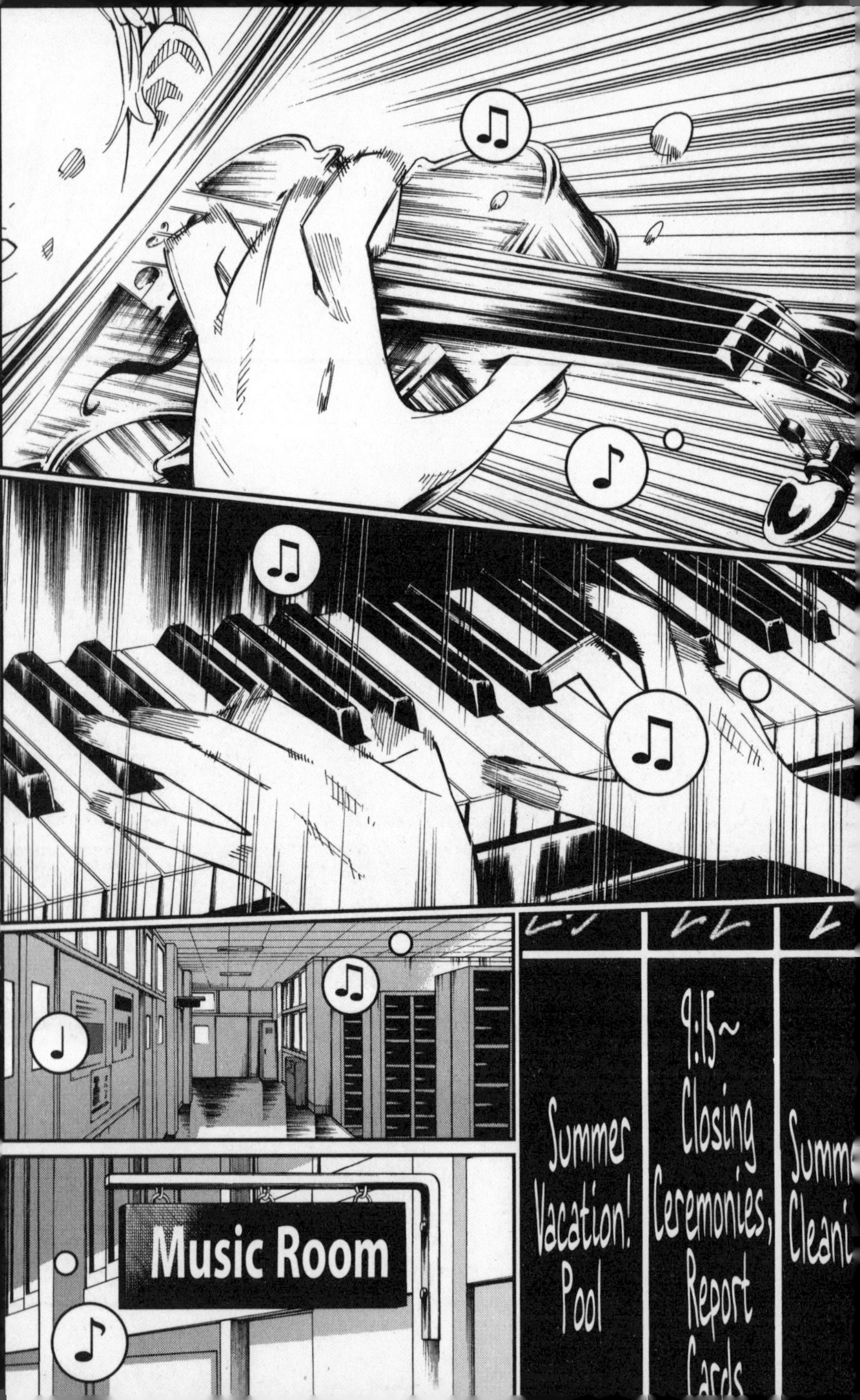
Summer Cleani
9:15~ Closing Ceremonies, Report Cards
Summer Vacation! Pool
Music Room

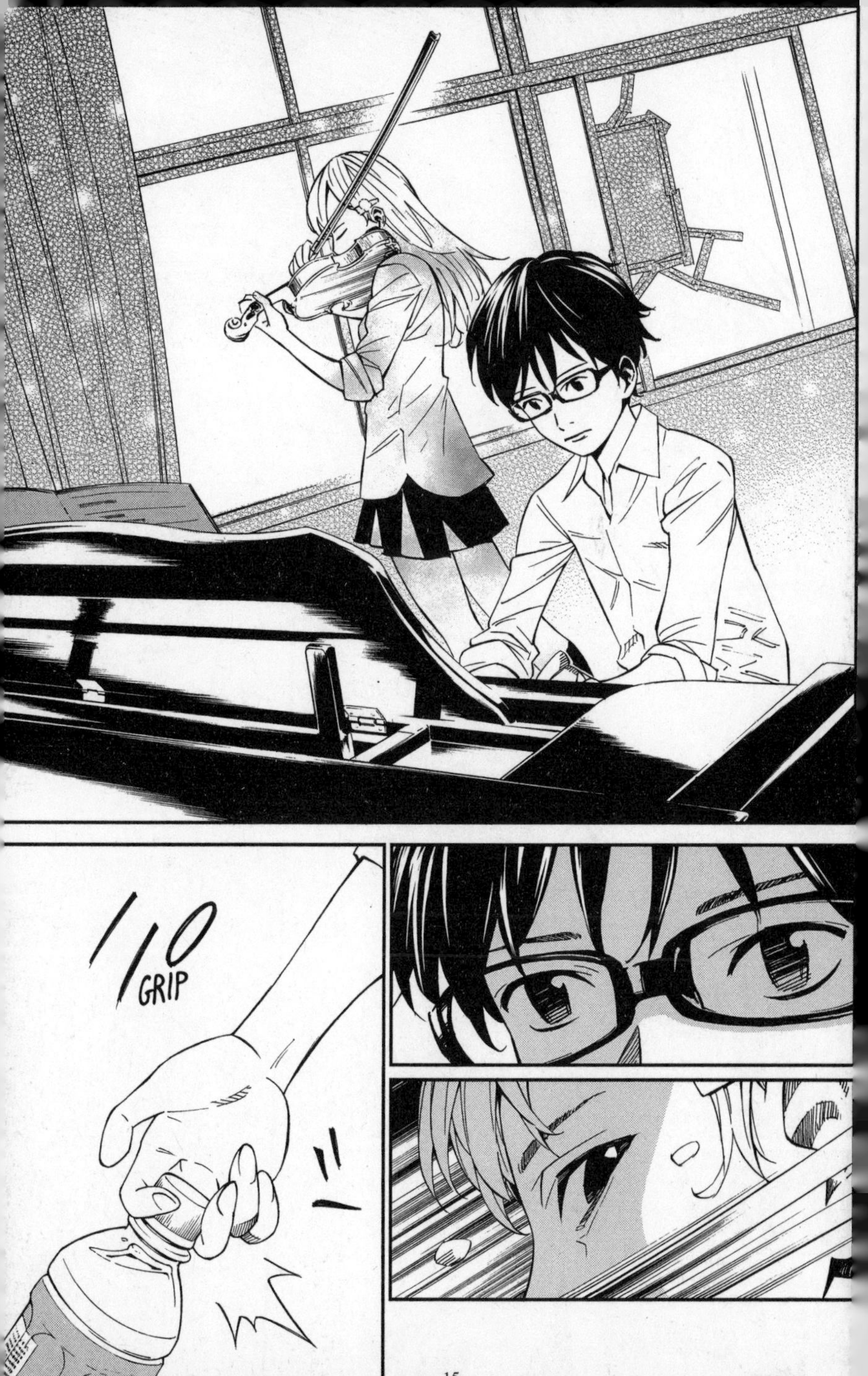
GRIP

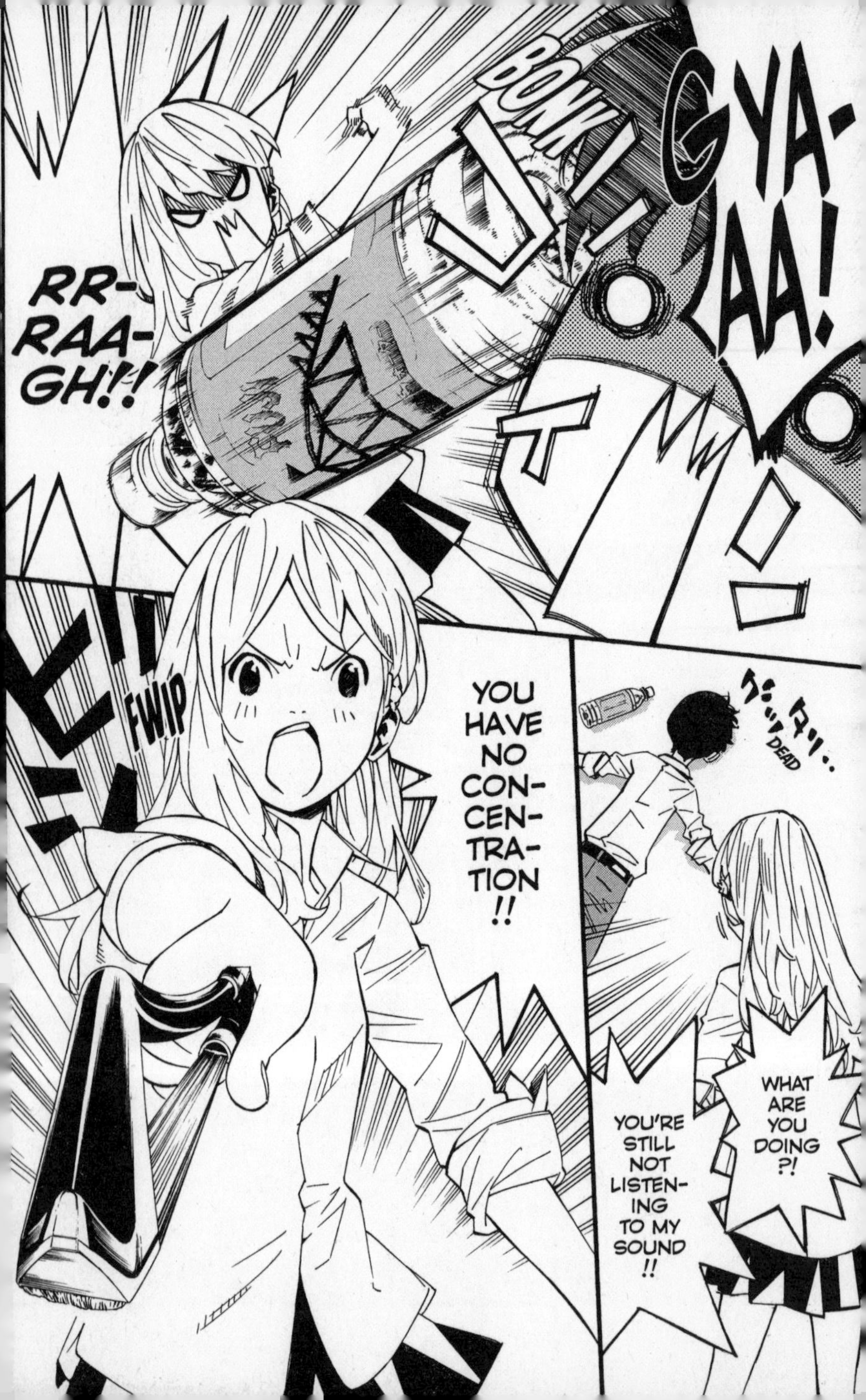
GYA-AA!
BONK!
RR-RAA-GH!!
DEAD
WHAT ARE YOU DOING?!
YOU'RE STILL NOT LISTEN-ING TO MY SOUND!!
YOU HAVE NO CON-CEN-TRA-TION!!
FWIP

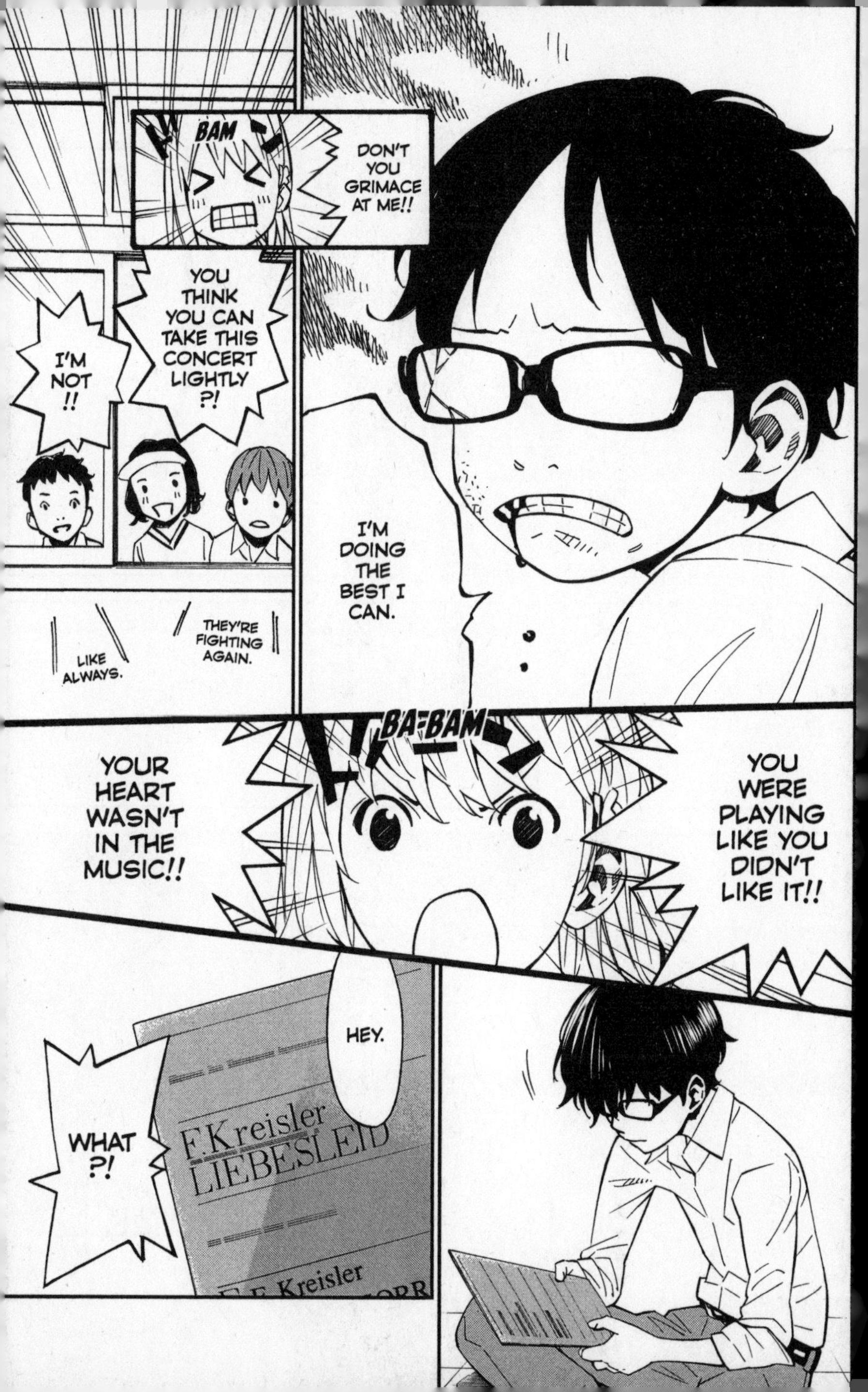
I'M DOING THE BEST I CAN.
BAM
DON'T YOU GRIMACE AT ME!!
YOU THINK YOU CAN TAKE THIS CONCERT LIGHTLY?!
I'M NOT!!
THEY'RE FIGHTING AGAIN.
LIKE ALWAYS.
BA-BAM
YOU WERE PLAYING LIKE YOU DIDN'T LIKE IT!!
YOUR HEART WASN'T IN THE MUSIC!!
HEY.
WHAT?!
F.Kreisler
LIEBESLEID
F. Kreisler

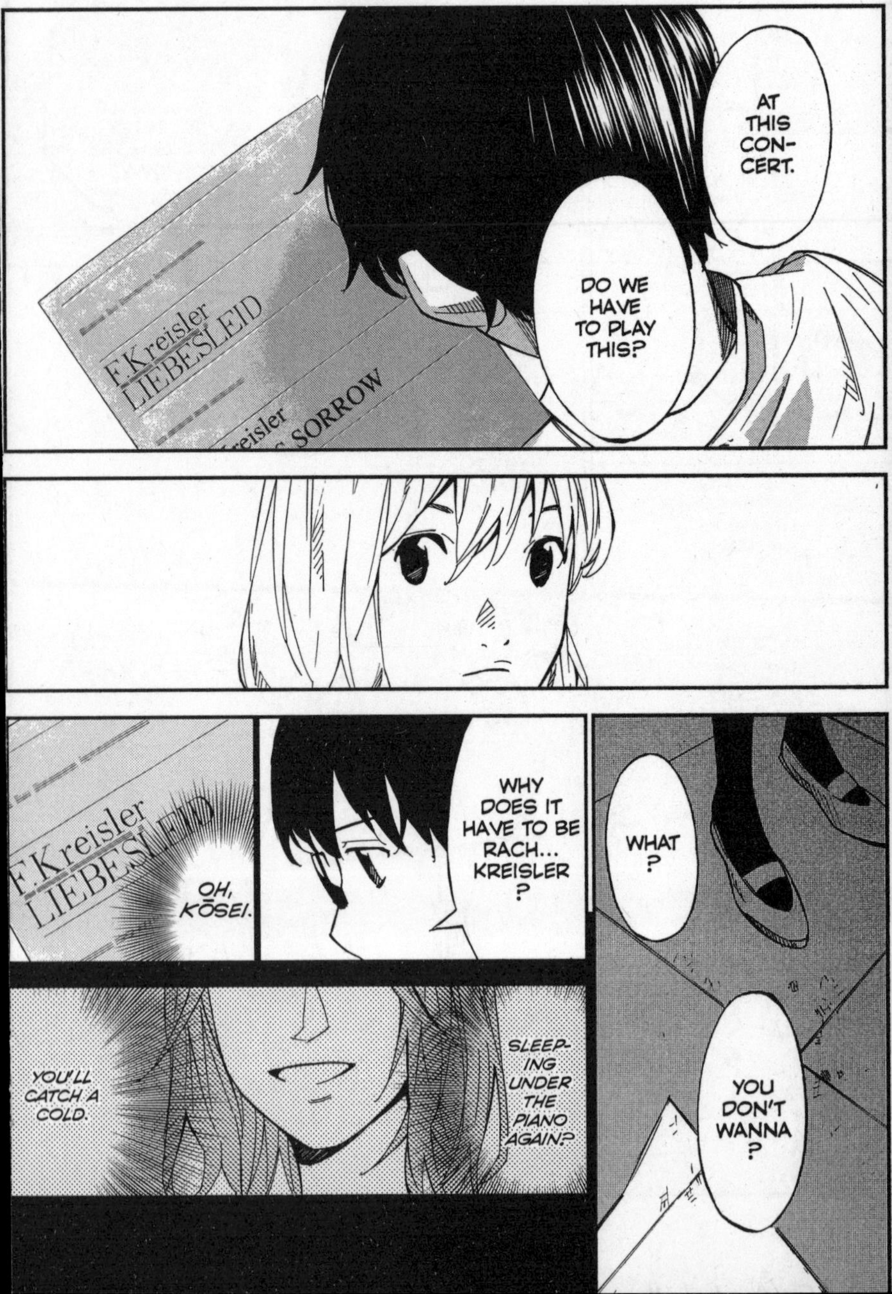
AT THIS CONCERT.
DO WE HAVE TO PLAY THIS?
F.Kreisler LIEBESLEID
SORROW
WHAT?
YOU DON'T WANNA?
WHY DOES IT HAVE TO BE RACH... KREISLER?
F.Kreisler LIEBESLEID
OH, KŌSEI.
SLEEPING UNDER THE PIANO AGAIN?
YOU'LL CATCH A COLD.

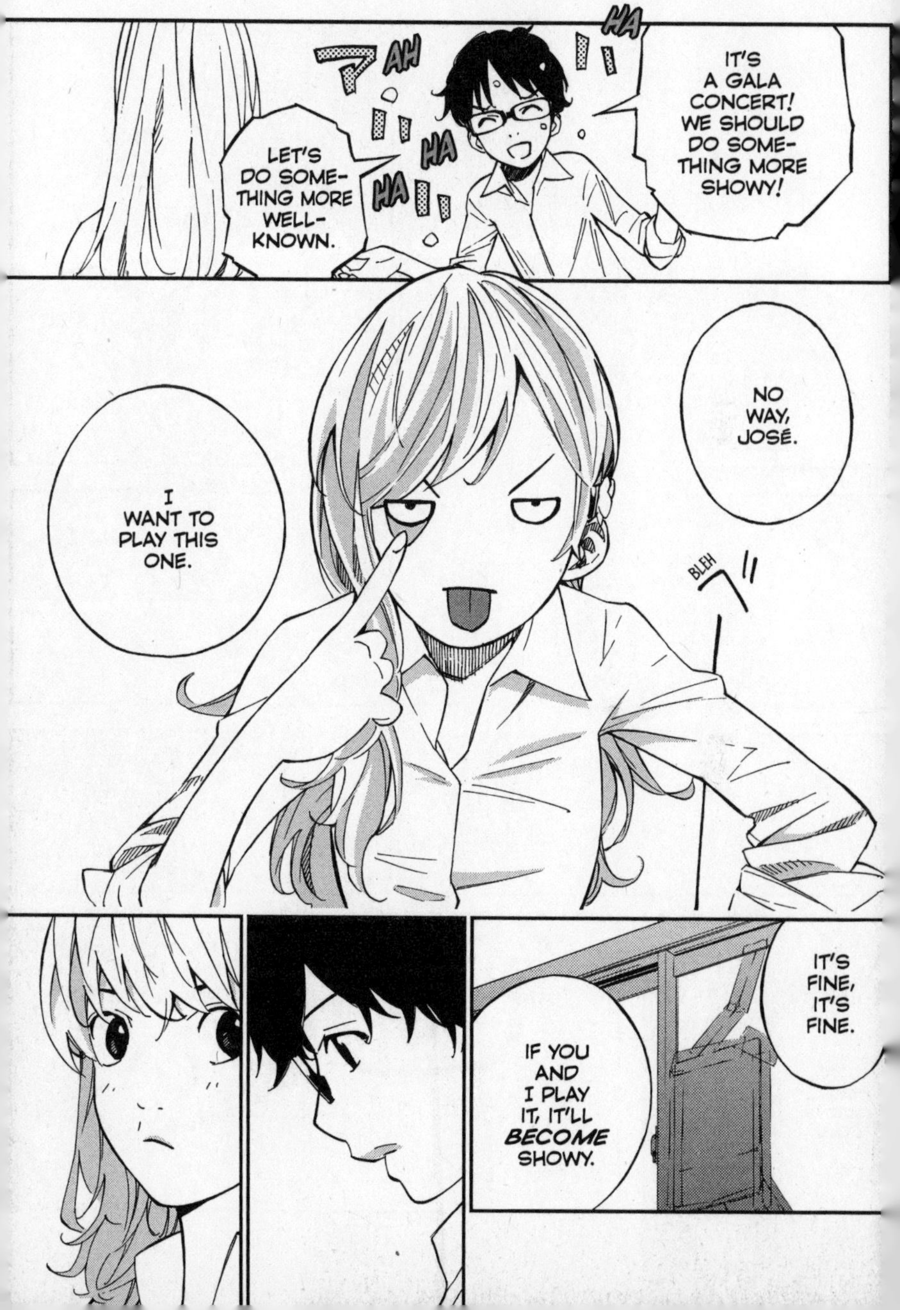
HA
IT'S A GALA CONCERT! WE SHOULD DO SOMETHING MORE SHOWY!
AH
HA
HA
LET'S DO SOMETHING MORE WELL-KNOWN.
NO WAY, JOSÉ.
BLEH
I WANT TO PLAY THIS ONE.
IT'S FINE, IT'S FINE.
IF YOU AND I PLAY IT, IT'LL *BECOME* SHOWY.

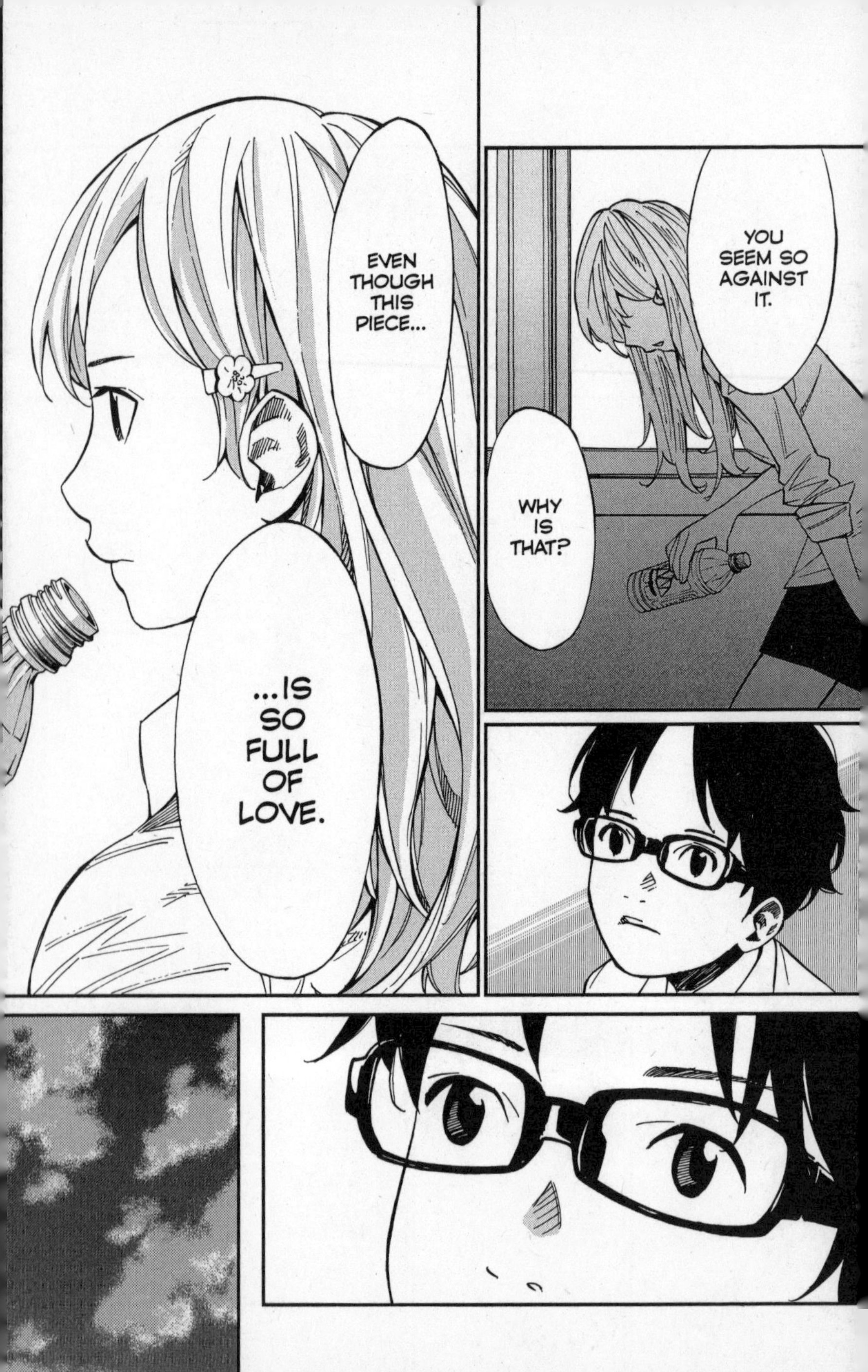

YOU SEEM SO AGAINST IT.
WHY IS THAT?
EVEN THOUGH THIS PIECE...
...IS SO FULL OF LOVE.

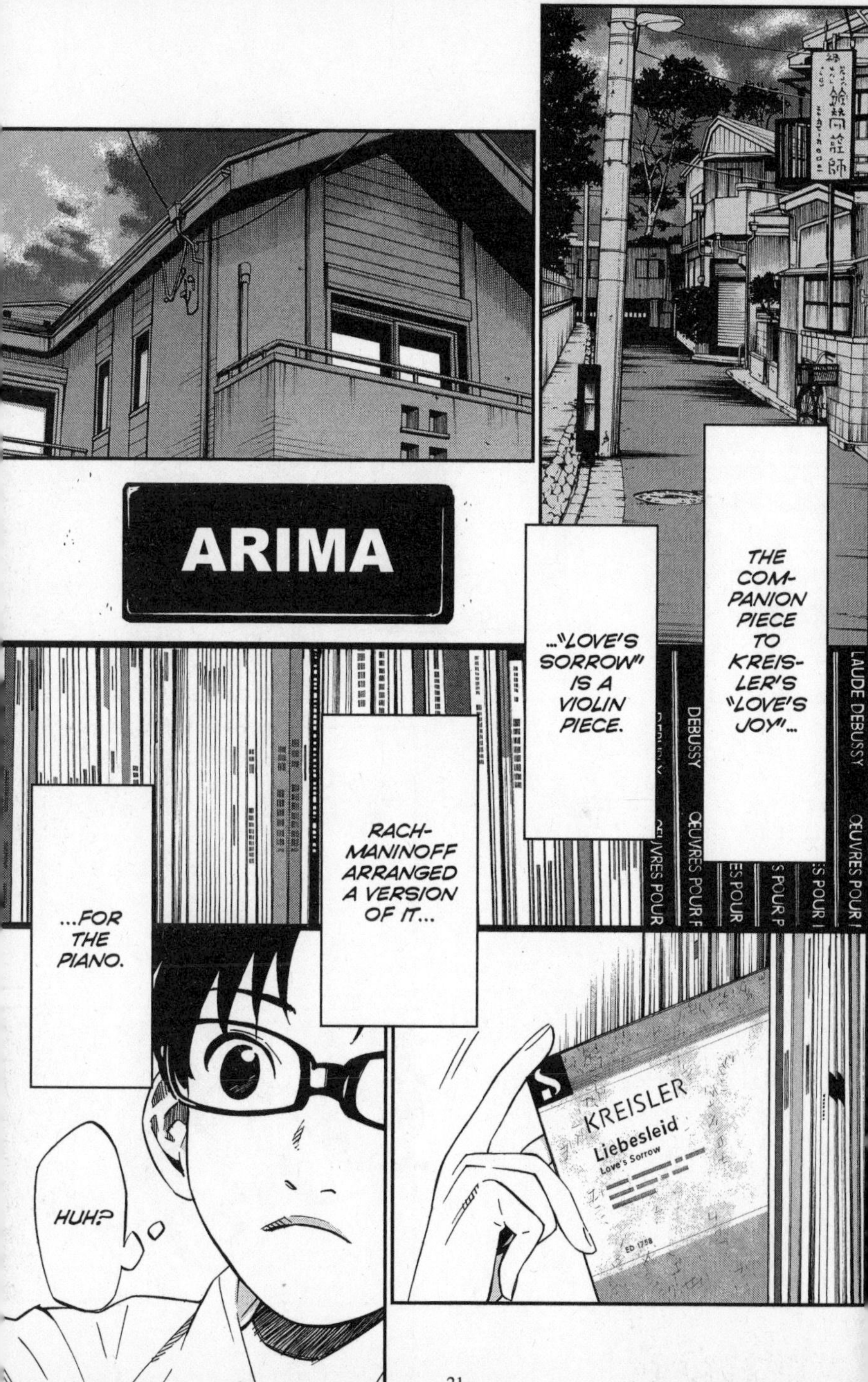
THE COMPANION PIECE TO KREISLER'S "LOVE'S JOY"...
..."LOVE'S SORROW" IS A VIOLIN PIECE.
ARIMA
LAUDE DEBUSSY
ŒUVRES POUR
DEBUSSY
ŒUVRES POUR
RACHMANINOFF ARRANGED A VERSION OF IT...
...FOR THE PIANO.
KREISLER
Liebesleid
Love's Sorrow
ED 1758
HUH?

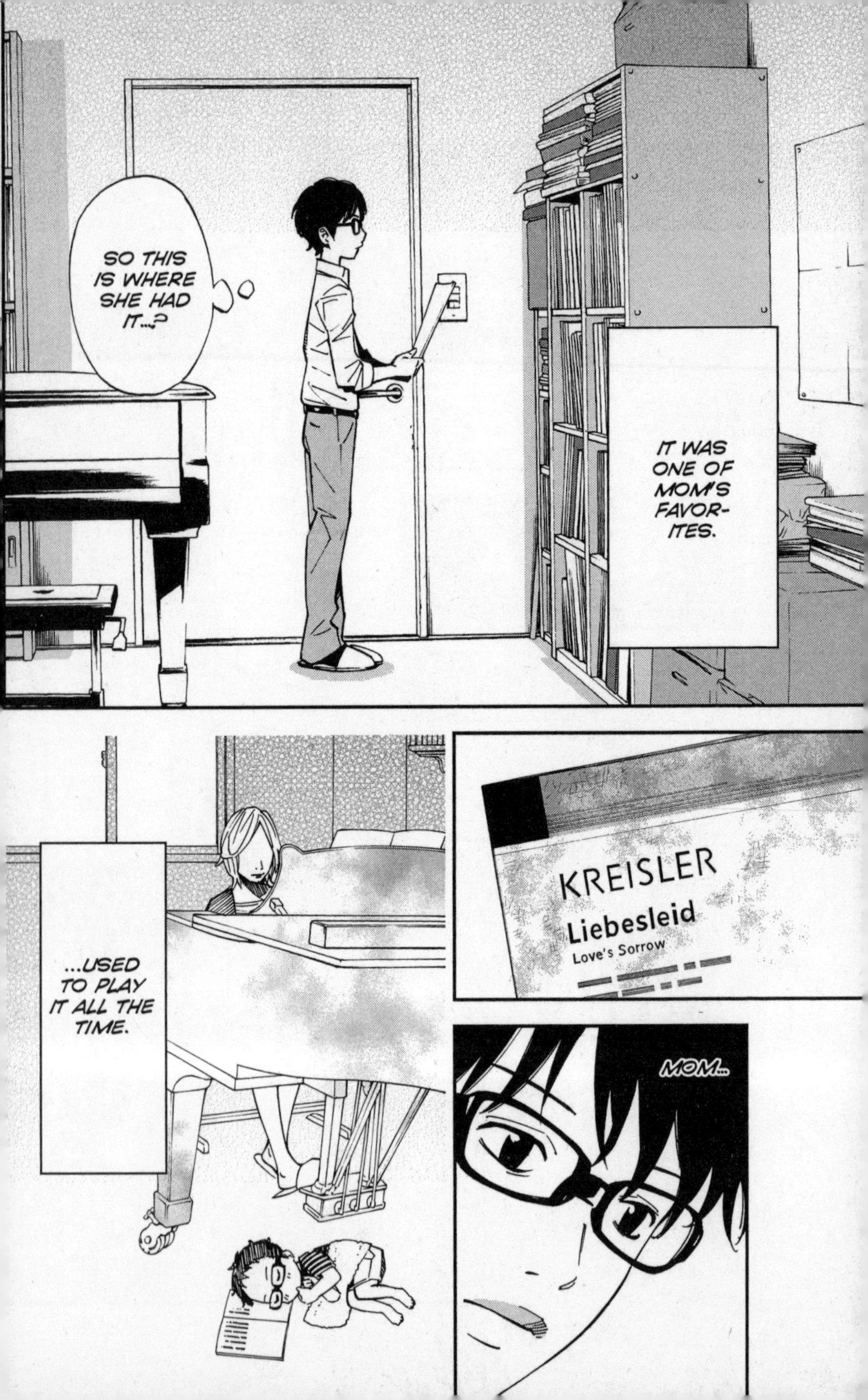
SO THIS IS WHERE SHE HAD IT...?
IT WAS ONE OF MOM'S FAVOR-ITES.
KREISLER
Liebesleid
Love's Sorrow
MOM...
...USED TO PLAY IT ALL THE TIME.

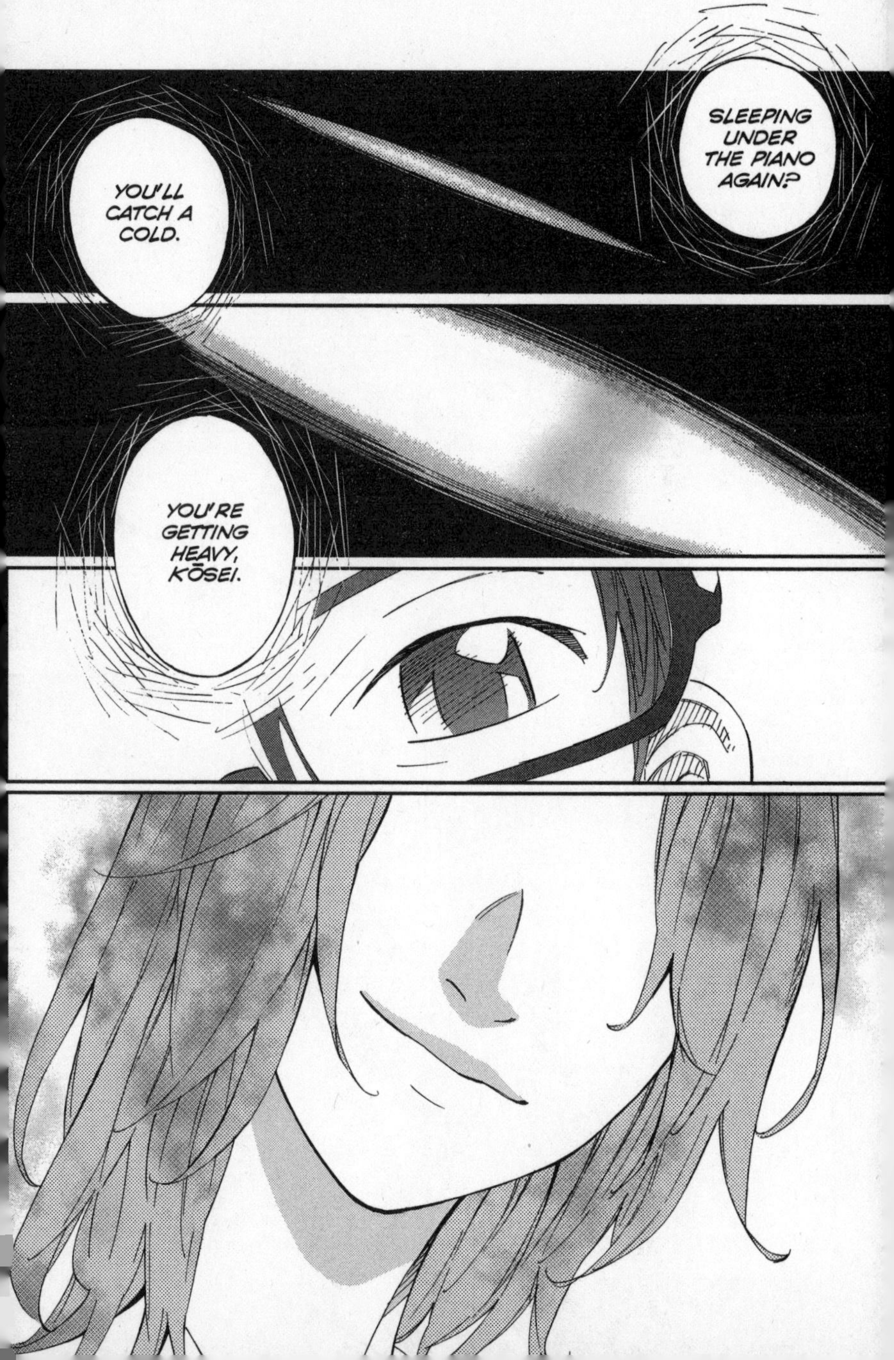
SLEEPING UNDER THE PIANO AGAIN?
YOU'LL CATCH A COLD.
YOU'RE GETTING HEAVY, KŌSEI.

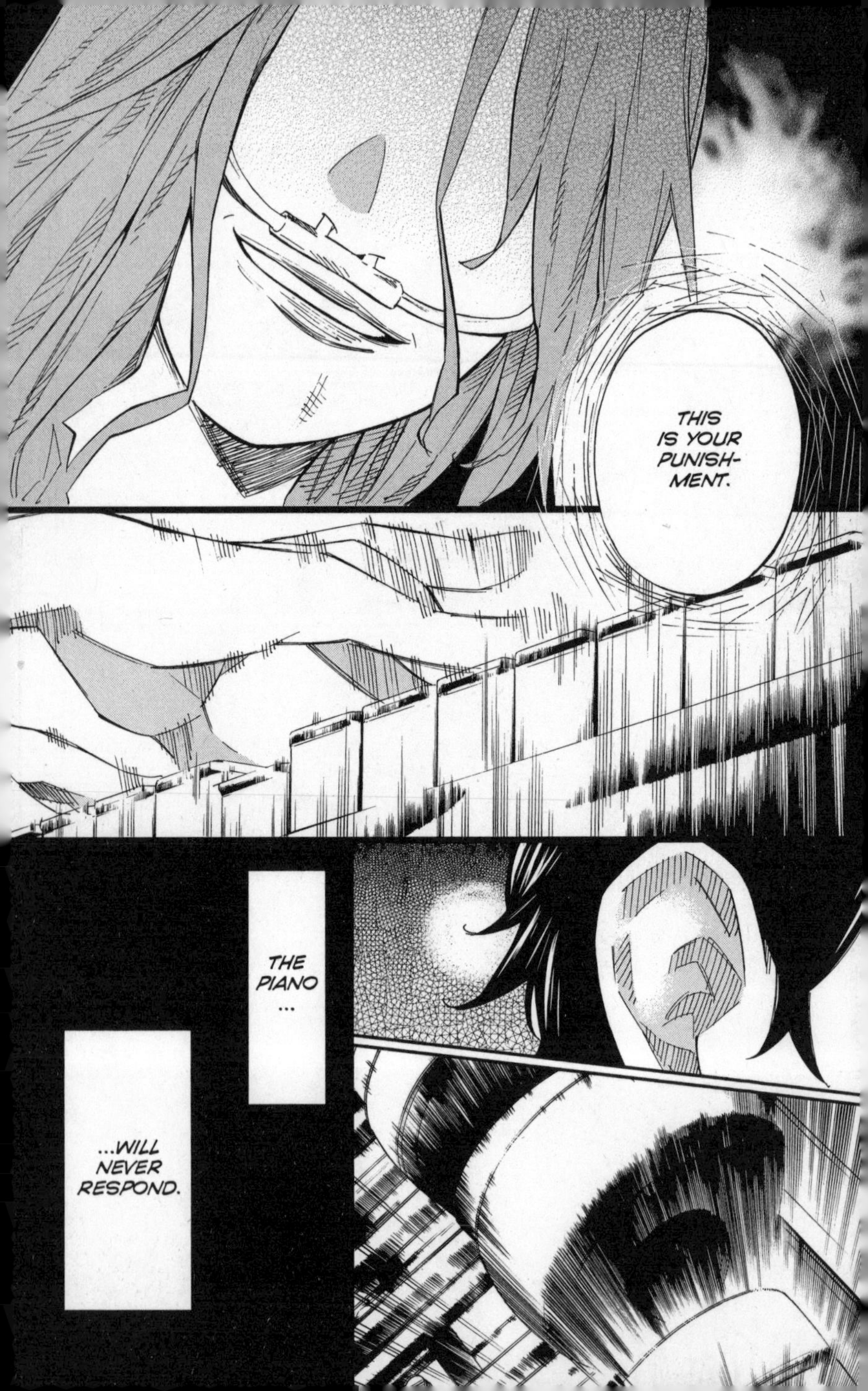
THIS IS YOUR PUNISH-MENT.
THE PIANO ...
...WILL NEVER RESPOND.

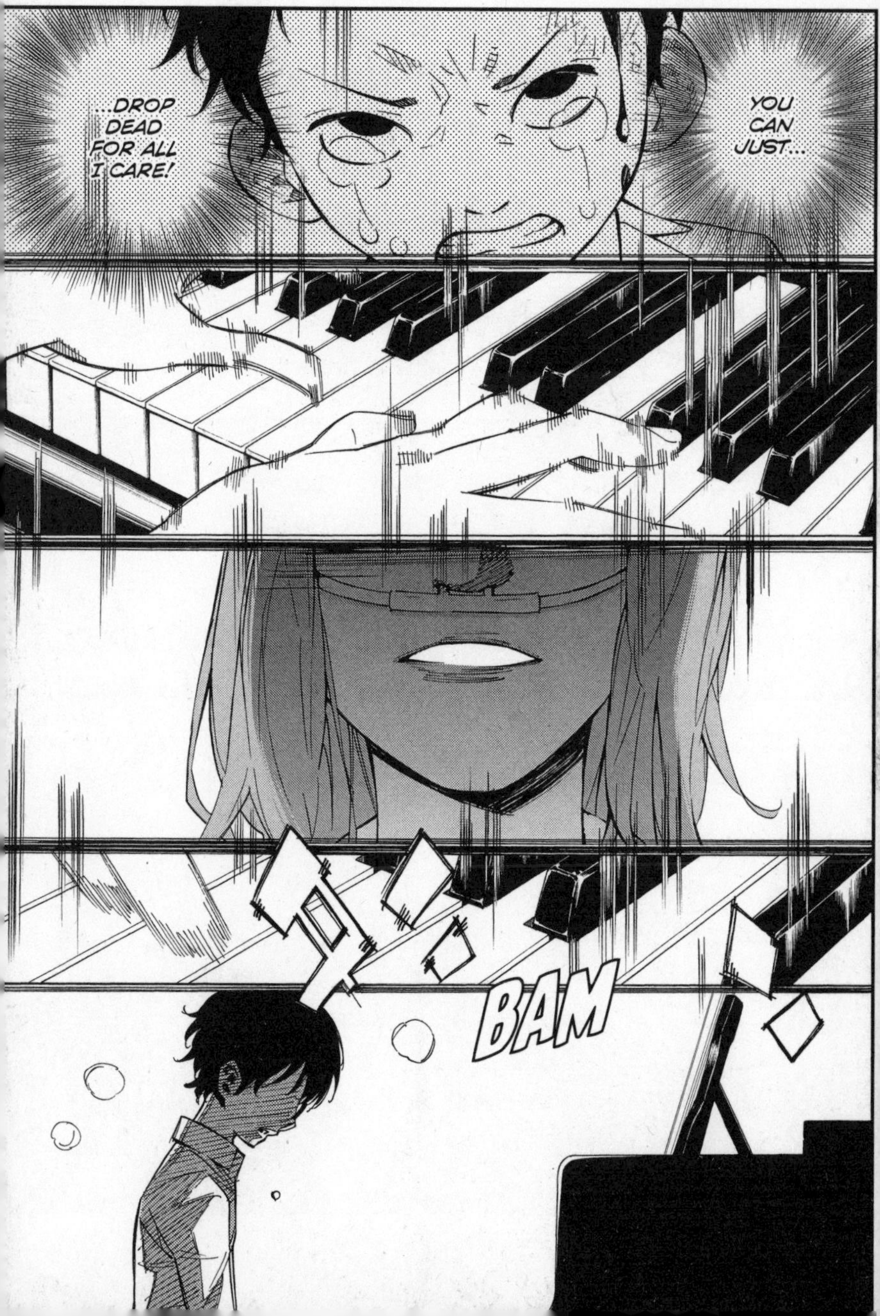
YOU CAN JUST...
...DROP DEAD FOR ALL I CARE!
BAM

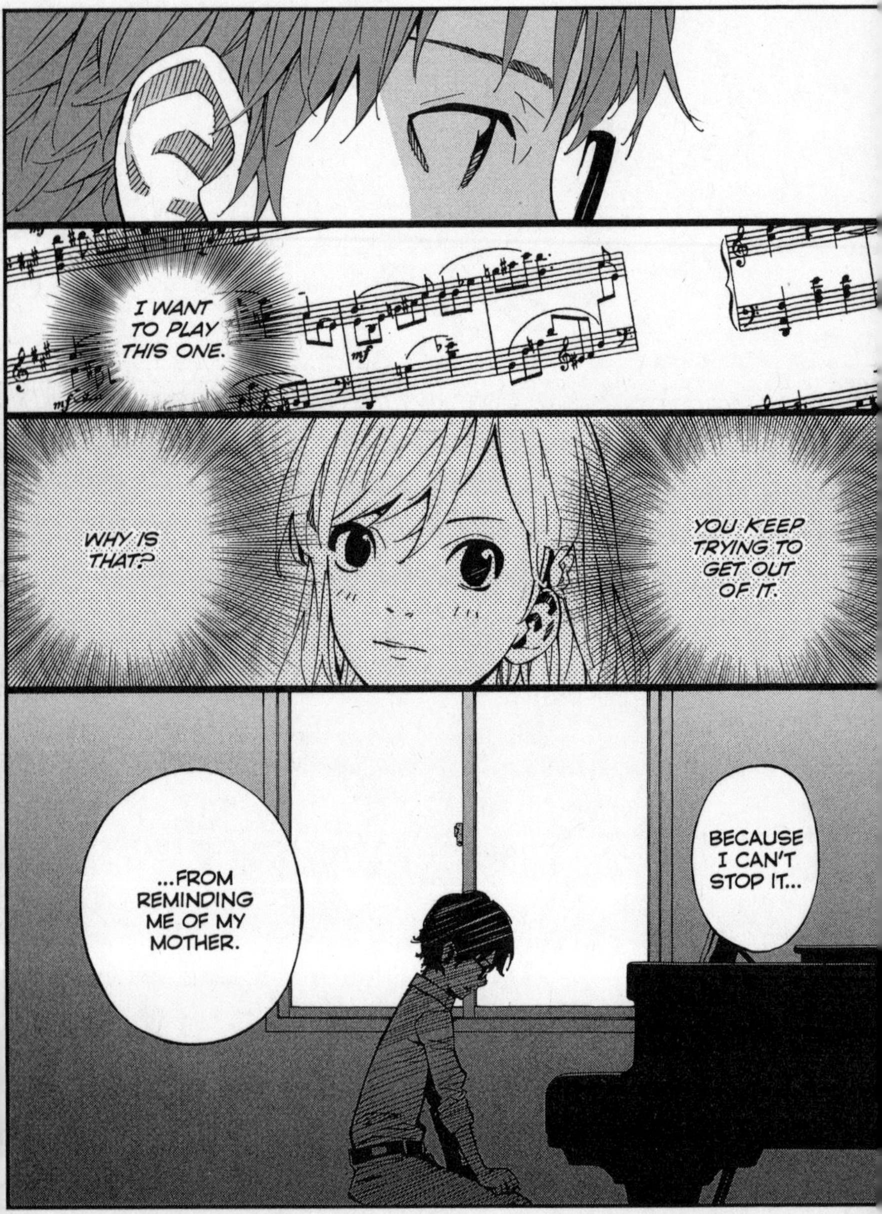
I WANT TO PLAY THIS ONE.
YOU KEEP TRYING TO GET OUT OF IT.
WHY IS THAT?
BECAUSE I CAN'T STOP IT...
...FROM REMINDING ME OF MY MOTHER.

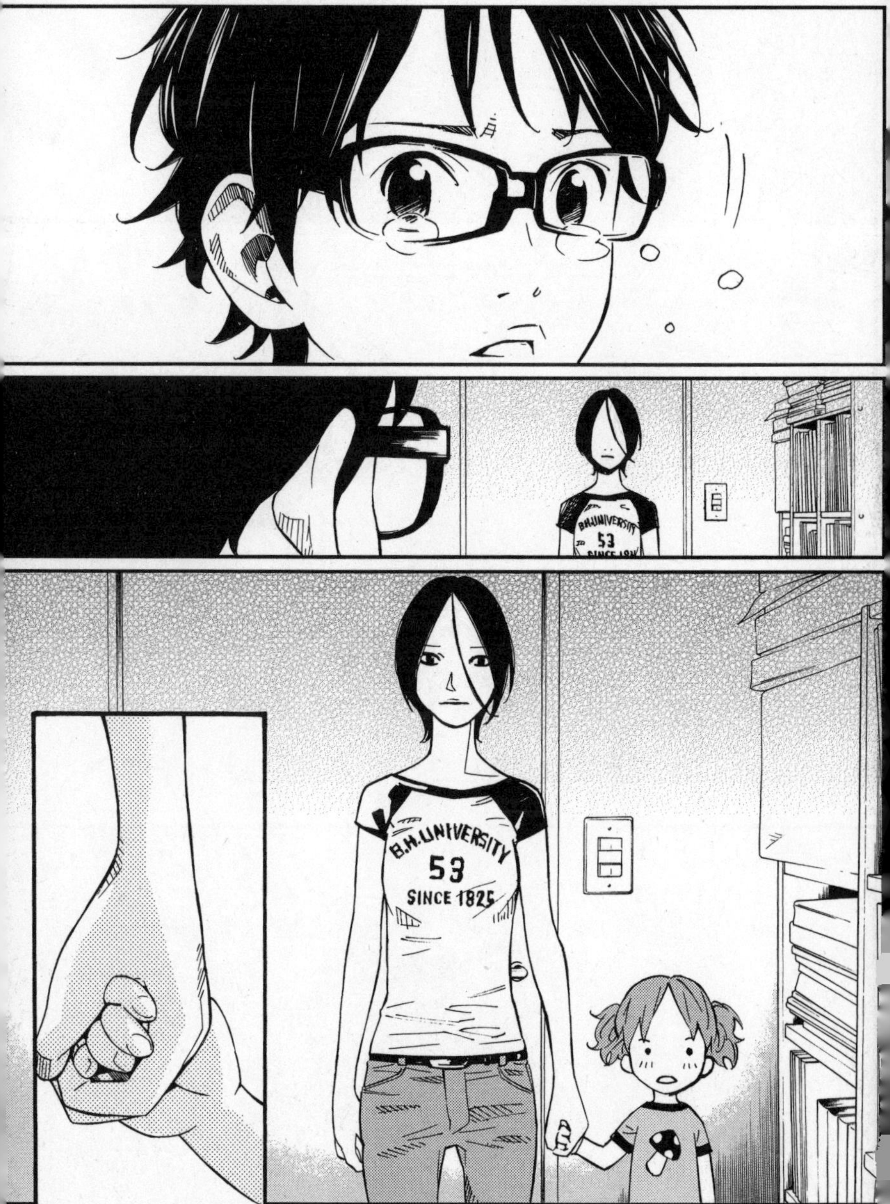
B.H.UNIVERSITY
53
SINCE 1825

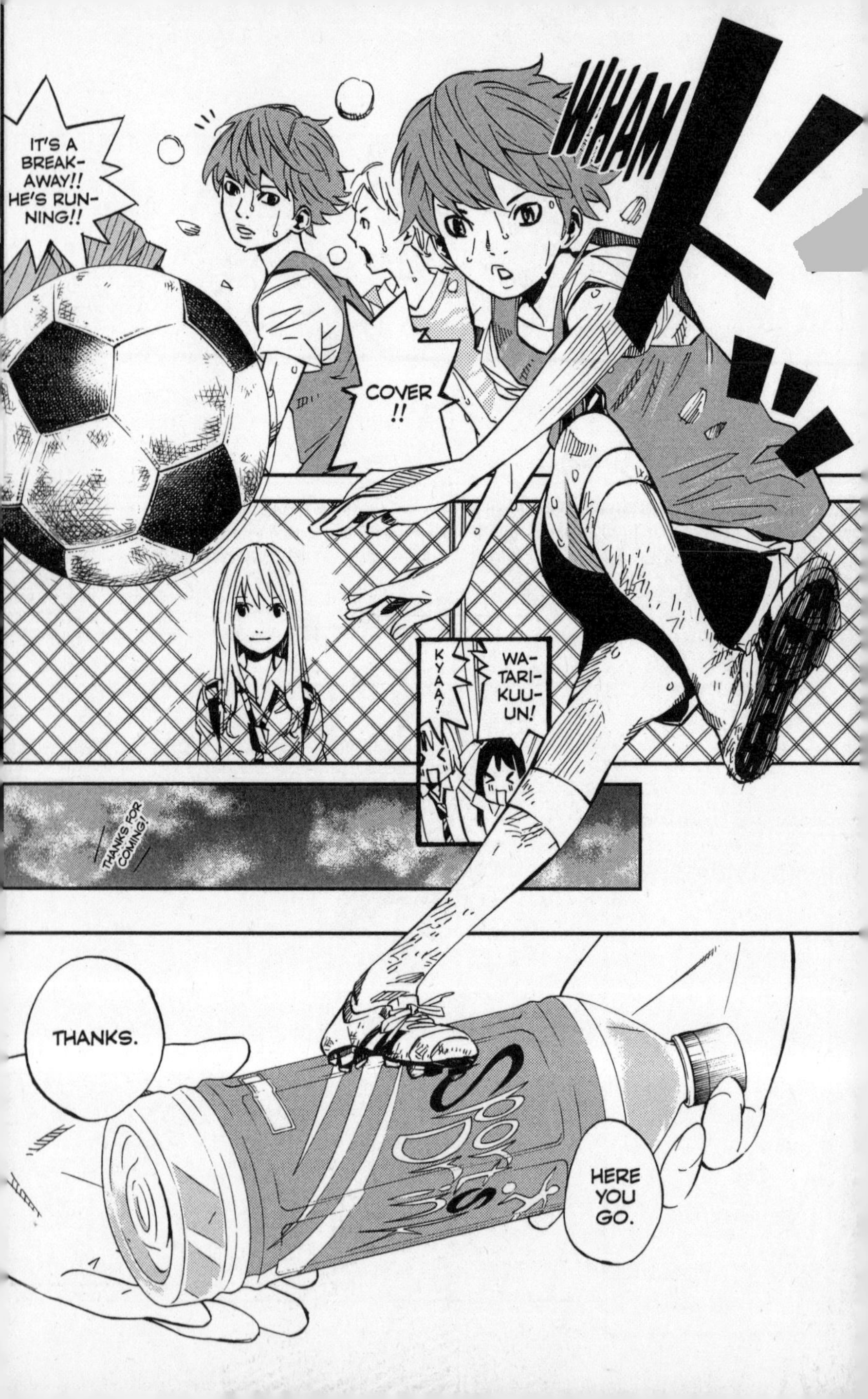
WHAM!!
COVER!!
IT'S A BREAK-AWAY!! HE'S RUN-NING!!
WA-TARI-KUUU-UN!
KYAA!
THANKS FOR COMING!
HERE YOU GO.
THANKS.

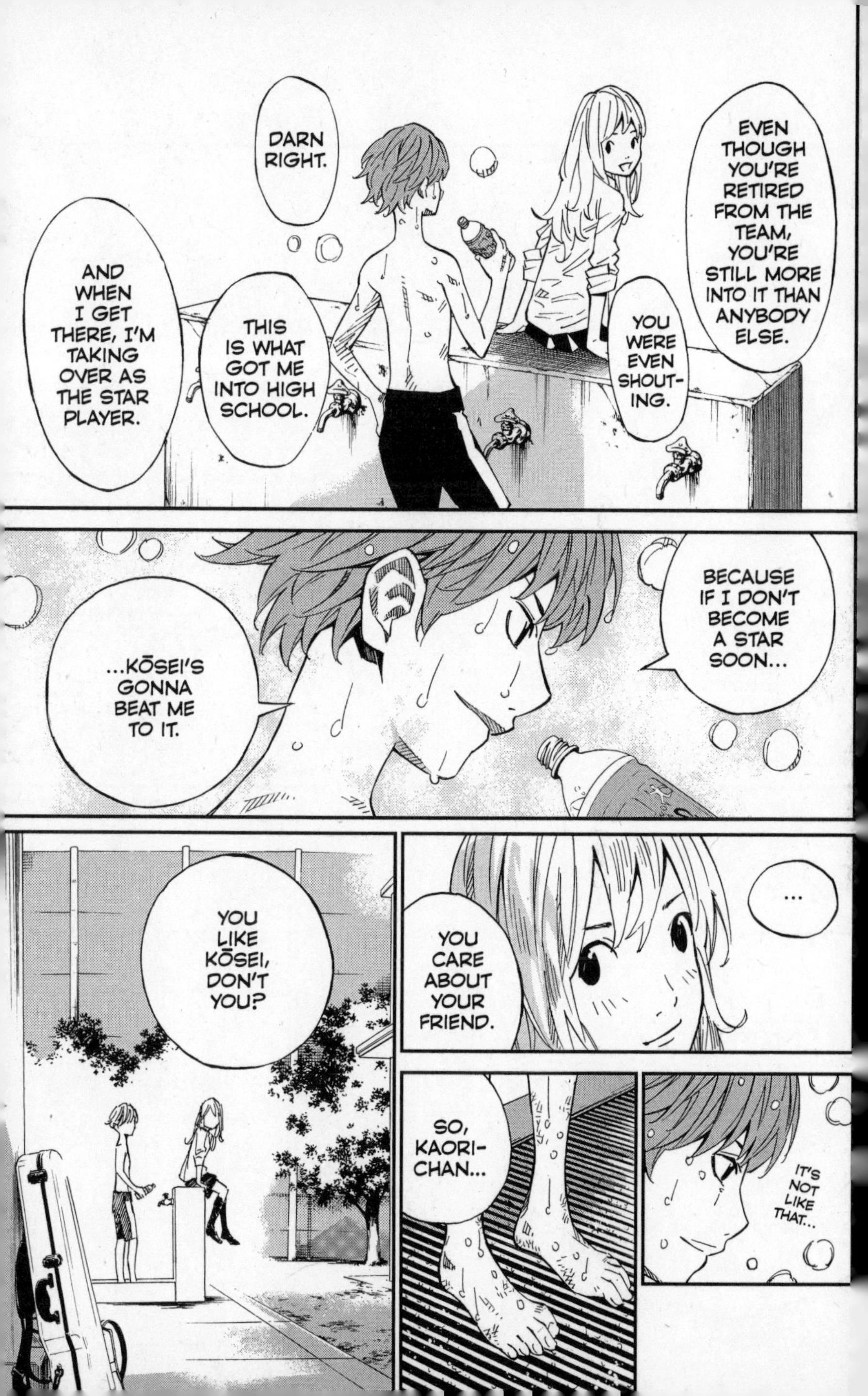
EVEN THOUGH YOU'RE RETIRED FROM THE TEAM, YOU'RE STILL MORE INTO IT THAN ANYBODY ELSE.
YOU WERE EVEN SHOUTING.
DARN RIGHT.
THIS IS WHAT GOT ME INTO HIGH SCHOOL.
AND WHEN I GET THERE, I'M TAKING OVER AS THE STAR PLAYER.
BECAUSE IF I DON'T BECOME A STAR SOON...
...KŌSEI'S GONNA BEAT ME TO IT.
...
YOU CARE ABOUT YOUR FRIEND.
IT'S NOT LIKE THAT...
SO, KAORI-CHAN...
YOU LIKE KŌSEI, DON'T YOU?

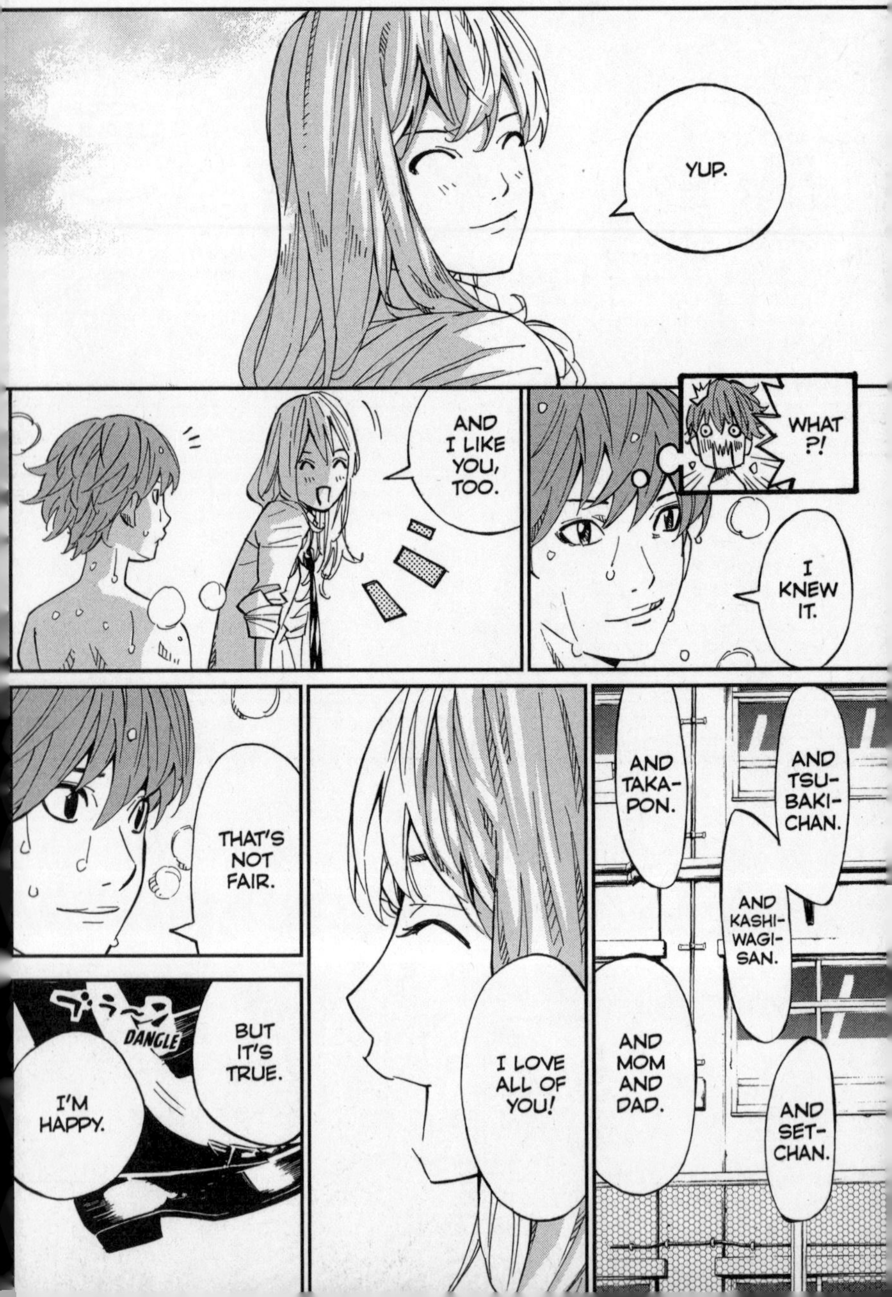
YUP.
WHAT?!
I KNEW IT.
AND I LIKE YOU, TOO.
AND TSUBAKI-CHAN.
AND TAKA-PON.
AND KASHIWAGI-SAN.
AND SET-CHAN.
AND MOM AND DAD.
I LOVE ALL OF YOU!
THAT'S NOT FAIR.
BUT IT'S TRUE.
DANGLE
I'M HAPPY.

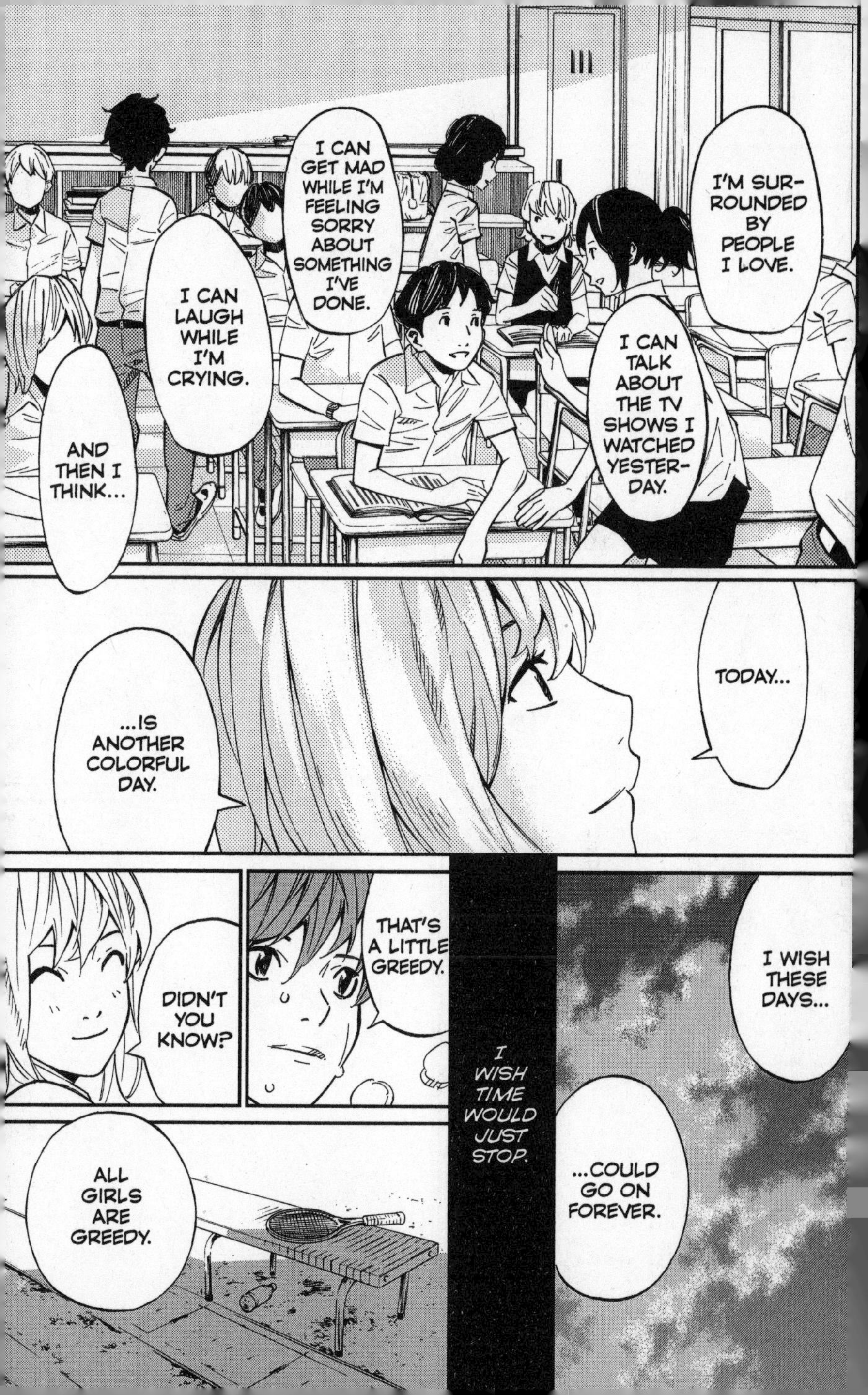
I'M SURROUNDED BY PEOPLE I LOVE.
I CAN TALK ABOUT THE TV SHOWS I WATCHED YESTERDAY.
I CAN GET MAD WHILE I'M FEELING SORRY ABOUT SOMETHING I'VE DONE.
I CAN LAUGH WHILE I'M CRYING.
AND THEN I THINK...
TODAY...
...IS ANOTHER COLORFUL DAY.
I WISH THESE DAYS...
...COULD GO ON FOREVER.
I WISH TIME WOULD JUST STOP.
THAT'S A LITTLE GREEDY.
DIDN'T YOU KNOW?
ALL GIRLS ARE GREEDY.

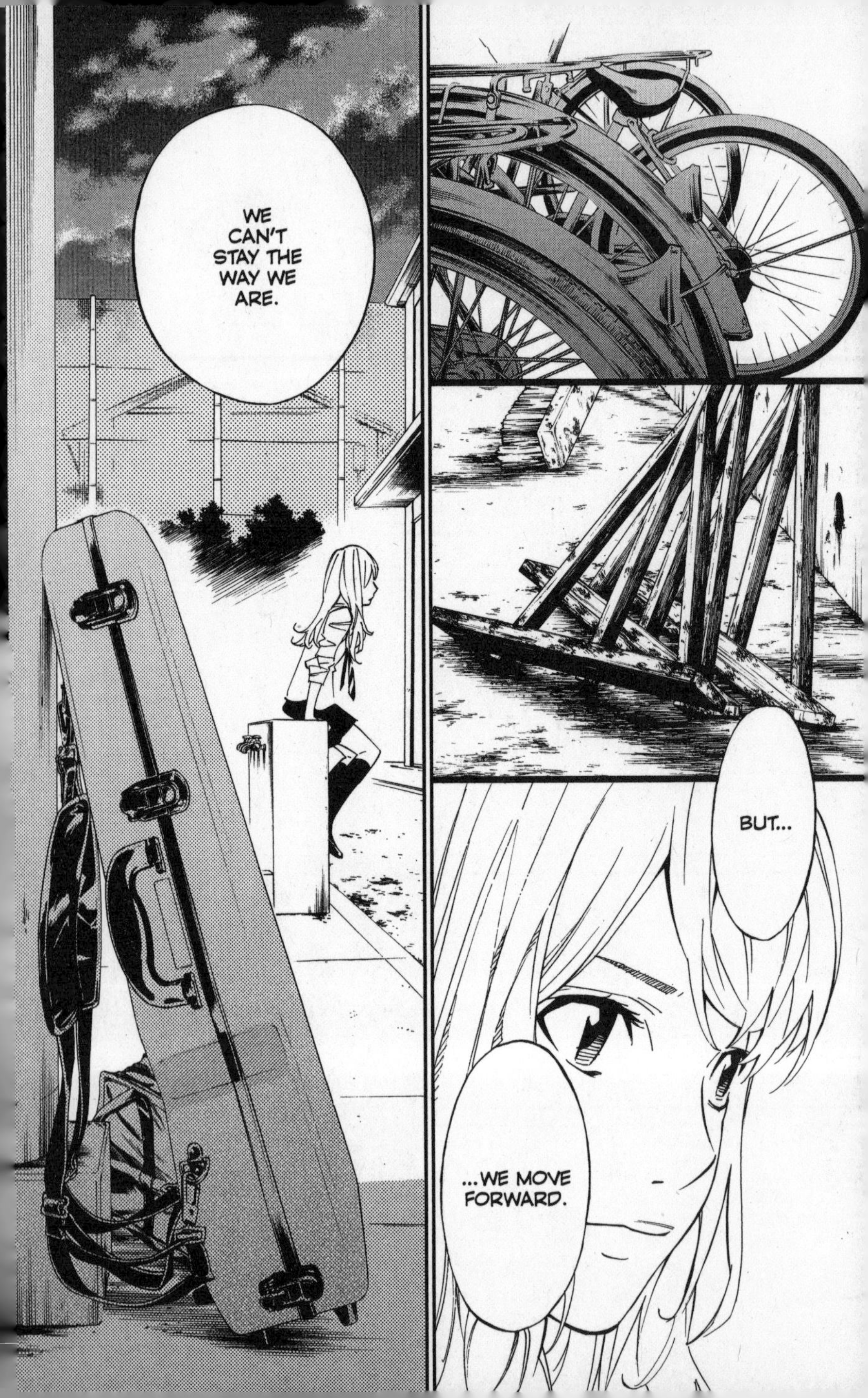
BUT...
...WE MOVE FORWARD.
WE CAN'T STAY THE WAY WE ARE.

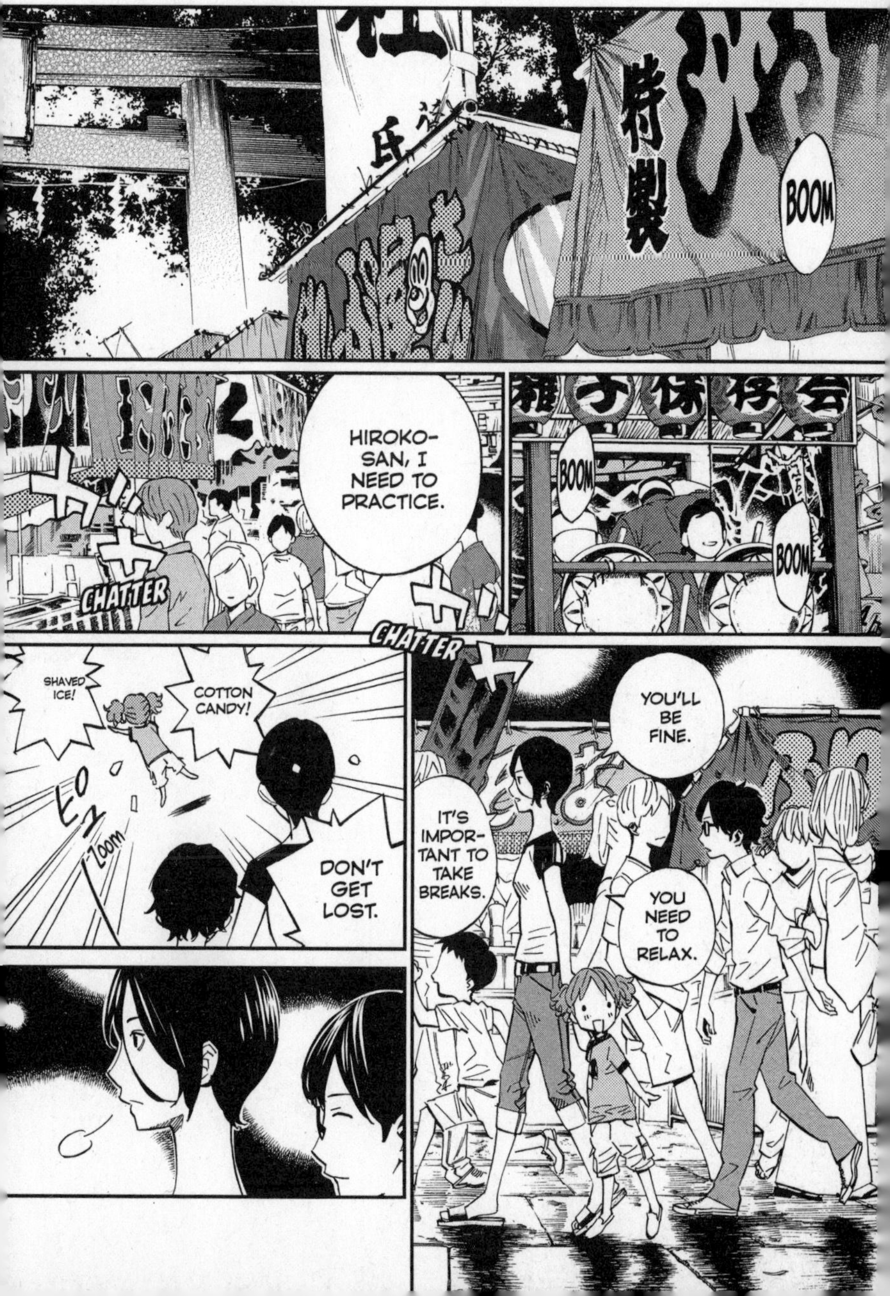
BOOM
BOOM
BOOM
HIROKO-SAN, I NEED TO PRACTICE.
CHATTER
CHATTER
YOU'LL BE FINE.
IT'S IMPORTANT TO TAKE BREAKS.
YOU NEED TO RELAX.
COTTON CANDY!
SHAVED ICE!
ZOOM
DON'T GET LOST.

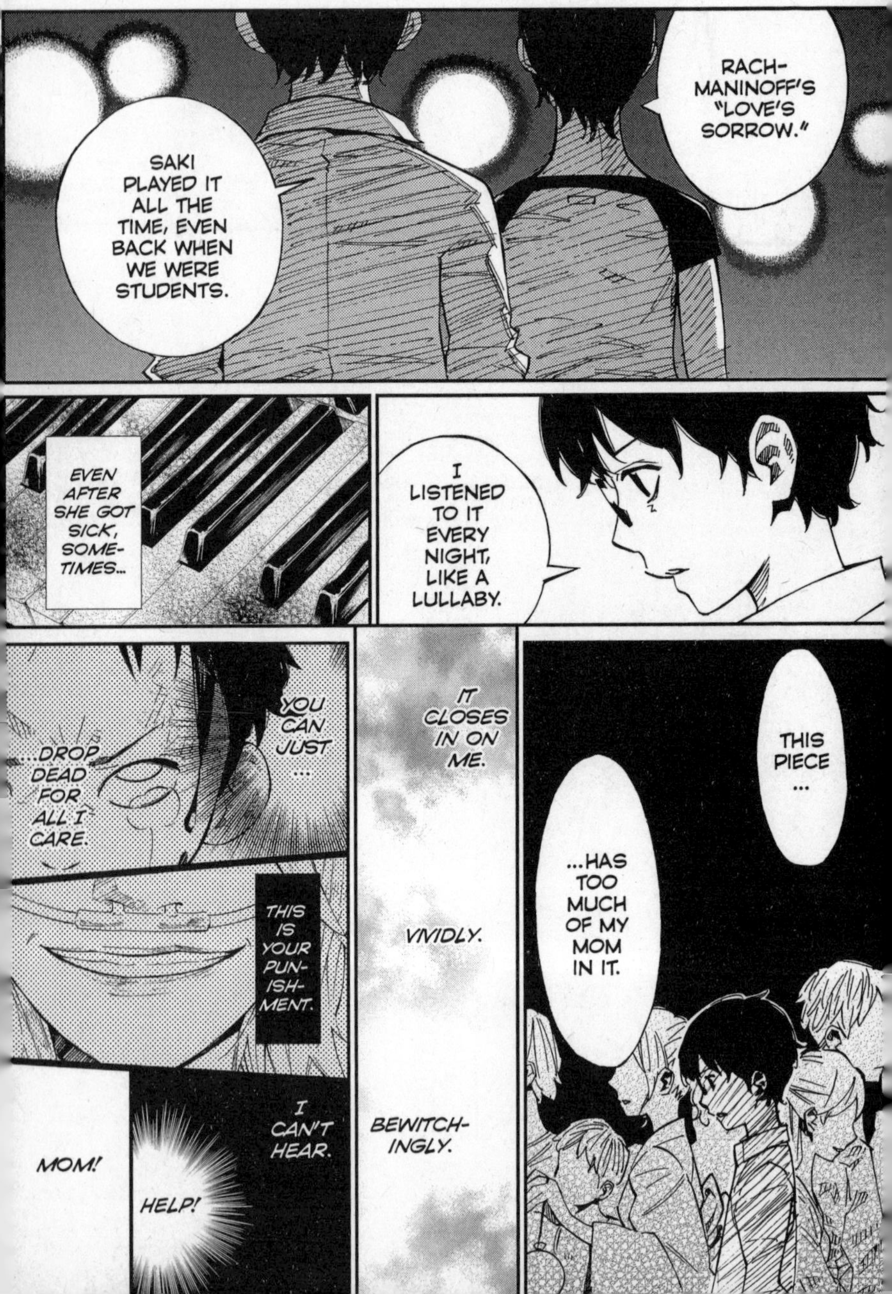
RACHMANINOFF'S "LOVE'S SORROW."
SAKI PLAYED IT ALL THE TIME, EVEN BACK WHEN WE WERE STUDENTS.
I LISTENED TO IT EVERY NIGHT, LIKE A LULLABY.
EVEN AFTER SHE GOT SICK, SOMETIMES...
THIS PIECE ...
...HAS TOO MUCH OF MY MOM IN IT.
IT CLOSES IN ON ME.
VIVIDLY.
BEWITCHINGLY.
YOU CAN JUST ...
...DROP DEAD FOR ALL I CARE.
THIS IS YOUR PUNISHMENT.
I CAN'T HEAR.
HELP!
MOM!

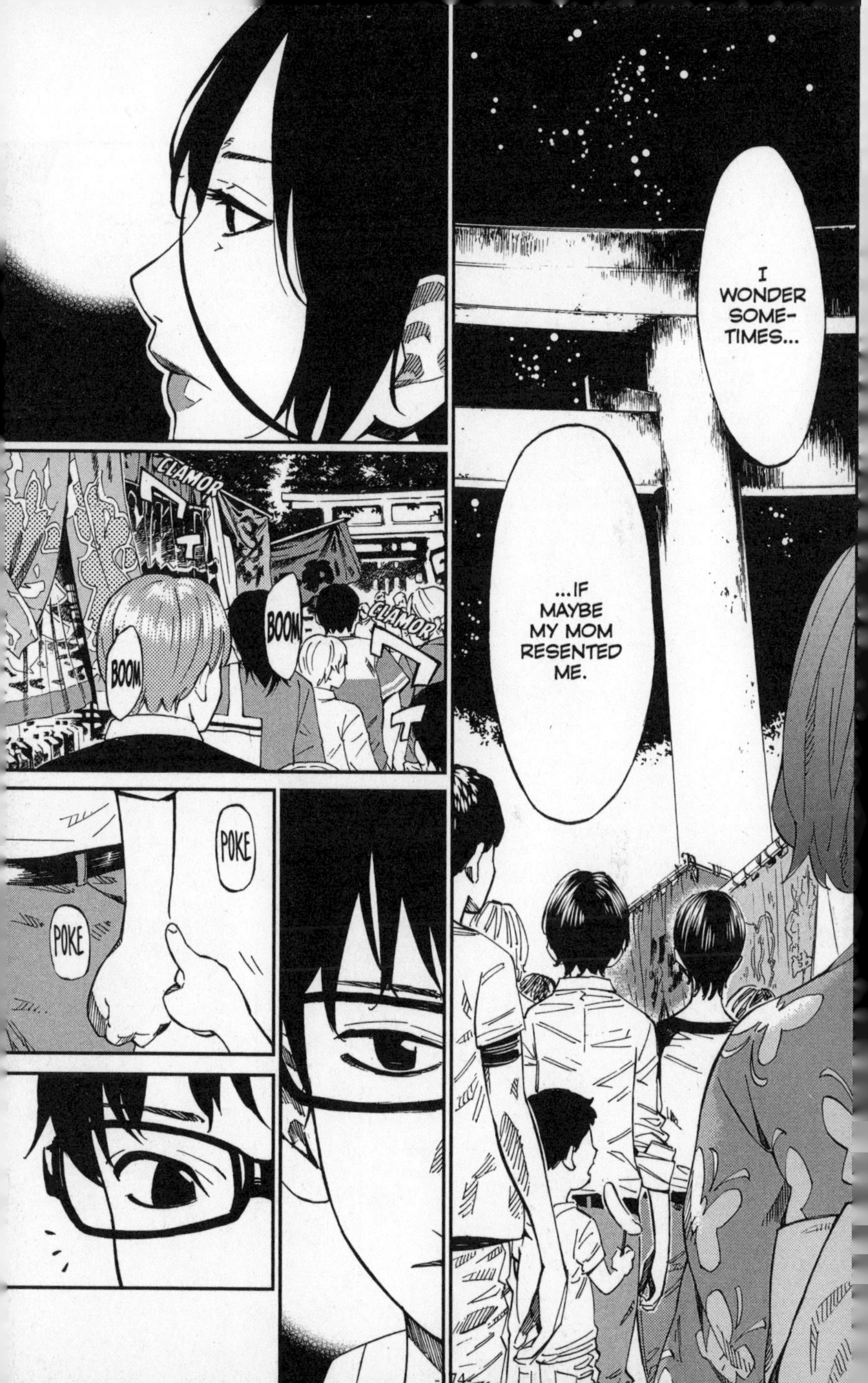
I WONDER SOME-TIMES...
...IF MAYBE MY MOM RESENTED ME.
CLAMOR
CLAMOR
BOOM
BOOM
POKE
POKE

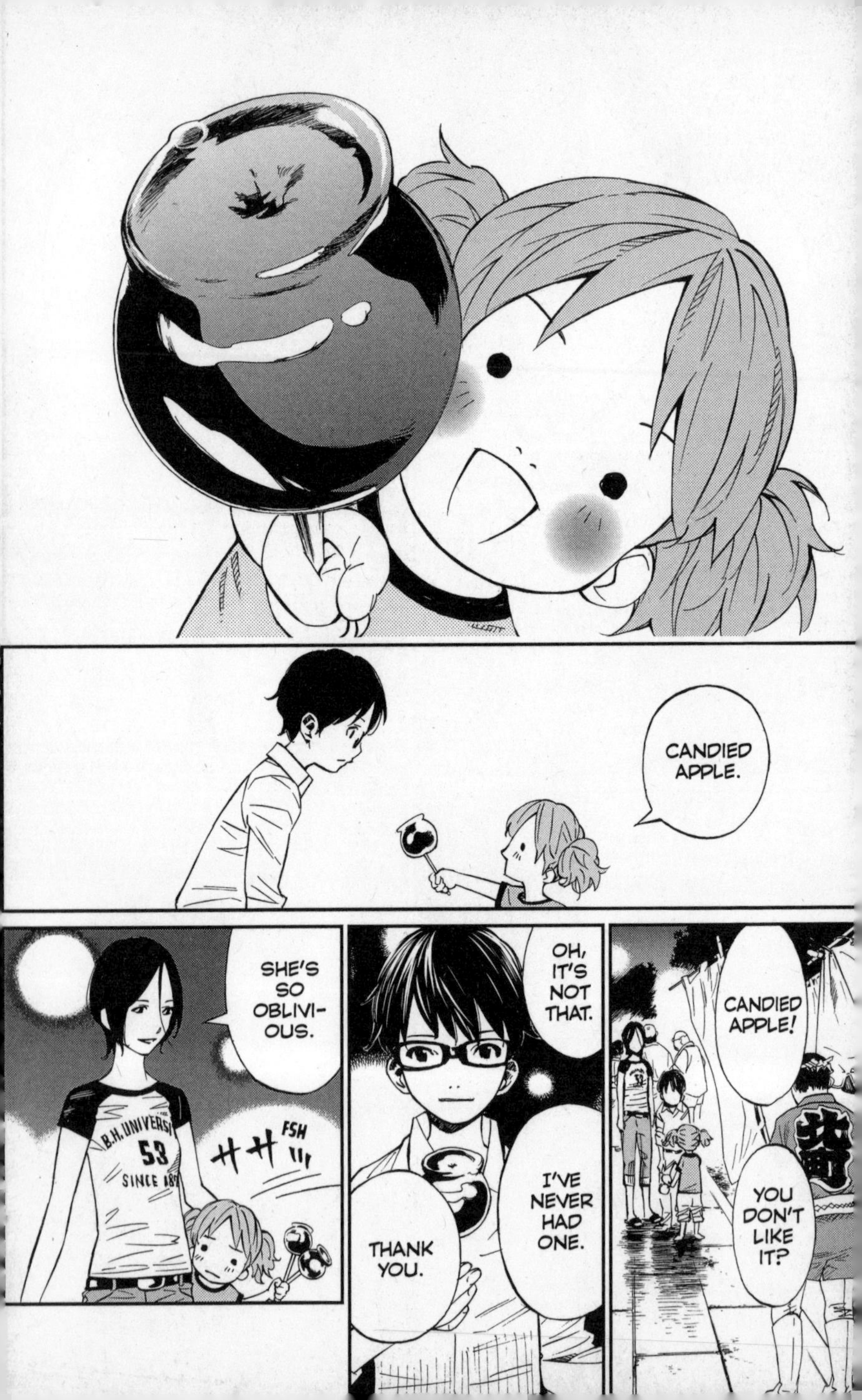
CANDIED APPLE.
CANDIED APPLE!
YOU DON'T LIKE IT?
OH, IT'S NOT THAT.
I'VE NEVER HAD ONE.
THANK YOU.
SHE'S SO OBLIVI-OUS.
FSH

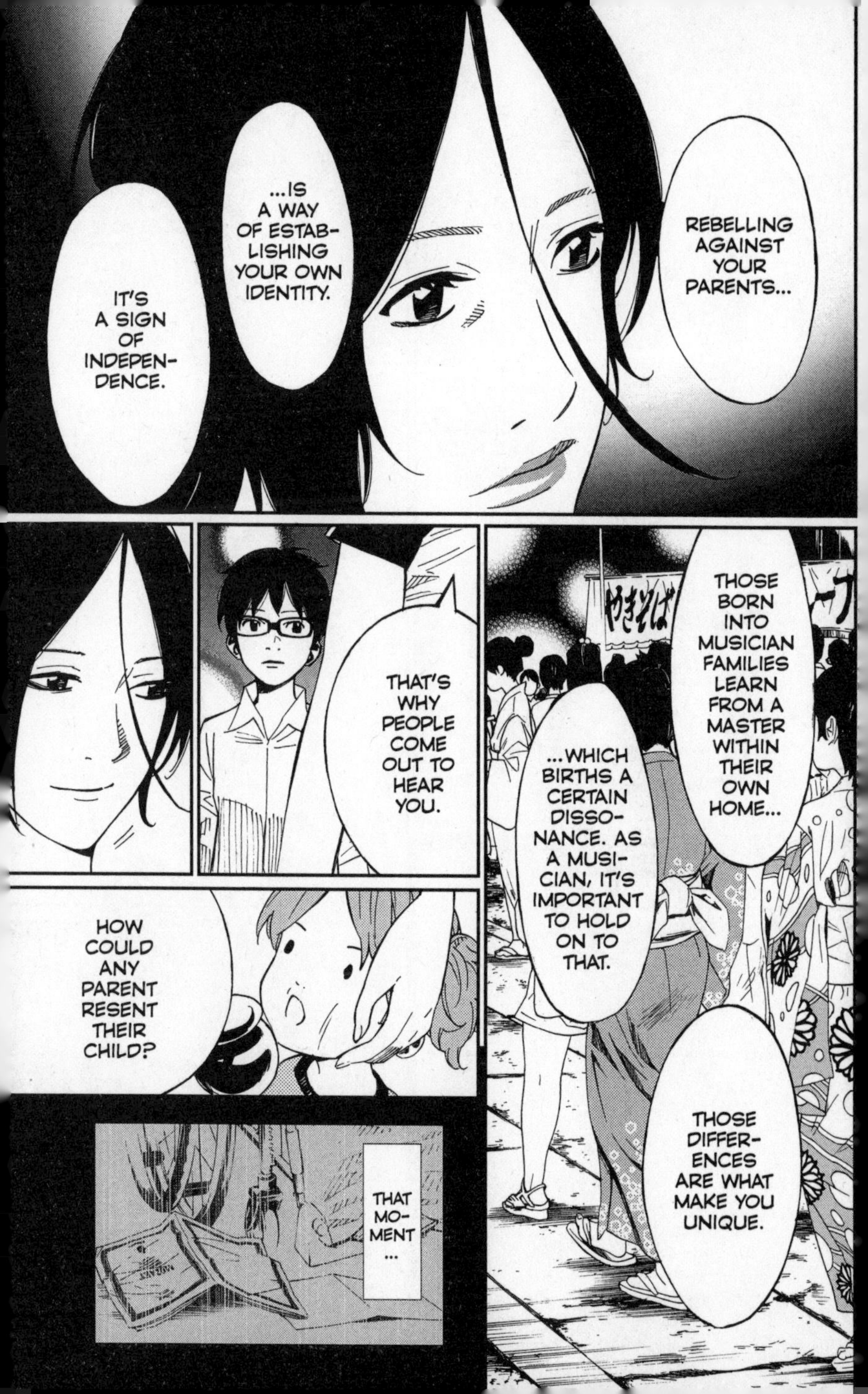
REBELLING AGAINST YOUR PARENTS...
...IS A WAY OF ESTAB-LISHING YOUR OWN IDENTITY.
IT'S A SIGN OF INDEPEN-DENCE.
やきそば
THOSE BORN INTO MUSICIAN FAMILIES LEARN FROM A MASTER WITHIN THEIR OWN HOME...
...WHICH BIRTHS A CERTAIN DISSO-NANCE. AS A MUSI-CIAN, IT'S IMPORTANT TO HOLD ON TO THAT.
THOSE DIFFER-ENCES ARE WHAT MAKE YOU UNIQUE.
THAT'S WHY PEOPLE COME OUT TO HEAR YOU.
HOW COULD ANY PARENT RESENT THEIR CHILD?
THAT MO-MENT...

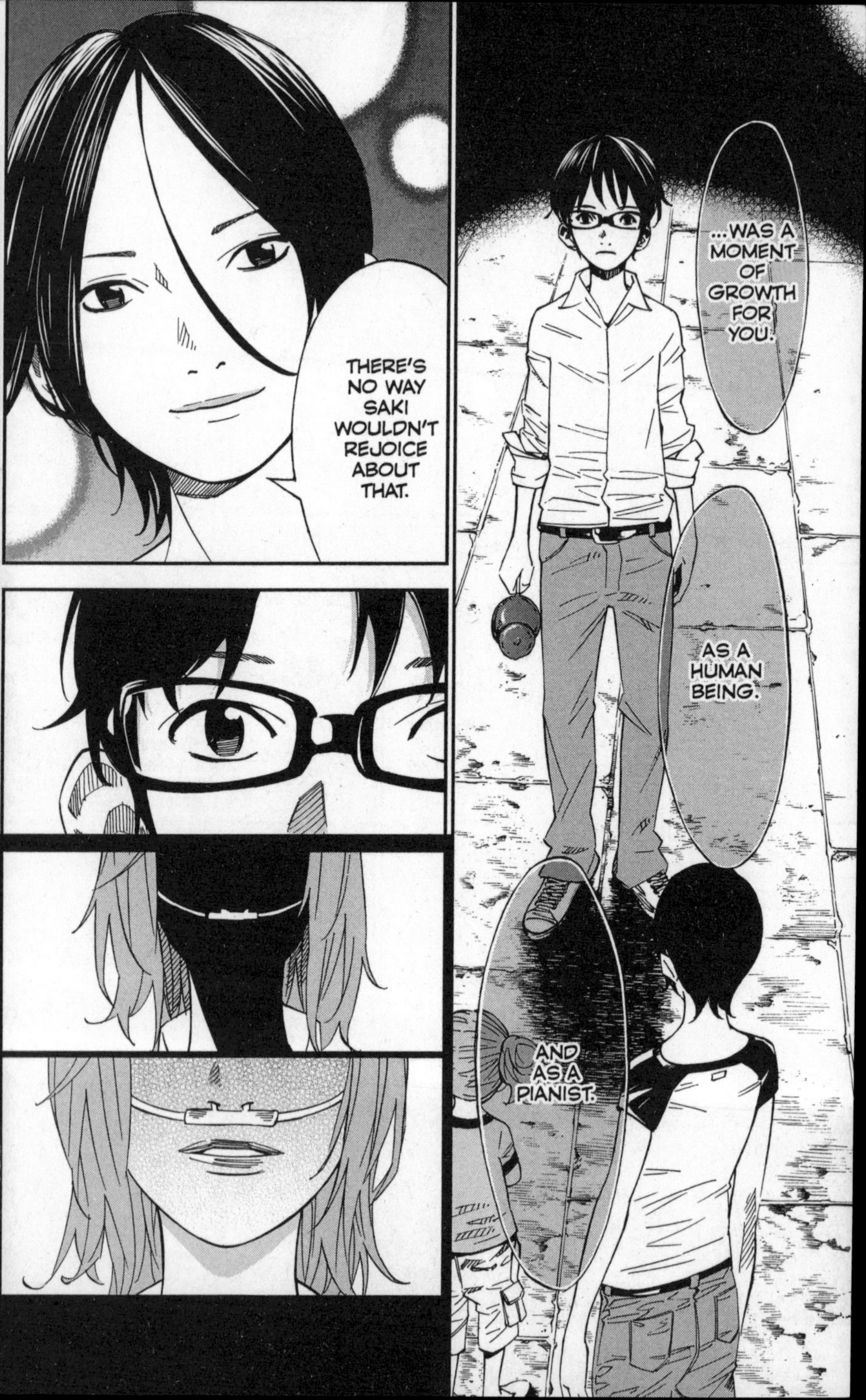
...WAS A MOMENT OF GROWTH FOR YOU.
AS A HUMAN BEING.
AND AS A PIANIST.
THERE'S NO WAY SAKI WOULDN'T REJOICE ABOUT THAT.

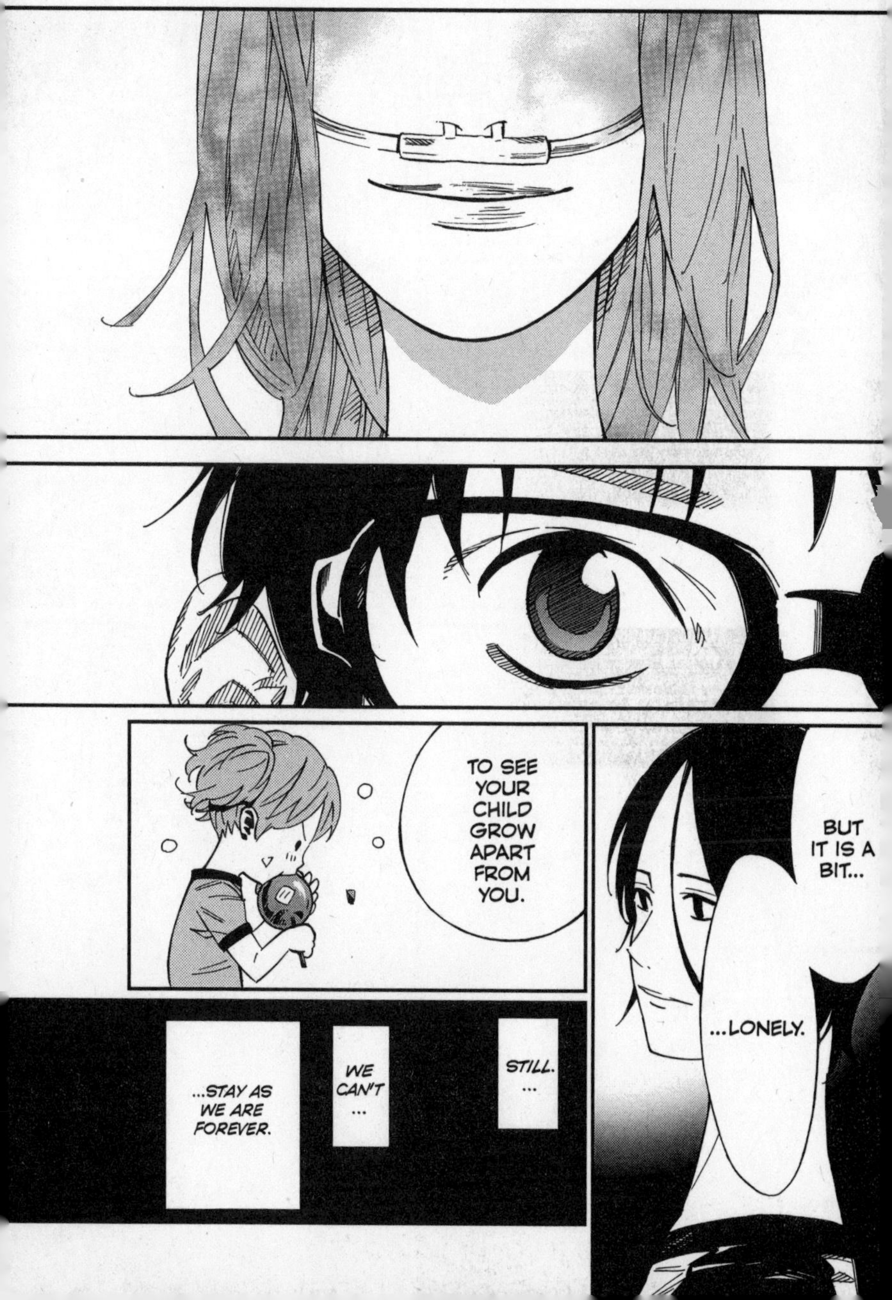
BUT IT IS A BIT...
...LONELY.
TO SEE YOUR CHILD GROW APART FROM YOU.
STILL. ...
WE CAN'T ...
...STAY AS WE ARE FOREVER.

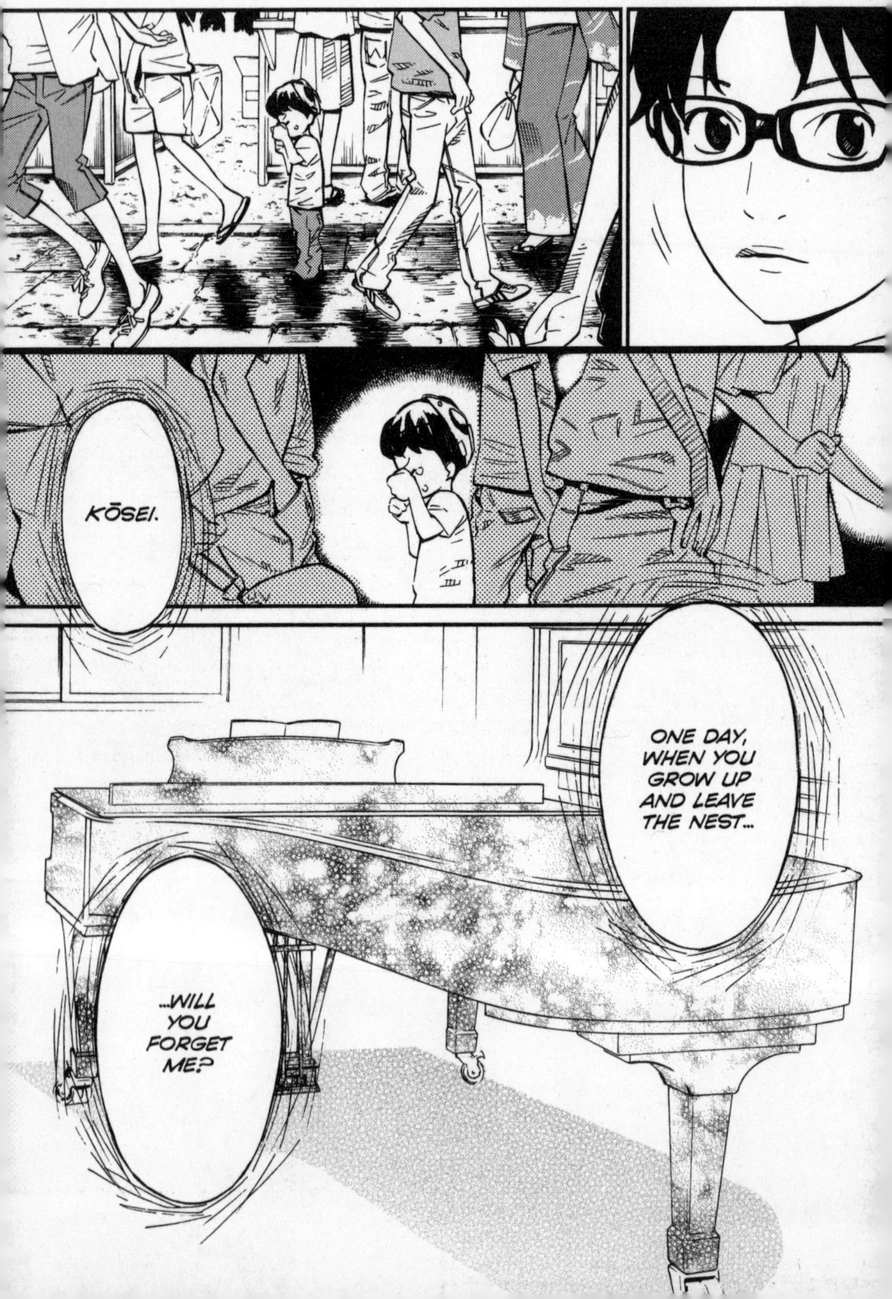
KŌSEI.
ONE DAY, WHEN YOU GROW UP AND LEAVE THE NEST...
...WILL YOU FORGET ME?

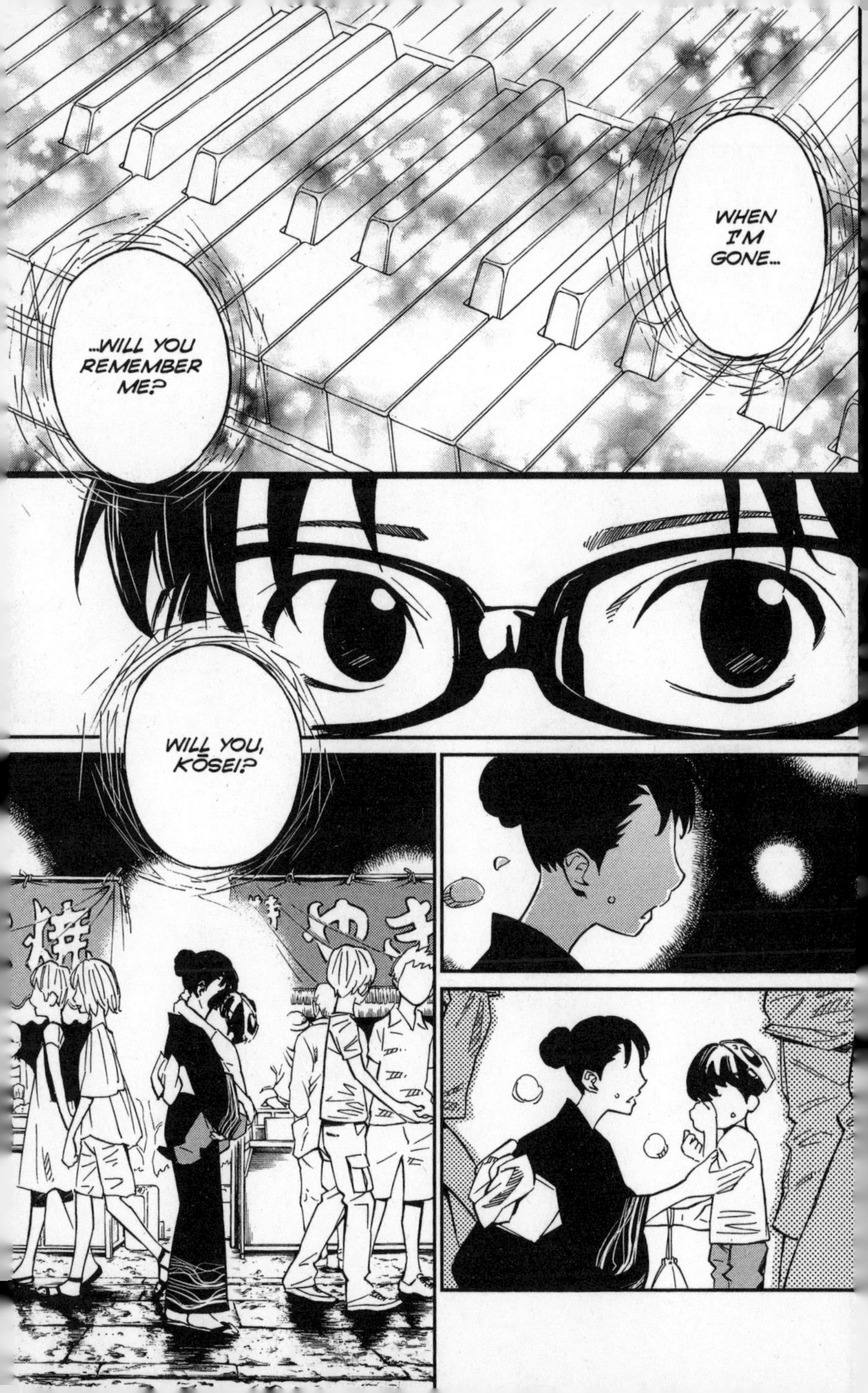
WHEN I'M GONE...
...WILL YOU REMEMBER ME?
WILL YOU, KŌSEI?

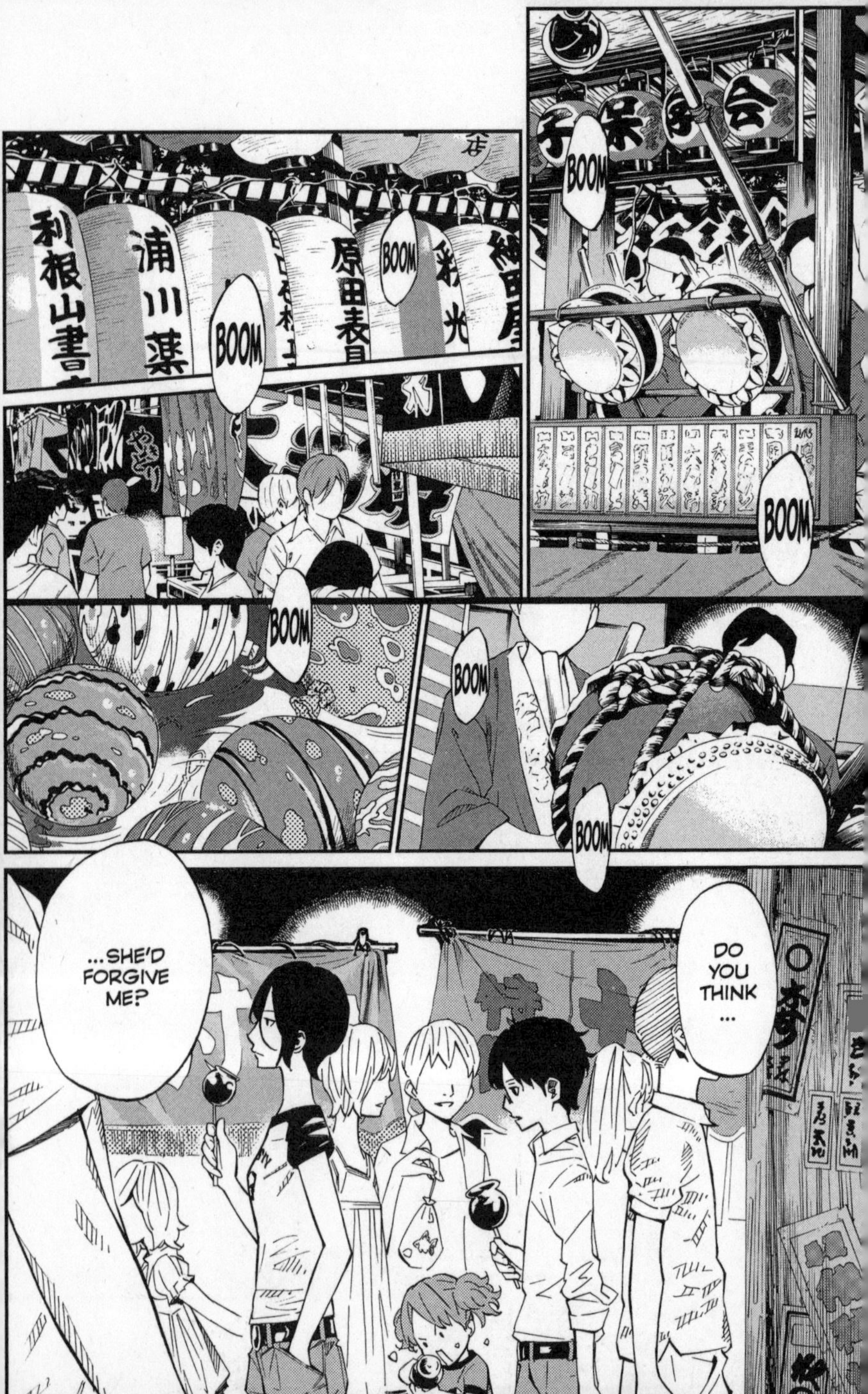
BOOM
BOOM
BOOM
BOOM
BOOM
BOOM
BOOM
BOOM
DO YOU THINK ...
...SHE'D FORGIVE ME?

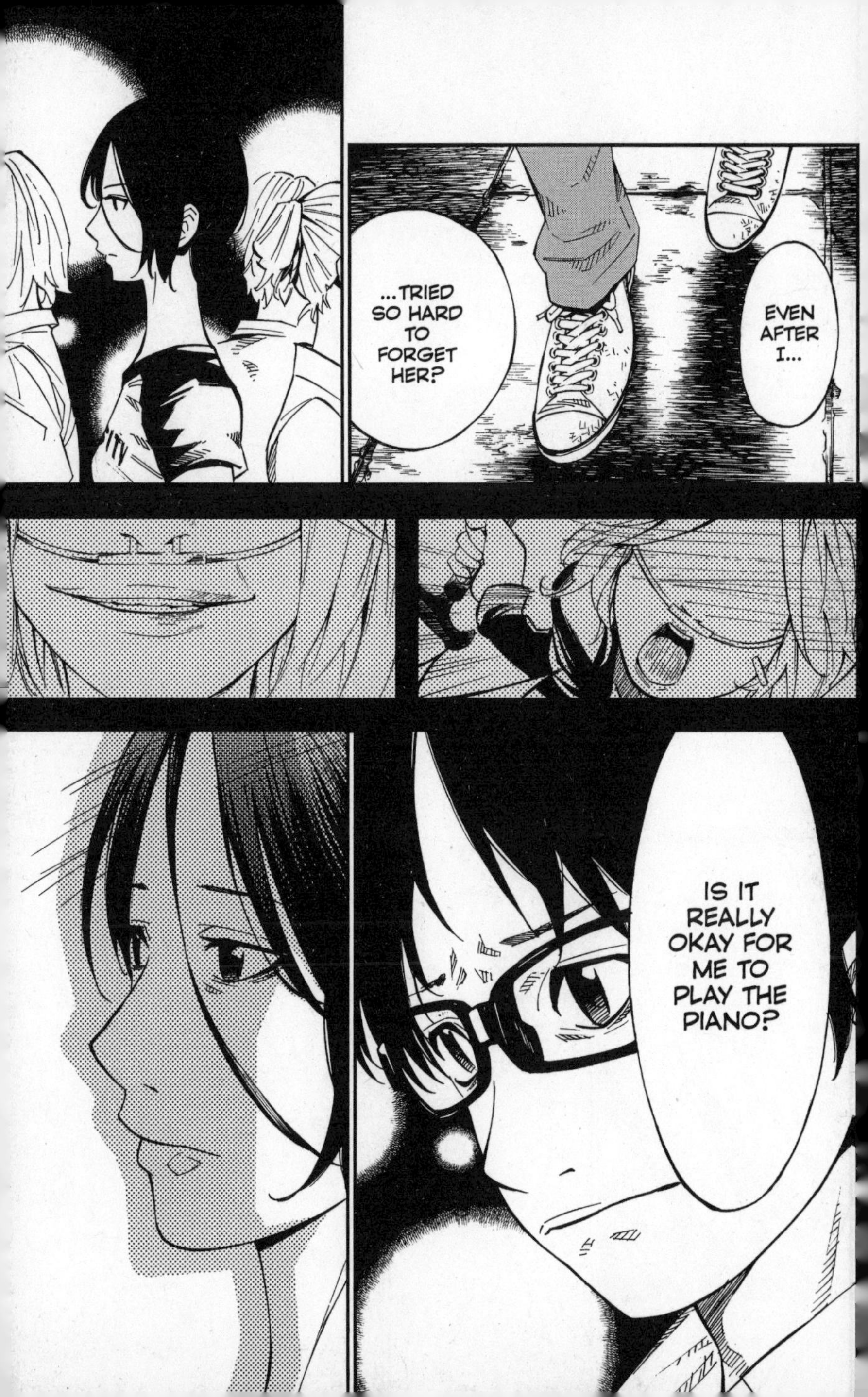
EVEN AFTER I...
...TRIED SO HARD TO FORGET HER?
IS IT REALLY OKAY FOR ME TO PLAY THE PIANO?

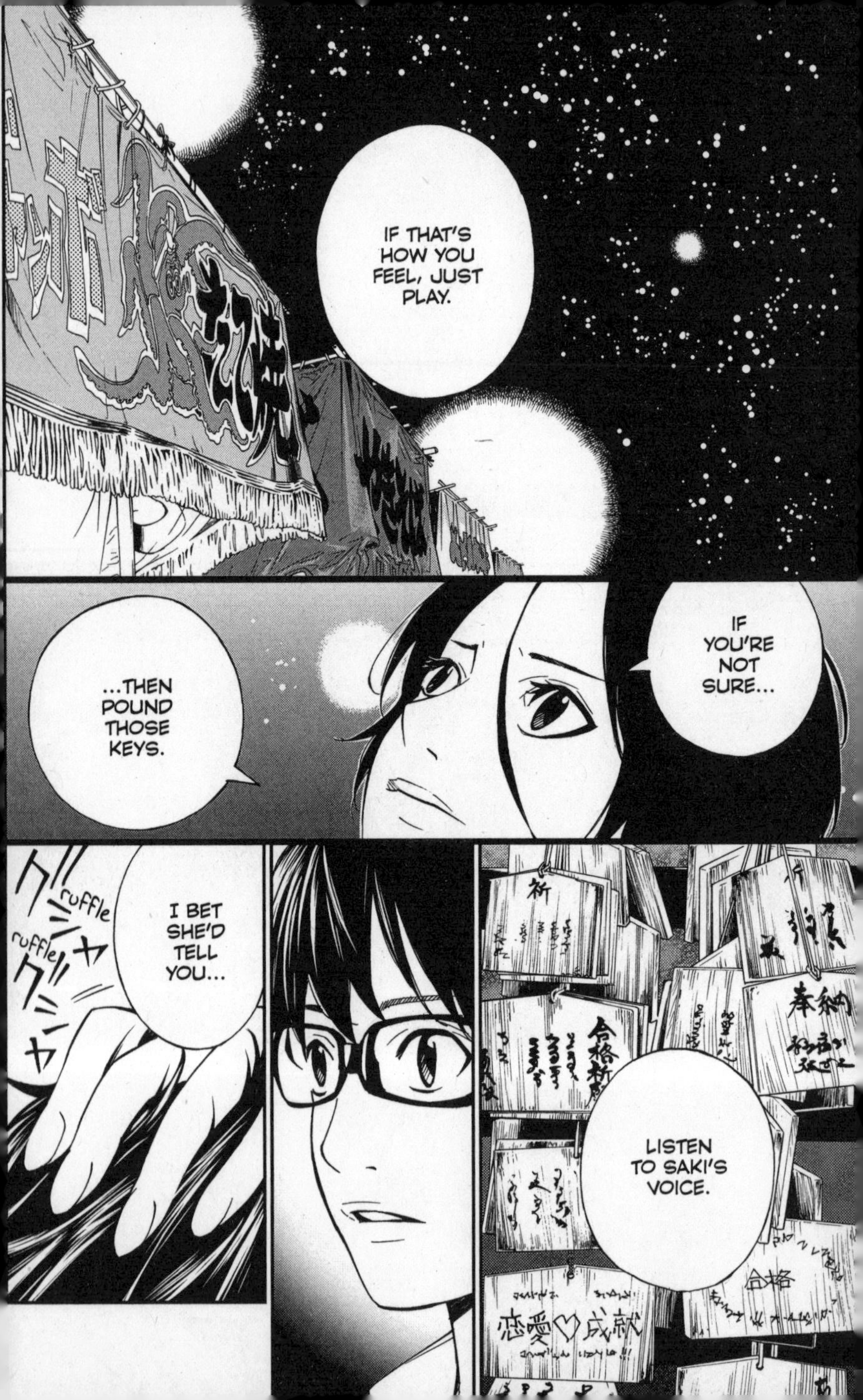
IF THAT'S HOW YOU FEEL, JUST PLAY.
IF YOU'RE NOT SURE...
...THEN POUND THOSE KEYS.
LISTEN TO SAKI'S VOICE.
奉納
合格
恋愛♡成就
I BET SHE'D TELL YOU...
ruffle
ruffle

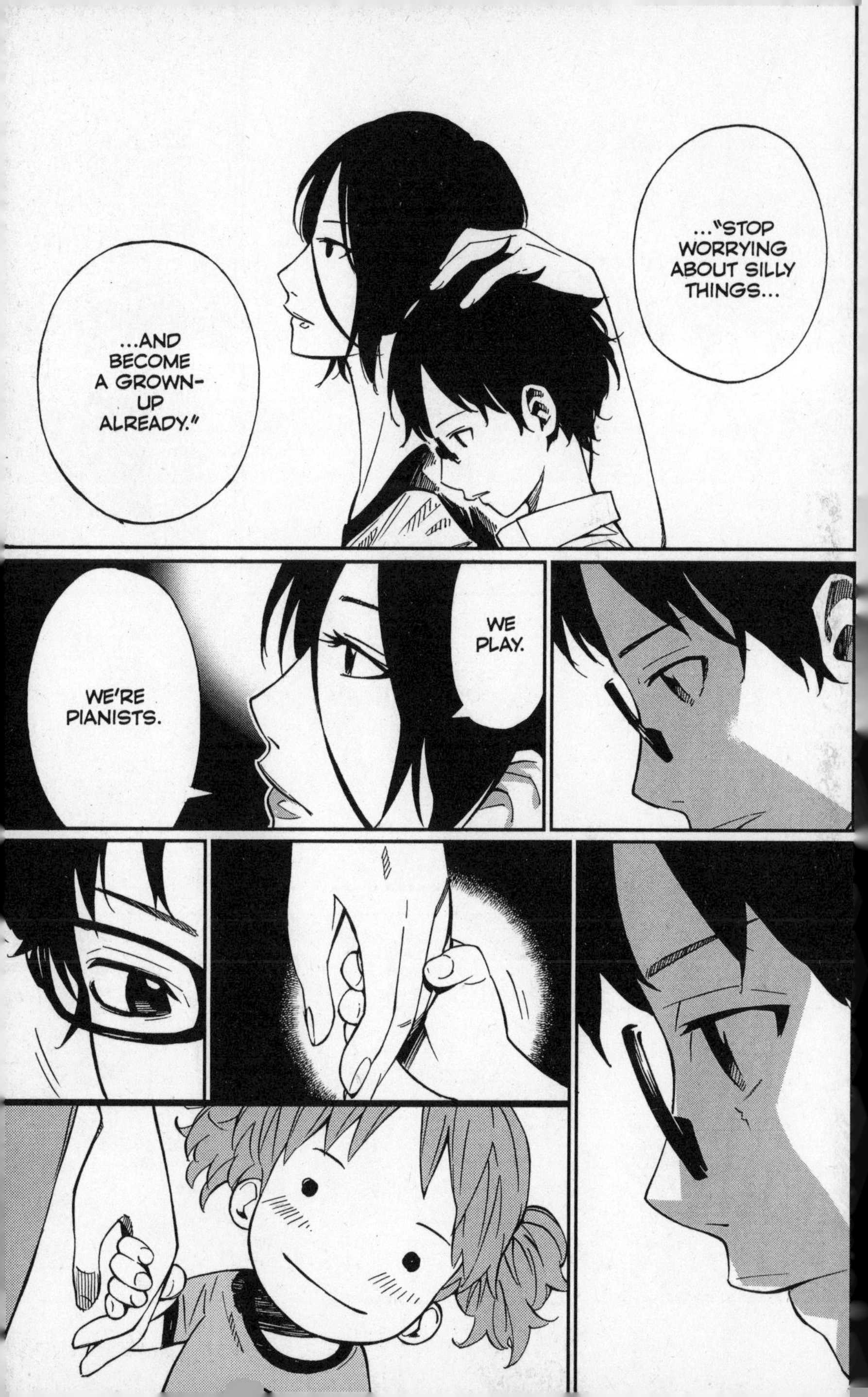
..."STOP WORRYING ABOUT SILLY THINGS...
...AND BECOME A GROWN-UP ALREADY."
WE PLAY.
WE'RE PIANISTS.

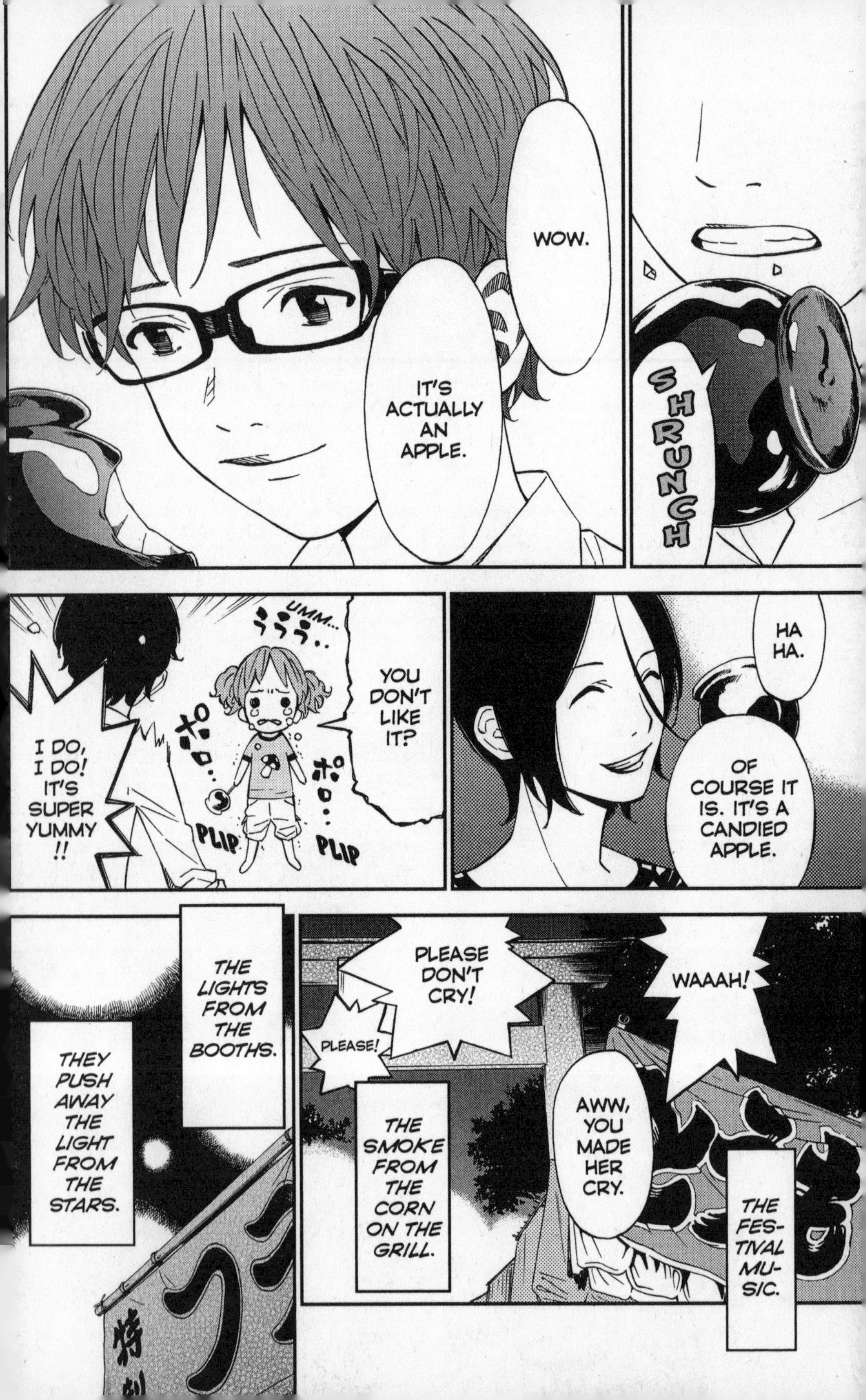
SHRUNCH
WOW.
IT'S ACTUALLY AN APPLE.
HA HA.
OF COURSE IT IS. IT'S A CANDIED APPLE.
UMM... ううう..
YOU DON'T LIKE IT?
ポロ..
PLIP
ポロ..
PLIP
I DO, I DO! IT'S SUPER YUMMY!!
WAAAH!
PLEASE DON'T CRY!
PLEASE!
THE FES-TIVAL MU-SIC.
AWW, YOU MADE HER CRY.
THE SMOKE FROM THE CORN ON THE GRILL.
THE LIGHTS FROM THE BOOTHS.
THEY PUSH AWAY THE LIGHT FROM THE STARS.

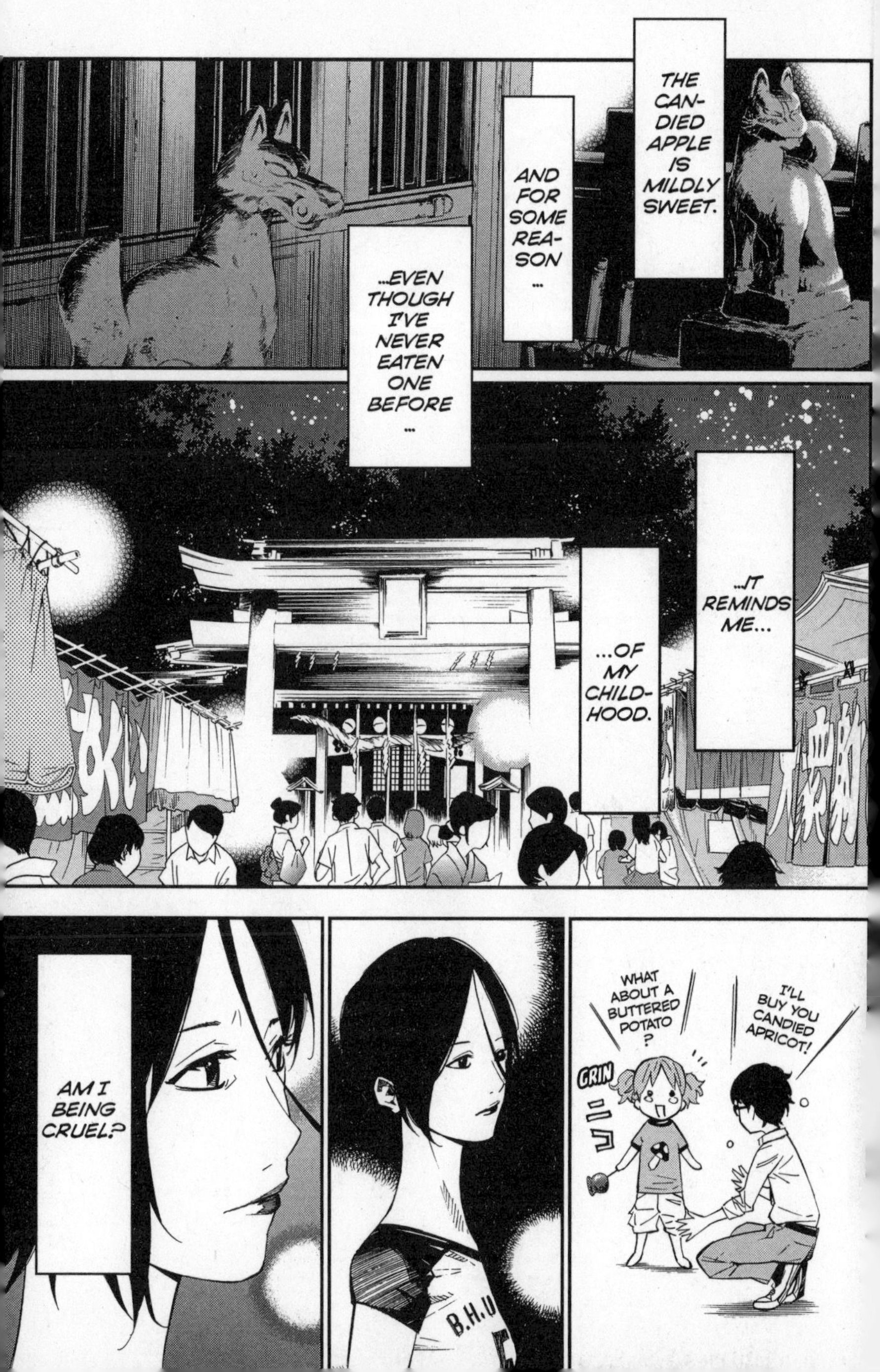
THE CAN-DIED APPLE IS MILDLY SWEET.
AND FOR SOME REA-SON ...
...EVEN THOUGH I'VE NEVER EATEN ONE BEFORE ...
...IT REMINDS ME...
...OF MY CHILD-HOOD.
I'LL BUY YOU CANDIED APRICOT!
WHAT ABOUT A BUTTERED POTATO ?
GRIN
AM I BEING CRUEL?

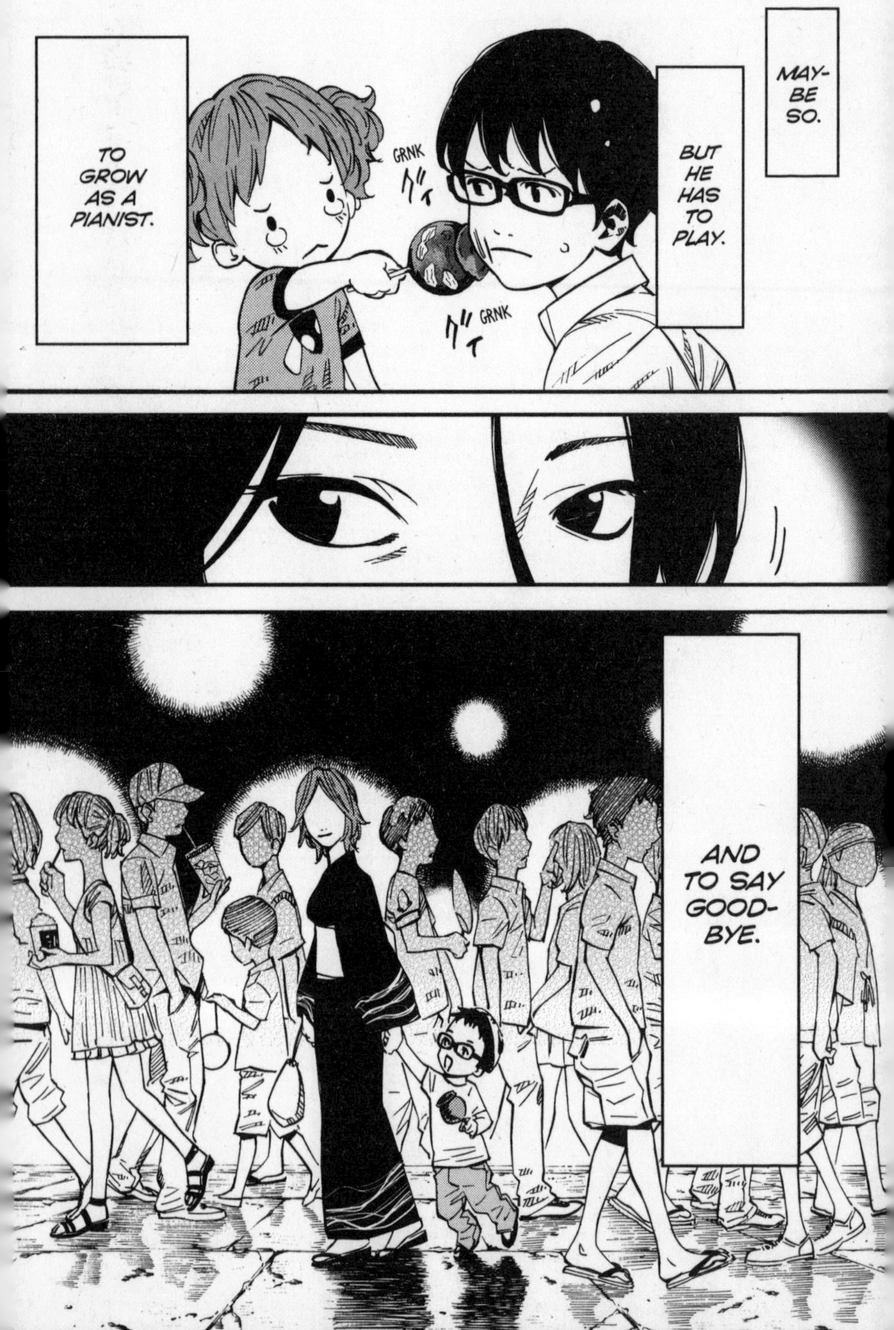
MAYBE SO.
BUT HE HAS TO PLAY.
GRNK
GRNK
TO GROW AS A PIANIST.
AND TO SAY GOODBYE.

CANDIED APPLE / END

Your Lie in April

I met the girl under full-bloomed cherry blossoms, and my fate has begun to change.

Your Lie in April

I met the girl under full-bloomed cherry blossoms, and my fate has begun to change.

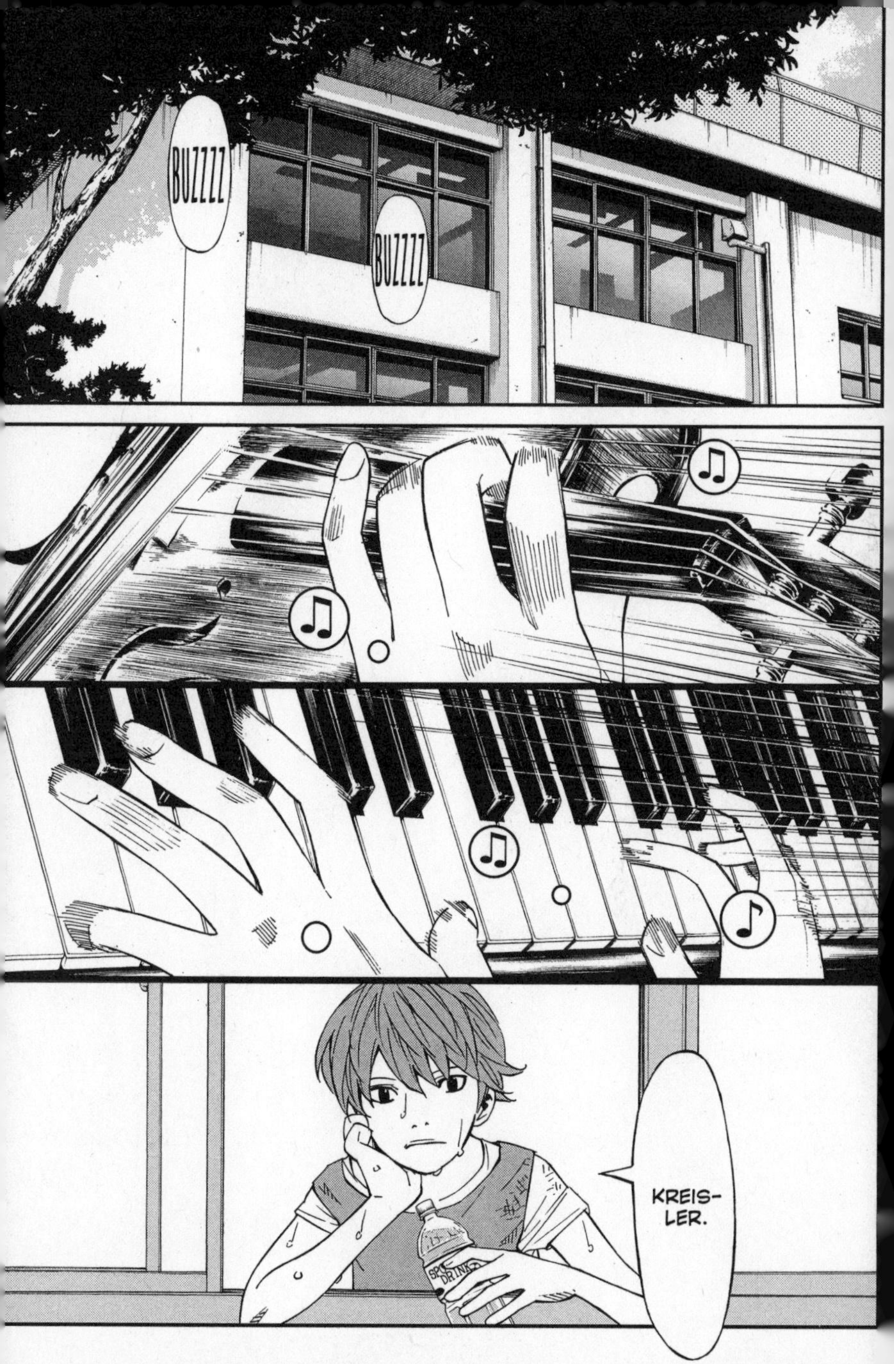
BUZZZZ
BUZZZZ
KREIS-LER.

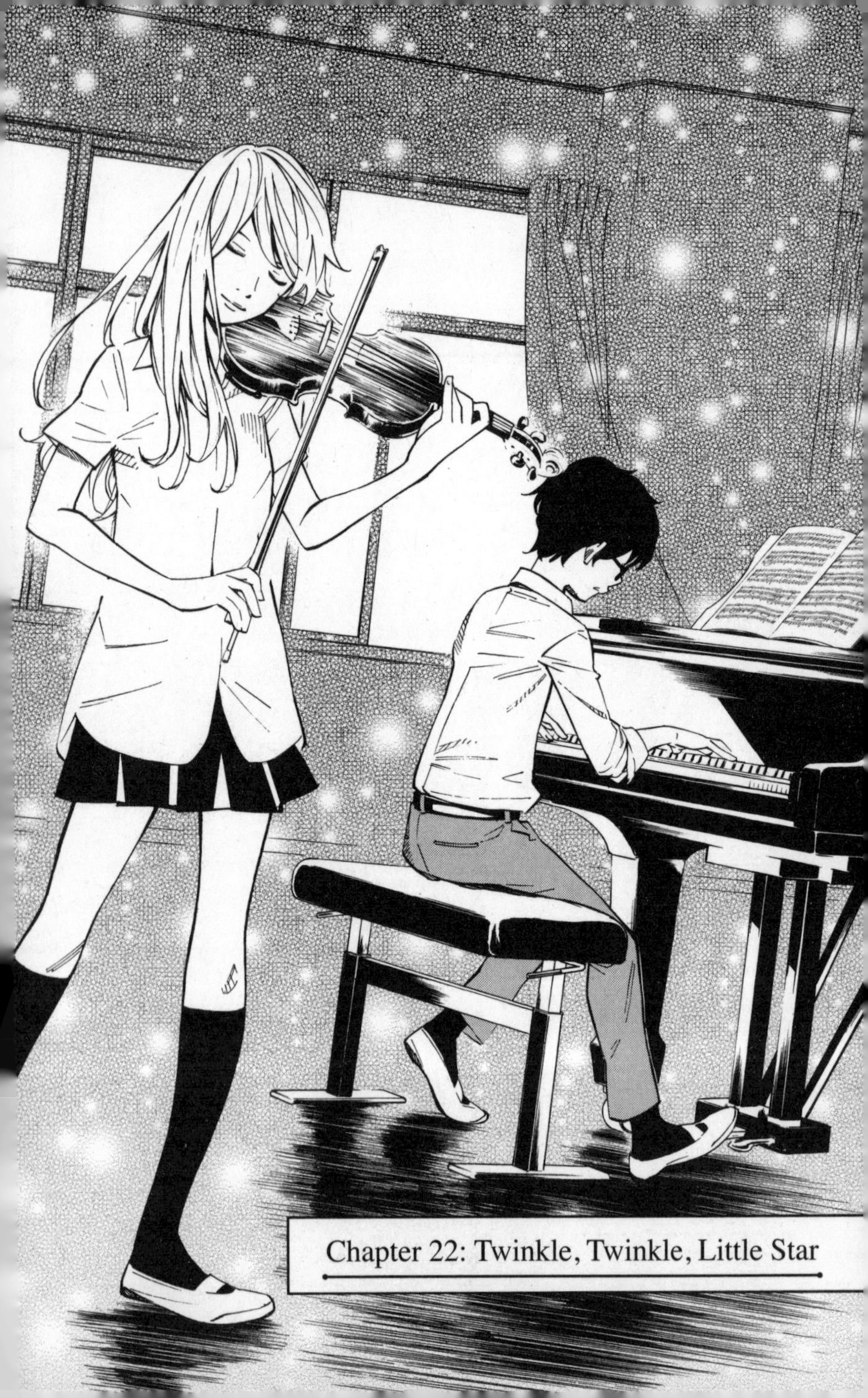
Chapter 22: Twinkle, Twinkle, Little Star

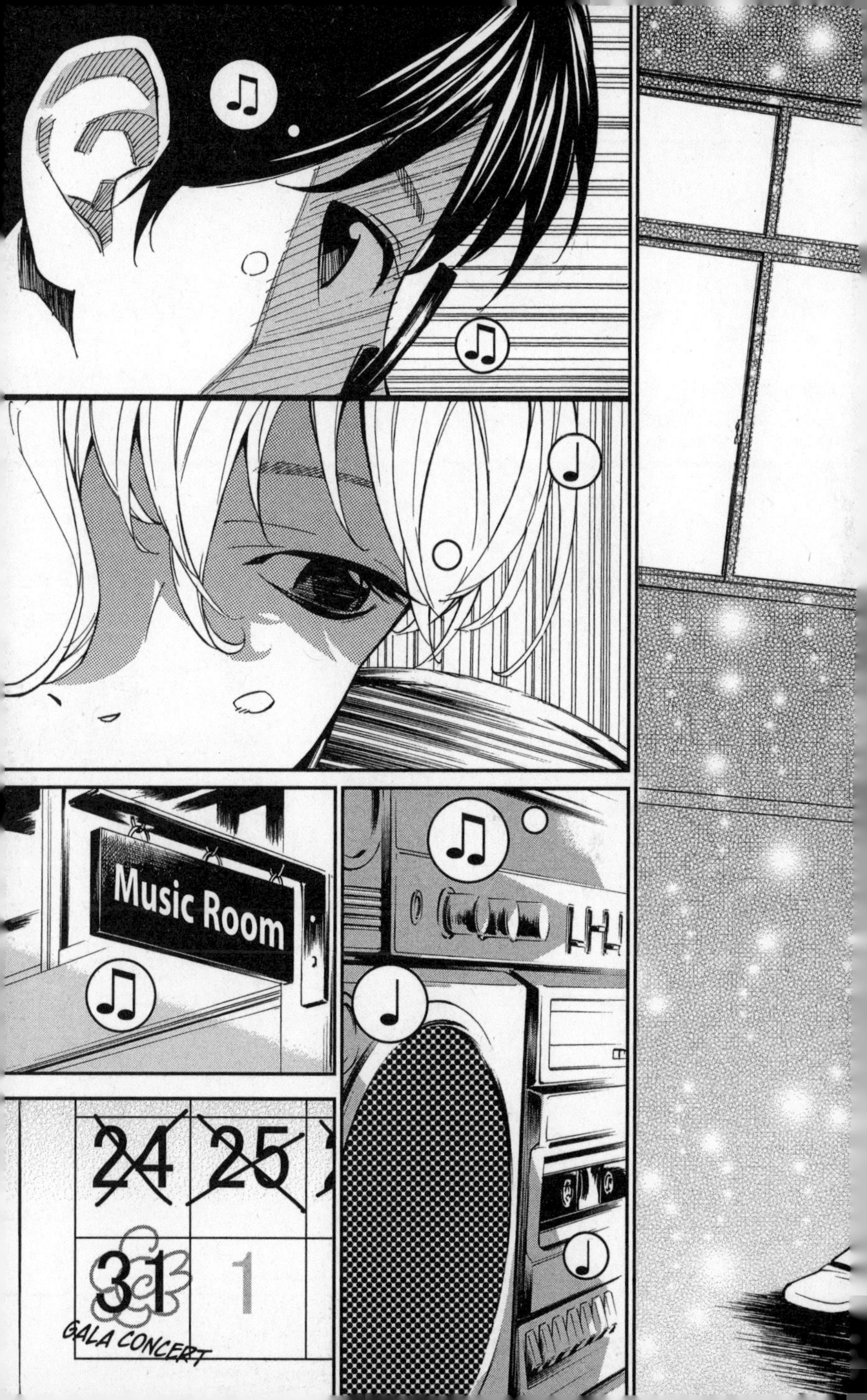
Music Room
24 25
31 1
GALA CONCERT

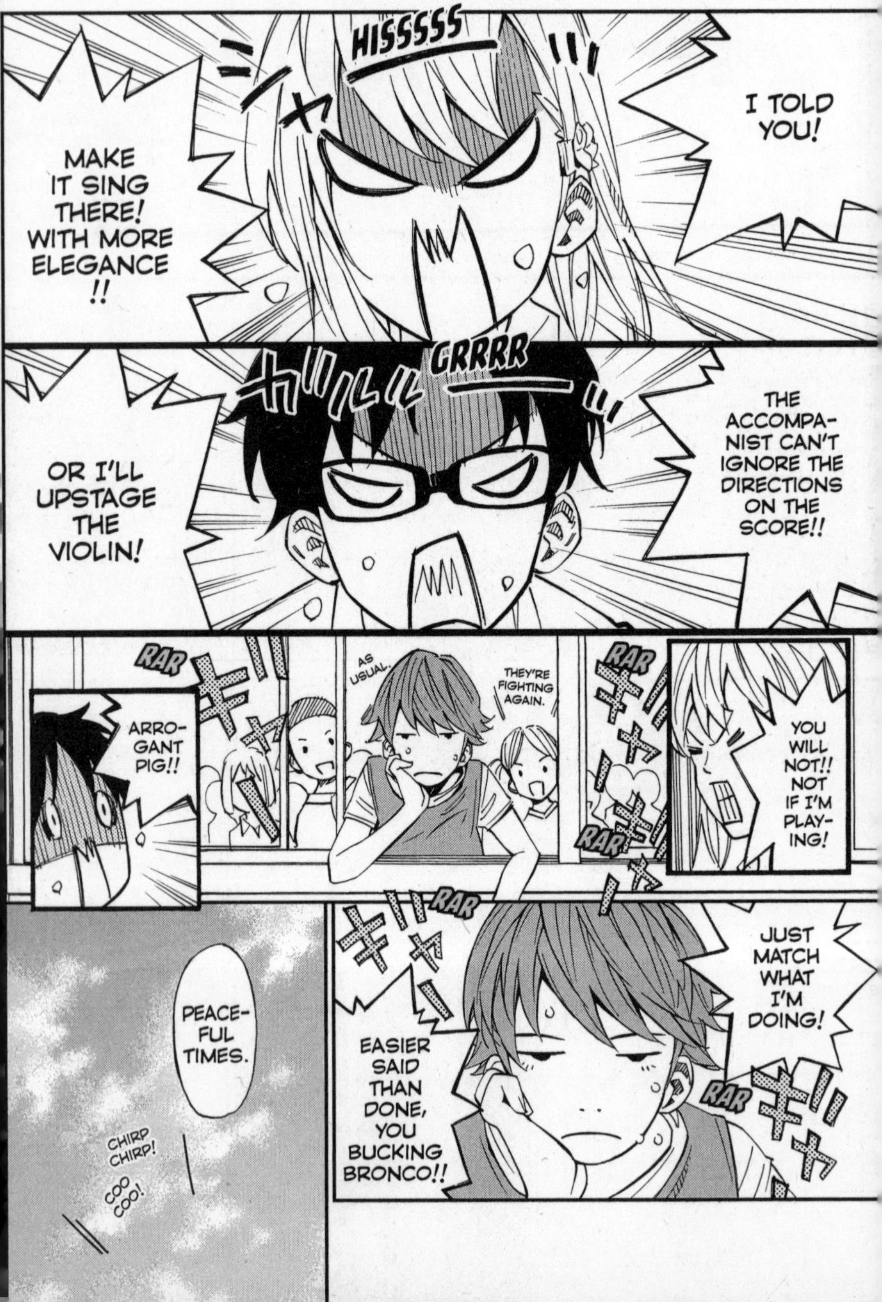
I TOLD YOU!
HISSSSS
MAKE IT SING THERE! WITH MORE ELEGANCE!!
THE ACCOMPANIST CAN'T IGNORE THE DIRECTIONS ON THE SCORE!!
GRRRR
OR I'LL UPSTAGE THE VIOLIN!
YOU WILL NOT!! NOT IF I'M PLAYING!
RAR
RAR
THEY'RE FIGHTING AGAIN.
AS USUAL.
RAR
ARROGANT PIG!!
JUST MATCH WHAT I'M DOING!
RAR
RAR
EASIER SAID THAN DONE, YOU BUCKING BRONCO!!
PEACEFUL TIMES.
CHIRP CHIRP!
COO COO!

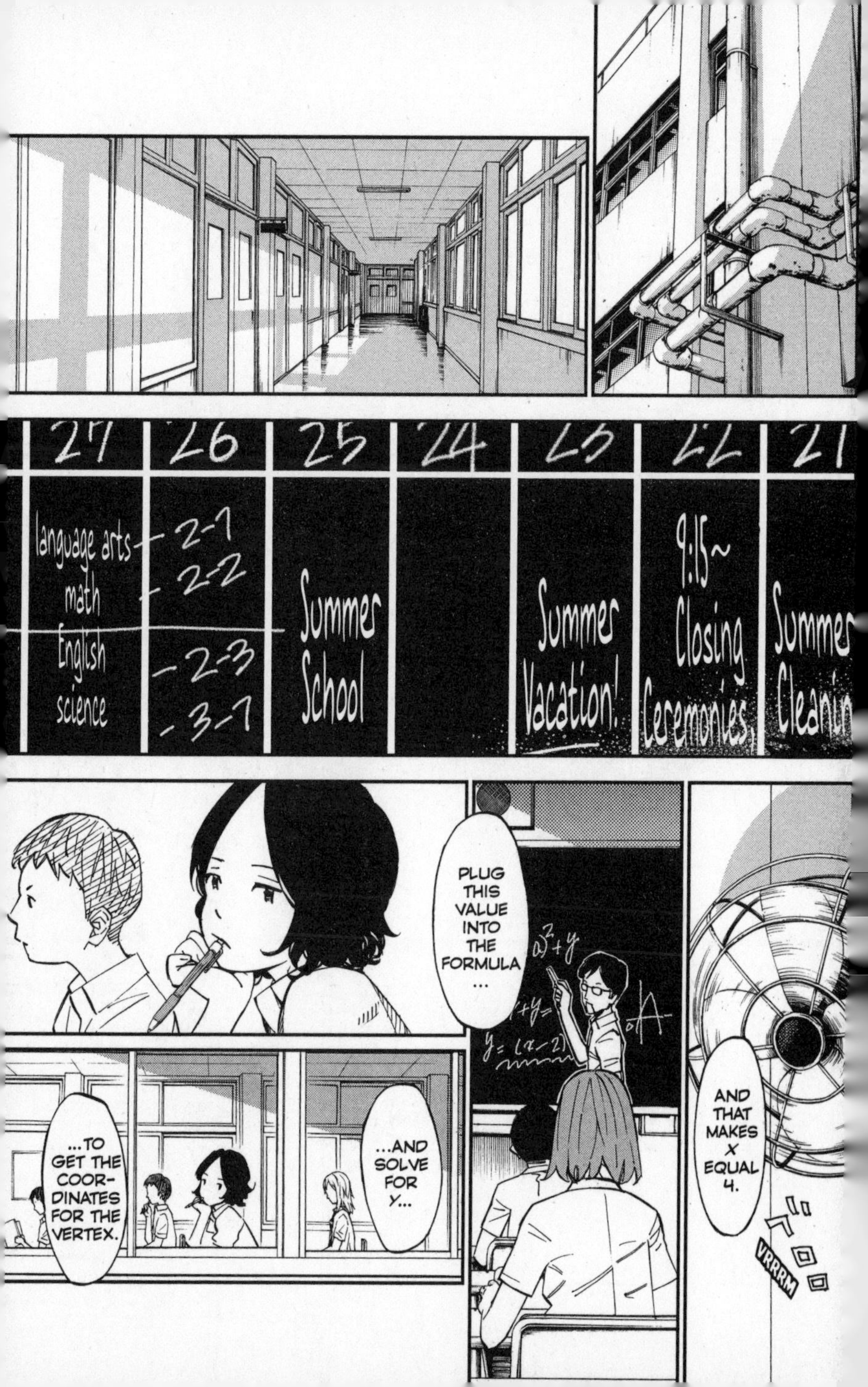
21
Summer Cleanin
22
9:15~
Closing Ceremonies,
23
Summer Vacation!
24
25
Summer School
26
2-1
2-2
2-3
3-1
27
language arts
math
English
science
AND THAT MAKES X EQUAL 4.
VRRRM
PLUG THIS VALUE INTO THE FORMULA ...
...AND SOLVE FOR Y...
...TO GET THE COORDINATES FOR THE VERTEX.

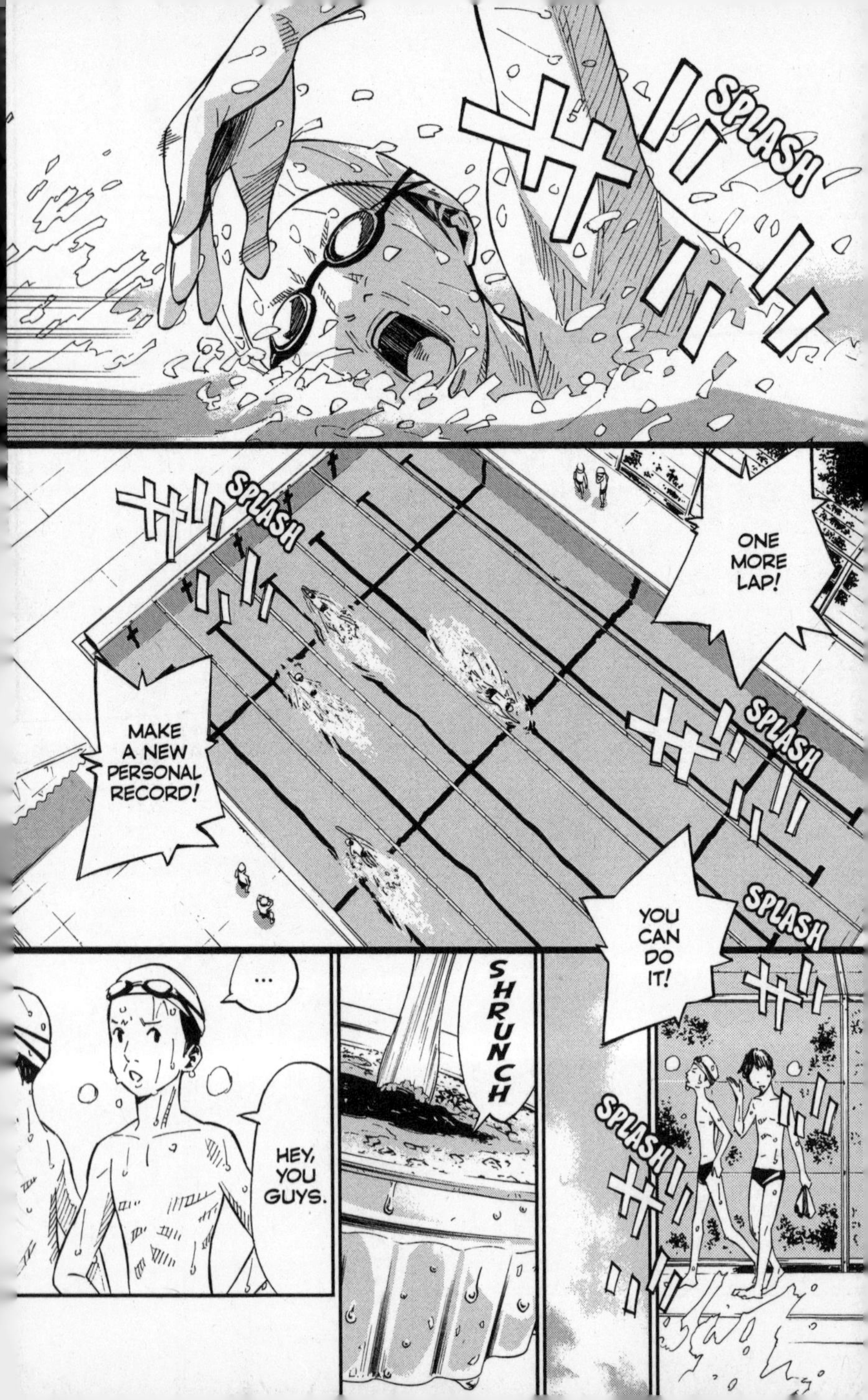
SPLASH
ONE MORE LAP!
SPLASH
SPLASH
MAKE A NEW PERSONAL RECORD!
SPLASH
YOU CAN DO IT!
SPLASH
SHRUNCH
...
HEY, YOU GUYS.

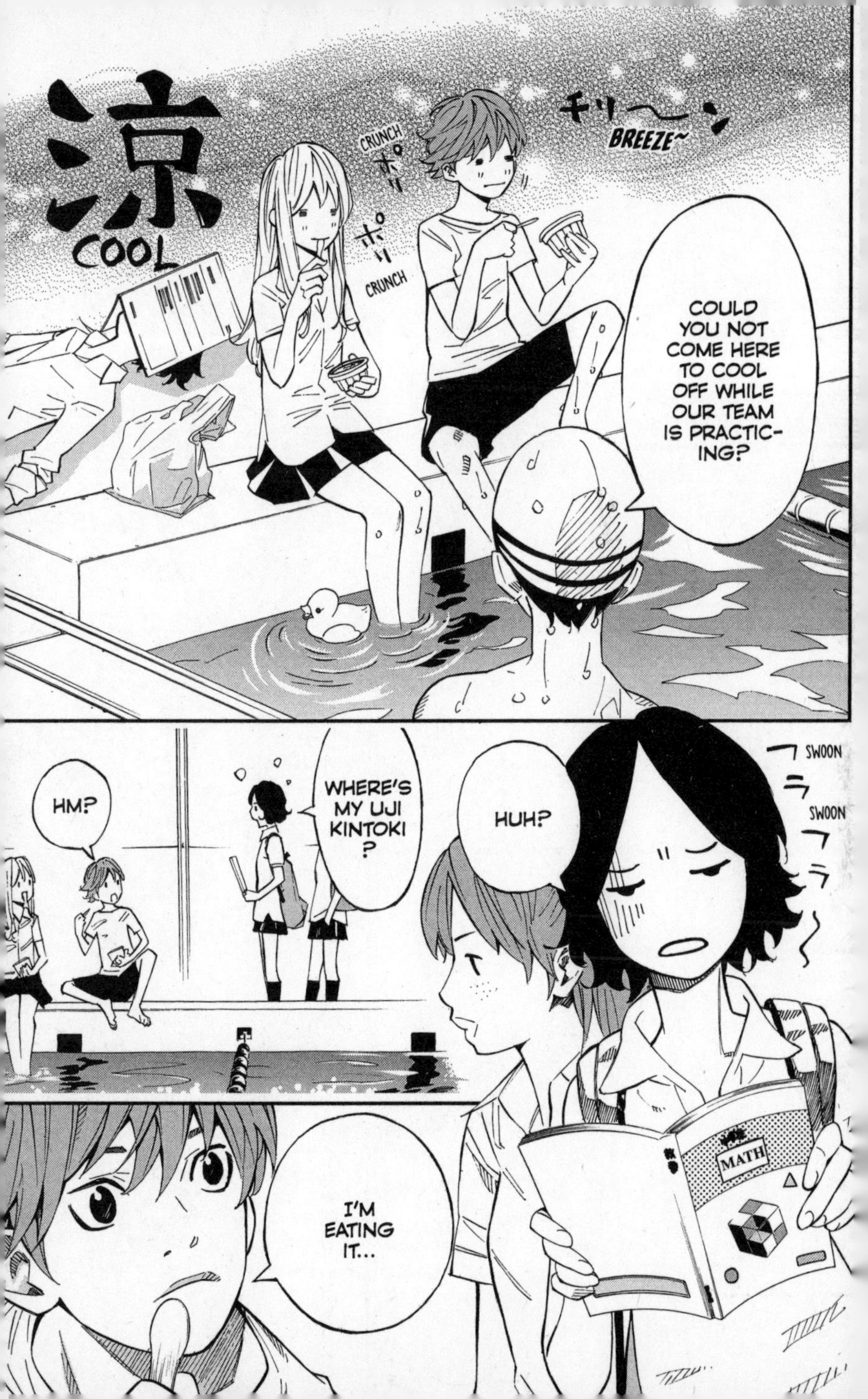

COULD YOU NOT COME HERE TO COOL OFF WHILE OUR TEAM IS PRACTIC-ING?
BREEZE~
CRUNCH
CRUNCH
涼
COOL
SWOON
SWOON
HUH?
WHERE'S MY UJI KINTOKI?
HM?
I'M EATING IT...

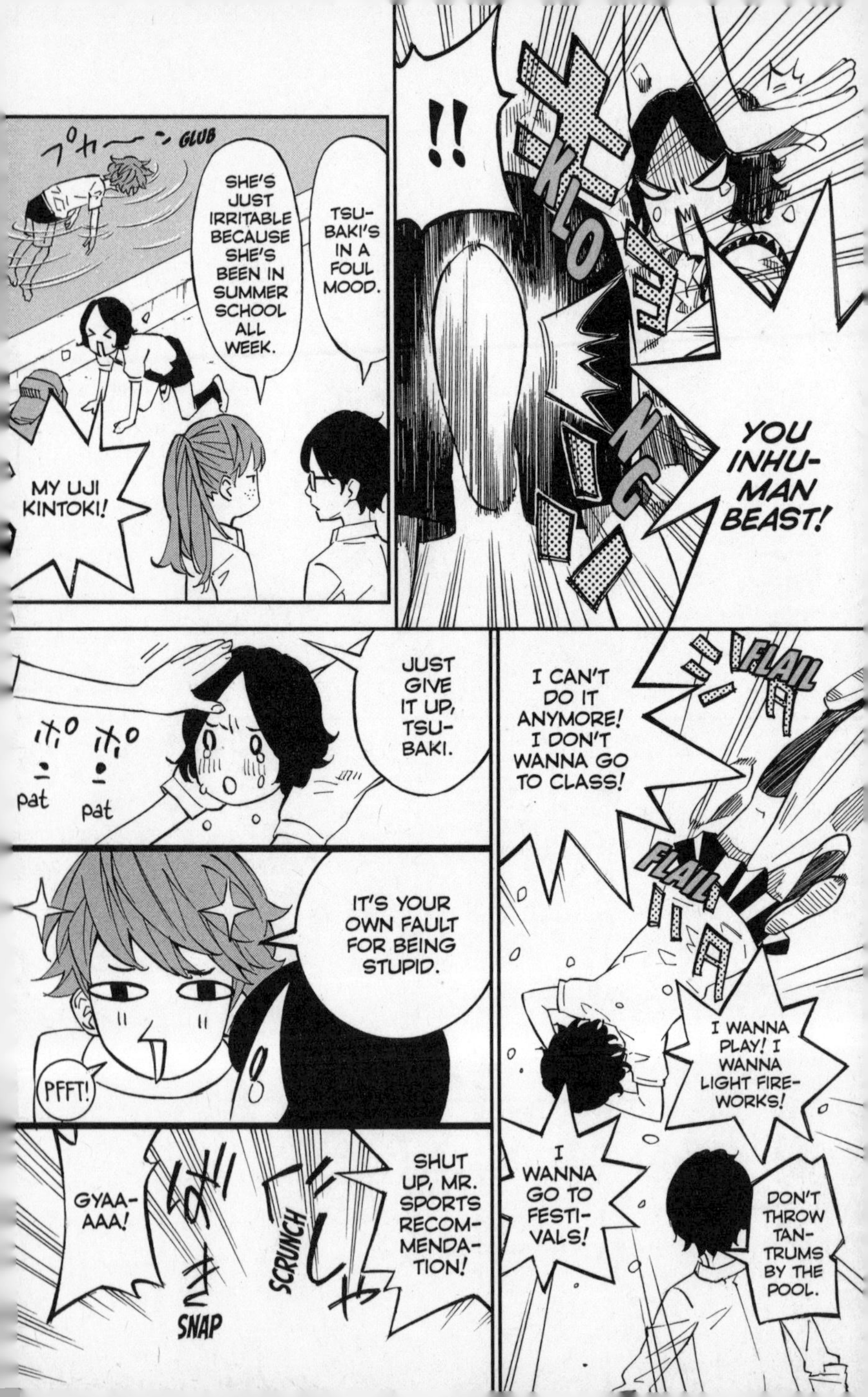
!!
KLONNG
YOU INHUMAN BEAST!
プカ〜ン GLUB
TSUBAKI'S IN A FOUL MOOD.
SHE'S JUST IRRITABLE BECAUSE SHE'S BEEN IN SUMMER SCHOOL ALL WEEK.
MY UJI KINTOKI!
FLAIL
I CAN'T DO IT ANYMORE! I DON'T WANNA GO TO CLASS!
FLAIL
I WANNA PLAY! I WANNA LIGHT FIREWORKS!
I WANNA GO TO FESTIVALS!
DON'T THROW TANTRUMS BY THE POOL.
JUST GIVE IT UP, TSUBAKI.
pat
pat
IT'S YOUR OWN FAULT FOR BEING STUPID.
PFFT!
SHUT UP, MR. SPORTS RECOMMENDATION!
SCRUNCH
SNAP
GYAAAAA!

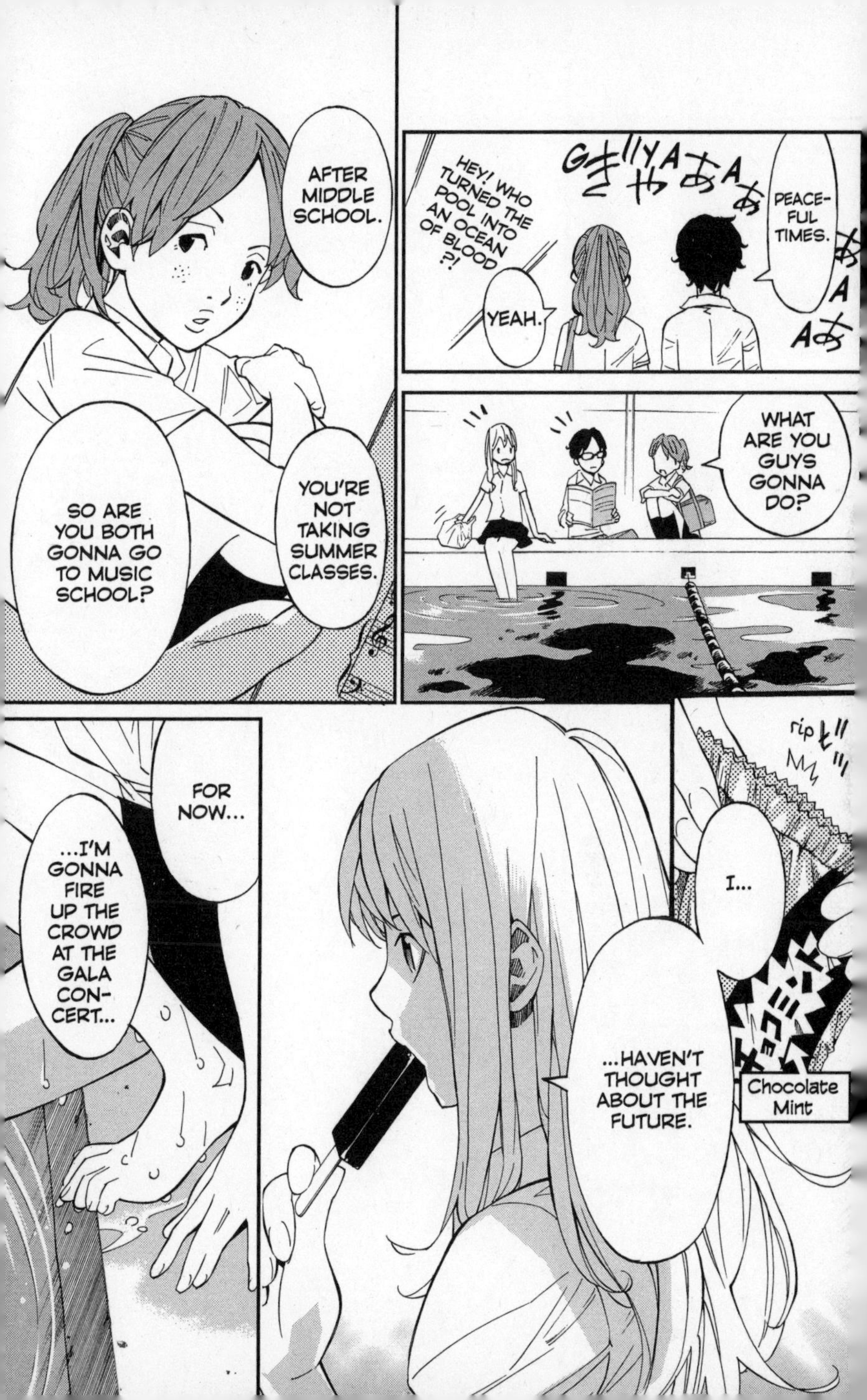
PEACE-FUL TIMES.
GYAAAA
HEY! WHO TURNED THE POOL INTO AN OCEAN OF BLOOD?!
YEAH.
WHAT ARE YOU GUYS GONNA DO?
AFTER MIDDLE SCHOOL.
YOU'RE NOT TAKING SUMMER CLASSES.
SO ARE YOU BOTH GONNA GO TO MUSIC SCHOOL?
rip
I...
...HAVEN'T THOUGHT ABOUT THE FUTURE.
Chocolate Mint
FOR NOW...
...I'M GONNA FIRE UP THE CROWD AT THE GALA CON-CERT...

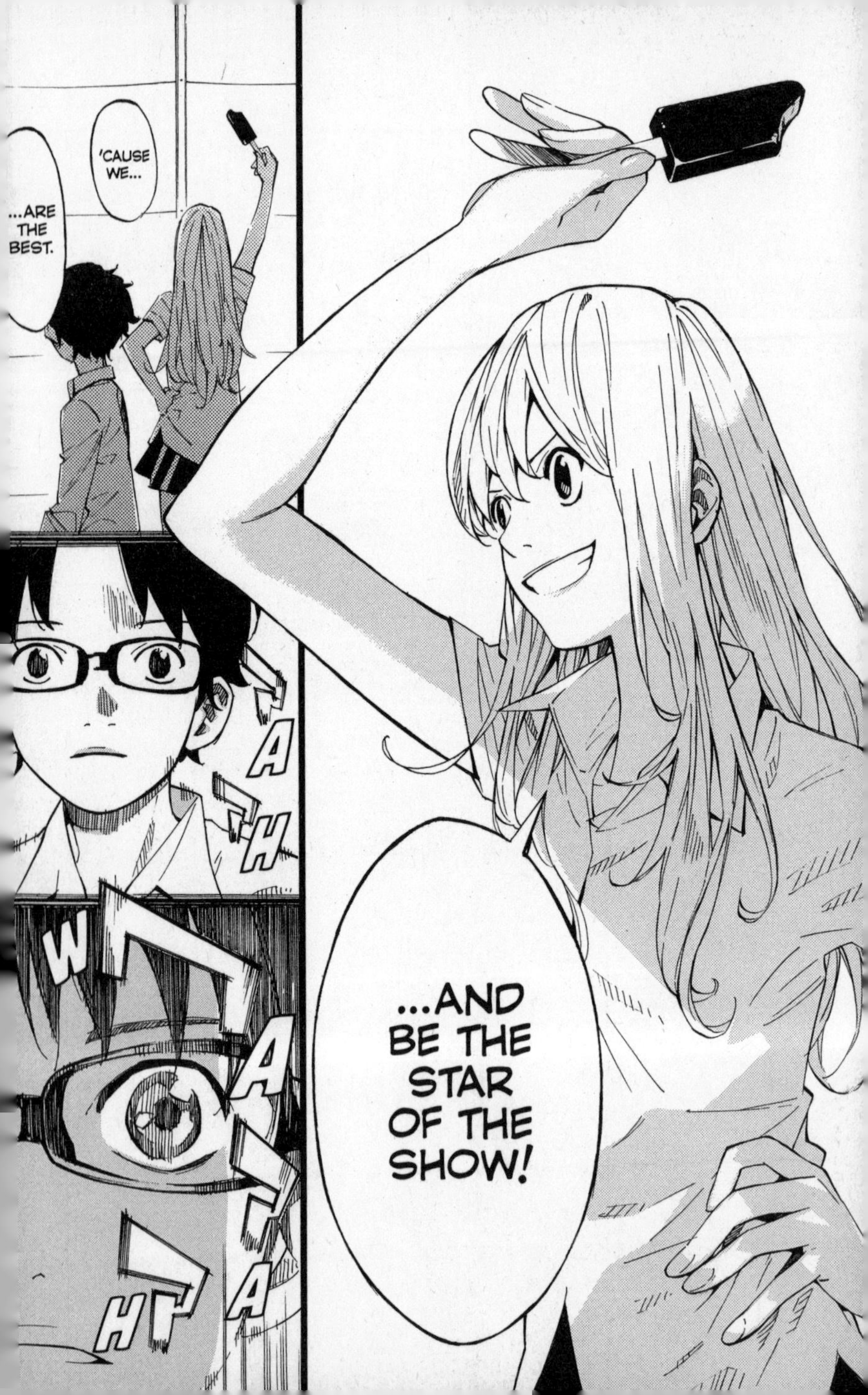

...AND BE THE STAR OF THE SHOW!
'CAUSE WE...
...ARE THE BEST.
AH
WAAH

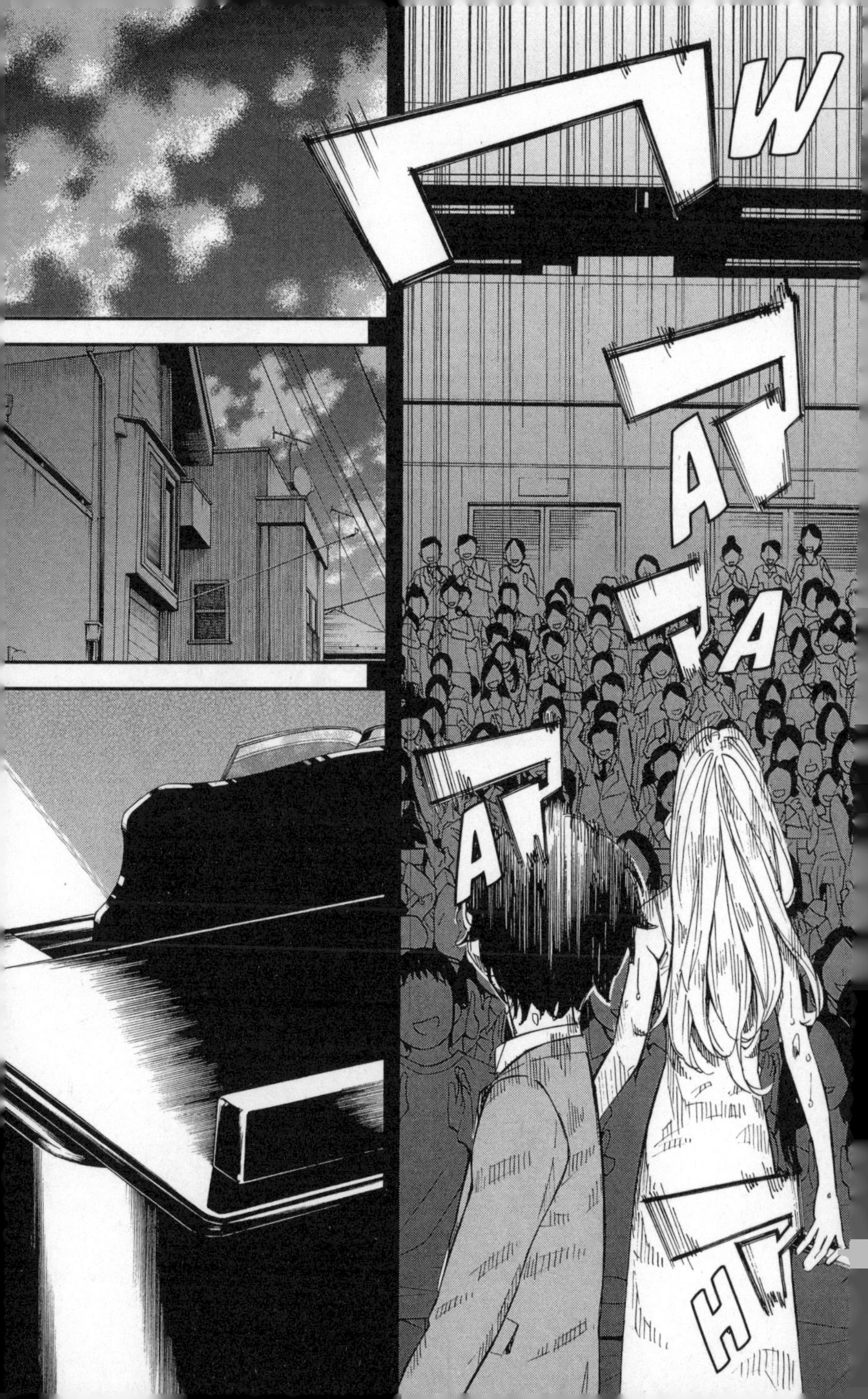
WAAAH

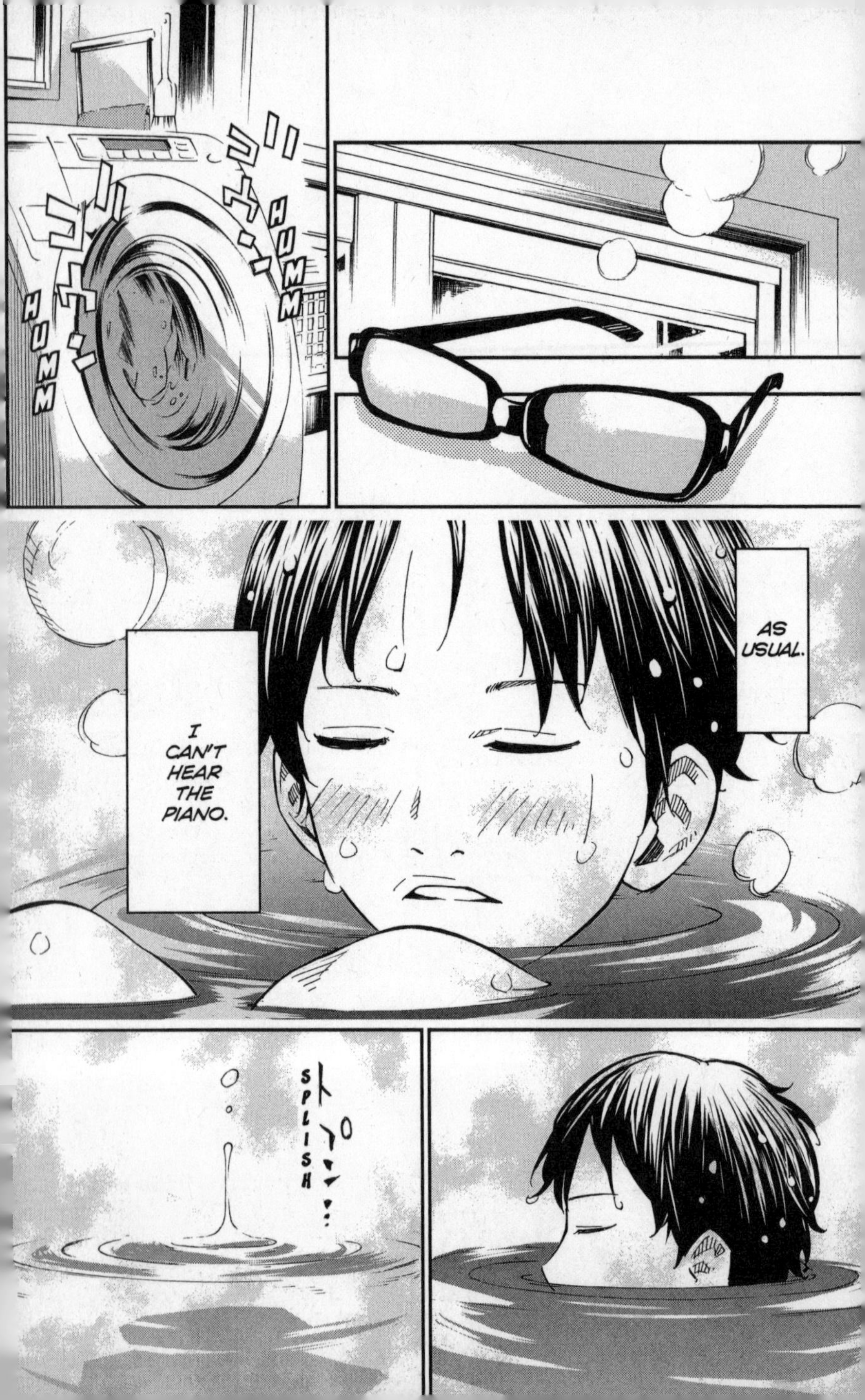
HUMM
HUMM
AS USUAL.
I CAN'T HEAR THE PIANO.
SPLISH

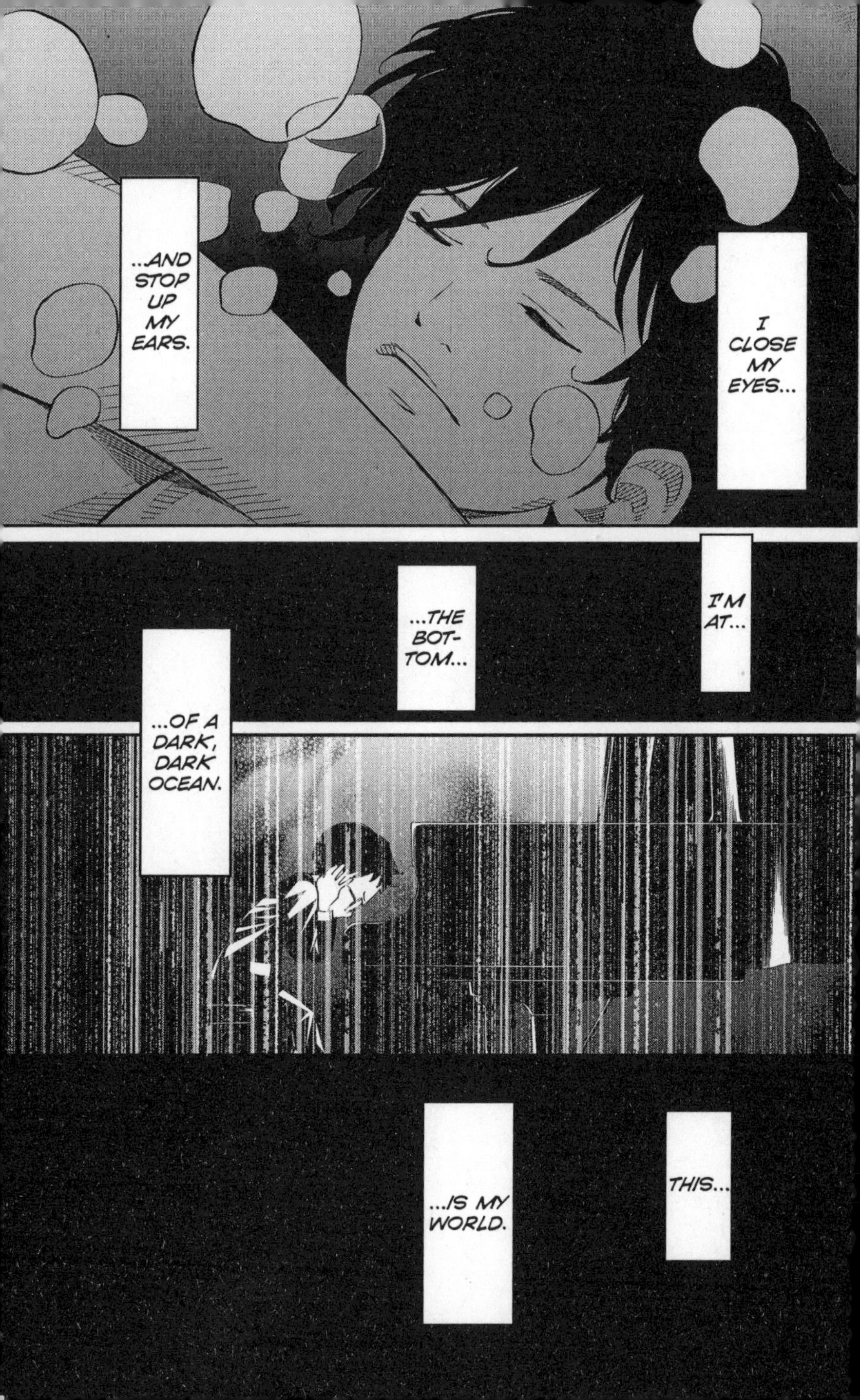
I CLOSE MY EYES...
...AND STOP UP MY EARS.
I'M AT...
...THE BOT-TOM...
...OF A DARK, DARK OCEAN.
THIS...
...IS MY WORLD.

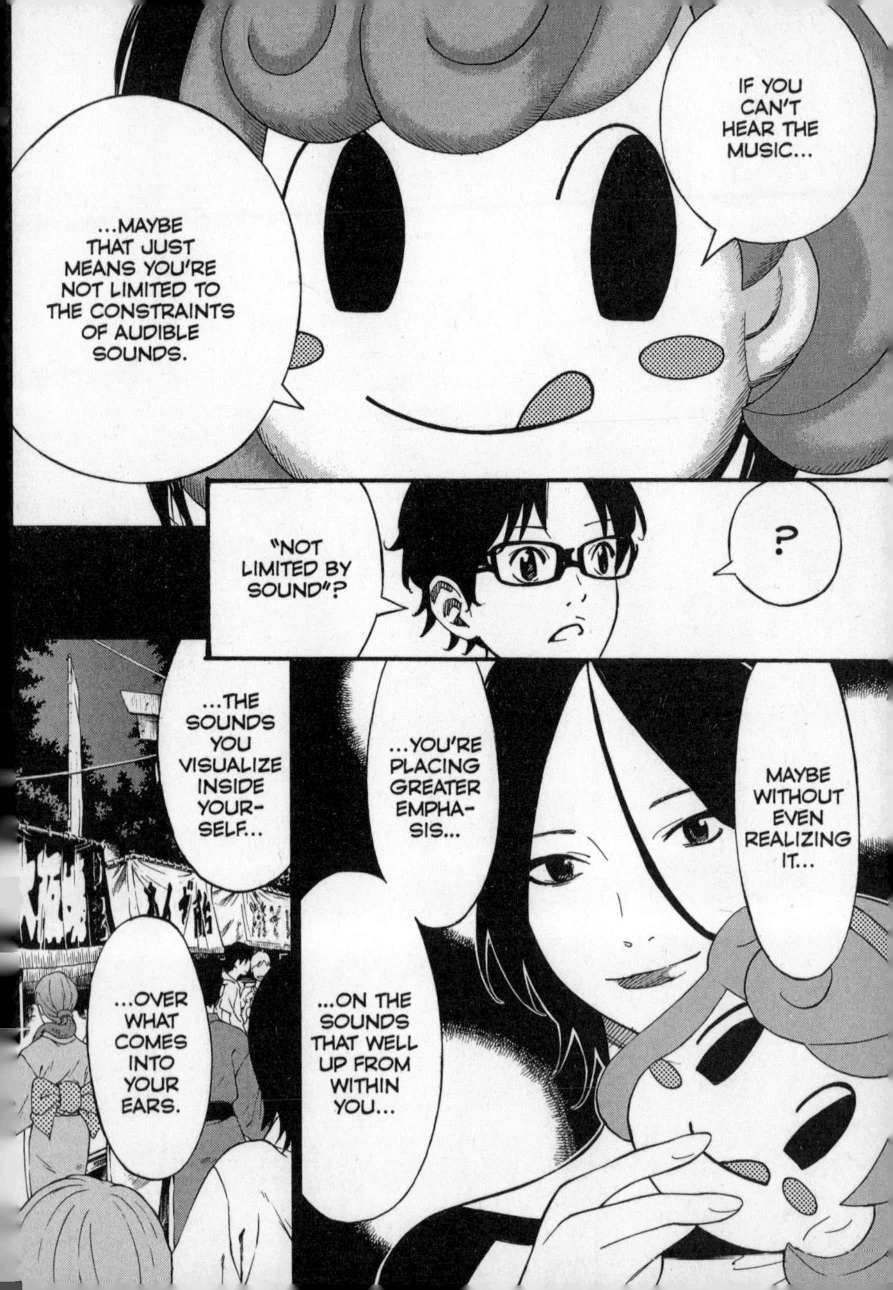
IF YOU CAN'T HEAR THE MUSIC...
...MAYBE THAT JUST MEANS YOU'RE NOT LIMITED TO THE CONSTRAINTS OF AUDIBLE SOUNDS.
?
"NOT LIMITED BY SOUND"?
MAYBE WITHOUT EVEN REALIZING IT...
...YOU'RE PLACING GREATER EMPHA-SIS...
...ON THE SOUNDS THAT WELL UP FROM WITHIN YOU...
...THE SOUNDS YOU VISUALIZE INSIDE YOUR-SELF...
...OVER WHAT COMES INTO YOUR EARS.

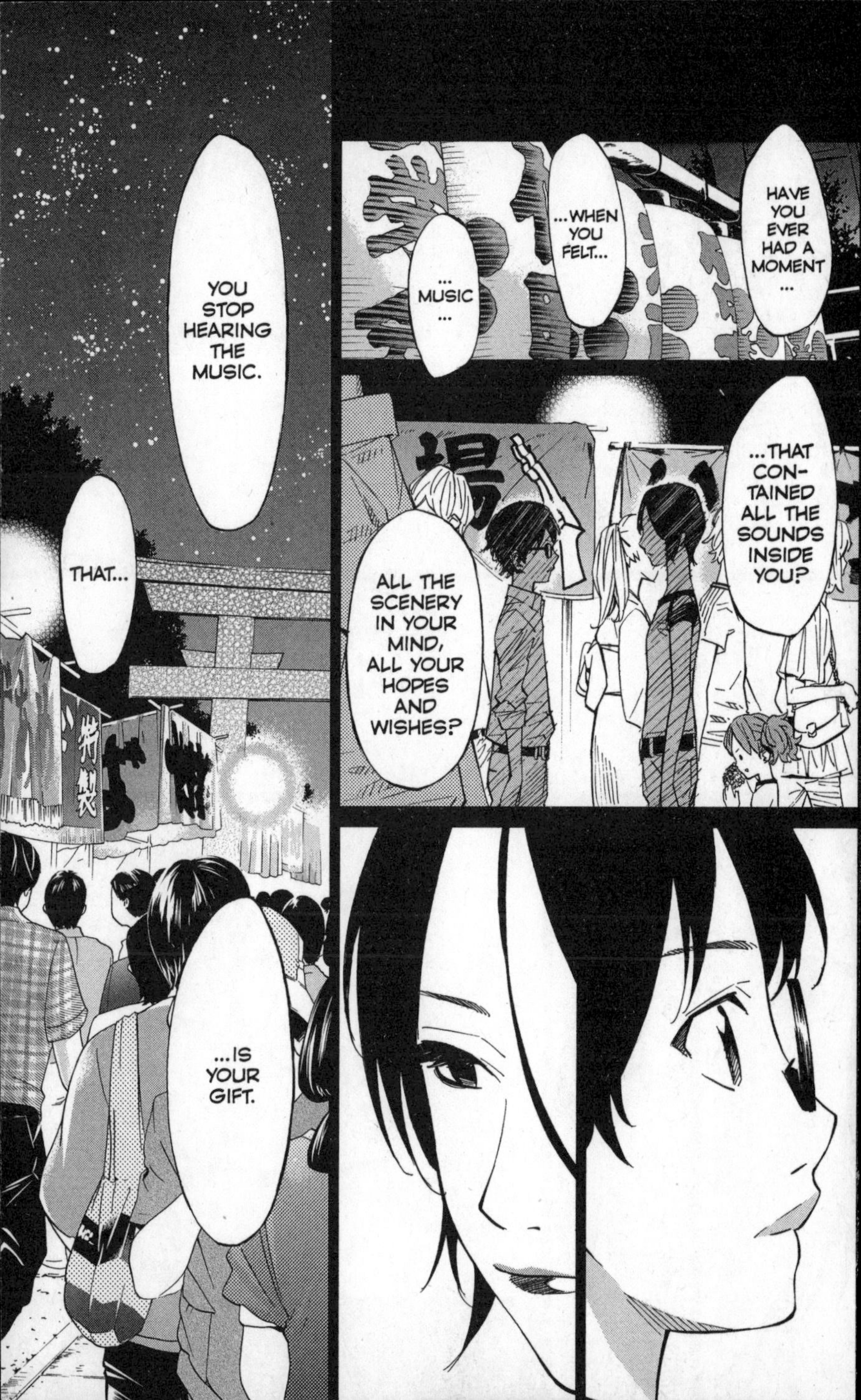
HAVE YOU EVER HAD A MOMENT ...
...WHEN YOU FELT...
... MUSIC ...
...THAT CON-TAINED ALL THE SOUNDS INSIDE YOU?
ALL THE SCENERY IN YOUR MIND, ALL YOUR HOPES AND WISHES?
YOU STOP HEARING THE MUSIC.
THAT...
...IS YOUR GIFT.

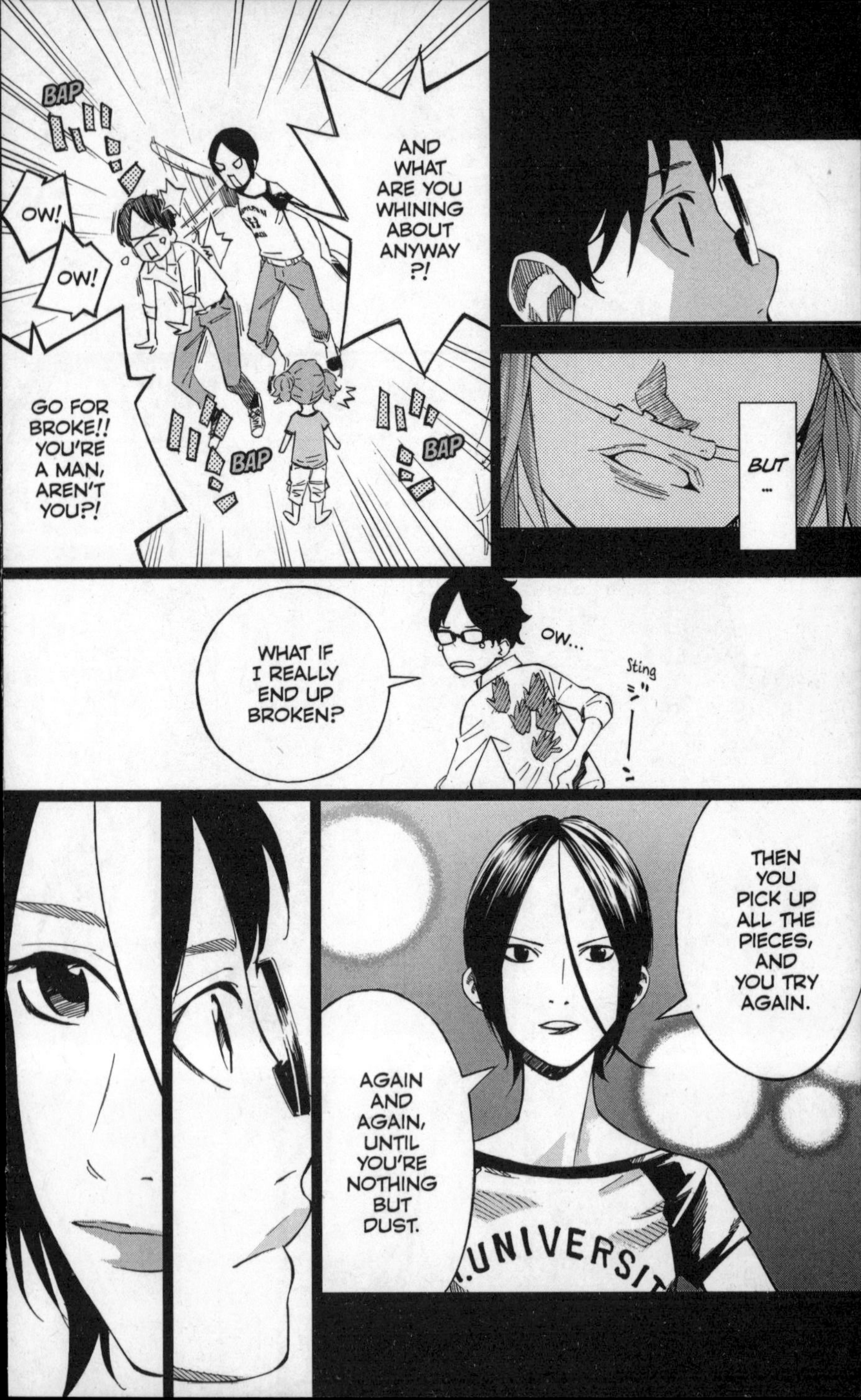
BUT ...
AND WHAT ARE YOU WHINING ABOUT ANYWAY ?!
BAP
OW!
OW!
BAP
GO FOR BROKE!! YOU'RE A MAN, AREN'T YOU?!
BAP
Sting
OW...
WHAT IF I REALLY END UP BROKEN?
THEN YOU PICK UP ALL THE PIECES, AND YOU TRY AGAIN.
AGAIN AND AGAIN, UNTIL YOU'RE NOTHING BUT DUST.
UNIVERSIT

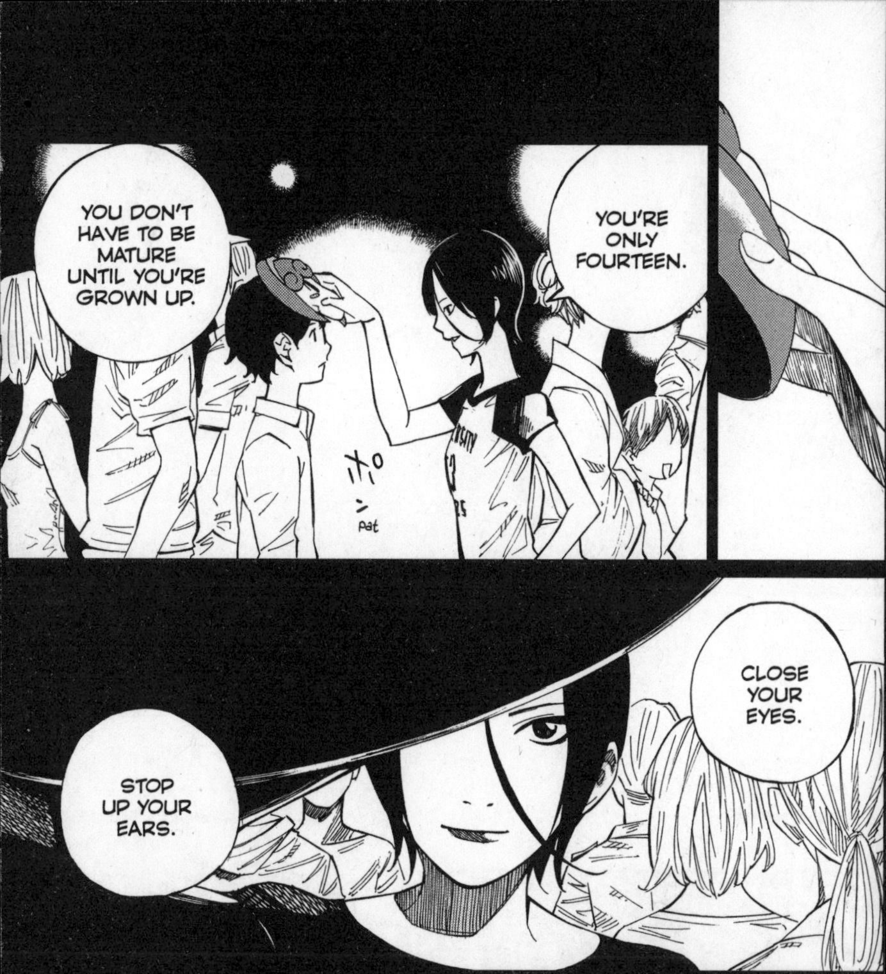
YOU'RE ONLY FOURTEEN.
YOU DON'T HAVE TO BE MATURE UNTIL YOU'RE GROWN UP.
pat
CLOSE YOUR EYES.
STOP UP YOUR EARS.

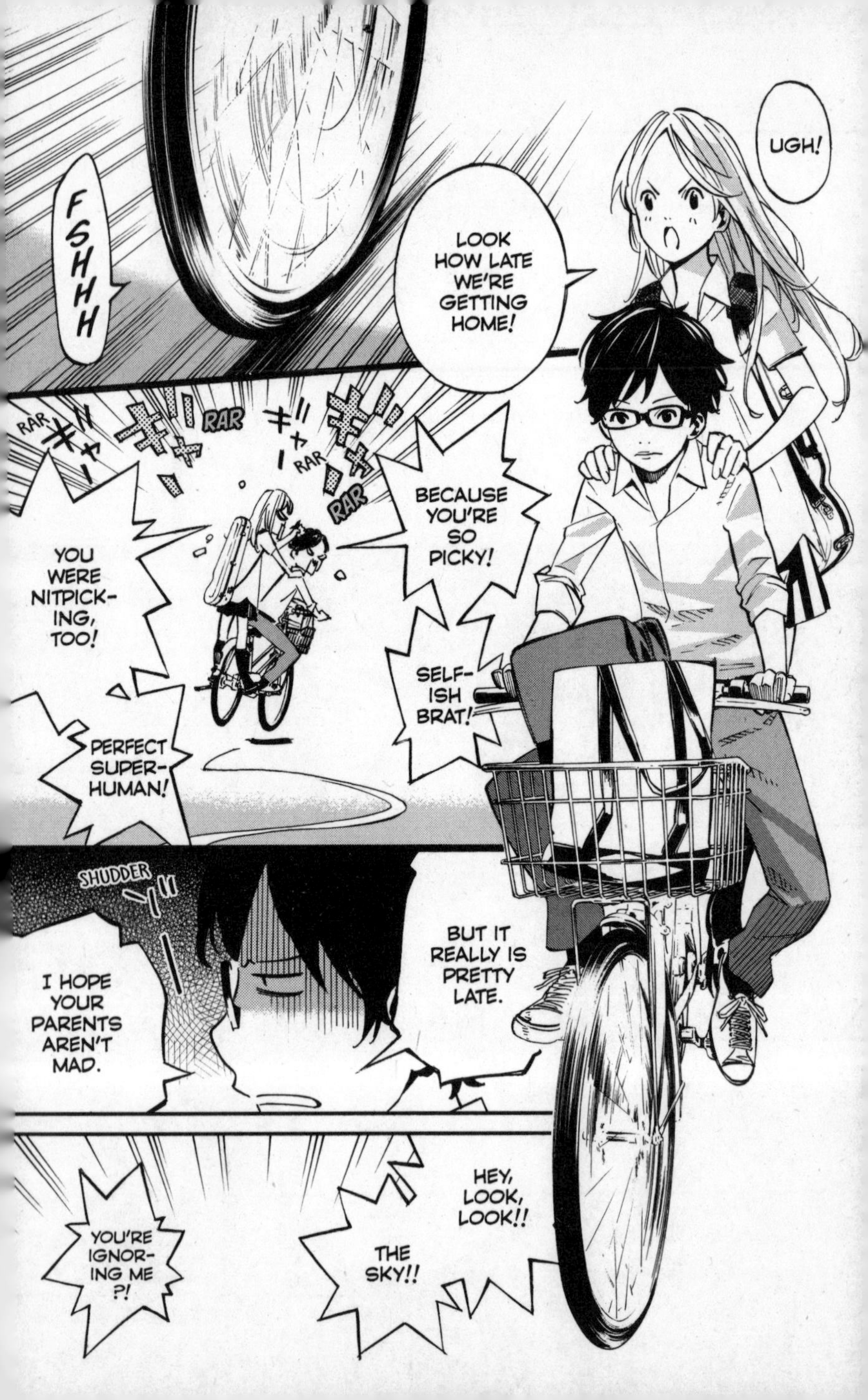
UGH!
LOOK HOW LATE WE'RE GETTING HOME!
FSHHH
RAR
RAR
RAR
RAR
BECAUSE YOU'RE SO PICKY!
SELF-ISH BRAT!
YOU WERE NITPICK-ING, TOO!
PERFECT SUPER-HUMAN!
BUT IT REALLY IS PRETTY LATE.
SHUDDER
I HOPE YOUR PARENTS AREN'T MAD.
HEY, LOOK, LOOK!!
THE SKY!!
YOU'RE IGNOR-ING ME ?!

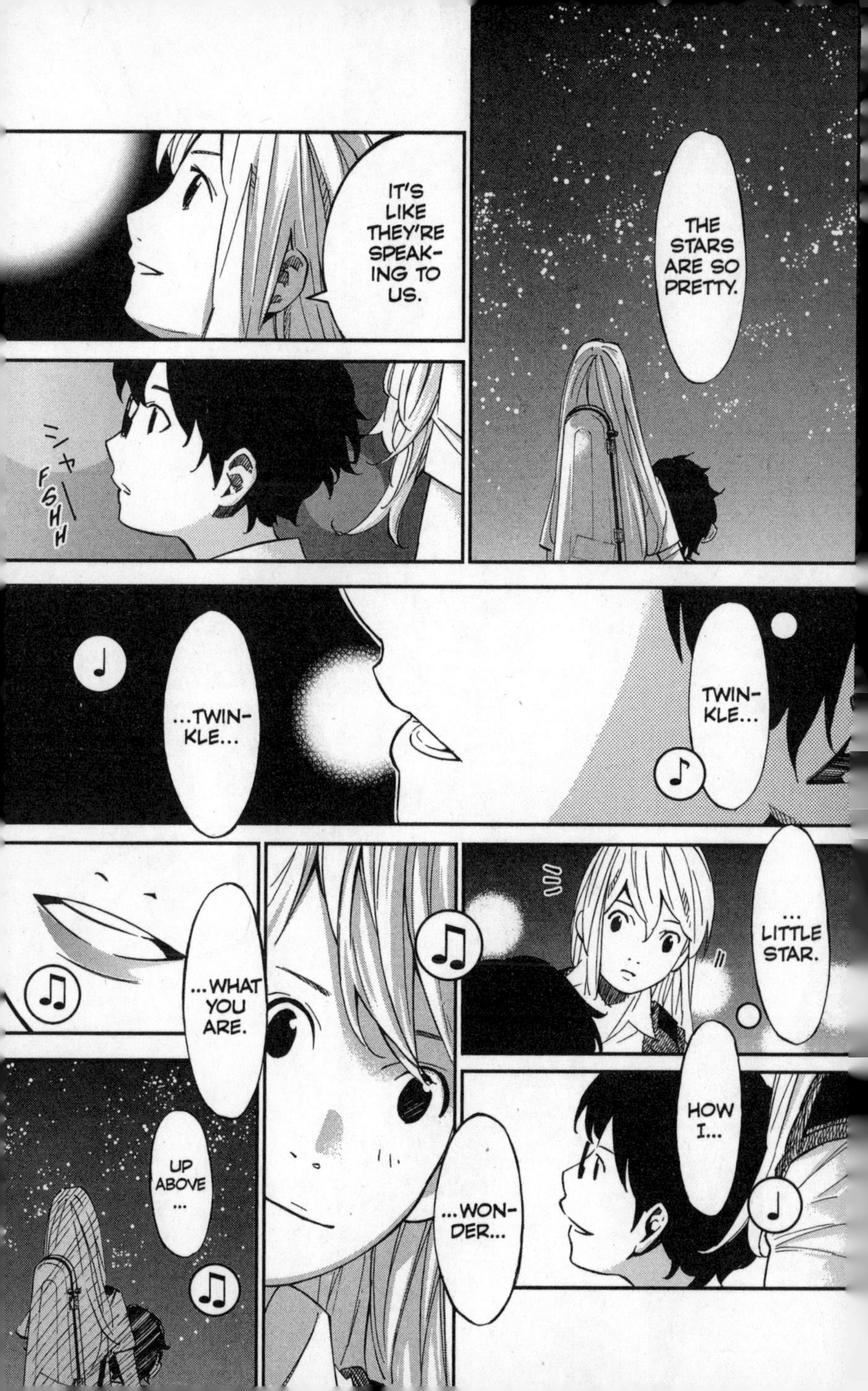
THE STARS ARE SO PRETTY.
IT'S LIKE THEY'RE SPEAK-ING TO US.
FSHH
TWIN-KLE...
...TWIN-KLE...
... LITTLE STAR.
HOW I...
...WON-DER...
...WHAT YOU ARE.
UP ABOVE ...

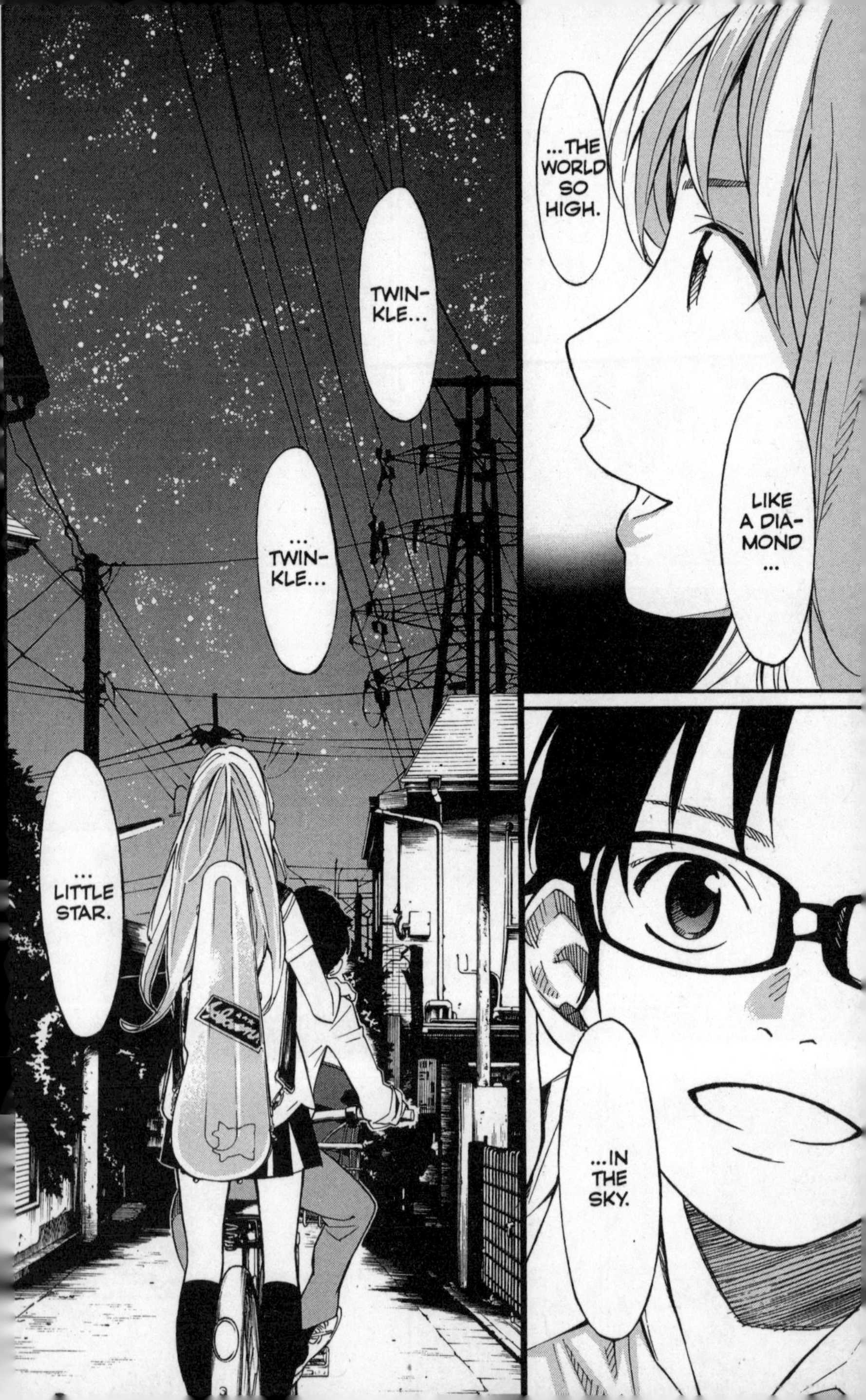
TWINKLE...
...TWINKLE...
...LITTLE STAR.
...THE WORLD SO HIGH.
LIKE A DIAMOND...
...IN THE SKY.

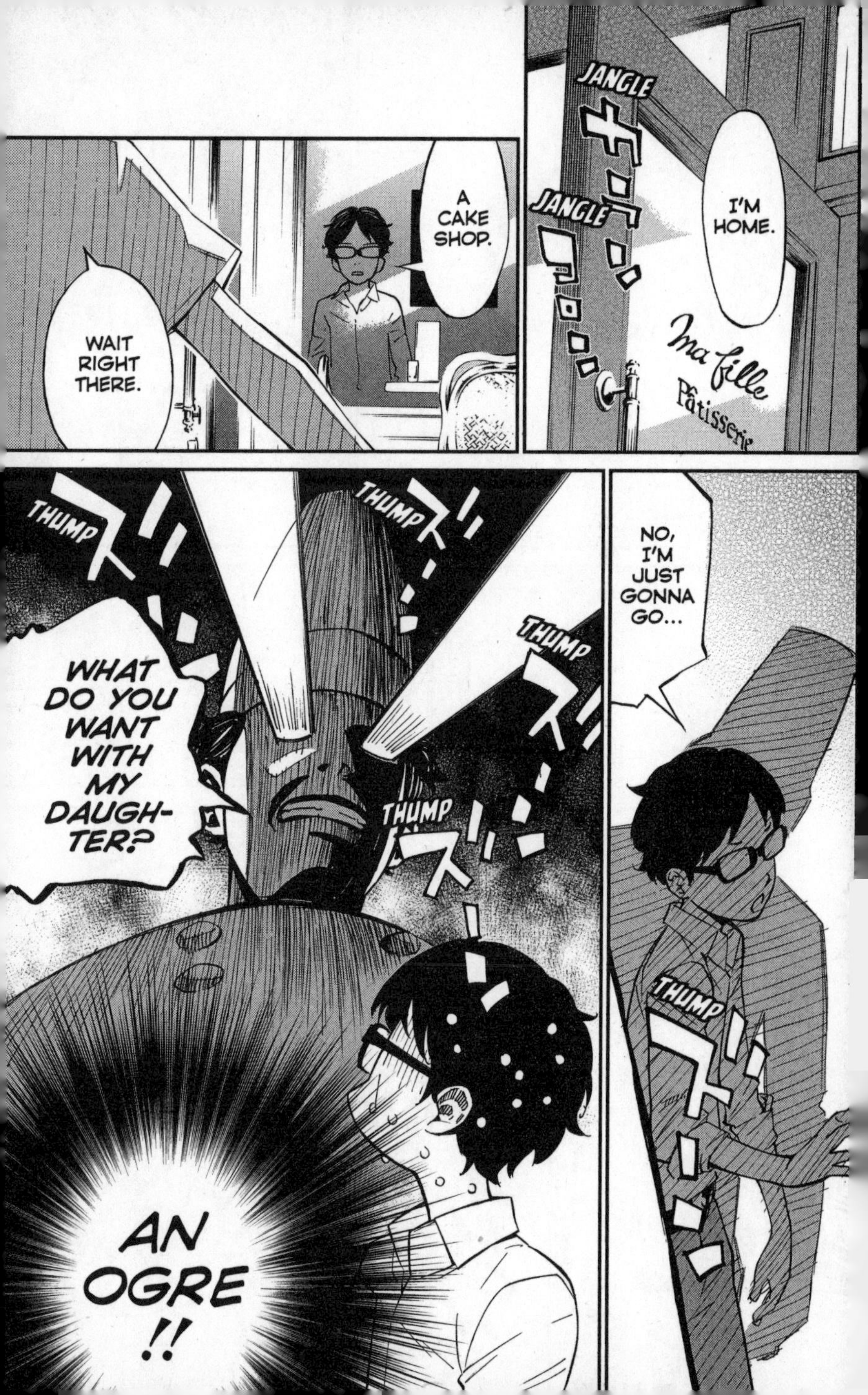
JANGLE
JANGLE
I'M HOME.
Ma fille
Pâtisserie
A CAKE SHOP.
WAIT RIGHT THERE.
NO, I'M JUST GONNA GO...
THUMP
THUMP
THUMP
THUMP
THUMP
WHAT DO YOU WANT WITH MY DAUGHTER?
AN OGRE!!

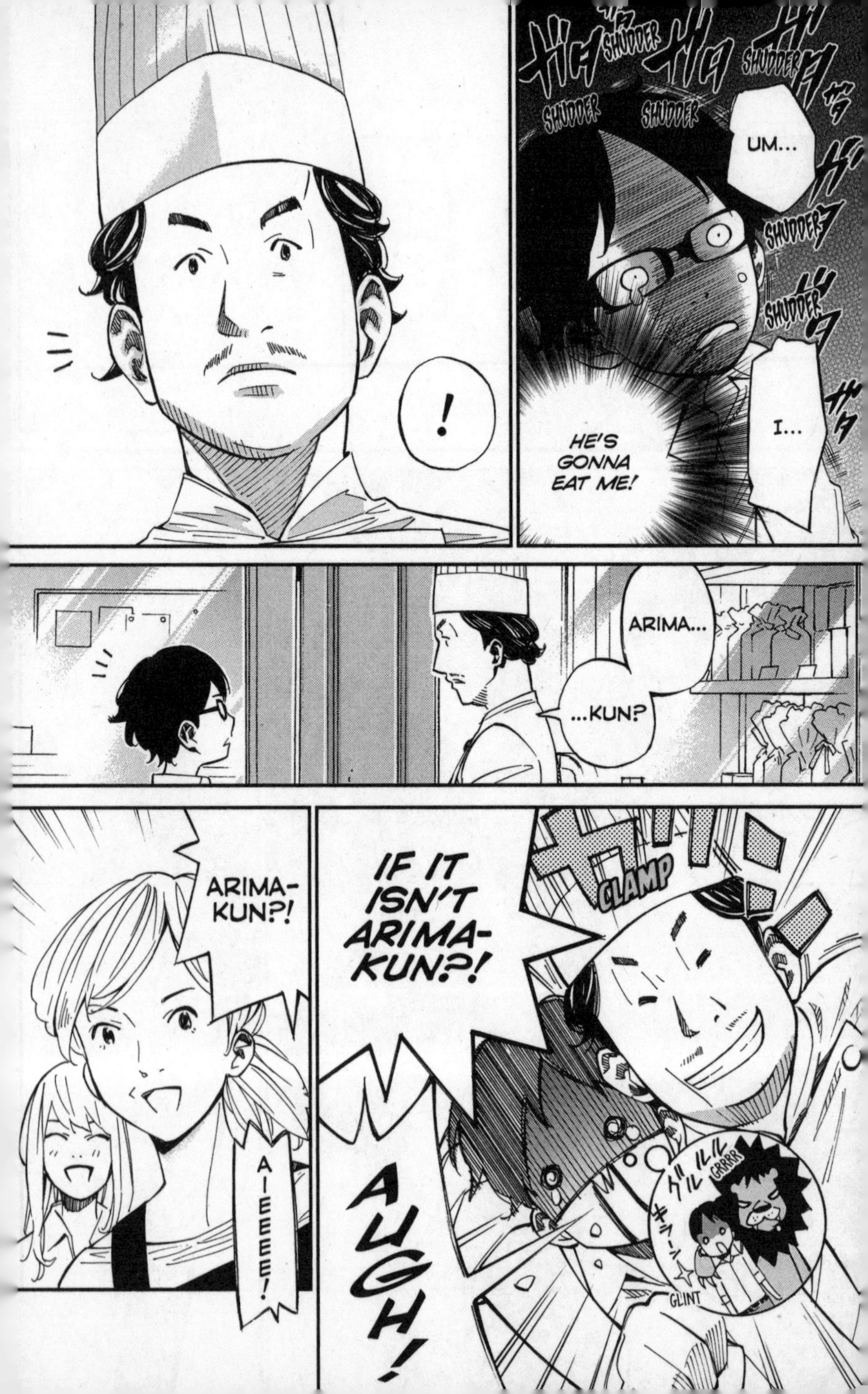
SHUDDER
SHUDDER
SHUDDER
SHUDDER
UM...
SHUDDER
SHUDDER
I...
HE'S GONNA EAT ME!
!
ARIMA...
...KUN?
CLAMP
IF IT ISN'T ARIMA-KUN?!
GRRRR
GLINT
AUGH!
ARIMA-KUN?!
AIEEEE!

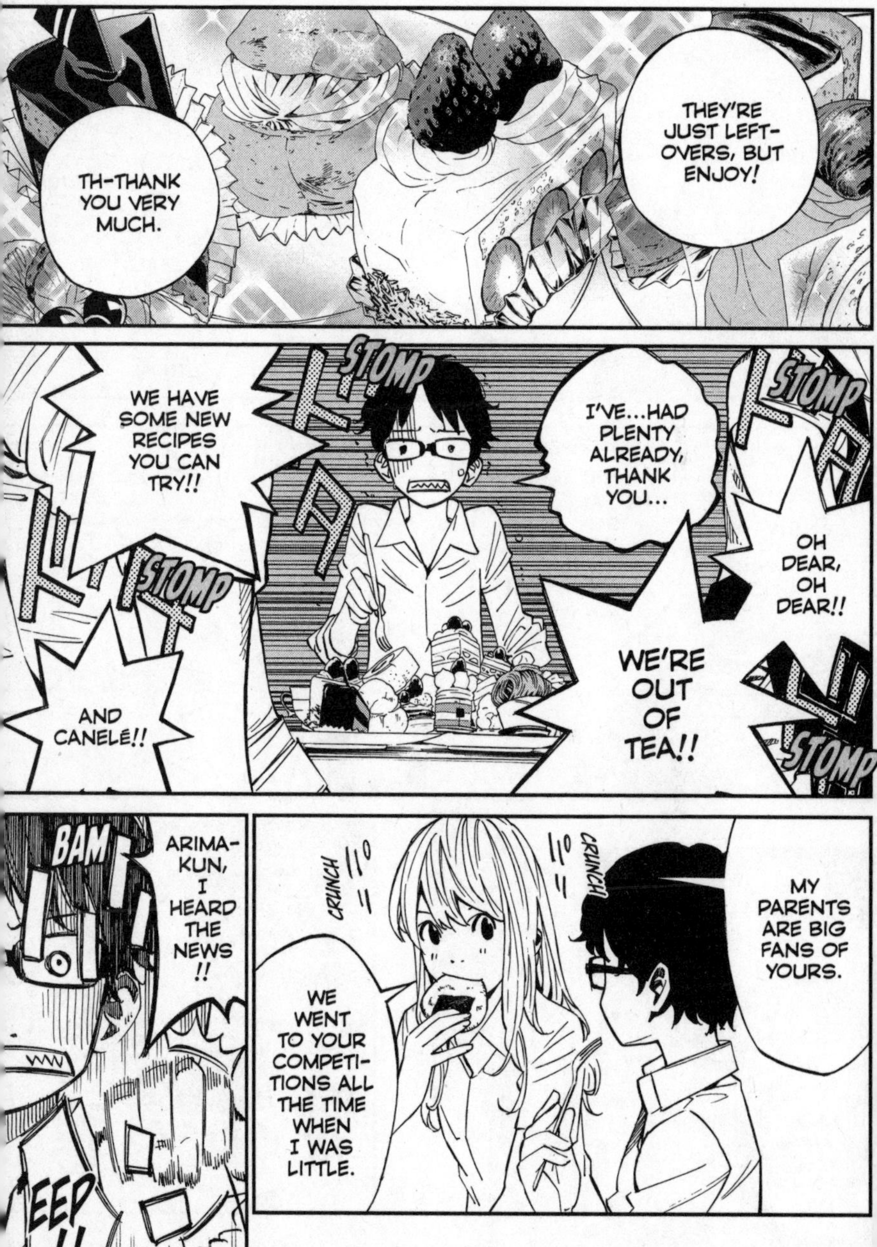
THEY'RE JUST LEFT-OVERS, BUT ENJOY!
TH-THANK YOU VERY MUCH.
STOMP
I'VE...HAD PLENTY ALREADY, THANK YOU...
OH DEAR, OH DEAR!!
WE'RE OUT OF TEA!!
STOMP
STOMP
WE HAVE SOME NEW RECIPES YOU CAN TRY!!
STOMP
AND CANELÉ!!
MY PARENTS ARE BIG FANS OF YOURS.
CRUNCH
CRUNCH
WE WENT TO YOUR COMPETITIONS ALL THE TIME WHEN I WAS LITTLE.
ARIMA-KUN, I HEARD THE NEWS!!
BAM
EEP!!

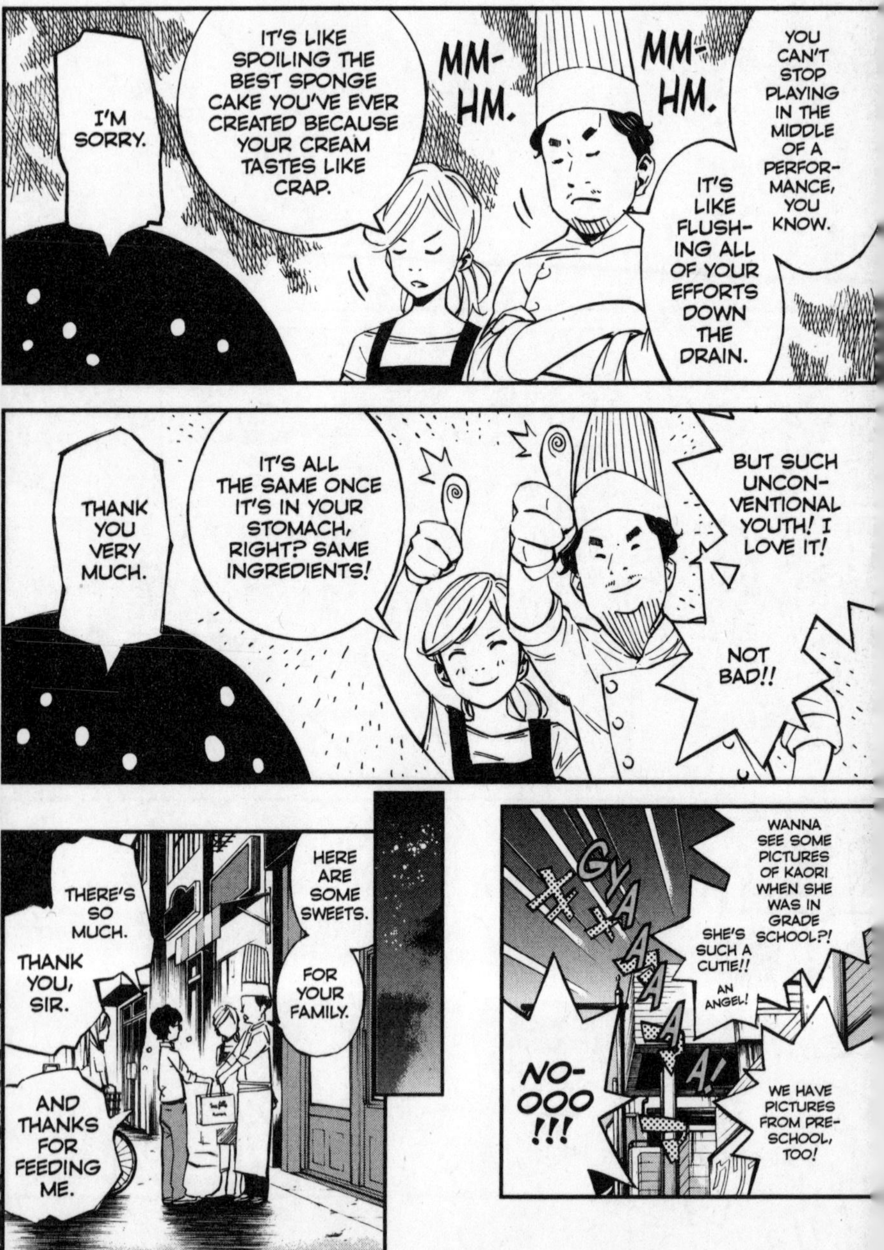

YOU CAN'T STOP PLAYING IN THE MIDDLE OF A PERFORMANCE, YOU KNOW.
MM-HM.
IT'S LIKE FLUSHING ALL OF YOUR EFFORTS DOWN THE DRAIN.
MM-HM.
IT'S LIKE SPOILING THE BEST SPONGE CAKE YOU'VE EVER CREATED BECAUSE YOUR CREAM TASTES LIKE CRAP.
I'M SORRY.
BUT SUCH UNCONVENTIONAL YOUTH! I LOVE IT!
NOT BAD!!
IT'S ALL THE SAME ONCE IT'S IN YOUR STOMACH, RIGHT? SAME INGREDIENTS!
THANK YOU VERY MUCH.
WANNA SEE SOME PICTURES OF KAORI WHEN SHE WAS IN GRADE SCHOOL?!
GYAAAAAA!
SHE'S SUCH A CUTIE!!
AN ANGEL!
WE HAVE PICTURES FROM PRESCHOOL, TOO!
NO-OOO!!!
HERE ARE SOME SWEETS.
FOR YOUR FAMILY.
THERE'S SO MUCH.
THANK YOU, SIR.
AND THANKS FOR FEEDING ME.

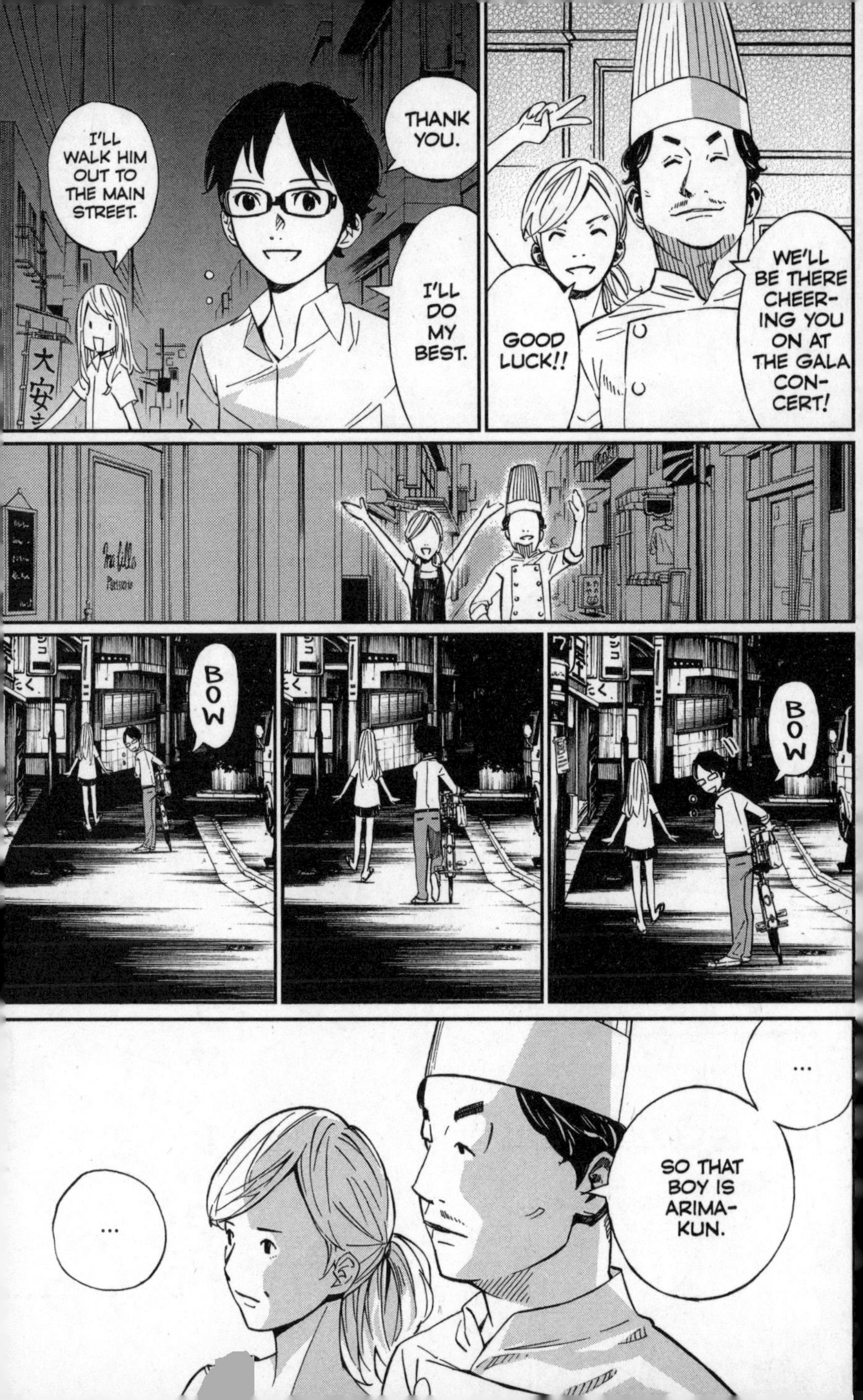
WE'LL BE THERE CHEERING YOU ON AT THE GALA CONCERT!
GOOD LUCK!!
THANK YOU.
I'LL DO MY BEST.
I'LL WALK HIM OUT TO THE MAIN STREET.
BOW
BOW
...
SO THAT BOY IS ARIMA-KUN.
...

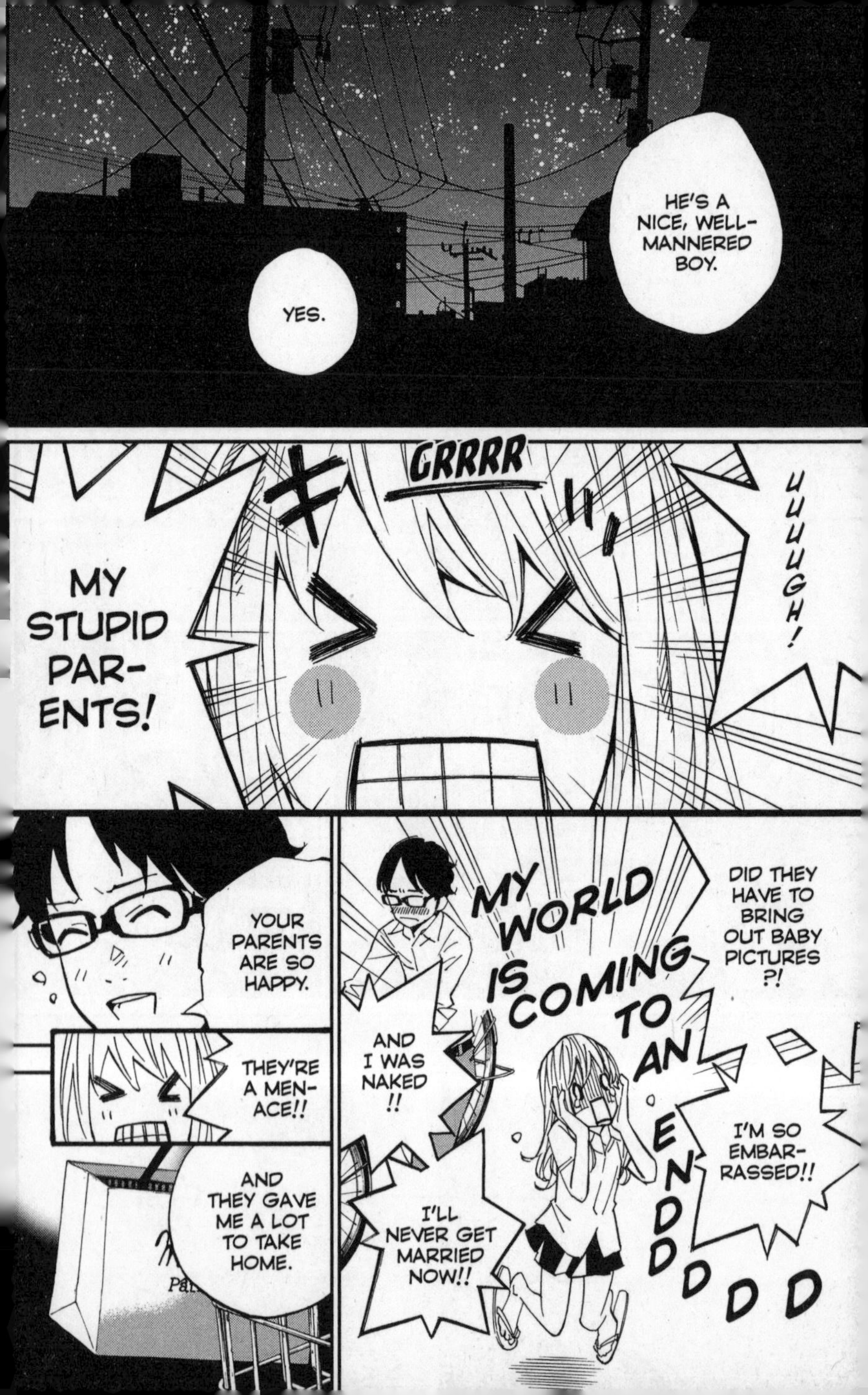
HE'S A NICE, WELL-MANNERED BOY.
YES.
UUUUGH!
GRRRR
MY STUPID PAR-ENTS!
DID THEY HAVE TO BRING OUT BABY PICTURES?!
MY WORLD IS COMING TO AN ENDDDDDD
AND I WAS NAKED!!
I'M SO EMBAR-RASSED!!
I'LL NEVER GET MARRIED NOW!!
YOUR PARENTS ARE SO HAPPY.
THEY'RE A MEN-ACE!!
AND THEY GAVE ME A LOT TO TAKE HOME.

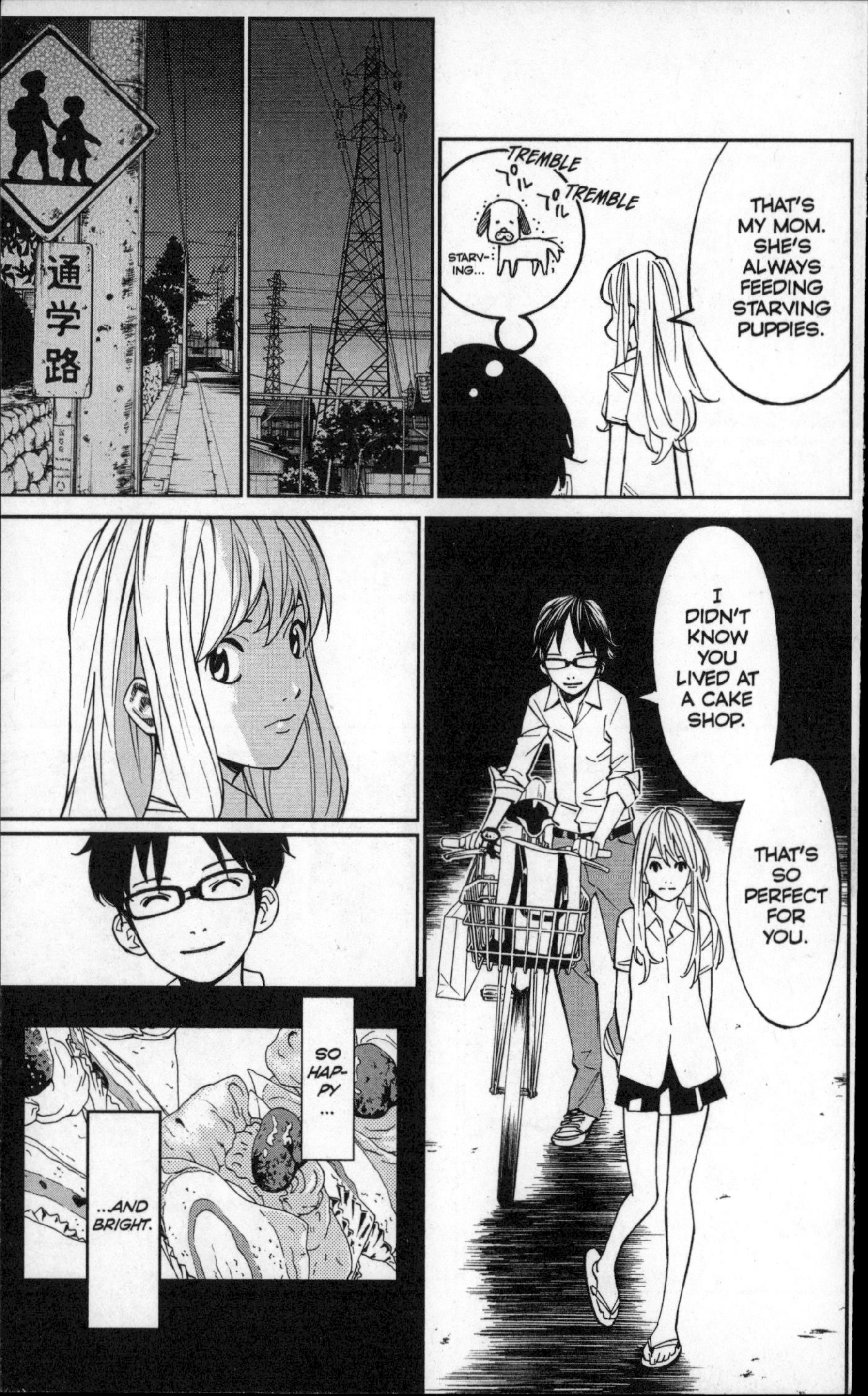
THAT'S MY MOM. SHE'S ALWAYS FEEDING STARVING PUPPIES.
TREMBLE
プル
プル
TREMBLE
STARV-ING...
通学路
I DIDN'T KNOW YOU LIVED AT A CAKE SHOP.
THAT'S SO PERFECT FOR YOU.
SO HAP-PY ...
...AND BRIGHT.

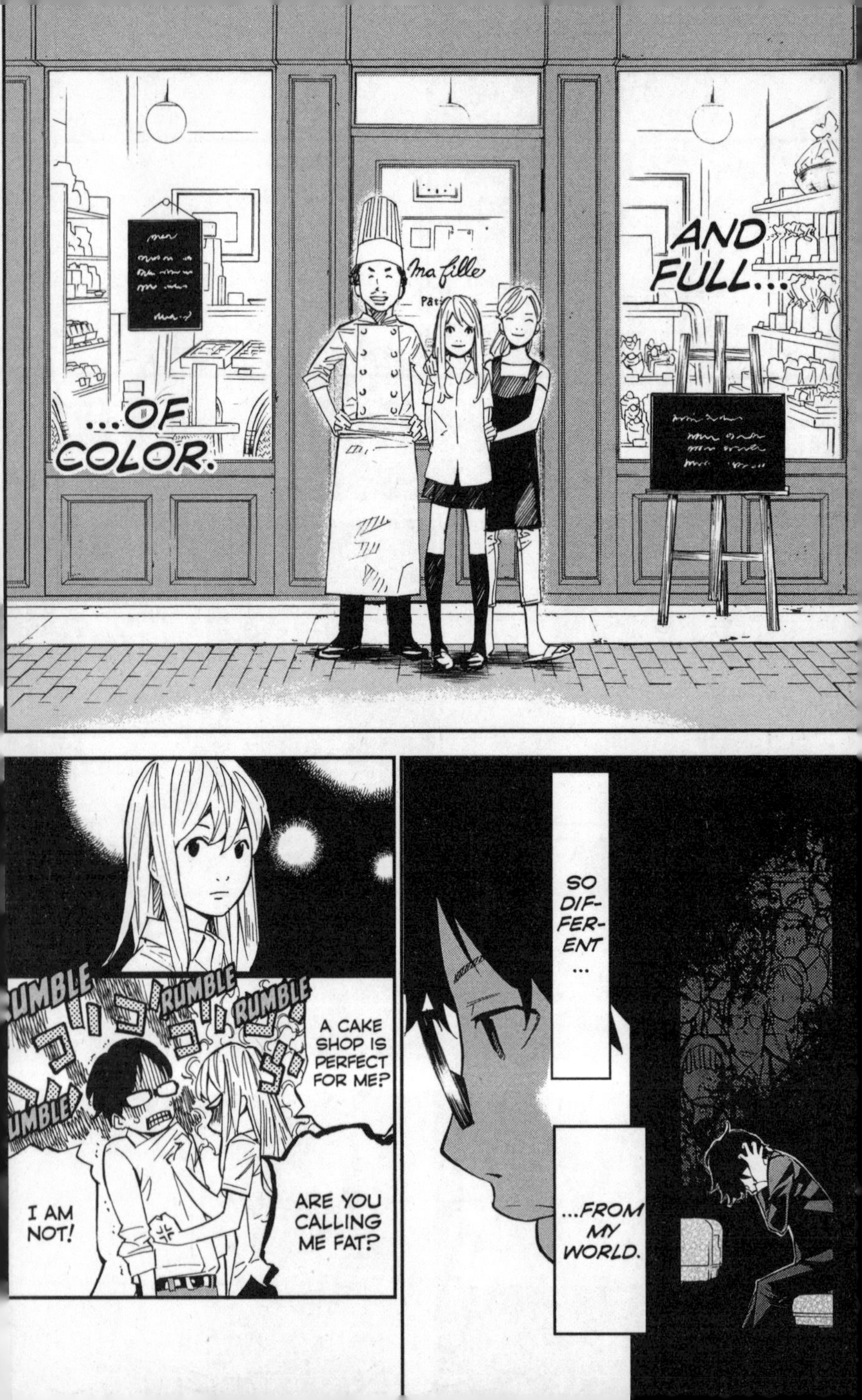
ma fille
AND FULL...
...OF COLOR.
SO DIF-FER-ENT...
...FROM MY WORLD.
RUMBLE
RUMBLE
RUMBLE
RUMBLE
A CAKE SHOP IS PERFECT FOR ME?
ARE YOU CALLING ME FAT?
I AM NOT!

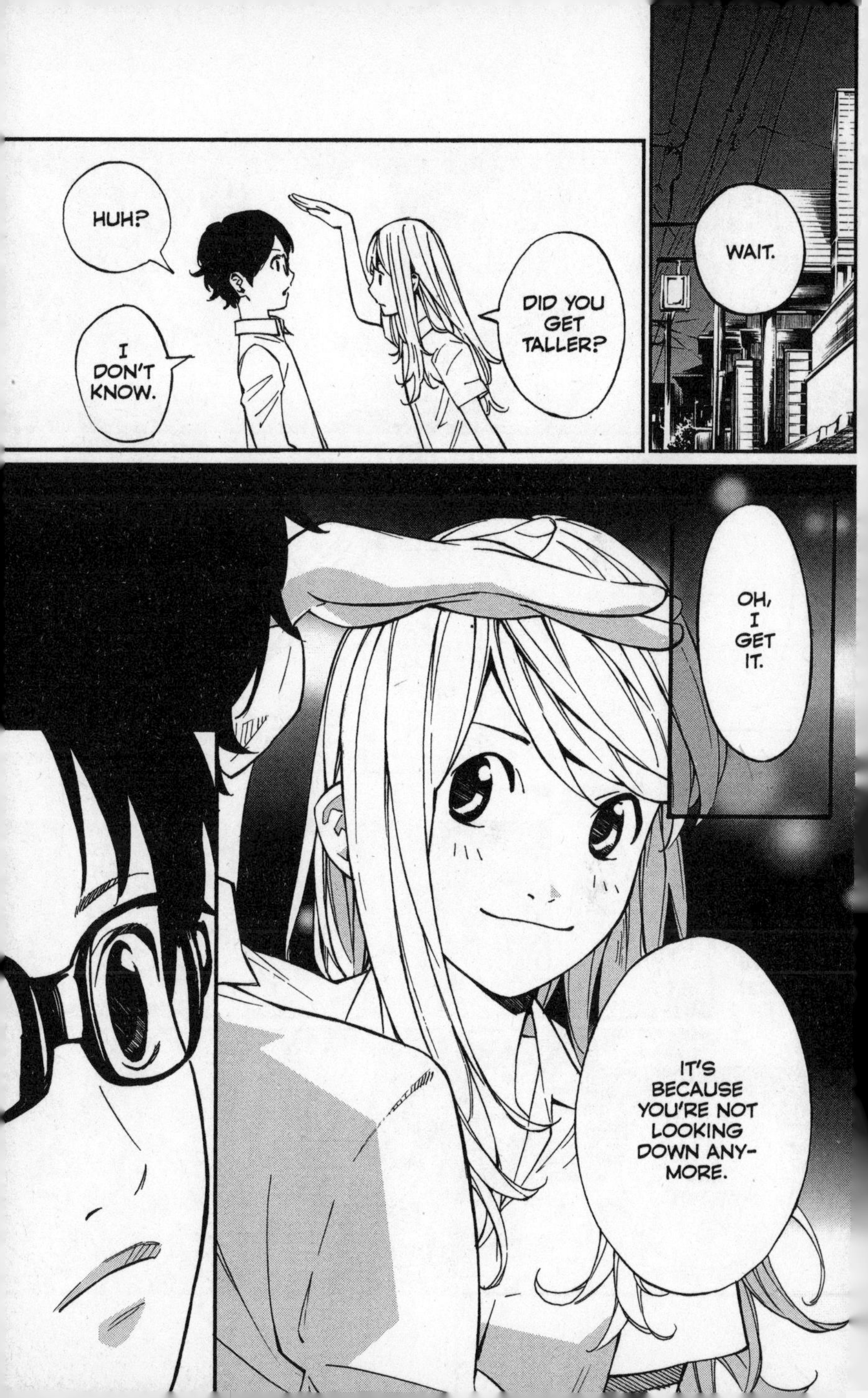
WAIT.
DID YOU GET TALLER?
HUH?
I DON'T KNOW.
OH, I GET IT.
IT'S BECAUSE YOU'RE NOT LOOKING DOWN ANY-MORE.

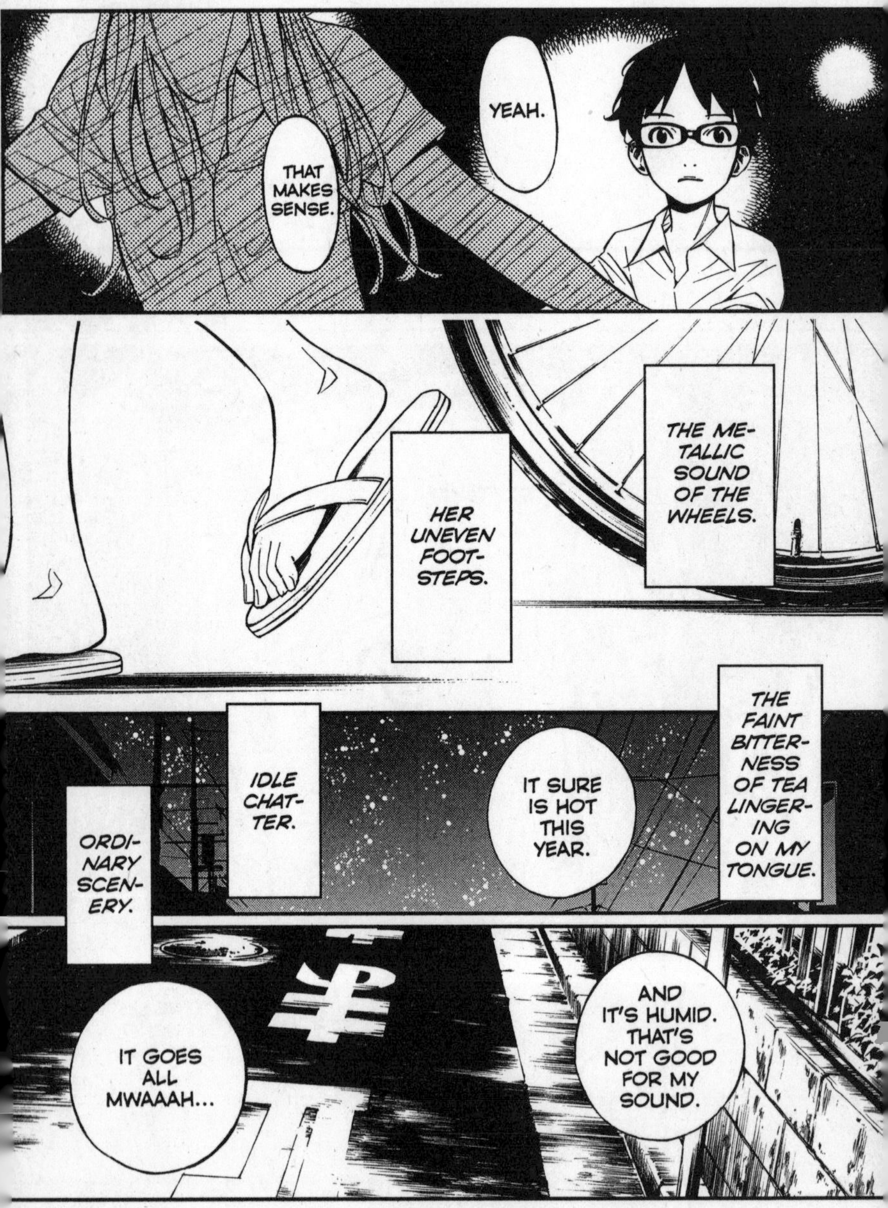
YEAH.
THAT MAKES SENSE.
THE METALLIC SOUND OF THE WHEELS.
HER UNEVEN FOOTSTEPS.
THE FAINT BITTERNESS OF TEA LINGERING ON MY TONGUE.
IT SURE IS HOT THIS YEAR.
IDLE CHATTER.
ORDINARY SCENERY.
AND IT'S HUMID. THAT'S NOT GOOD FOR MY SOUND.
IT GOES ALL MWAAAH...

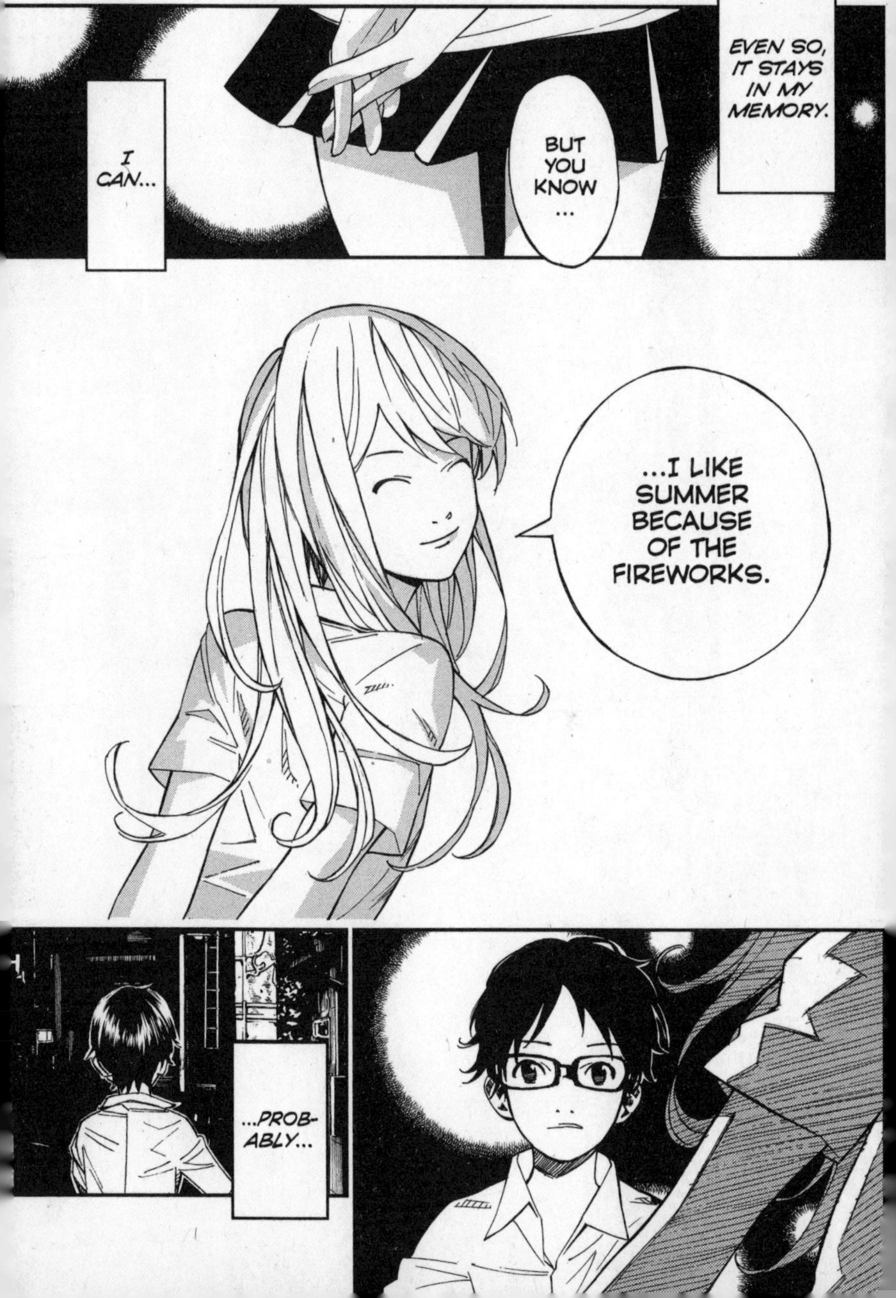
EVEN SO, IT STAYS IN MY MEMORY.
BUT YOU KNOW ...
I CAN...
...I LIKE SUMMER BECAUSE OF THE FIREWORKS.
...PROB-ABLY...

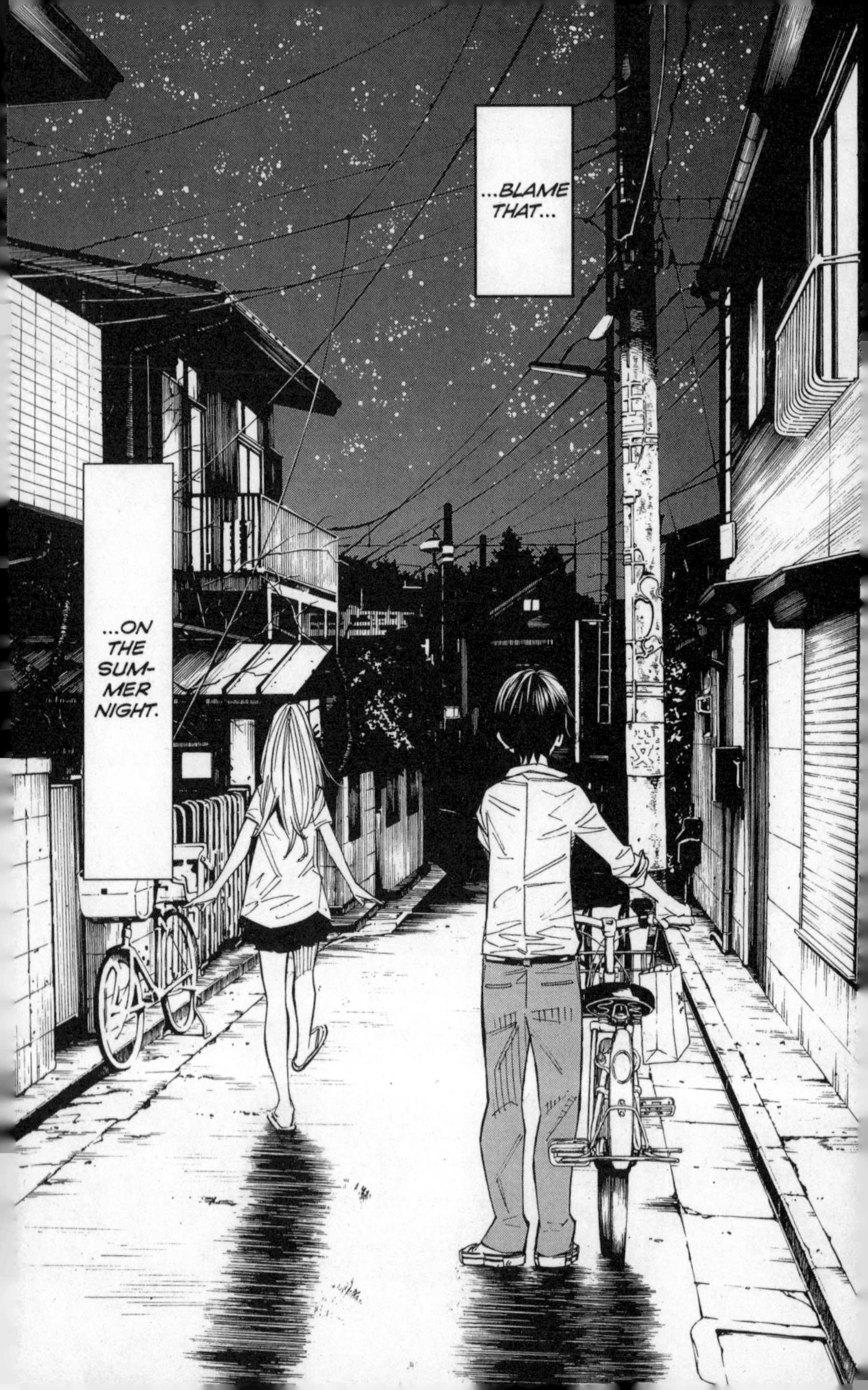
...BLAME THAT...
...ON THE SUM-MER NIGHT.

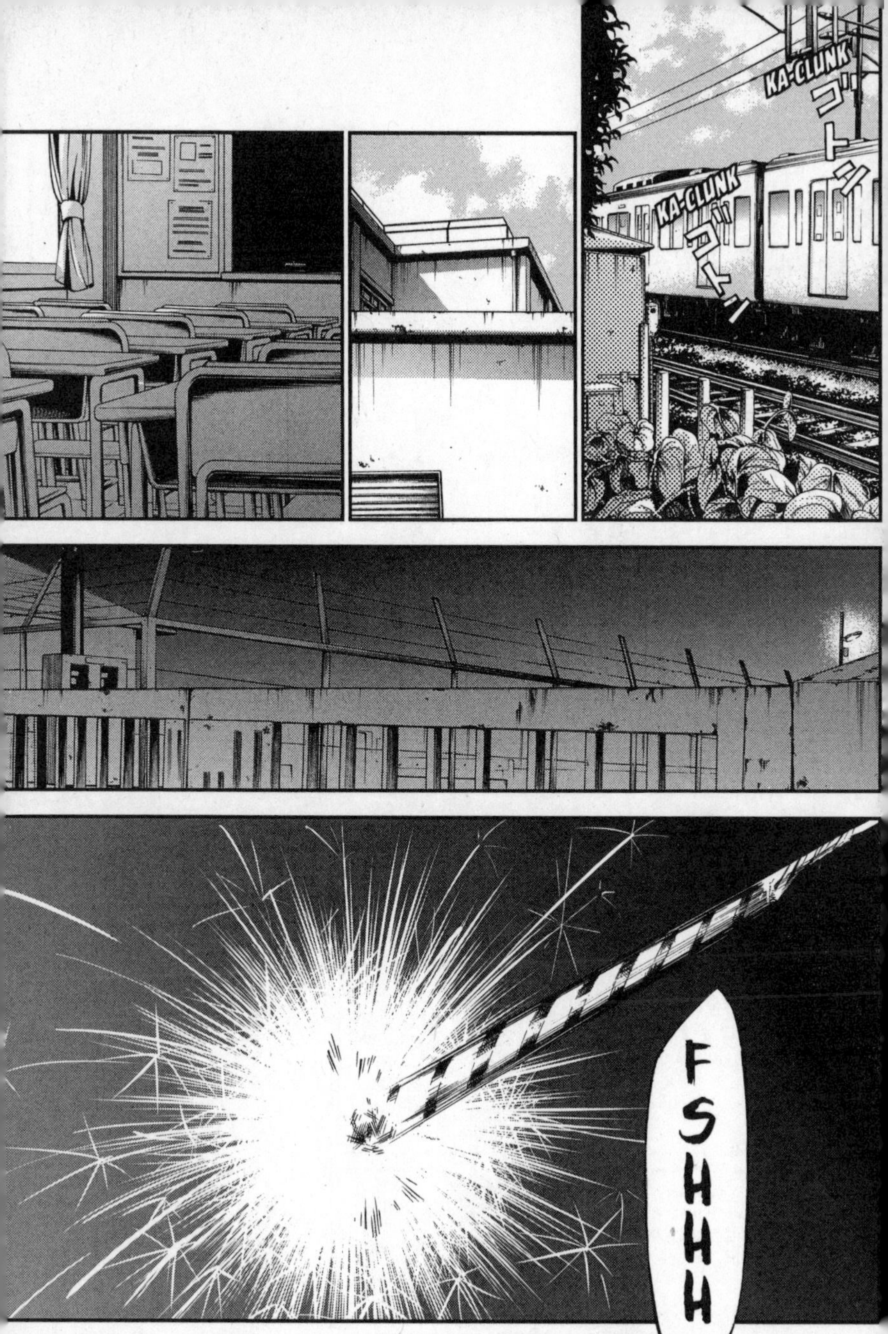
KA-CLUNK
KA-CLUNK
FSHHH

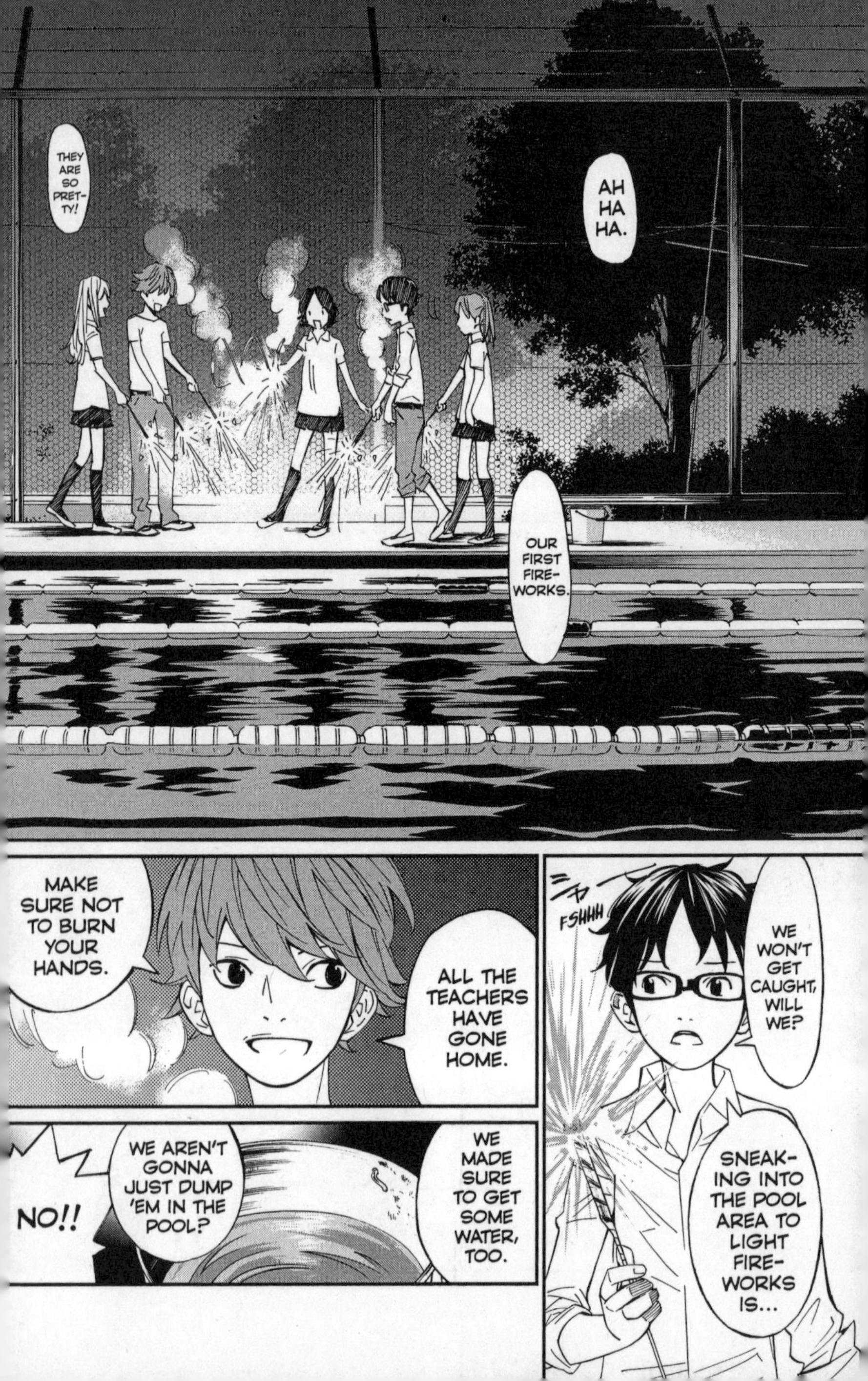
AH HA HA.
THEY ARE SO PRET-TY!
OUR FIRST FIRE-WORKS.
FSHHH
WE WON'T GET CAUGHT, WILL WE?
SNEAK-ING INTO THE POOL AREA TO LIGHT FIRE-WORKS IS...
ALL THE TEACHERS HAVE GONE HOME.
MAKE SURE NOT TO BURN YOUR HANDS.
WE MADE SURE TO GET SOME WATER, TOO.
WE AREN'T GONNA JUST DUMP 'EM IN THE POOL?
NO!!

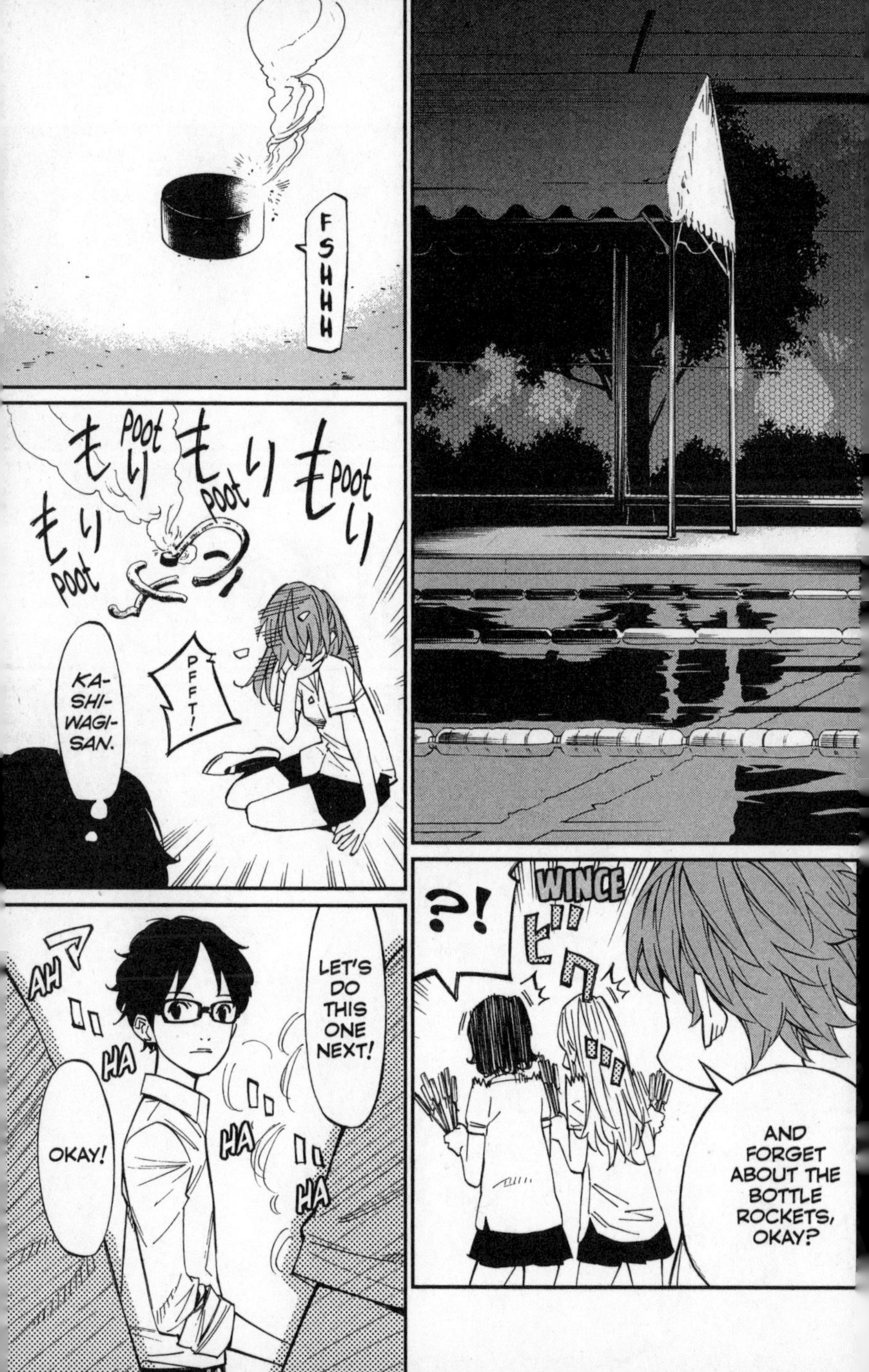
FSHHH
もり
Poot
もり
Poot
もり
Poot
もり
Poot
PFFT!
KA-SHI-WAGI-SAN.
AND FORGET ABOUT THE BOTTLE ROCKETS, OKAY?
WINCE
?!
LET'S DO THIS ONE NEXT!
AH
HA
OKAY!
HA
HA

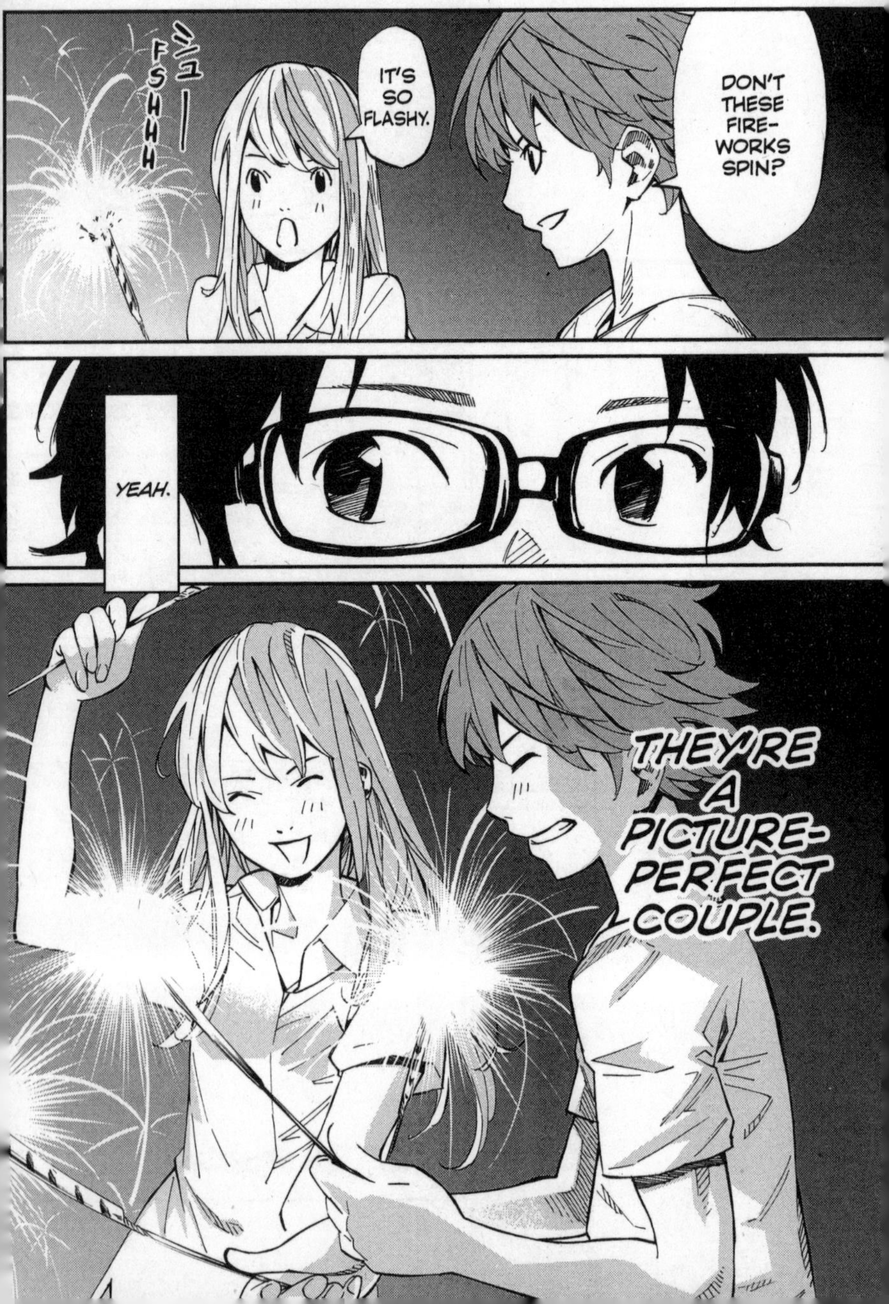
DON'T THESE FIRE-WORKS SPIN?
IT'S SO FLASHY.
シュー FSHHH
YEAH.
THEY'RE A PICTURE-PERFECT COUPLE.

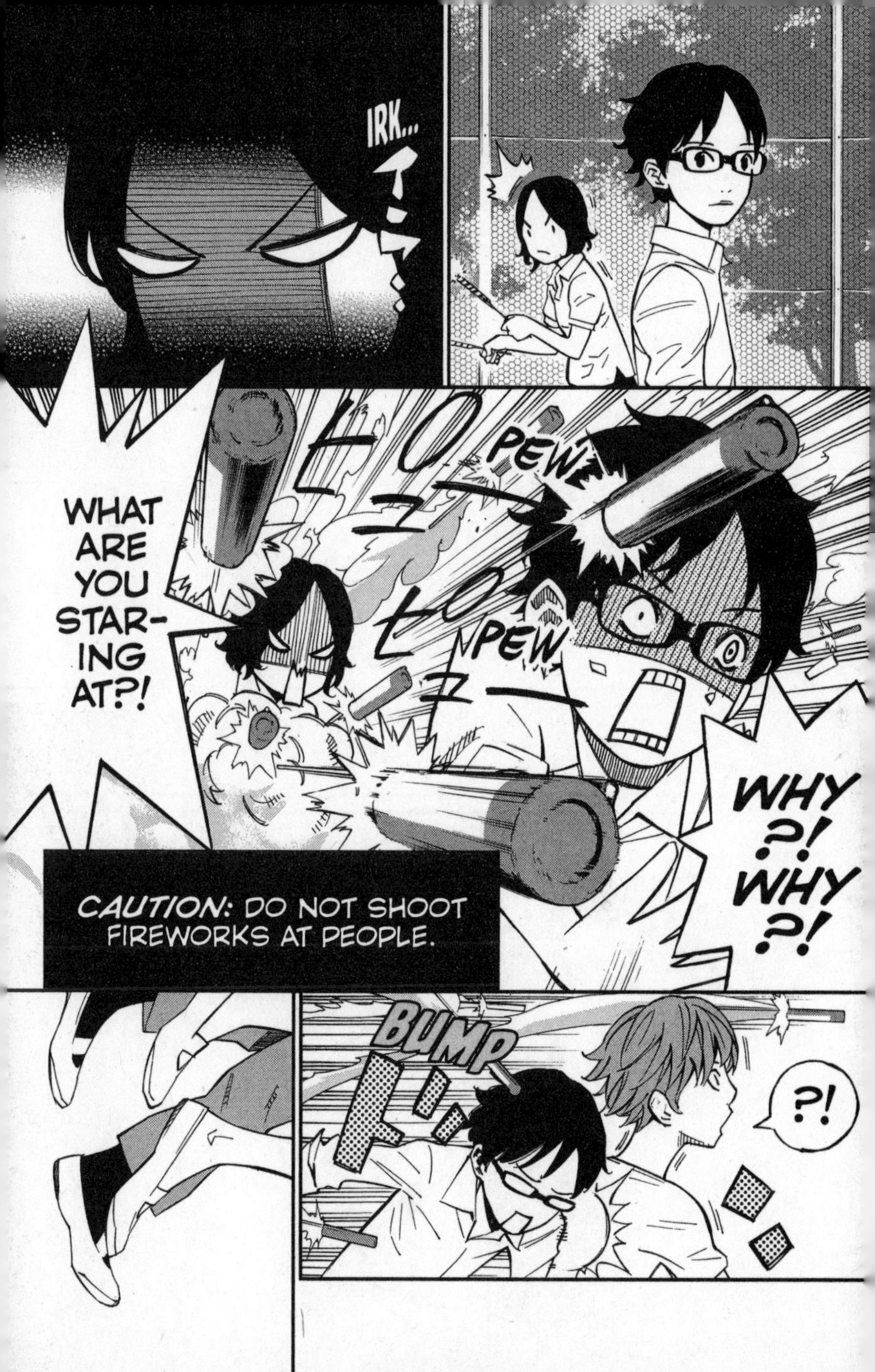
IRK...
PEW
PEW
WHY?! WHY?!
WHAT ARE YOU STARING AT?!
CAUTION: DO NOT SHOOT FIREWORKS AT PEOPLE.
BUMP
?!

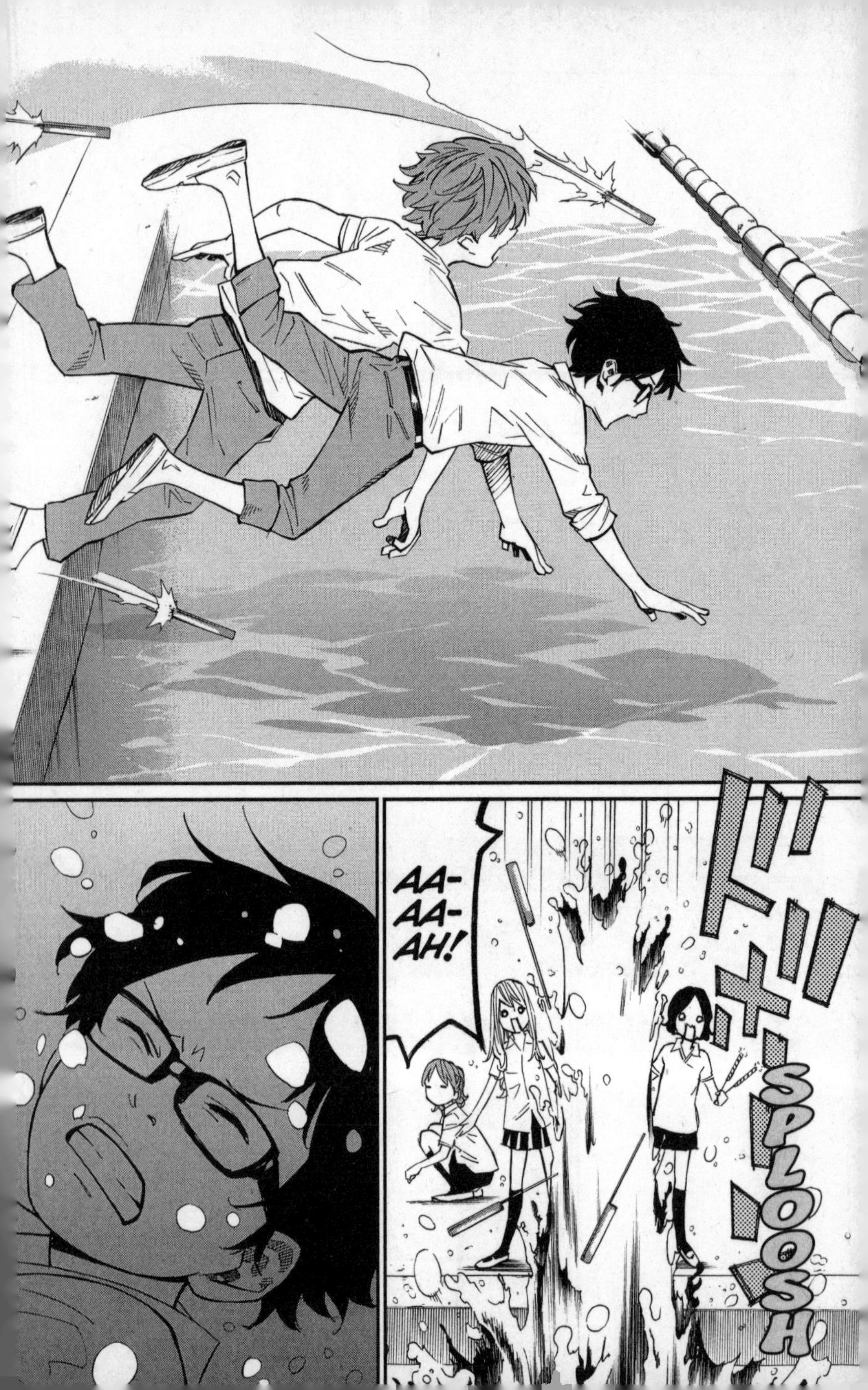
AA-
AA-
AAH!
SPLOOSH

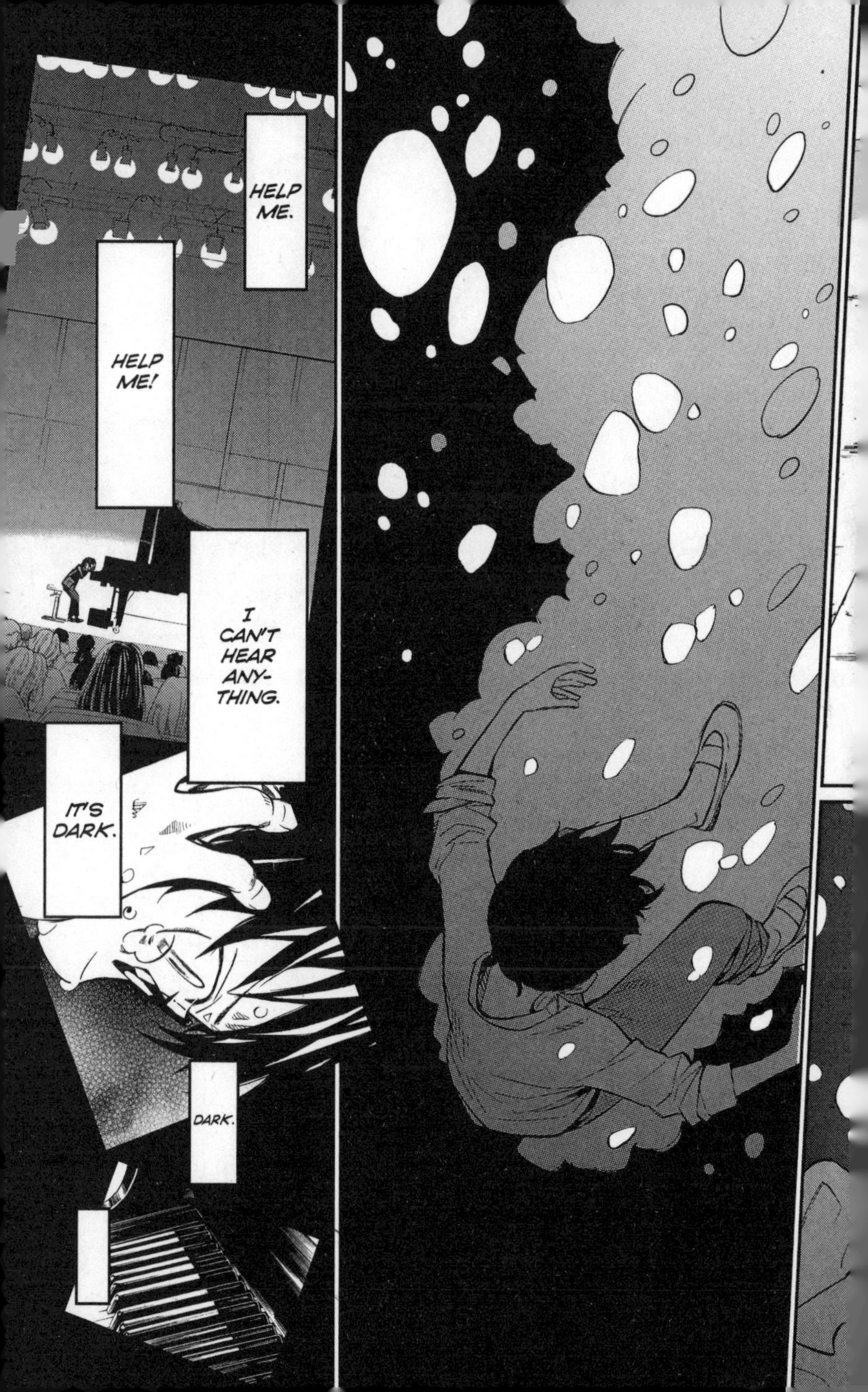
HELP ME.
HELP ME!
I CAN'T HEAR ANYTHING.
IT'S DARK.
DARK.

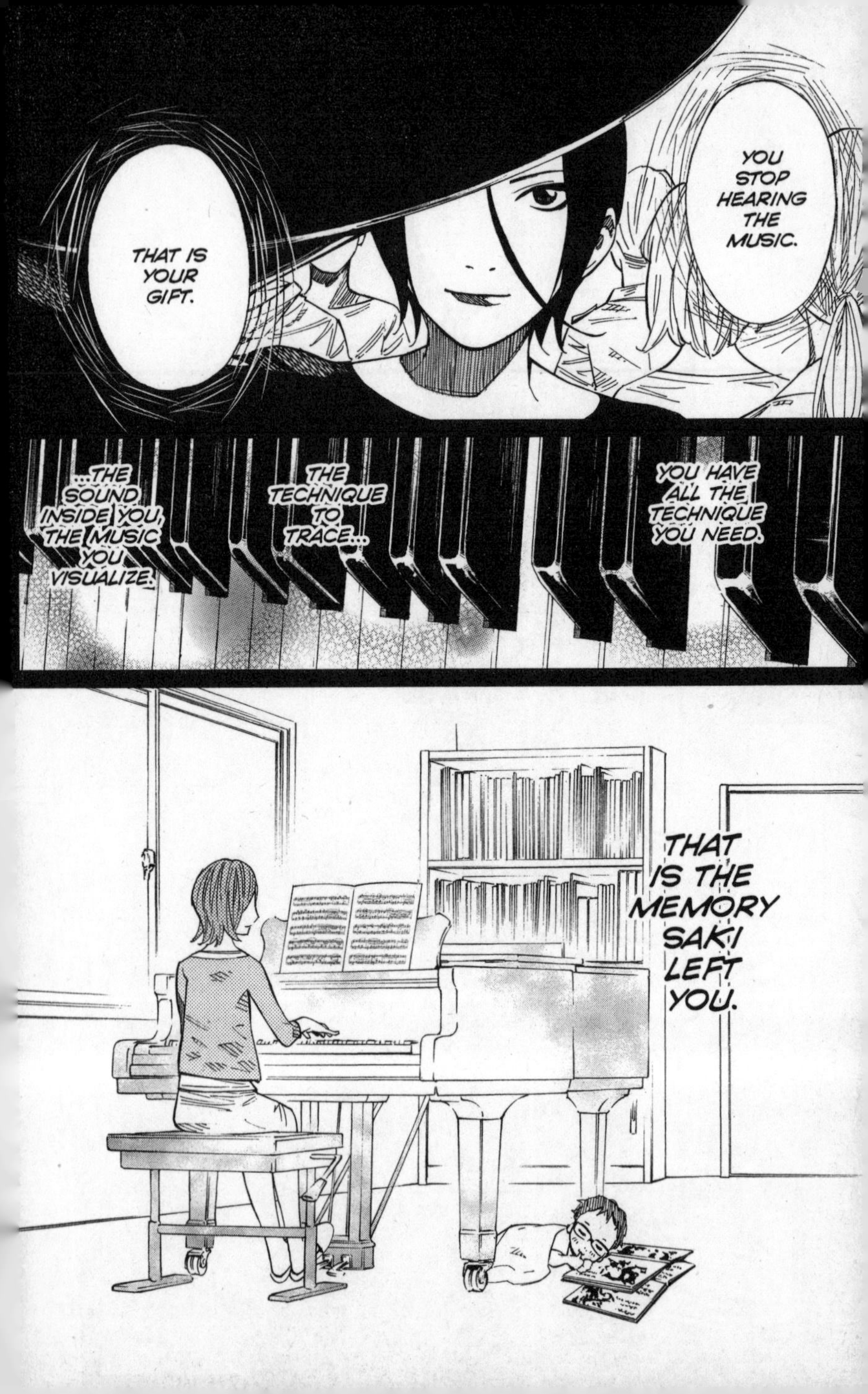
YOU STOP HEARING THE MUSIC.
THAT IS YOUR GIFT.
YOU HAVE ALL THE TECHNIQUE YOU NEED.
THE TECHNIQUE TO TRACE...
...THE SOUND INSIDE YOU, THE MUSIC YOU VISUALIZE.
THAT IS THE MEMORY SAKI LEFT YOU.

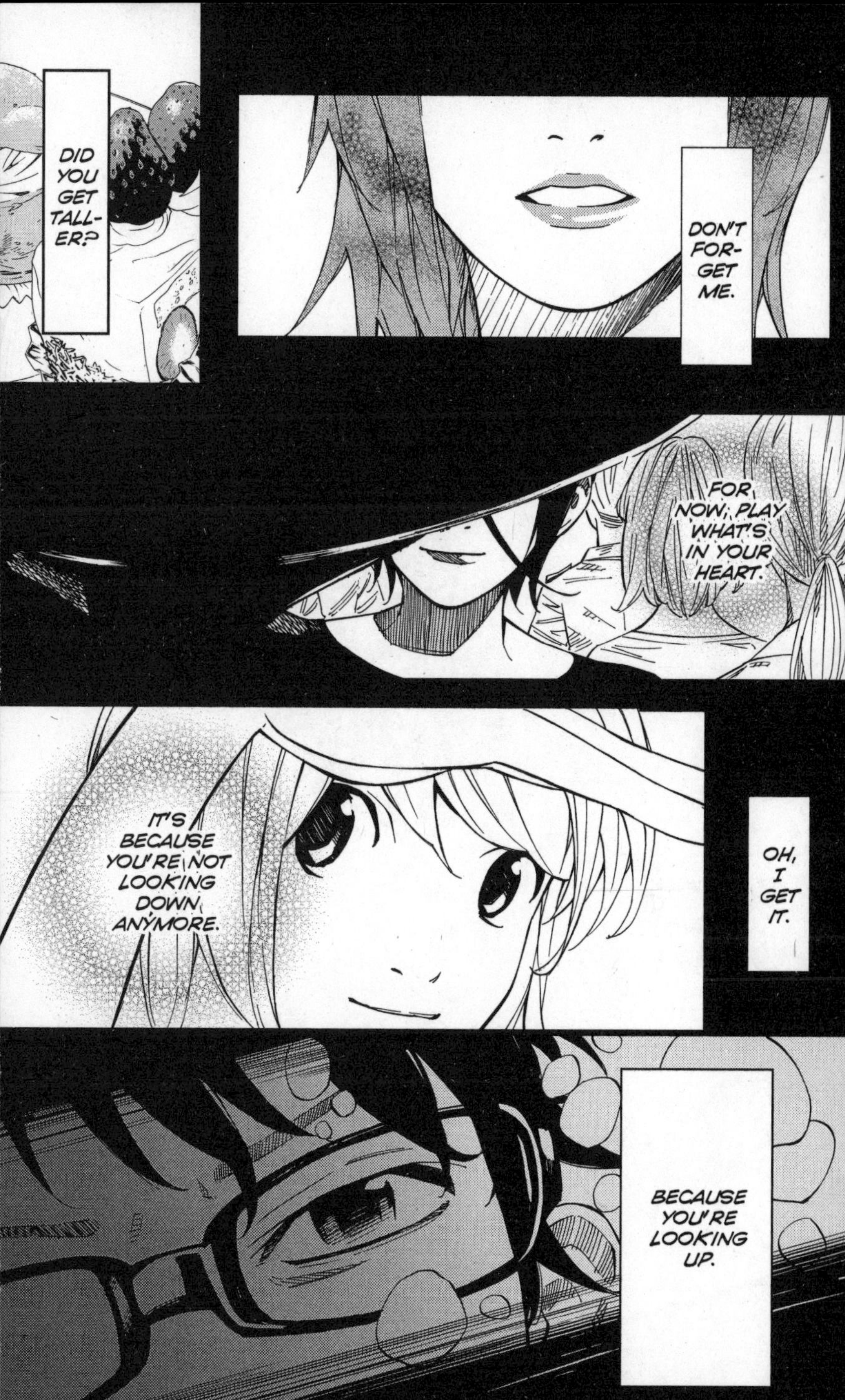
DON'T FORGET ME.
DID YOU GET TALLER?
FOR NOW, PLAY WHAT'S IN YOUR HEART.
OH, I GET IT.
IT'S BECAUSE YOU'RE NOT LOOKING DOWN ANYMORE.
BECAUSE YOU'RE LOOKING UP.

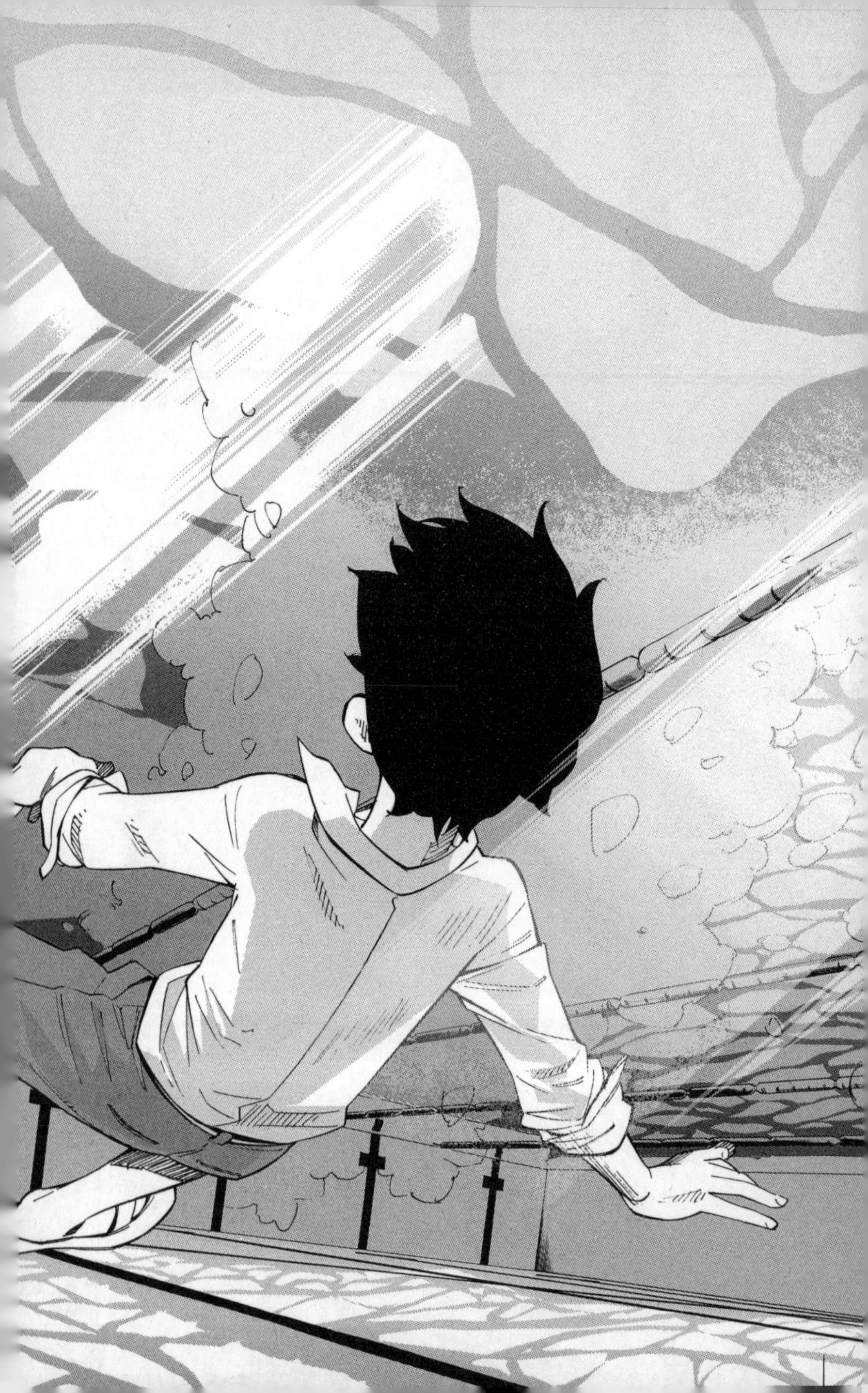

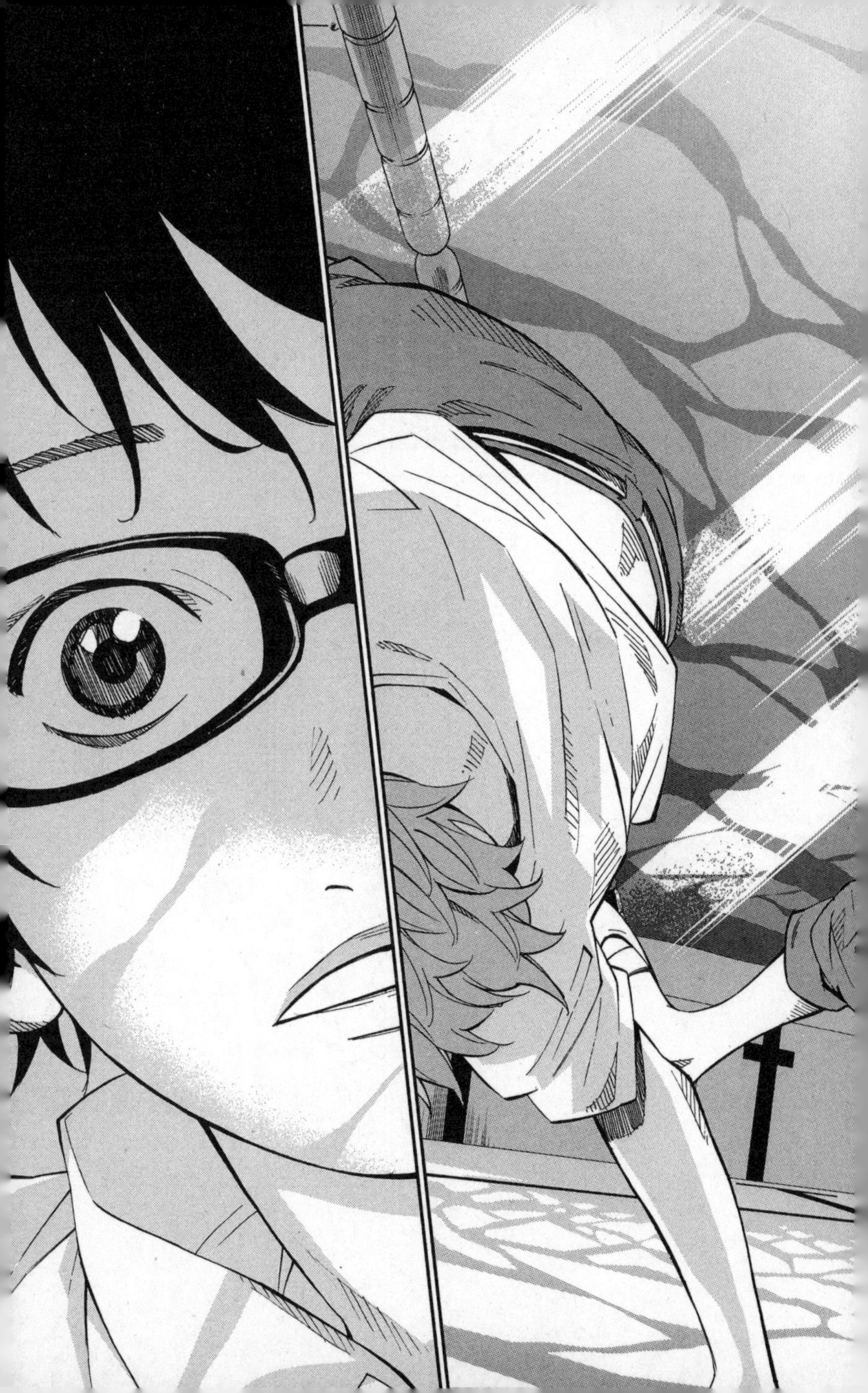

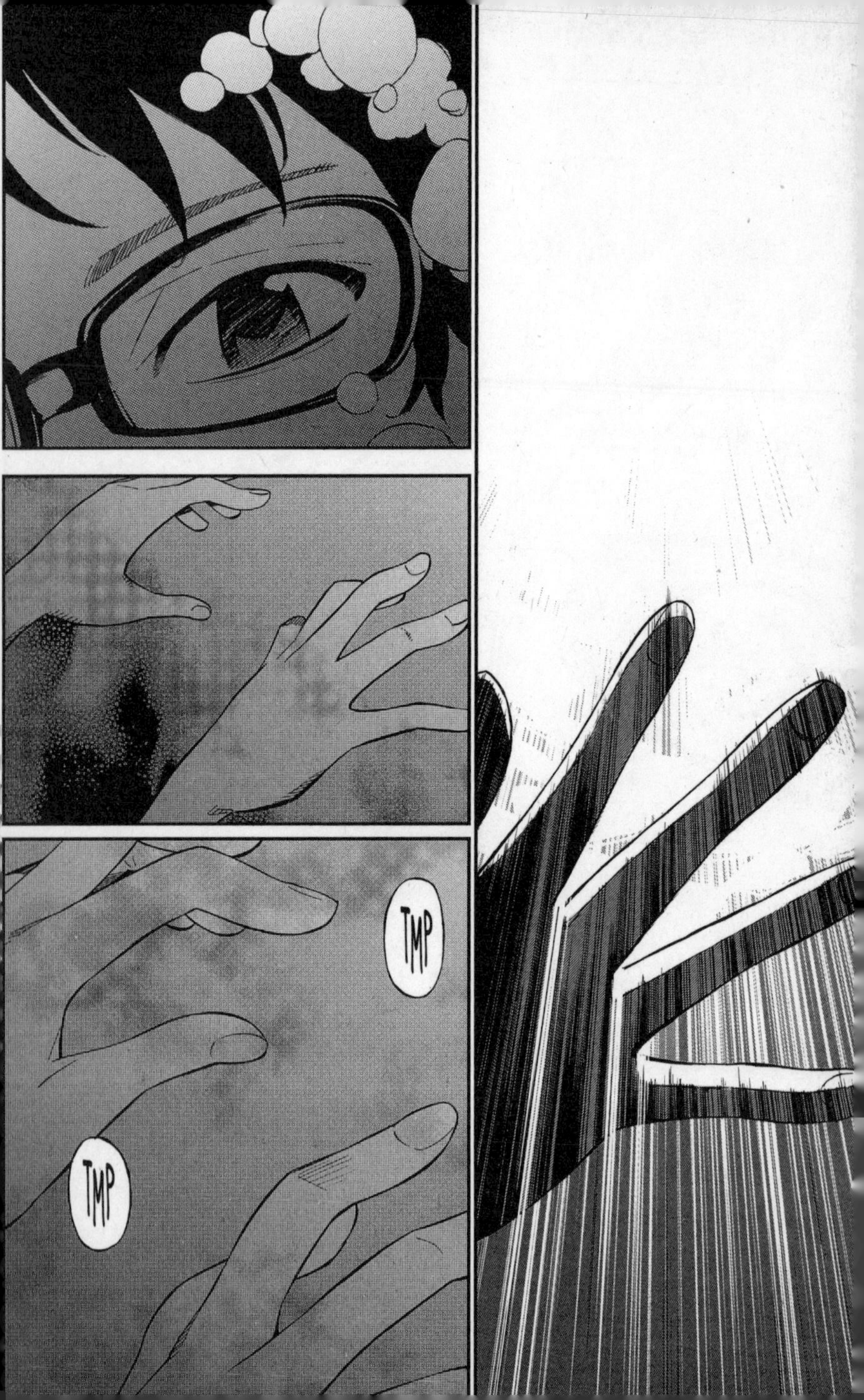
TMP
TMP

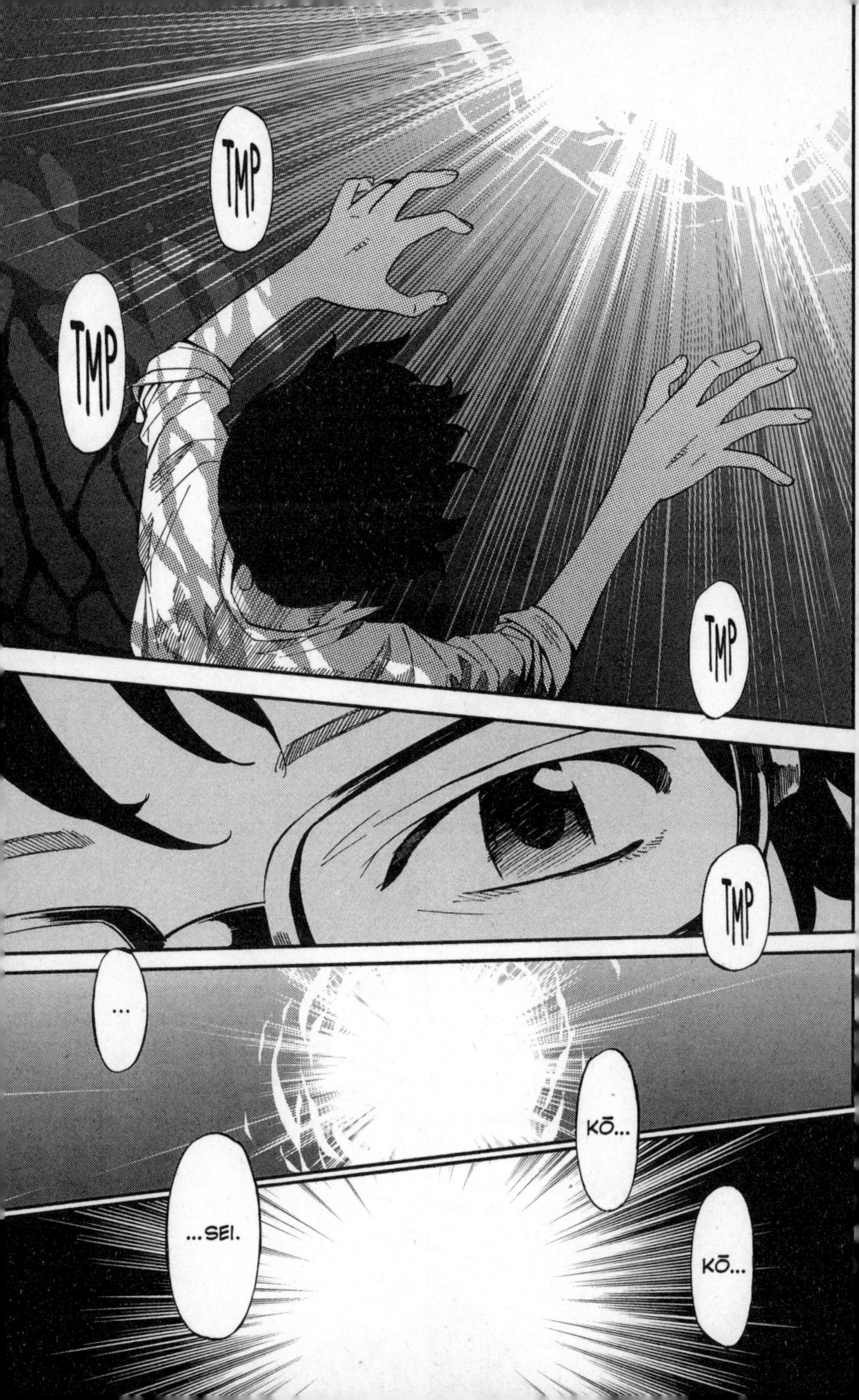
TMP
TMP
TMP
TMP
KŌ...
...
KŌ...
...SEI.

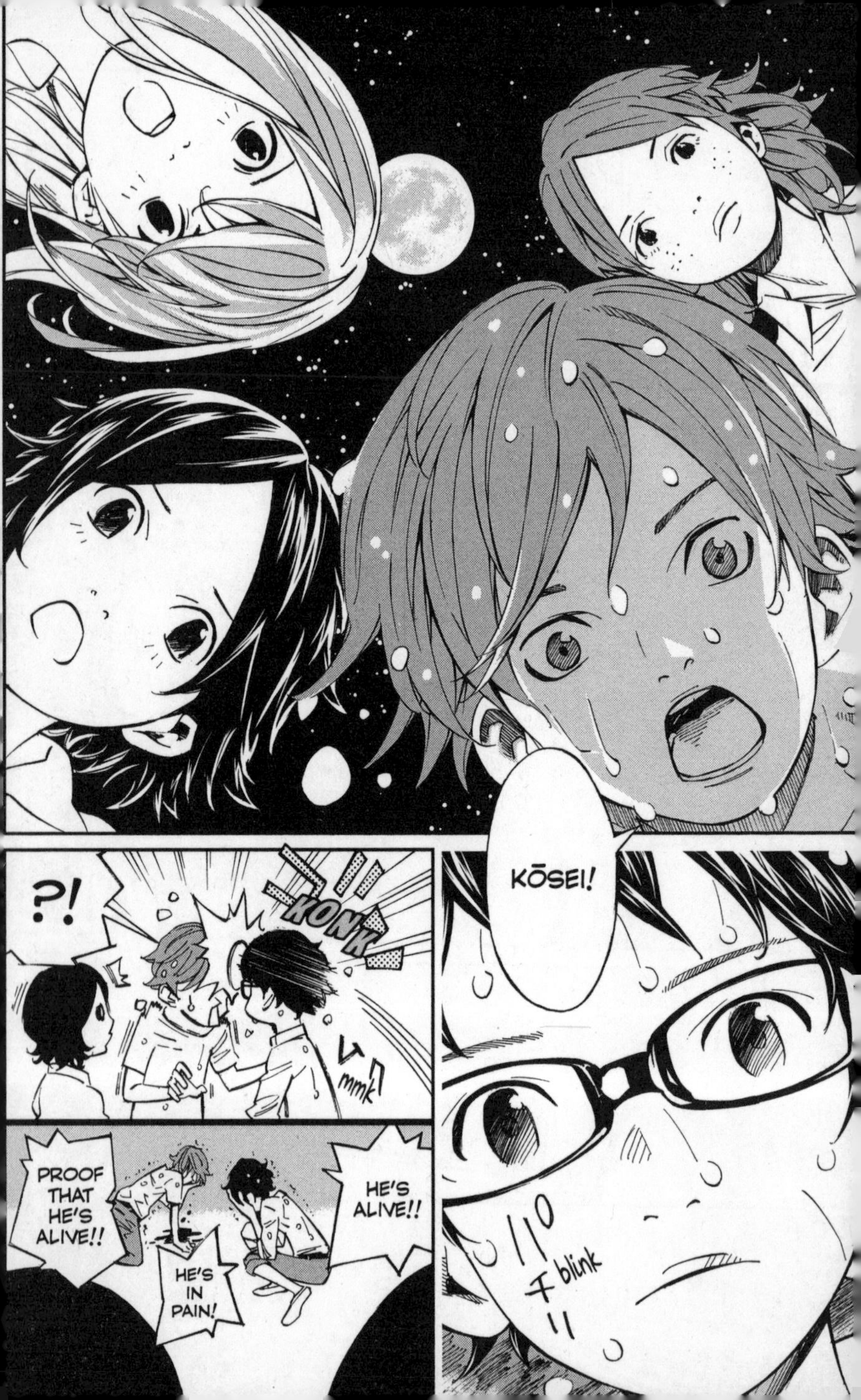
KŌSEI!
blink
KONK
?!
mmk
HE'S ALIVE!!
PROOF THAT HE'S ALIVE!!
HE'S IN PAIN!

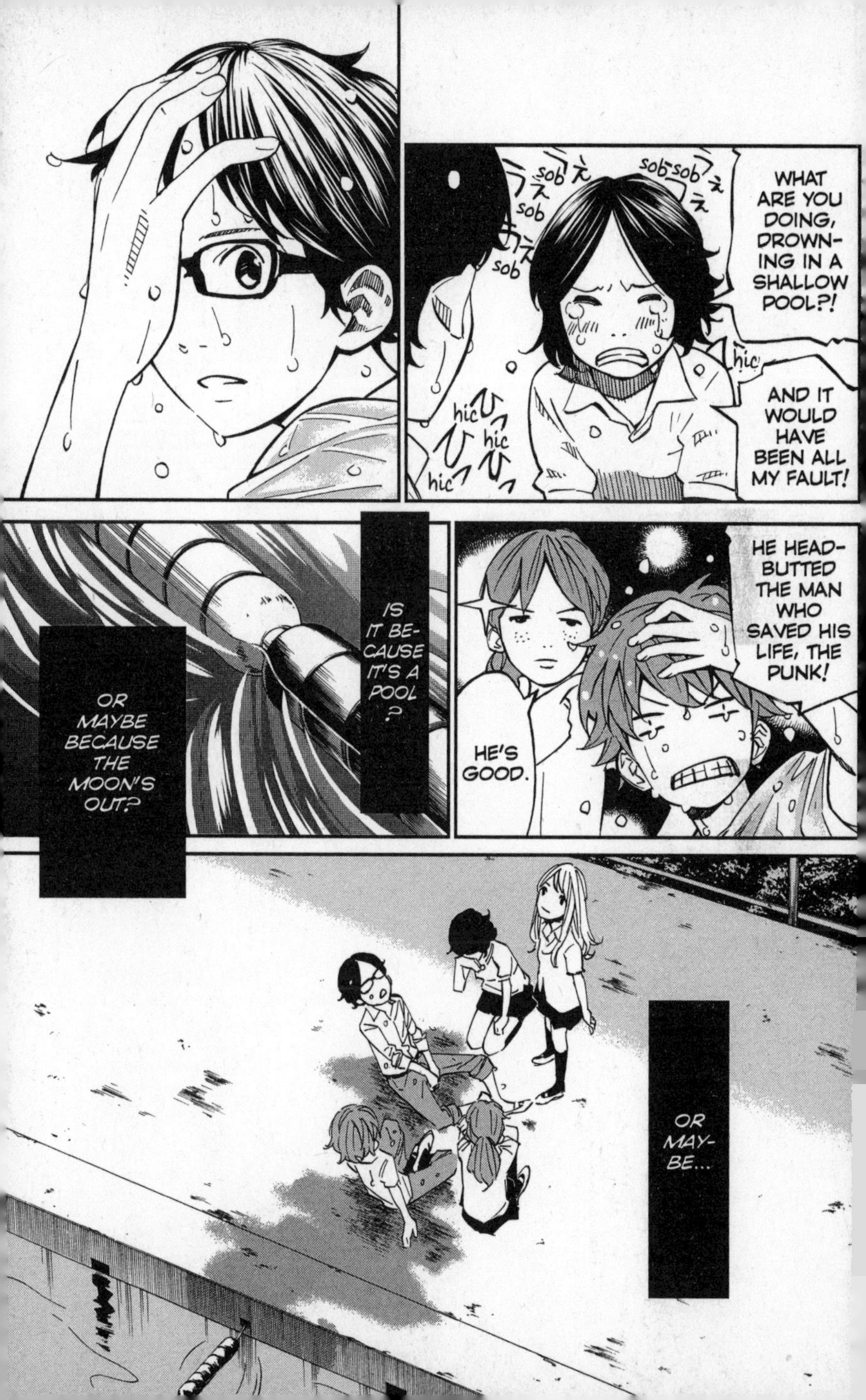

sob sob
WHAT ARE YOU DOING, DROWNING IN A SHALLOW POOL?!
sob sob
hic
AND IT WOULD HAVE BEEN ALL MY FAULT!
hic hic hic
HE HEAD-BUTTED THE MAN WHO SAVED HIS LIFE, THE PUNK!
HE'S GOOD.
IS IT BECAUSE IT'S A POOL?
OR MAYBE BECAUSE THE MOON'S OUT?
OR MAY-BE...

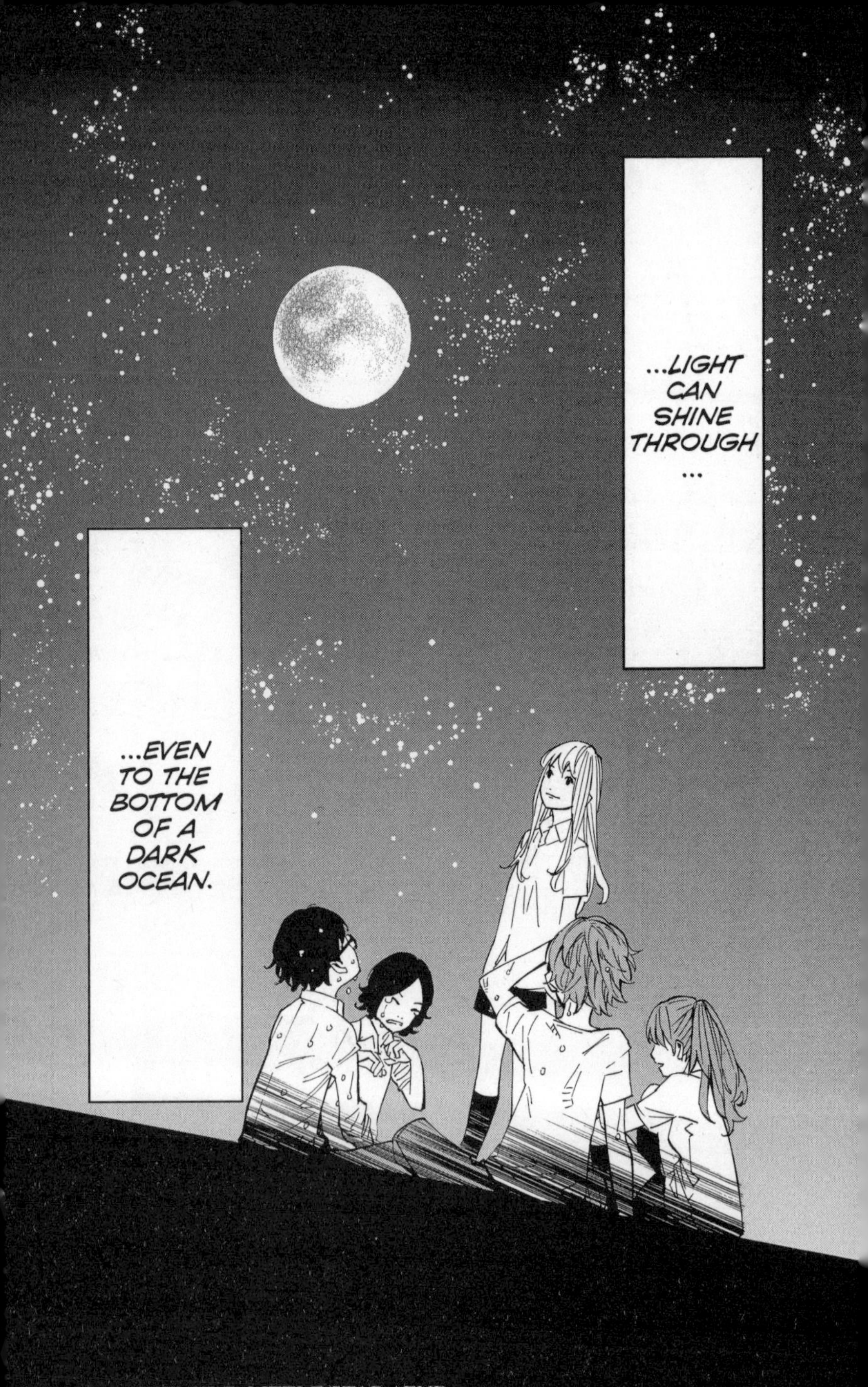
...LIGHT CAN SHINE THROUGH ...
...EVEN TO THE BOTTOM OF A DARK OCEAN.

TWINKLE, TWINKLE, LITTLE STAR / END

Your Lie in April

I met the girl under full-bloomed cherry blossoms, and my fate has begun to change.

Your Lie in April

I met the girl under full-bloomed cherry blossoms, and my fate has begun to change.

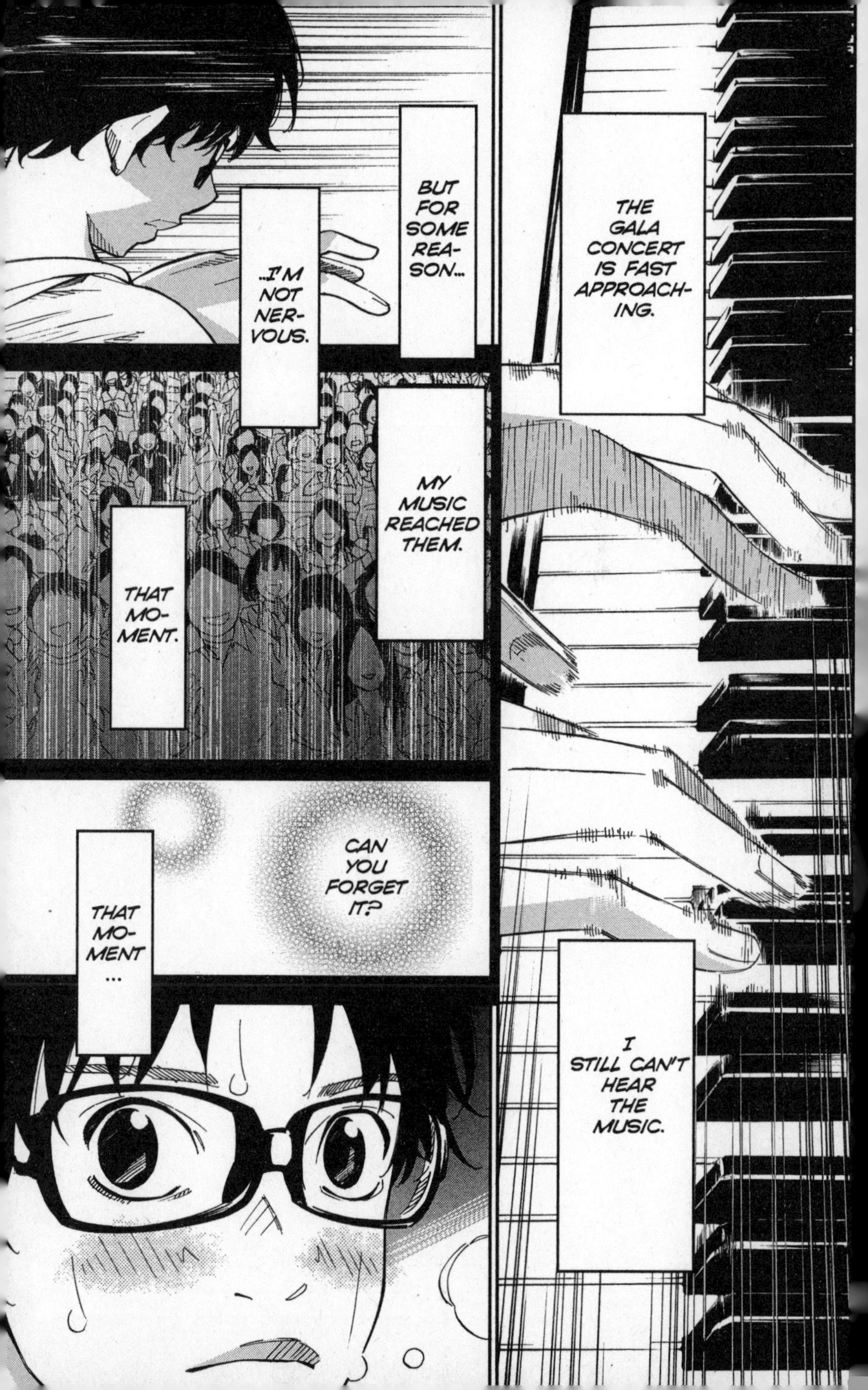
THE GALA CONCERT IS FAST APPROACHING.
I STILL CAN'T HEAR THE MUSIC.
BUT FOR SOME REASON...
...I'M NOT NERVOUS.
MY MUSIC REACHED THEM.
THAT MOMENT.
CAN YOU FORGET IT?
THAT MOMENT...

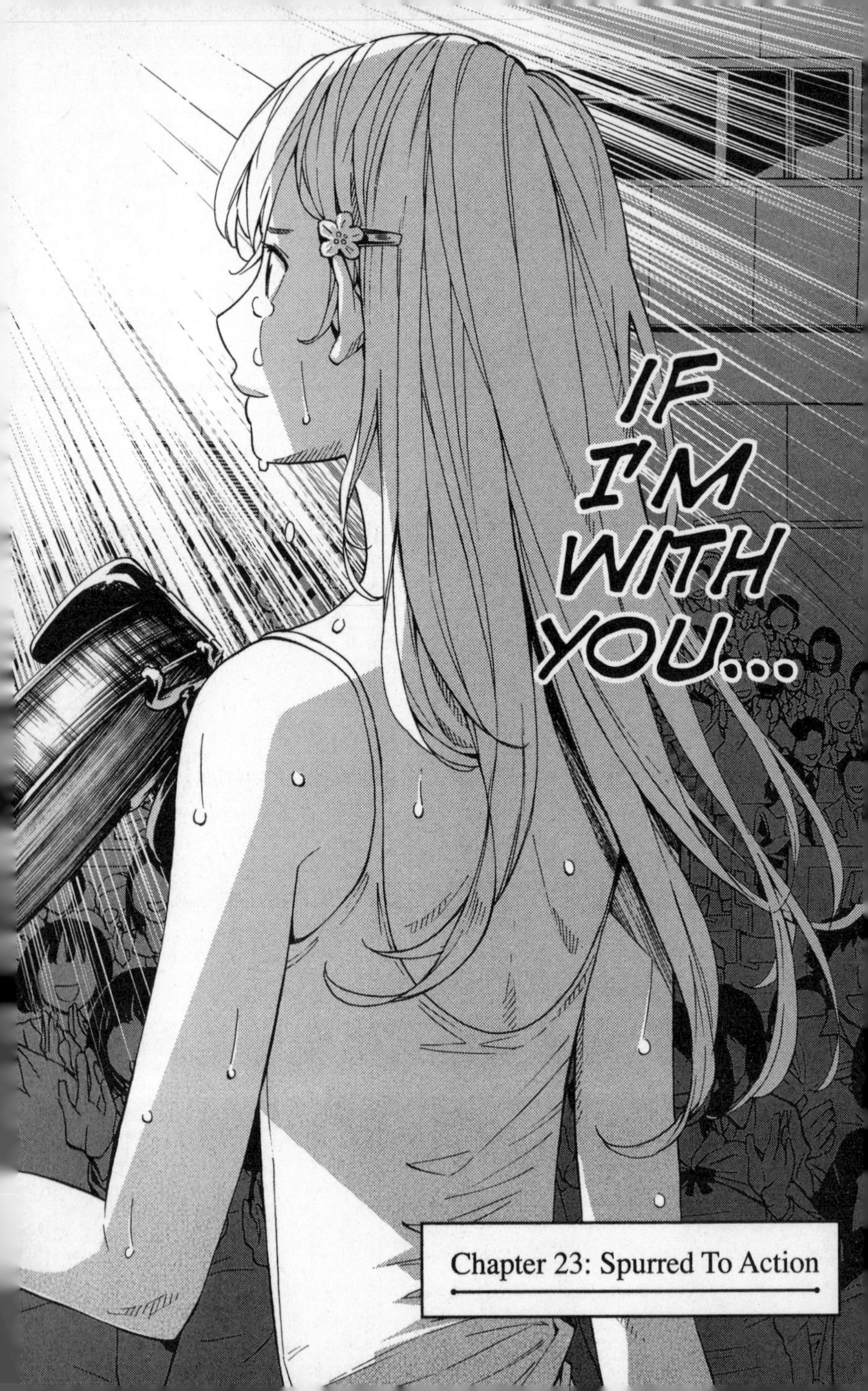
IF I'M WITH YOU...

Chapter 23: Spurred To Action

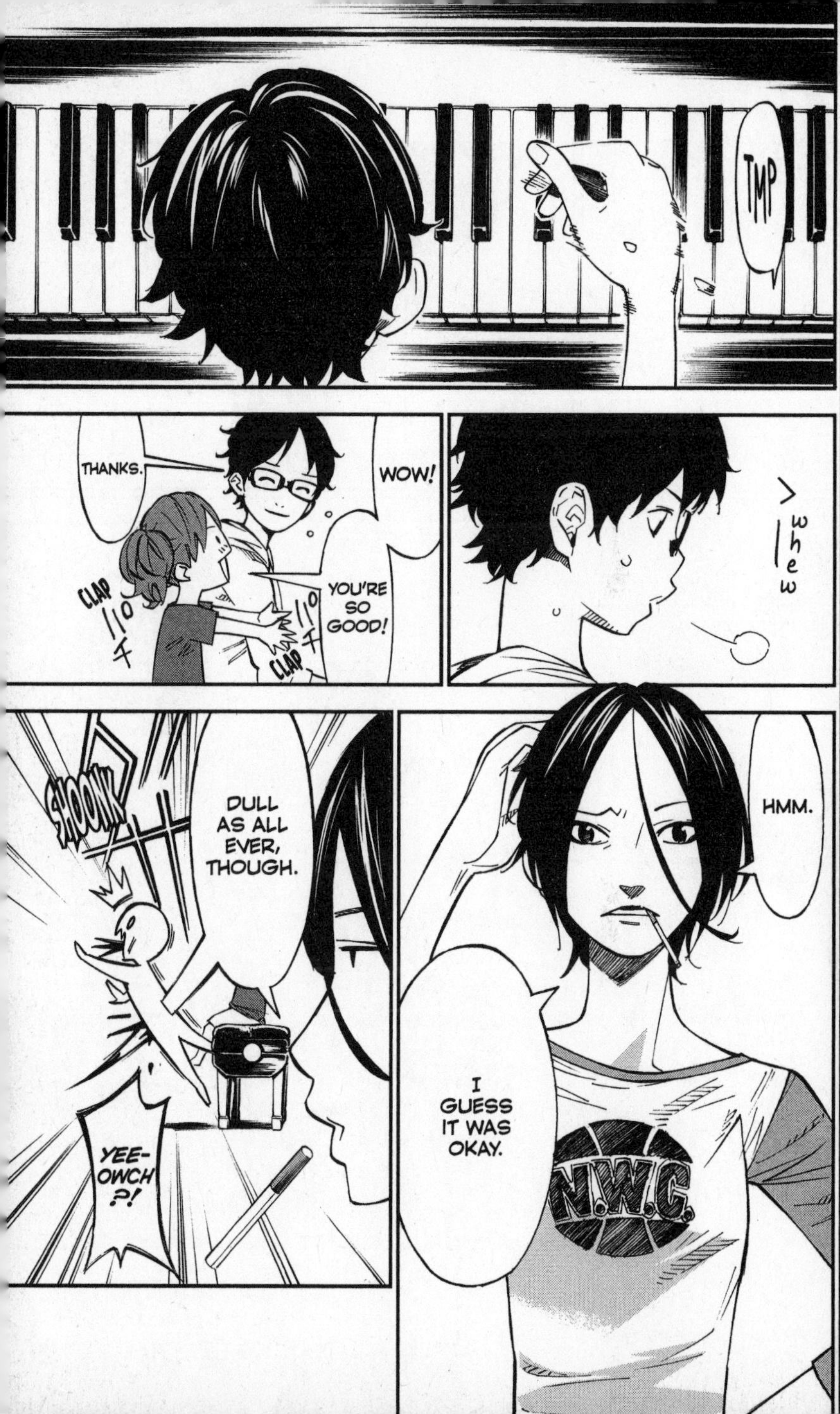

TMP
WHEW
WOW!
YOU'RE SO GOOD!
CLAP
CLAP
THANKS.
HMM.
I GUESS IT WAS OKAY.
DULL AS ALL EVER, THOUGH.
SHOONK
YEE-OWCH?!

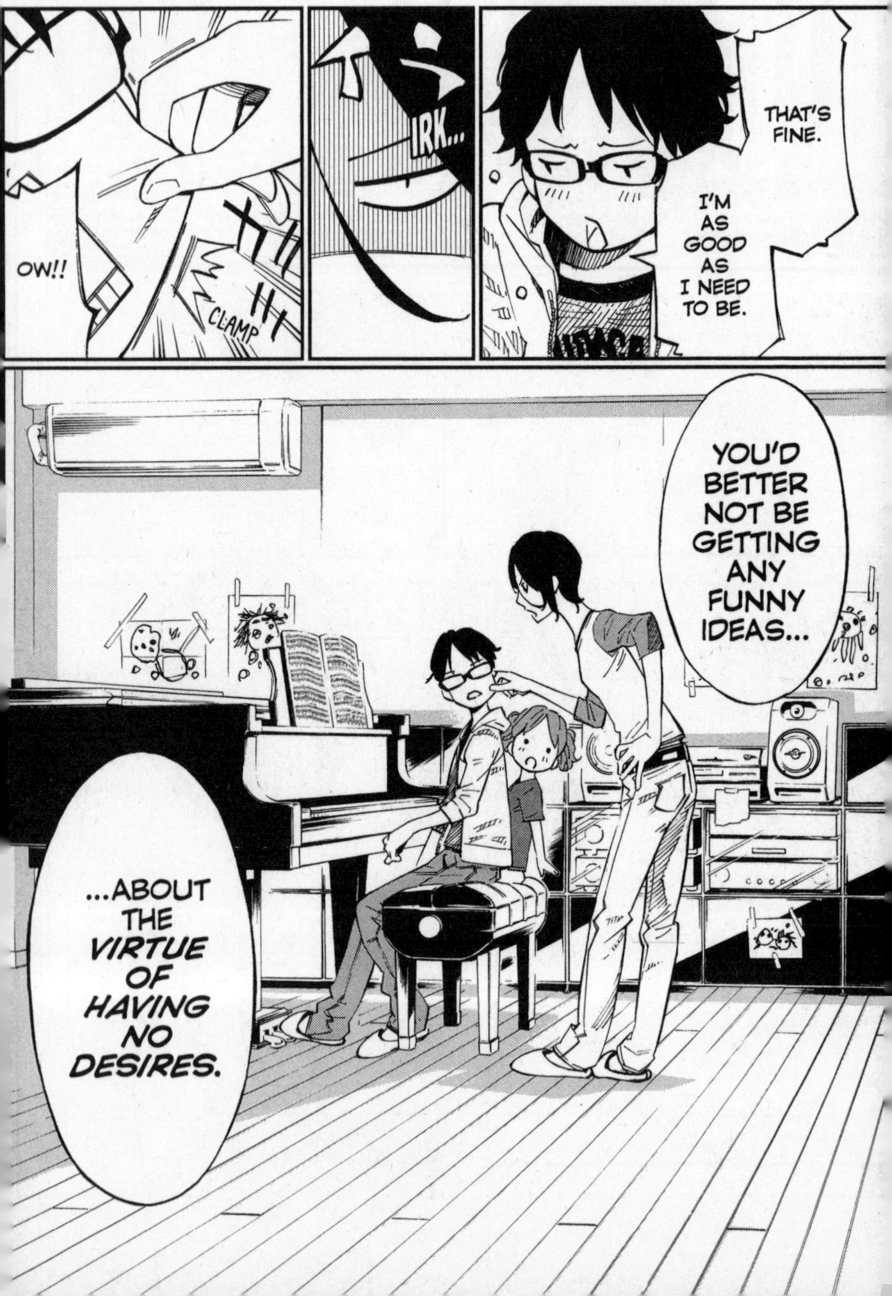
THAT'S FINE.
I'M AS GOOD AS I NEED TO BE.
IRK...
CLAMP
OW!!
YOU'D BETTER NOT BE GETTING ANY FUNNY IDEAS...
...ABOUT THE *VIRTUE OF HAVING NO DESIRES.*

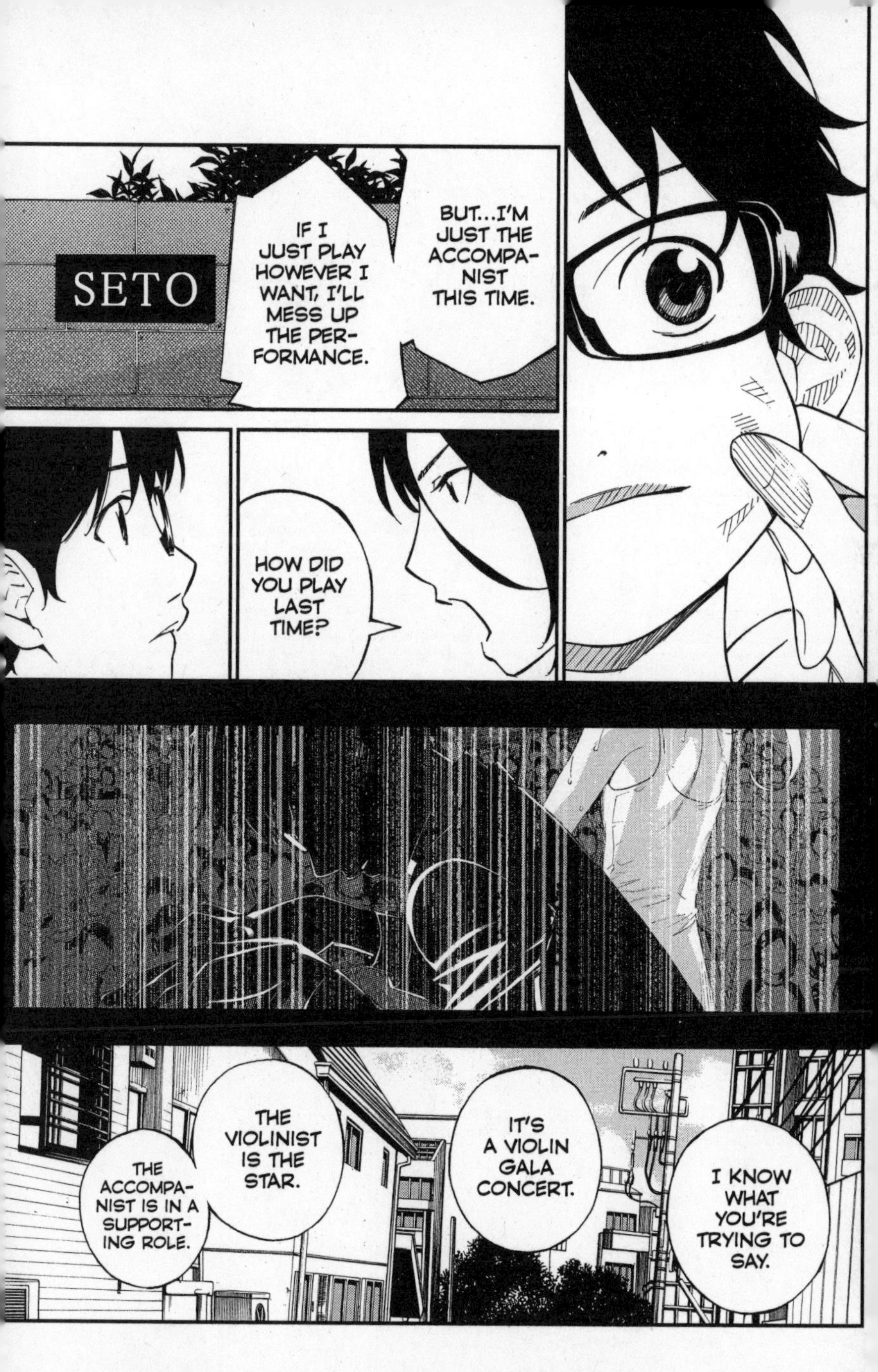
BUT...I'M JUST THE ACCOMPANIST THIS TIME.
IF I JUST PLAY HOWEVER I WANT, I'LL MESS UP THE PERFORMANCE.
SETO
HOW DID YOU PLAY LAST TIME?
I KNOW WHAT YOU'RE TRYING TO SAY.
IT'S A VIOLIN GALA CONCERT.
THE VIOLINIST IS THE STAR.
THE ACCOMPANIST IS IN A SUPPORTING ROLE.

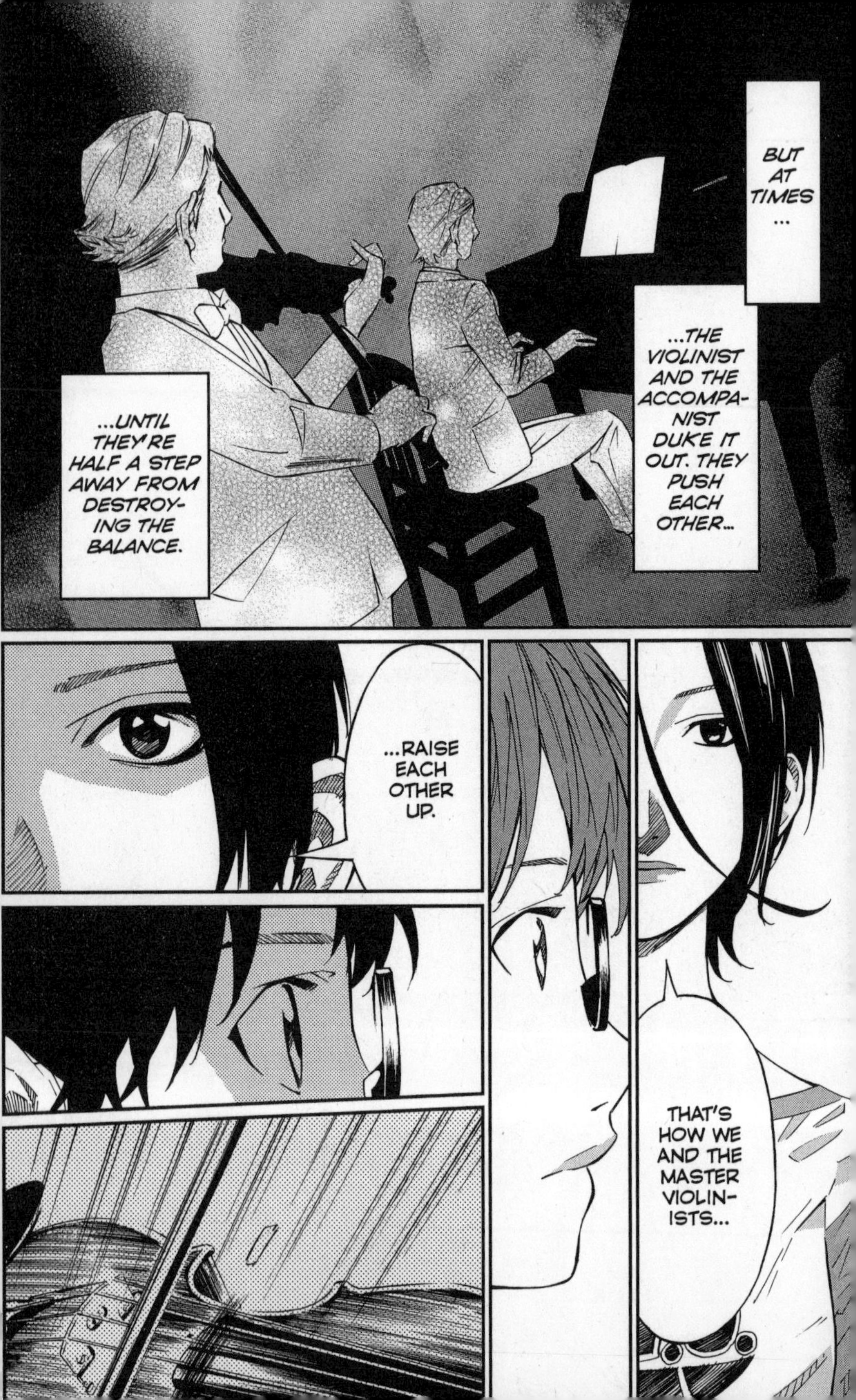
BUT AT TIMES...
...THE VIOLINIST AND THE ACCOMPANIST DUKE IT OUT. THEY PUSH EACH OTHER...
...UNTIL THEY'RE HALF A STEP AWAY FROM DESTROYING THE BALANCE.
THAT'S HOW WE AND THE MASTER VIOLINISTS...
...RAISE EACH OTHER UP.

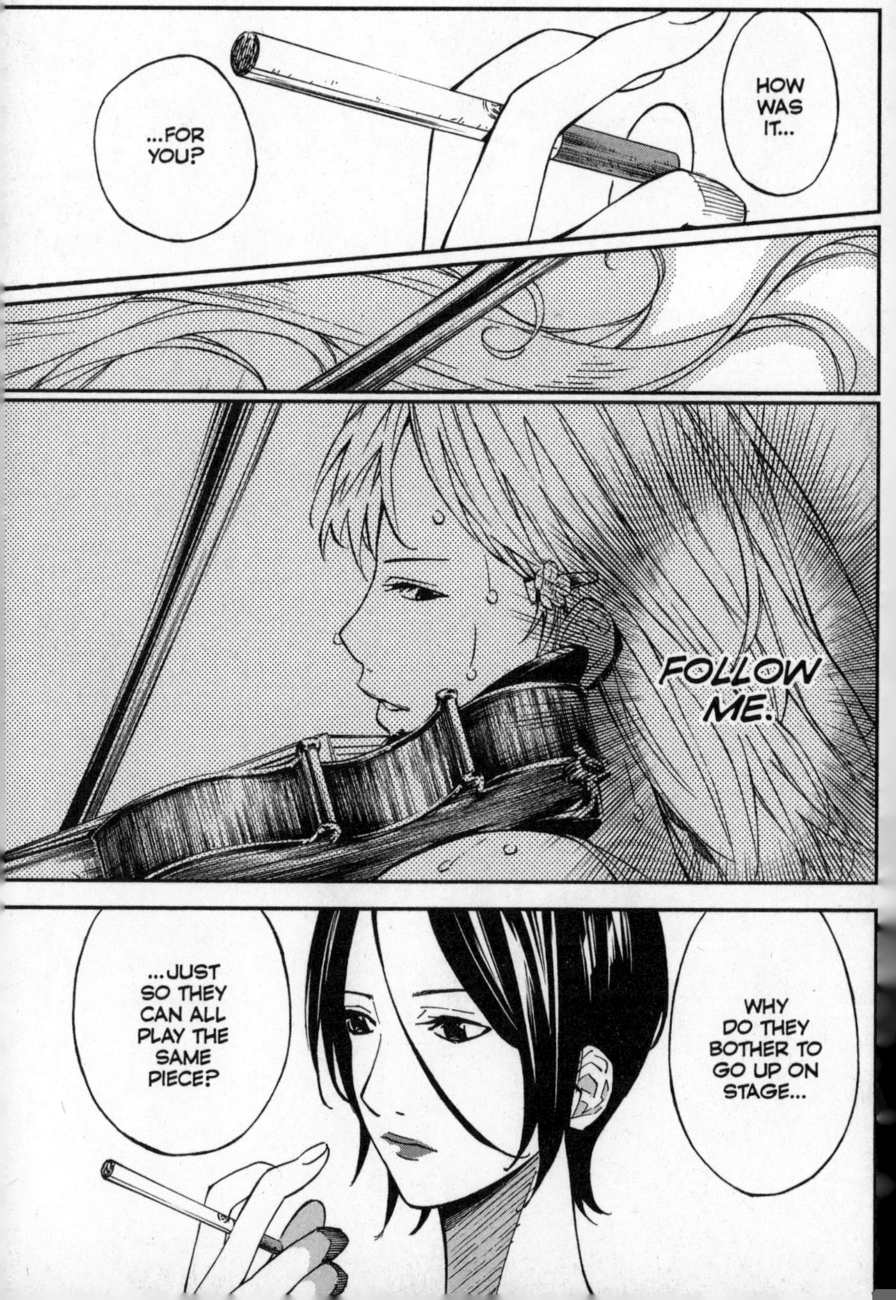
HOW WAS IT...
...FOR YOU?
FOLLOW ME.
WHY DO THEY BOTHER TO GO UP ON STAGE...
...JUST SO THEY CAN ALL PLAY THE SAME PIECE?

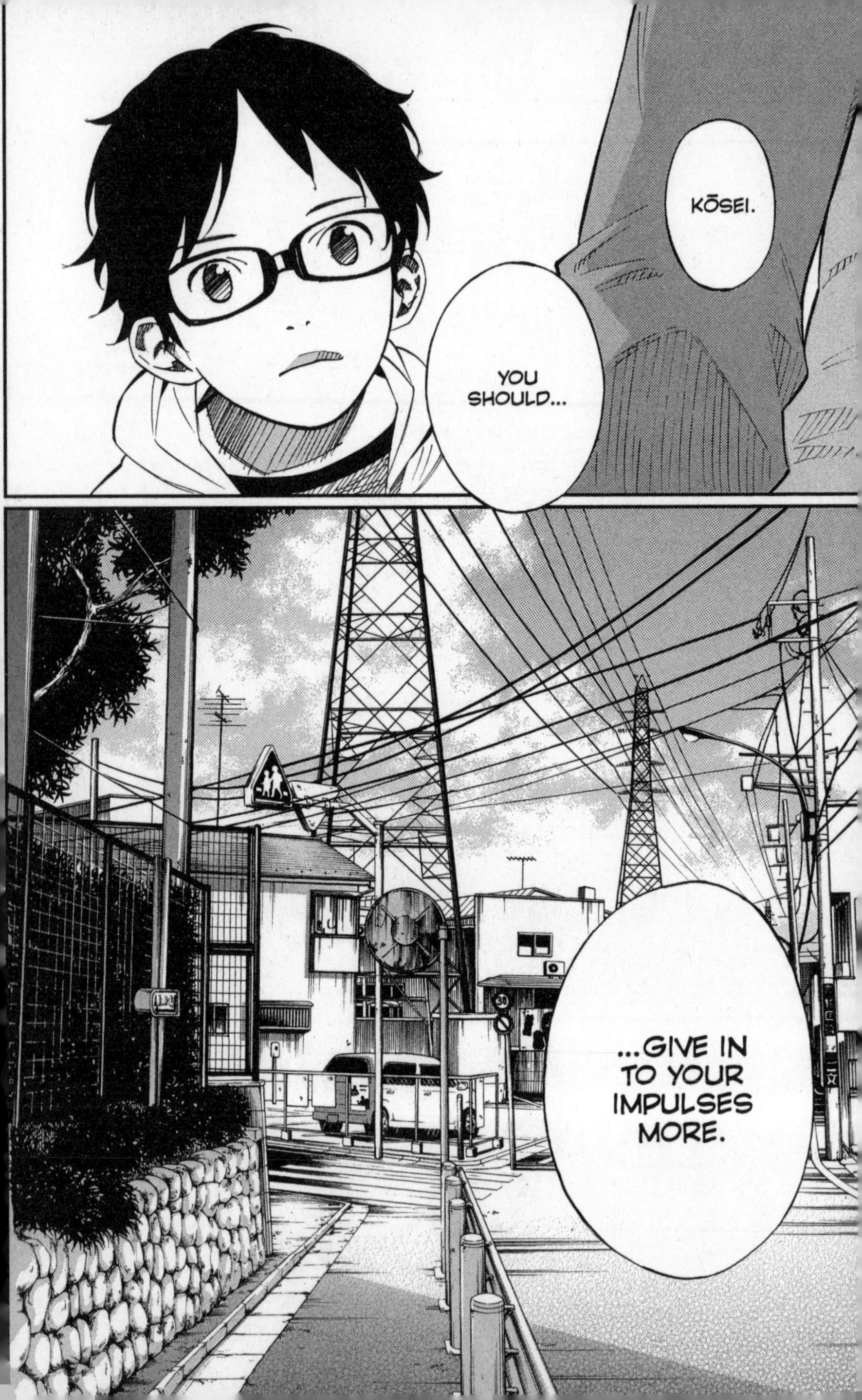
KŌSEI.
YOU SHOULD...
...GIVE IN TO YOUR IMPULSES MORE.

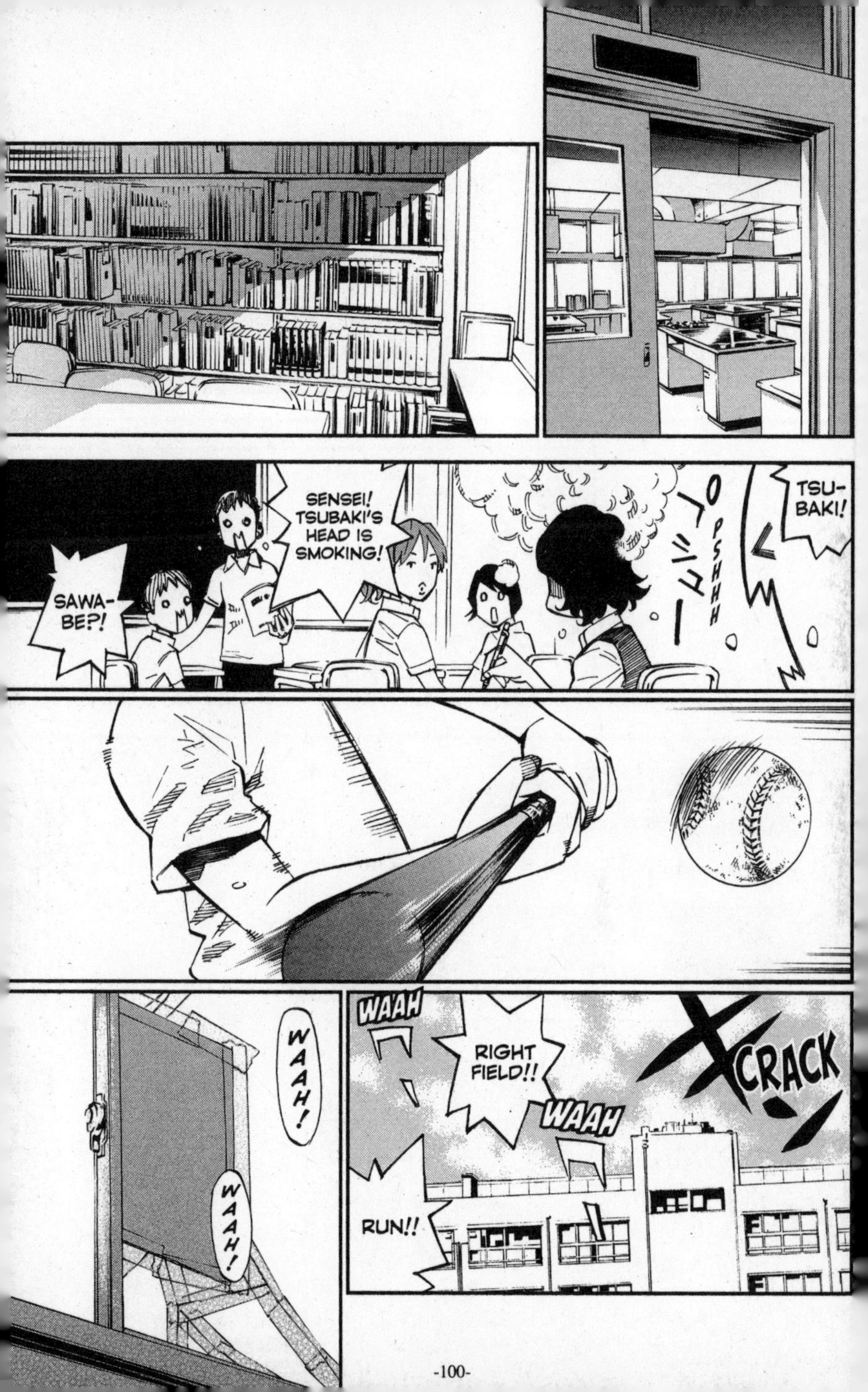
TSU-BAKI!
PSHHH
SENSEI! TSUBAKI'S HEAD IS SMOKING!
SAWA-BE?!
CRACK
WAAH
RIGHT FIELD!!
WAAH
RUN!!
WAAH!
WAAH!

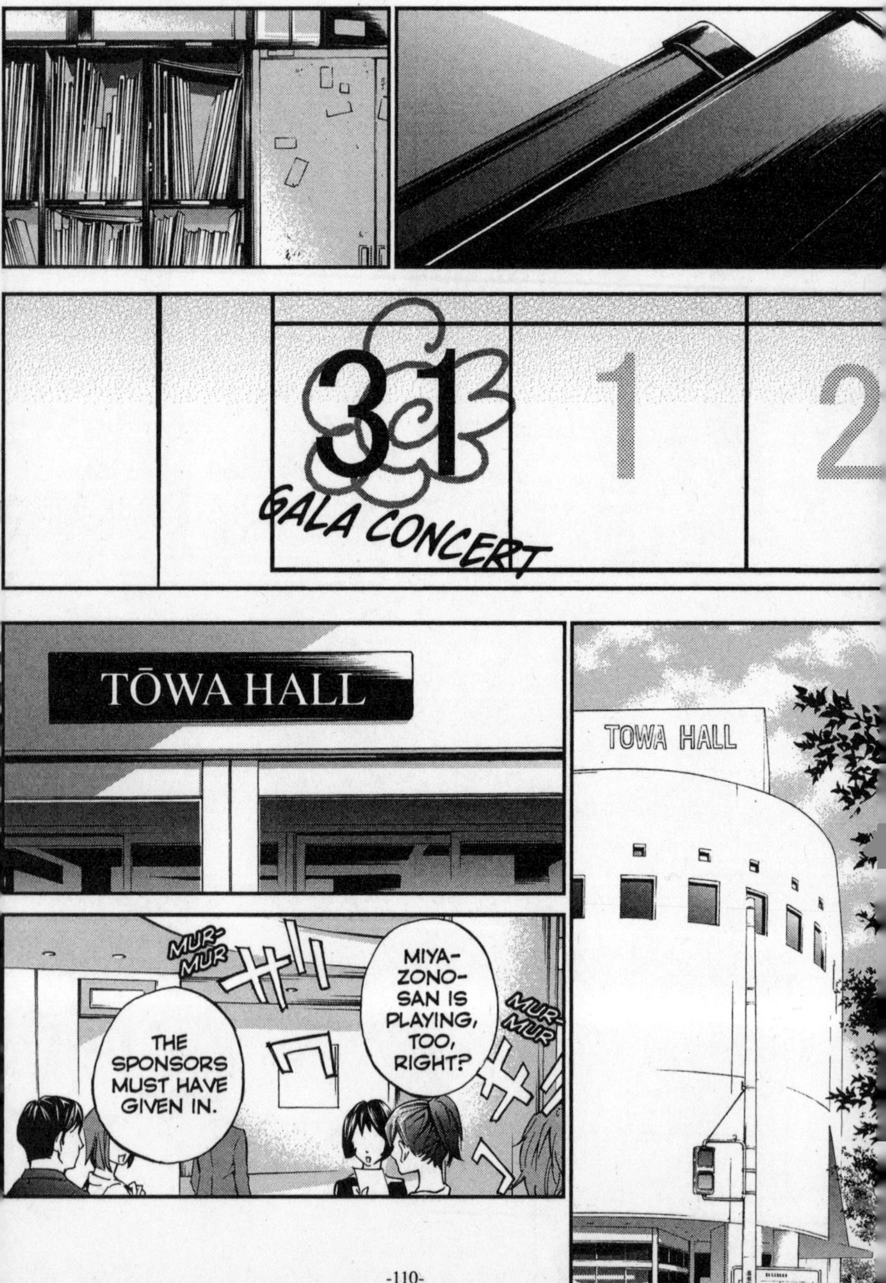
2
1
31
GALA CONCERT
TOWA HALL
TŌWA HALL
MUR-MUR
MIYA-ZONO-SAN IS PLAYING, TOO, RIGHT?
THE SPONSORS MUST HAVE GIVEN IN.
MUR-MUR

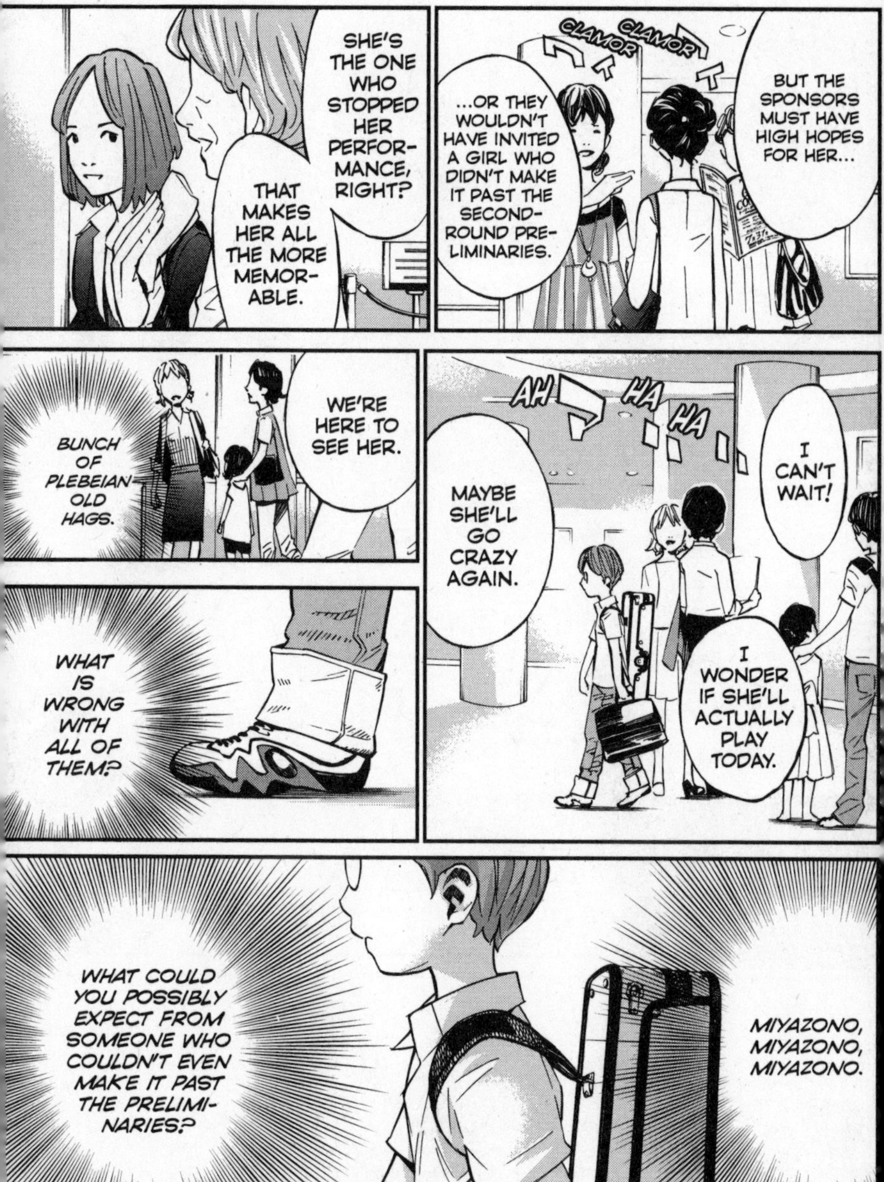
CLAMOR
CLAMOR
BUT THE SPONSORS MUST HAVE HIGH HOPES FOR HER...
...OR THEY WOULDN'T HAVE INVITED A GIRL WHO DIDN'T MAKE IT PAST THE SECOND-ROUND PRE-LIMINARIES.
SHE'S THE ONE WHO STOPPED HER PERFOR-MANCE, RIGHT?
THAT MAKES HER ALL THE MORE MEMOR-ABLE.
AH
HA
HA
I CAN'T WAIT!
MAYBE SHE'LL GO CRAZY AGAIN.
I WONDER IF SHE'LL ACTUALLY PLAY TODAY.
WE'RE HERE TO SEE HER.
BUNCH OF PLEBEIAN OLD HAGS.
WHAT IS WRONG WITH ALL OF THEM?
MIYAZONO, MIYAZONO, MIYAZONO.
WHAT COULD YOU POSSIBLY EXPECT FROM SOMEONE WHO COULDN'T EVEN MAKE IT PAST THE PRELIMI-NARIES?

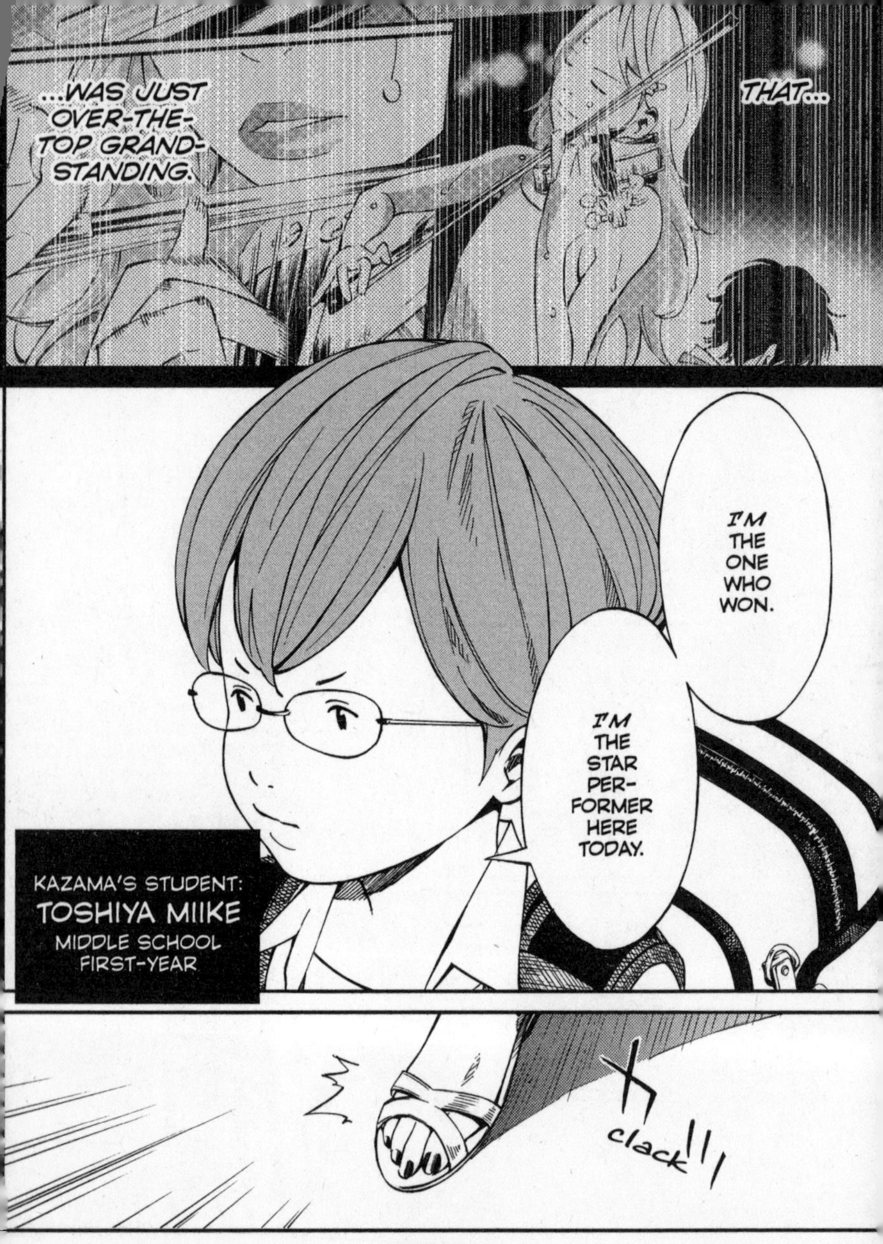
THAT...
...WAS JUST OVER-THE-TOP GRAND-STANDING.
I'M THE ONE WHO WON.
I'M THE STAR PER-FORMER HERE TODAY.
KAZAMA'S STUDENT: TOSHIYA MIIKE MIDDLE SCHOOL FIRST-YEAR
clack

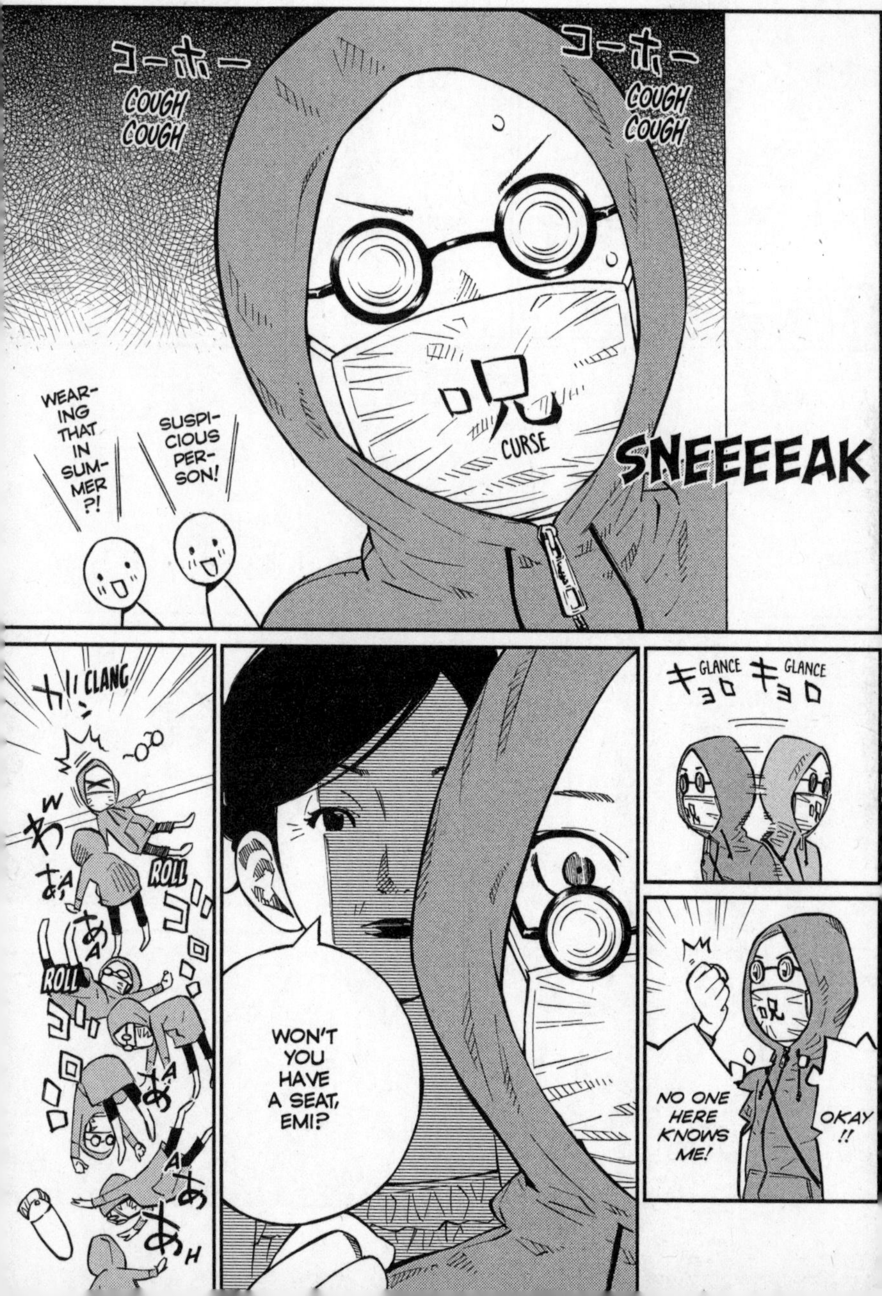
コーホー
COUGH COUGH
コーホー
COUGH COUGH
呪
CURSE
SNEEEEAK
SUSPI-CIOUS PER-SON!
WEAR-ING THAT IN SUM-MER?!
キョロ GLANCE キョロ GLANCE
OKAY!!
NO ONE HERE KNOWS ME!
WON'T YOU HAVE A SEAT, EMI?
カ!! CLANG
ROLL
ROLL

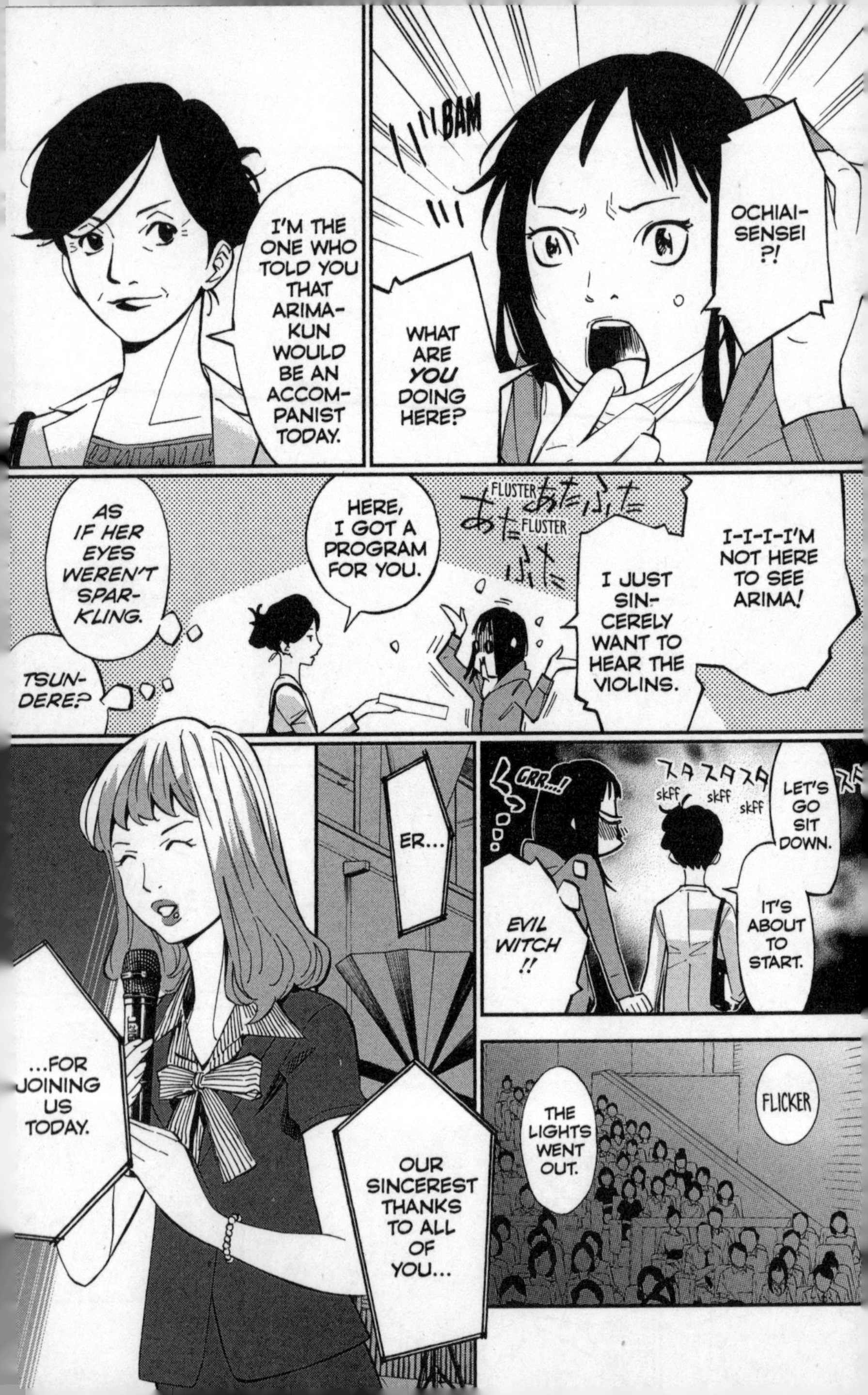
BAM
OCHIAI-SENSEI ?!
WHAT ARE YOU DOING HERE?
I'M THE ONE WHO TOLD YOU THAT ARIMA-KUN WOULD BE AN ACCOMPANIST TODAY.
I-I-I-I'M NOT HERE TO SEE ARIMA!
I JUST SINCERELY WANT TO HEAR THE VIOLINS.
FLUSTER FLUSTER
HERE, I GOT A PROGRAM FOR YOU.
AS IF HER EYES WEREN'T SPARKLING.
TSUNDERE?
LET'S GO SIT DOWN.
IT'S ABOUT TO START.
skff skff skff
GRR...!
EVIL WITCH !!
ER...
FLICKER
THE LIGHTS WENT OUT.
OUR SINCEREST THANKS TO ALL OF YOU...
...FOR JOINING US TODAY.

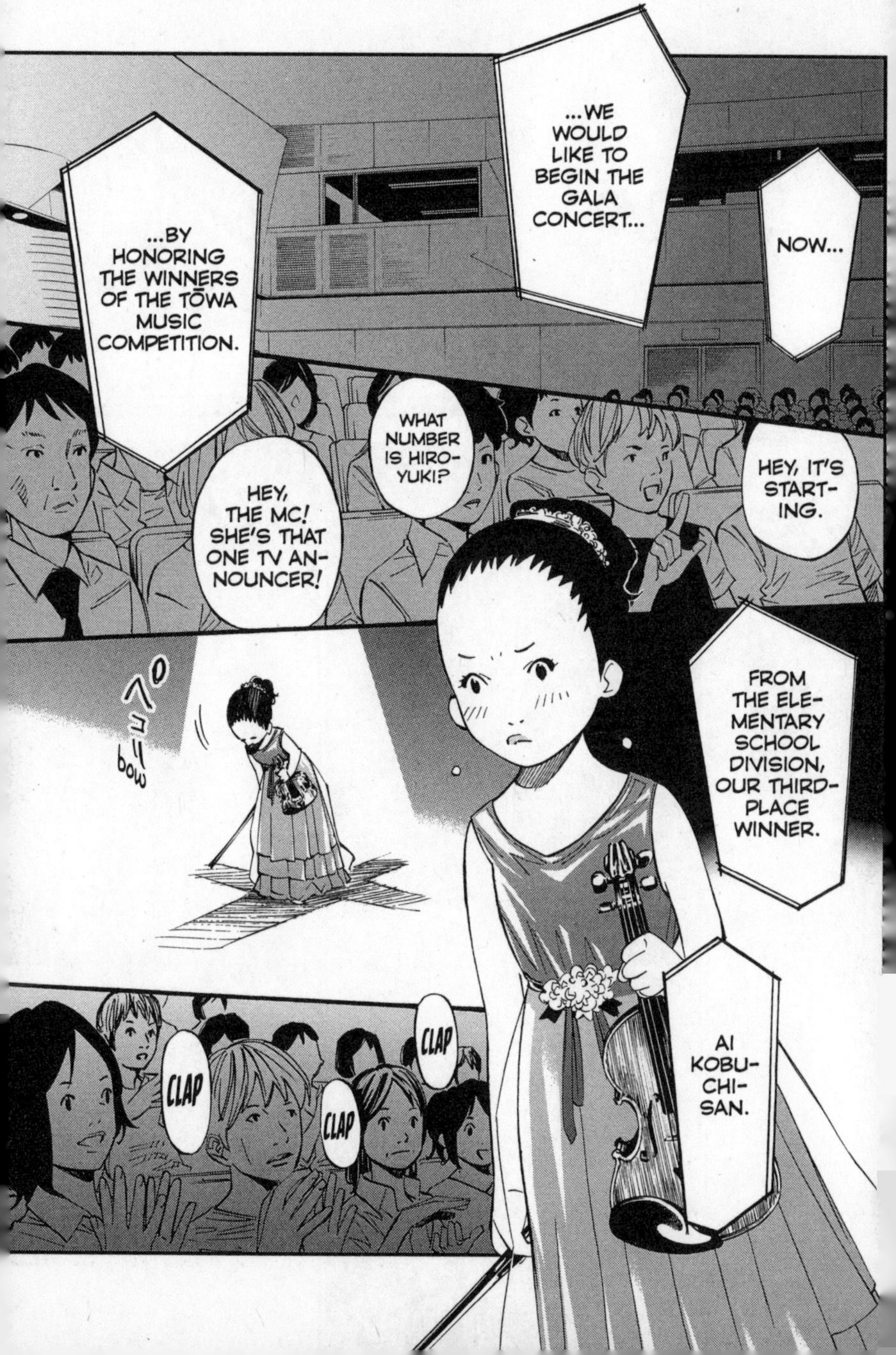
NOW...
...WE WOULD LIKE TO BEGIN THE GALA CONCERT...
...BY HONORING THE WINNERS OF THE TŌWA MUSIC COMPETITION.
HEY, IT'S START-ING.
WHAT NUMBER IS HIRO-YUKI?
HEY, THE MC! SHE'S THAT ONE TV AN-NOUNCER!
FROM THE ELE-MENTARY SCHOOL DIVISION, OUR THIRD-PLACE WINNER.
AI KOBU-CHI-SAN.
ペコリ
bow
CLAP
CLAP
CLAP

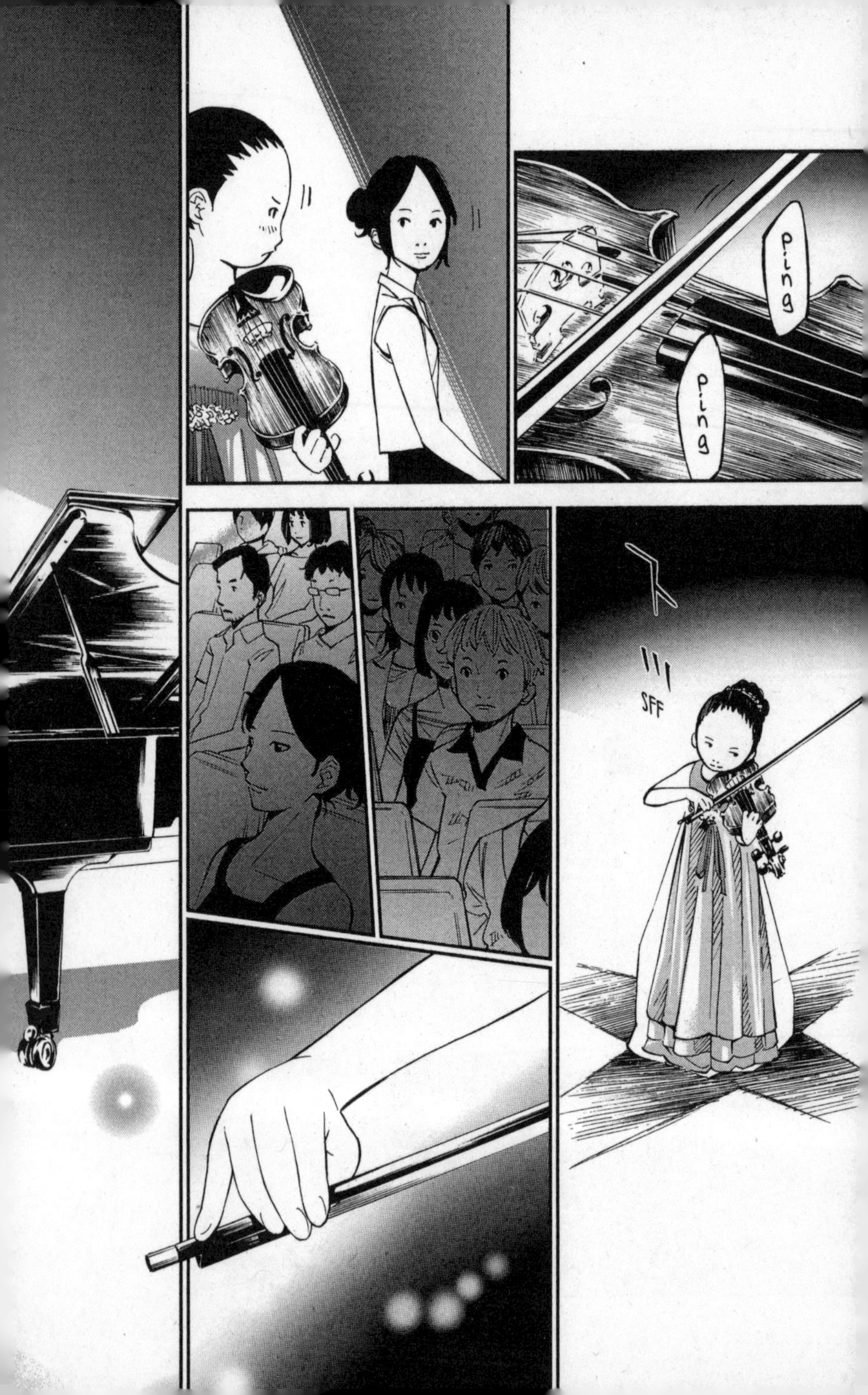
ping
ping
SFF

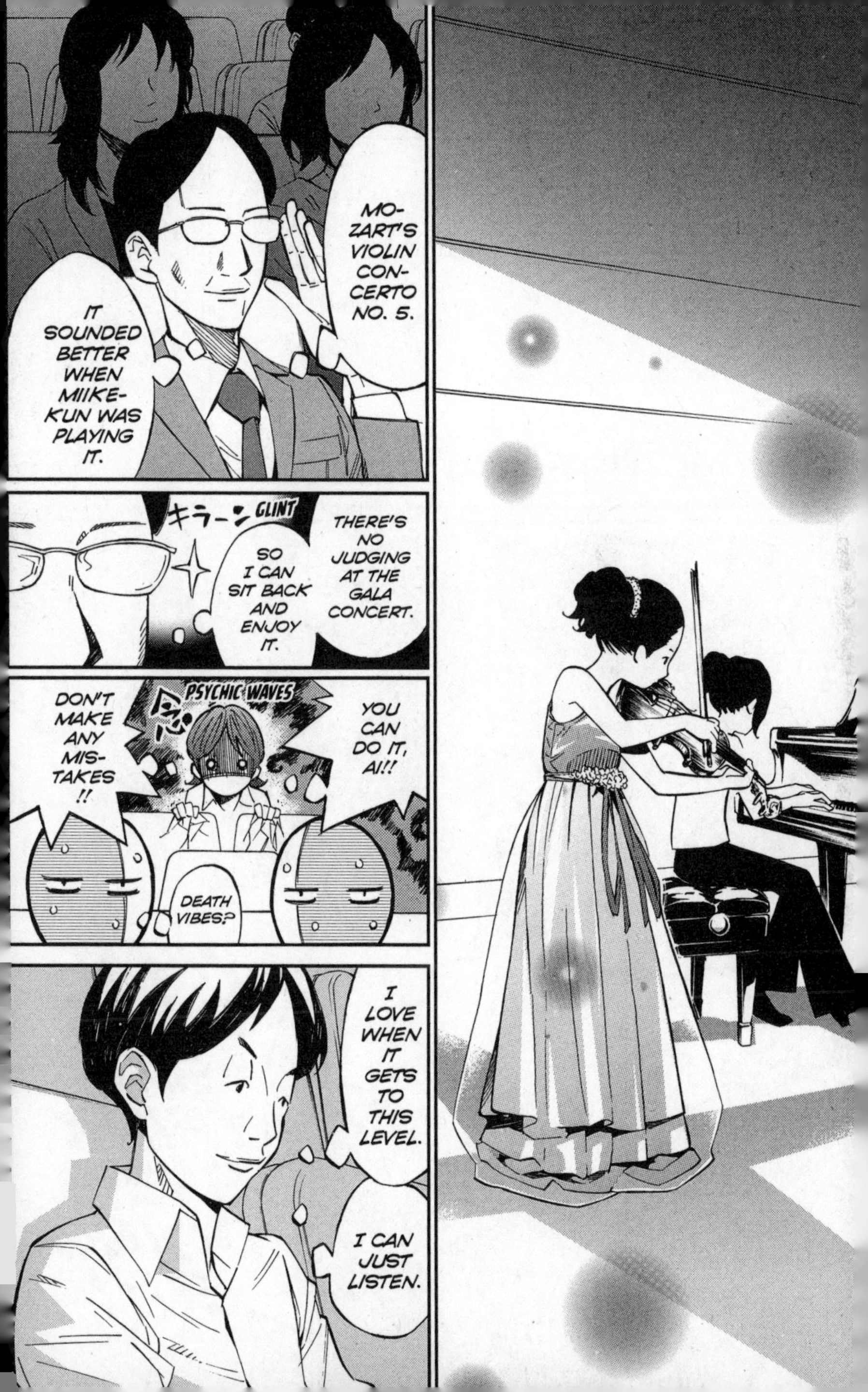
MO-ZART'S VIOLIN CONCERTO NO. 5.
IT SOUNDED BETTER WHEN MIIKE-KUN WAS PLAYING IT.
キラーン GLINT
THERE'S NO JUDGING AT THE GALA CONCERT.
SO I CAN SIT BACK AND ENJOY IT.
PSYCHIC WAVES
YOU CAN DO IT, AI!!
DON'T MAKE ANY MIS-TAKES!!
DEATH VIBES?
I LOVE WHEN IT GETS TO THIS LEVEL.
I CAN JUST LISTEN.

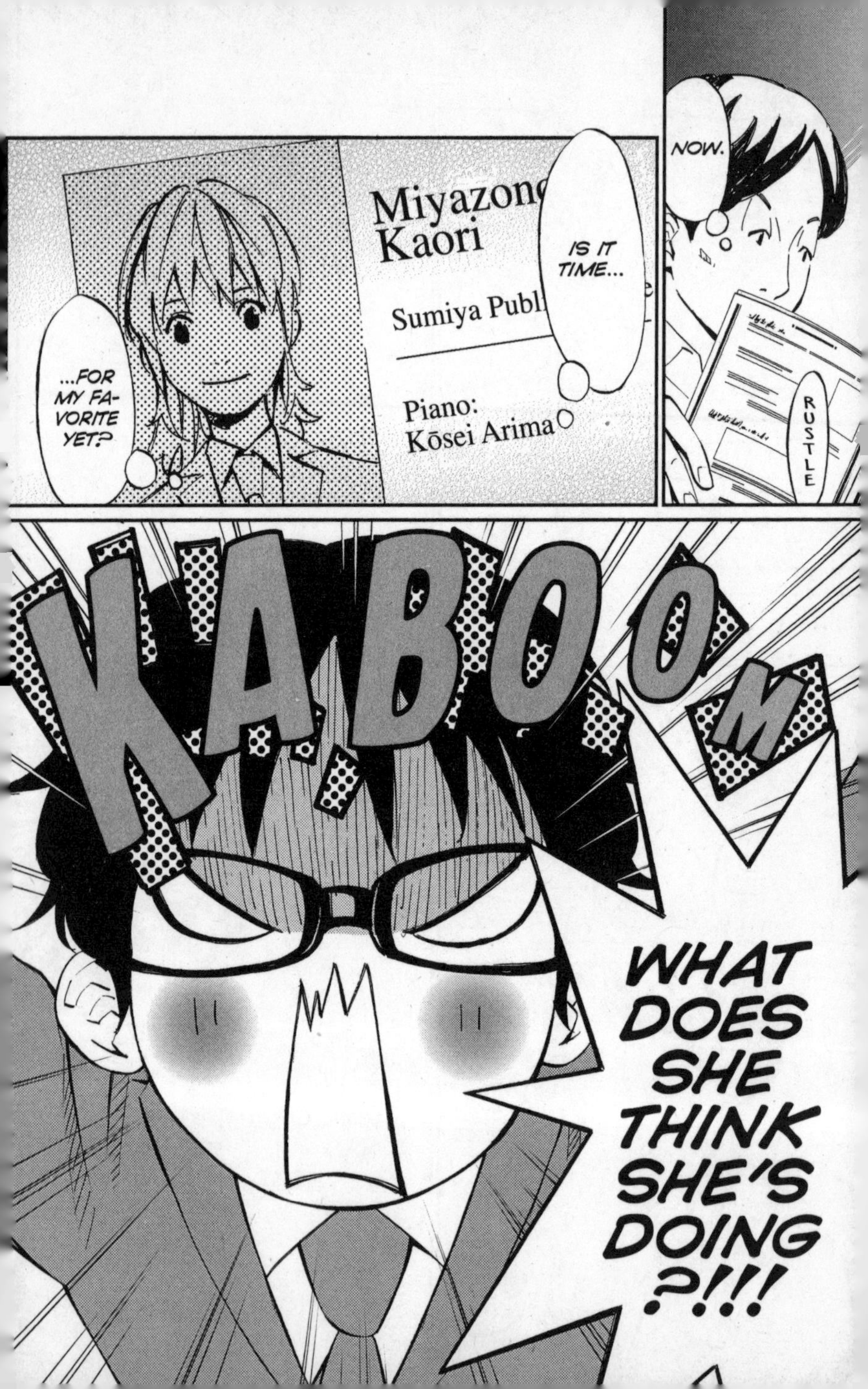
NOW.
RUSTLE
Miyazon
Kaori
Sumiya Publi
Piano:
Kōsei Arima
IS IT TIME...
...FOR MY FAVORITE YET?
KABOOM
WHAT DOES SHE THINK SHE'S DOING?!!!

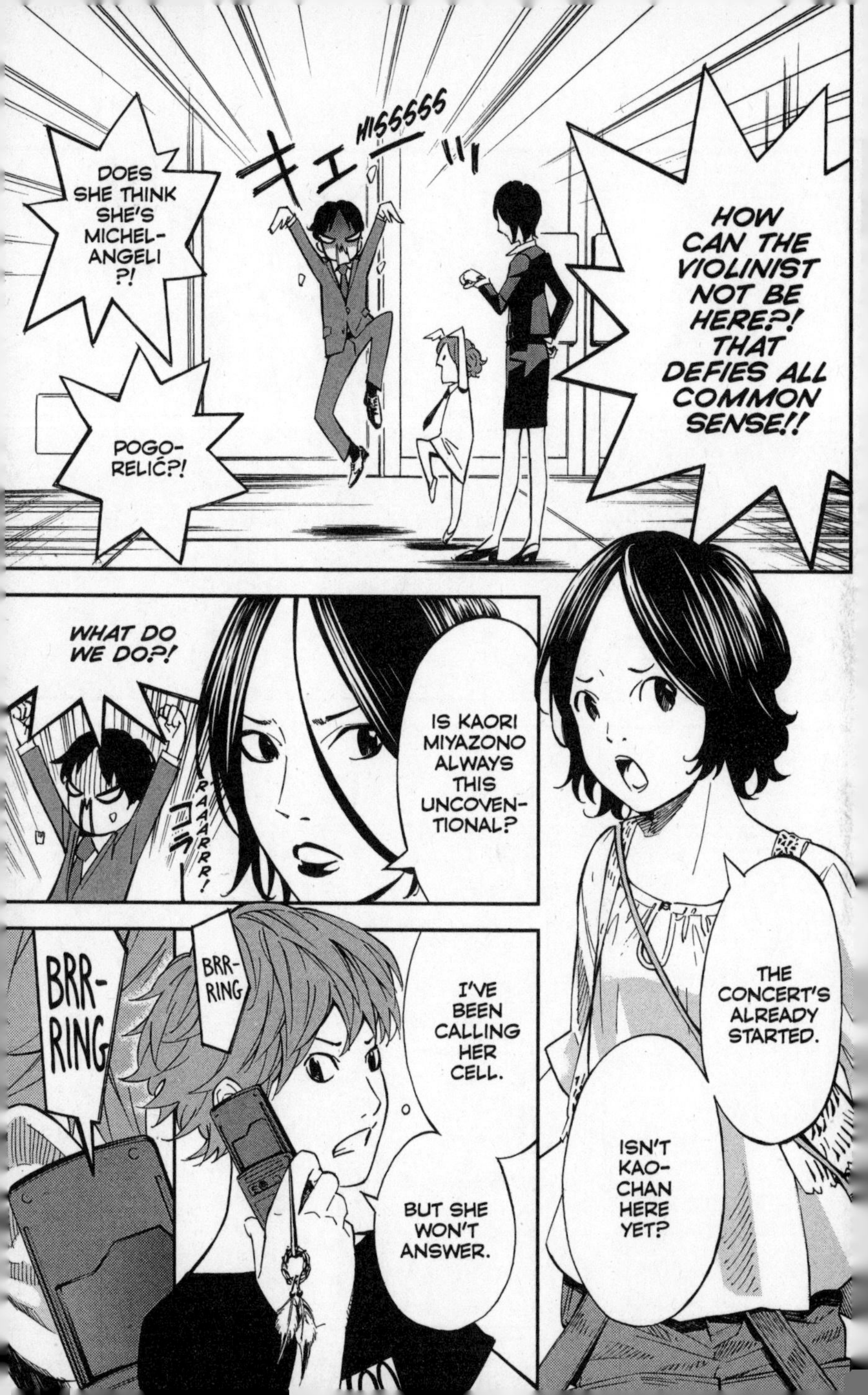
HOW CAN THE VIOLINIST NOT BE HERE?! THAT DEFIES ALL COMMON SENSE!!
HISSSSS
DOES SHE THINK SHE'S MICHEL-ANGELI ?!
POGO-RELIĆ?!
THE CONCERT'S ALREADY STARTED.
ISN'T KAO-CHAN HERE YET?
IS KAORI MIYAZONO ALWAYS THIS UNCOVEN-TIONAL?
WHAT DO WE DO?!
RAAAARRR!
I'VE BEEN CALLING HER CELL.
BUT SHE WON'T ANSWER.
BRR-RING
BRR-RING

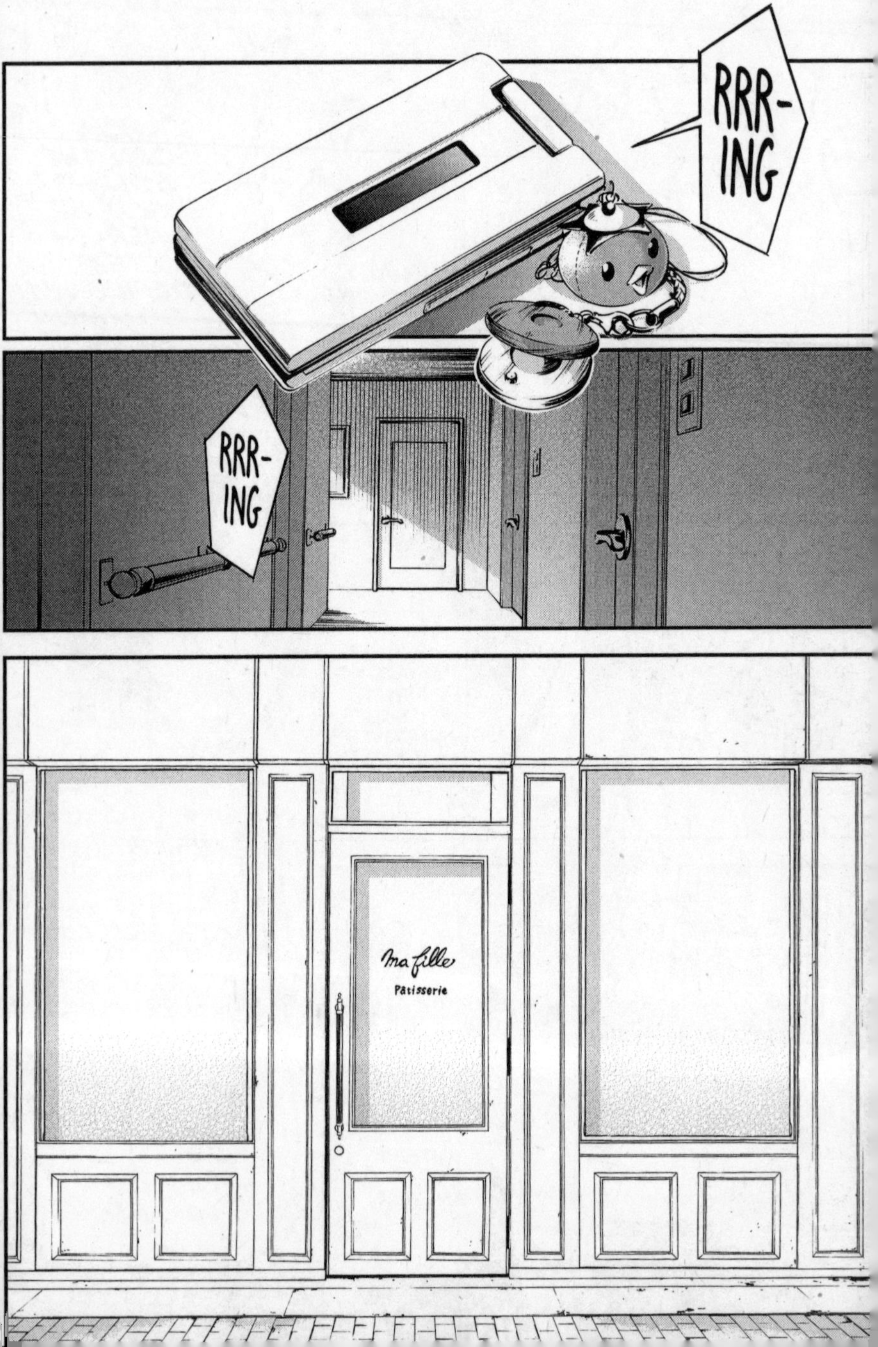
RRR-ING
RRR-ING
ma fille
Pâtisserie

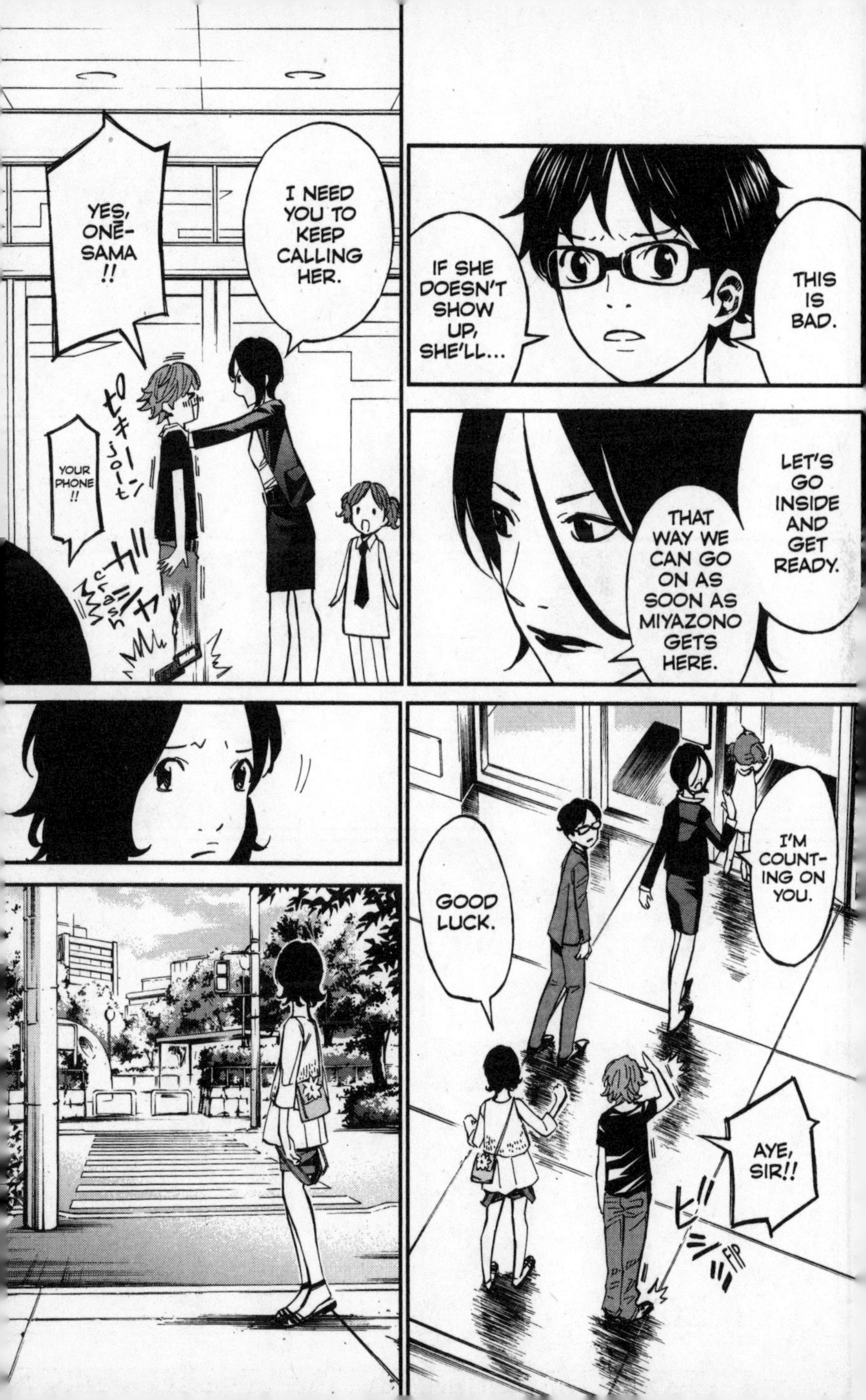
THIS IS BAD.
IF SHE DOESN'T SHOW UP, SHE'LL...
LET'S GO INSIDE AND GET READY.
THAT WAY WE CAN GO ON AS SOON AS MIYAZONO GETS HERE.
I NEED YOU TO KEEP CALLING HER.
YES, ONE-SAMA!!
jolt
YOUR PHONE!!
crash
I'M COUNTING ON YOU.
GOOD LUCK.
AYE, SIR!!
FLIP

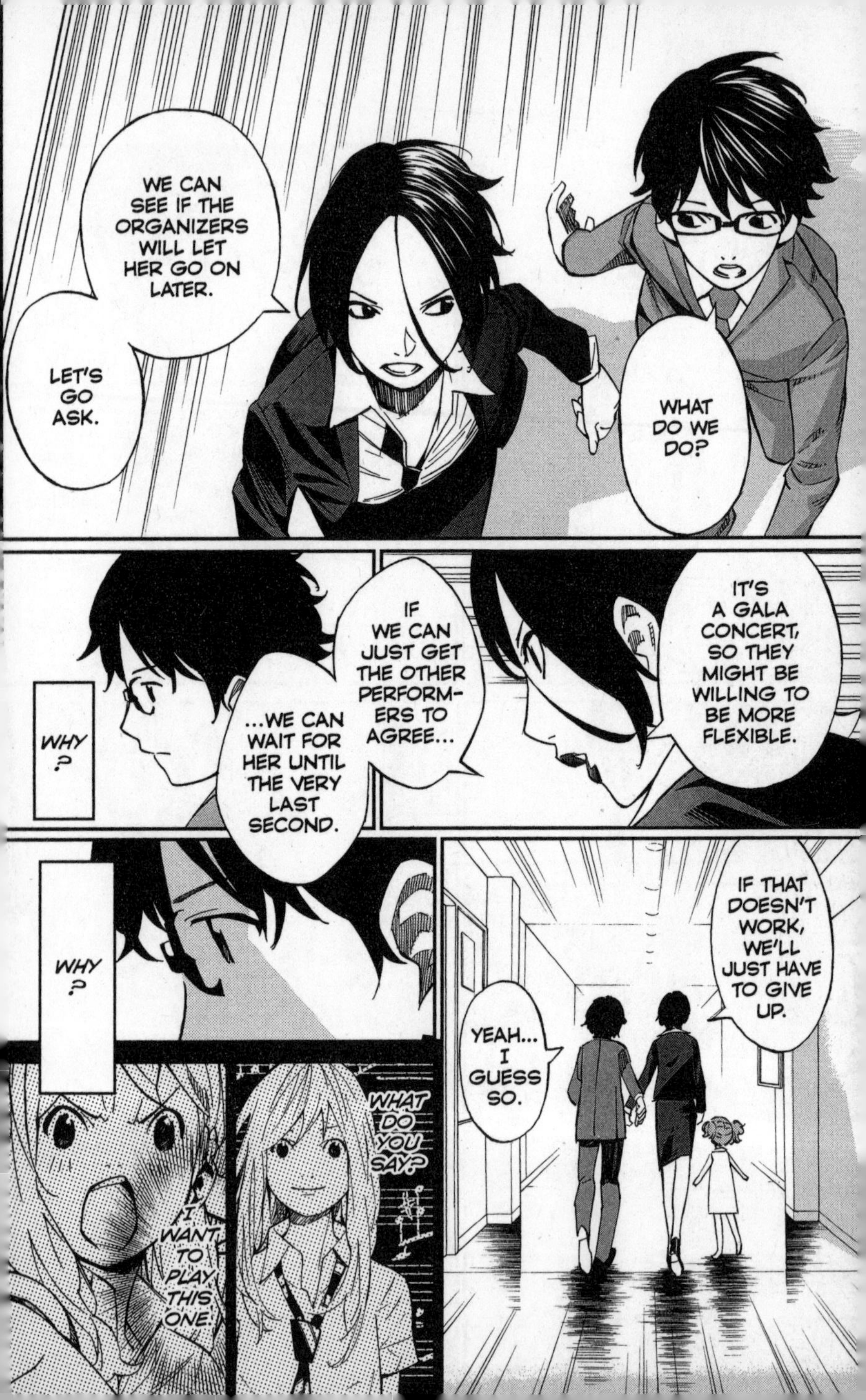
WHAT DO WE DO?
WE CAN SEE IF THE ORGANIZERS WILL LET HER GO ON LATER.
LET'S GO ASK.
IT'S A GALA CONCERT, SO THEY MIGHT BE WILLING TO BE MORE FLEXIBLE.
IF WE CAN JUST GET THE OTHER PERFORM-ERS TO AGREE...
...WE CAN WAIT FOR HER UNTIL THE VERY LAST SECOND.
WHY?
IF THAT DOESN'T WORK, WE'LL JUST HAVE TO GIVE UP.
YEAH... I GUESS SO.
WHY?
WHAT DO YOU SAY?
I WANT TO PLAY THIS ONE!

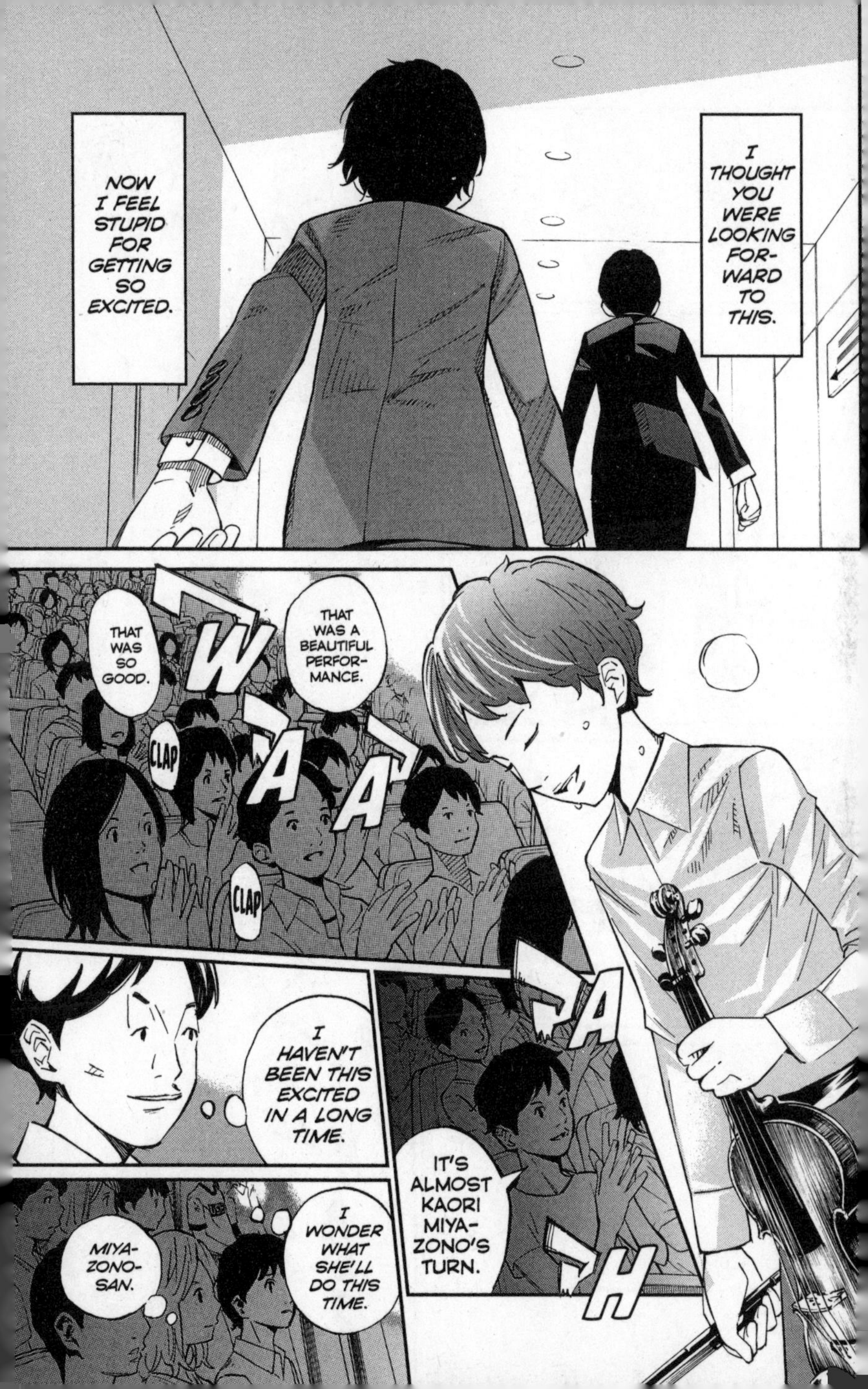
I THOUGHT YOU WERE LOOKING FOR-WARD TO THIS.
NOW I FEEL STUPID FOR GETTING SO EXCITED.
THAT WAS A BEAUTIFUL PERFOR-MANCE.
THAT WAS SO GOOD.
WAAAH
CLAP
CLAP
IT'S ALMOST KAORI MIYA-ZONO'S TURN.
I HAVEN'T BEEN THIS EXCITED IN A LONG TIME.
I WONDER WHAT SHE'LL DO THIS TIME.
MIYA-ZONO-SAN.

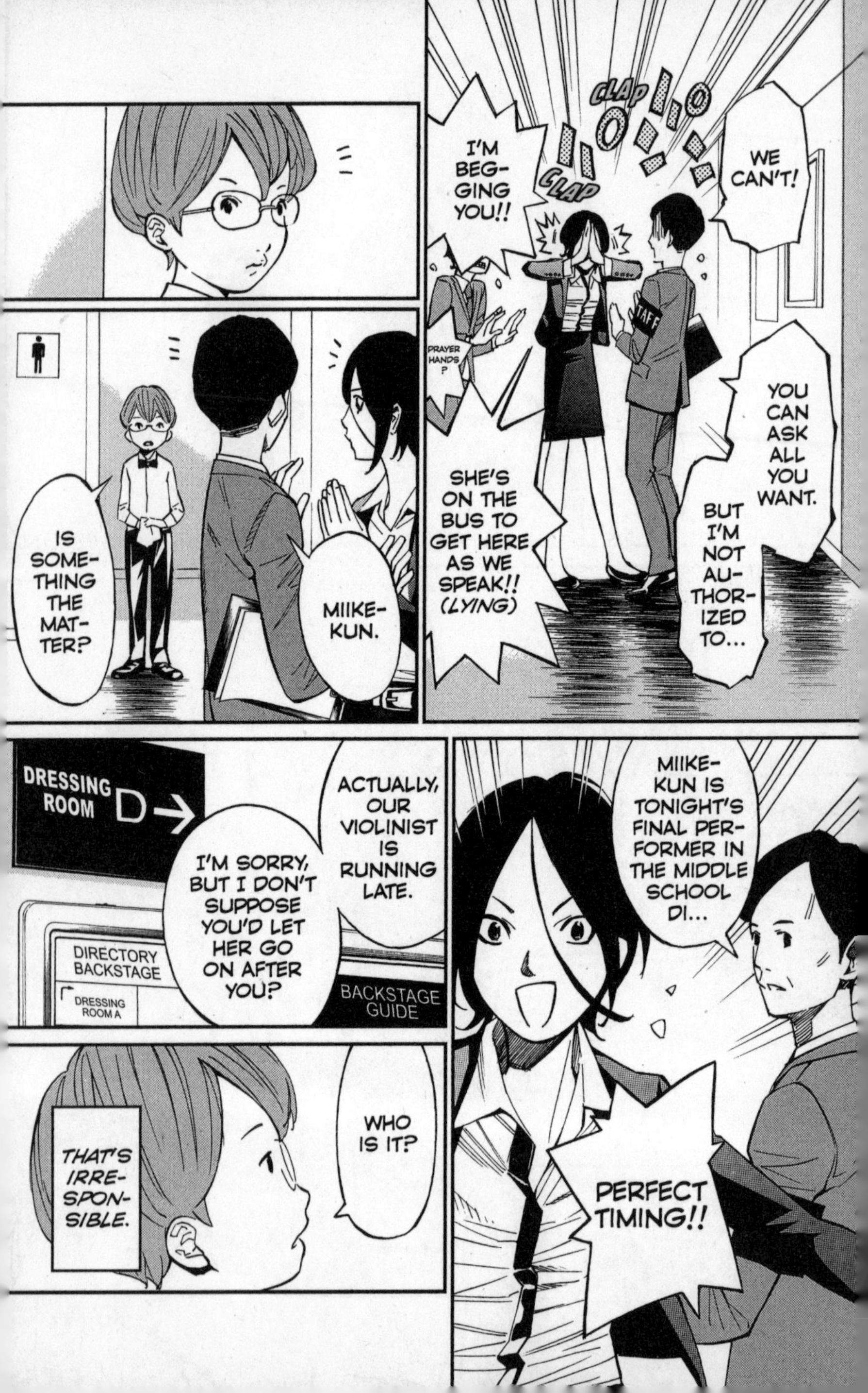
WE CAN'T!
CLAP
CLAP
I'M BEG-GING YOU!!
PRAYER HANDS?
YOU CAN ASK ALL YOU WANT.
BUT I'M NOT AU-THOR-IZED TO...
SHE'S ON THE BUS TO GET HERE AS WE SPEAK!! (LYING)
MIIKE-KUN.
IS SOME-THING THE MAT-TER?
MIIKE-KUN IS TONIGHT'S FINAL PER-FORMER IN THE MIDDLE SCHOOL DI...
PERFECT TIMING!!
ACTUALLY, OUR VIOLINIST IS RUNNING LATE.
I'M SORRY, BUT I DON'T SUPPOSE YOU'D LET HER GO ON AFTER YOU?
DRESSING ROOM D
DIRECTORY BACKSTAGE
DRESSING ROOM A
BACKSTAGE GUIDE
WHO IS IT?
THAT'S IRRE-SPON-SIBLE.

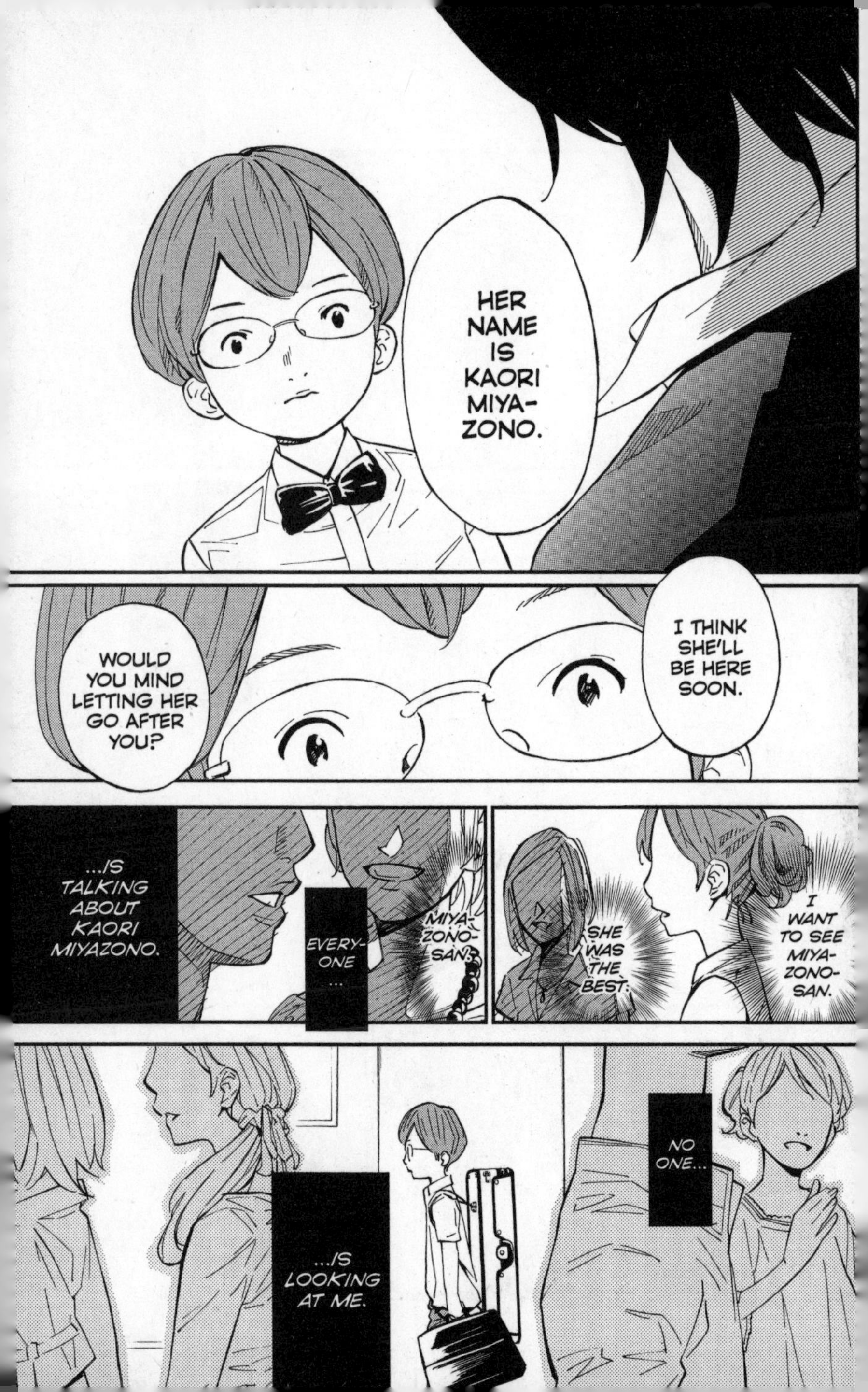
HER NAME IS KAORI MIYAZONO.
I THINK SHE'LL BE HERE SOON.
WOULD YOU MIND LETTING HER GO AFTER YOU?
I WANT TO SEE MIYAZONO-SAN.
SHE WAS THE BEST.
MIYAZONO-SAN?
EVERYONE...
...IS TALKING ABOUT KAORI MIYAZONO.
NO ONE...
...IS LOOKING AT ME.

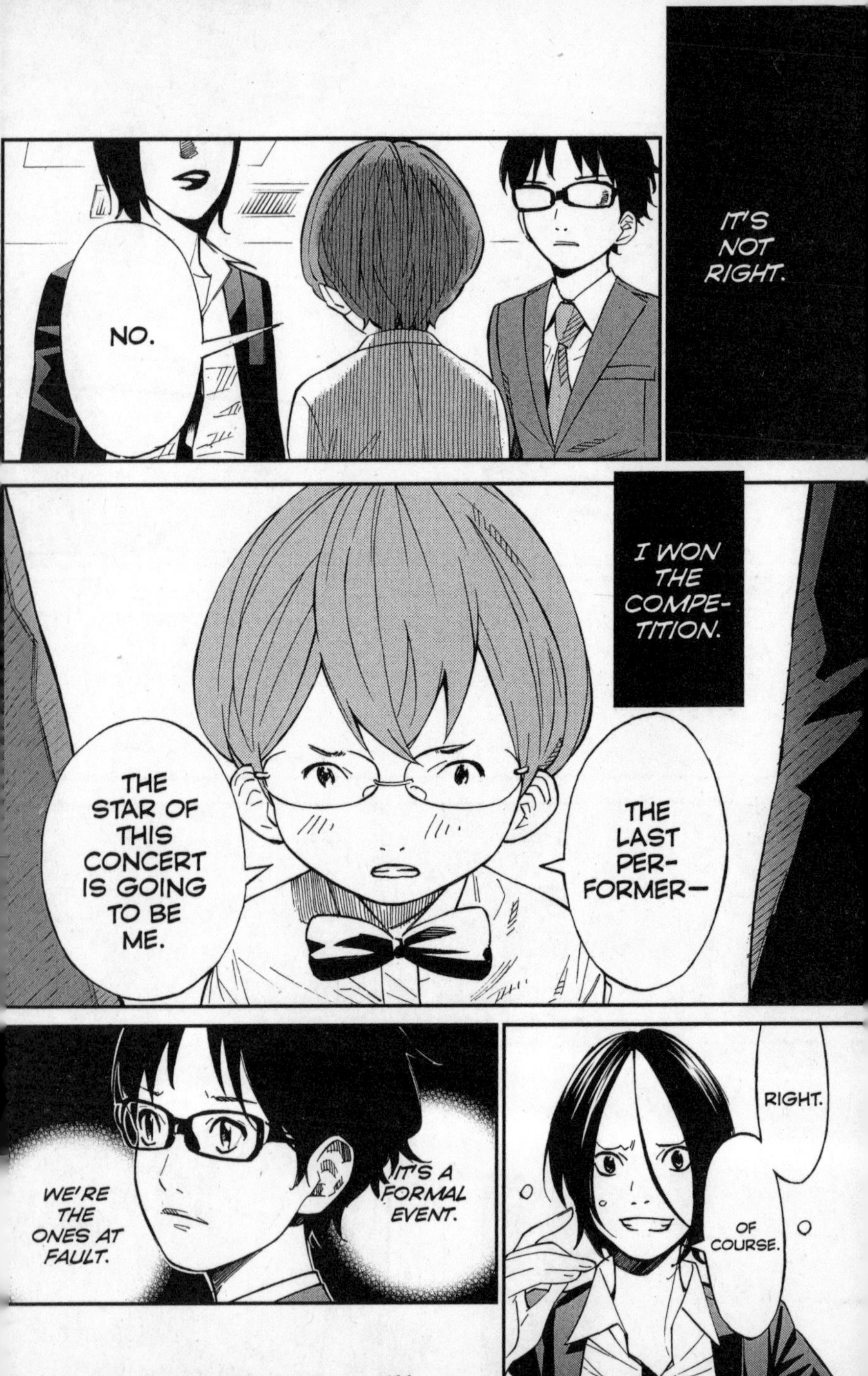
IT'S NOT RIGHT.
NO.
I WON THE COMPE-TITION.
THE LAST PER-FORMER—
THE STAR OF THIS CONCERT IS GOING TO BE ME.
RIGHT.
OF COURSE.
IT'S A FORMAL EVENT.
WE'RE THE ONES AT FAULT.

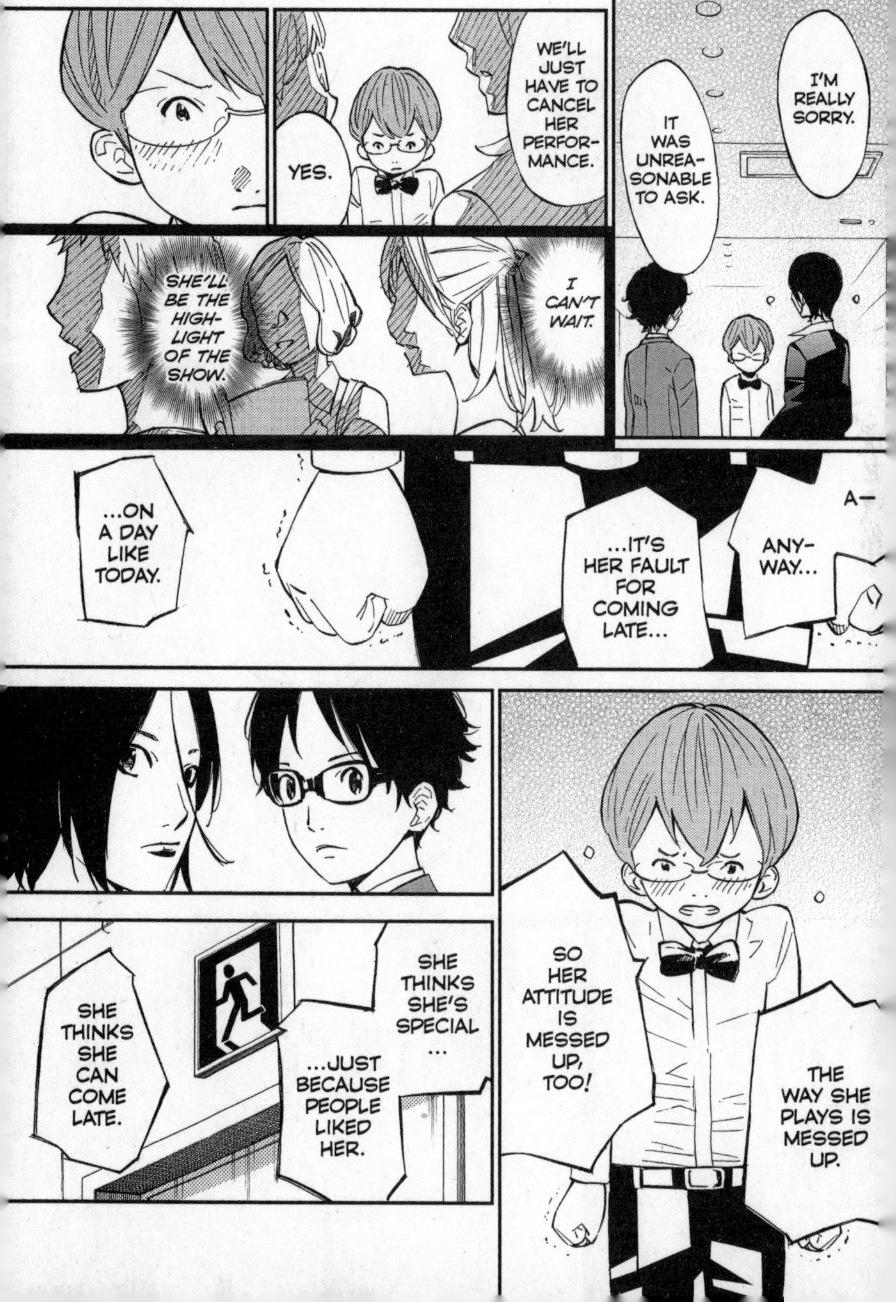
I'M REALLY SORRY.
IT WAS UNREASONABLE TO ASK.
WE'LL JUST HAVE TO CANCEL HER PERFORMANCE.
YES.
I CAN'T WAIT.
SHE'LL BE THE HIGHLIGHT OF THE SHOW.
A—
ANYWAY...
...IT'S HER FAULT FOR COMING LATE...
...ON A DAY LIKE TODAY.
THE WAY SHE PLAYS IS MESSED UP.
SO HER ATTITUDE IS MESSED UP, TOO!
SHE THINKS SHE'S SPECIAL...
...JUST BECAUSE PEOPLE LIKED HER.
SHE THINKS SHE CAN COME LATE.

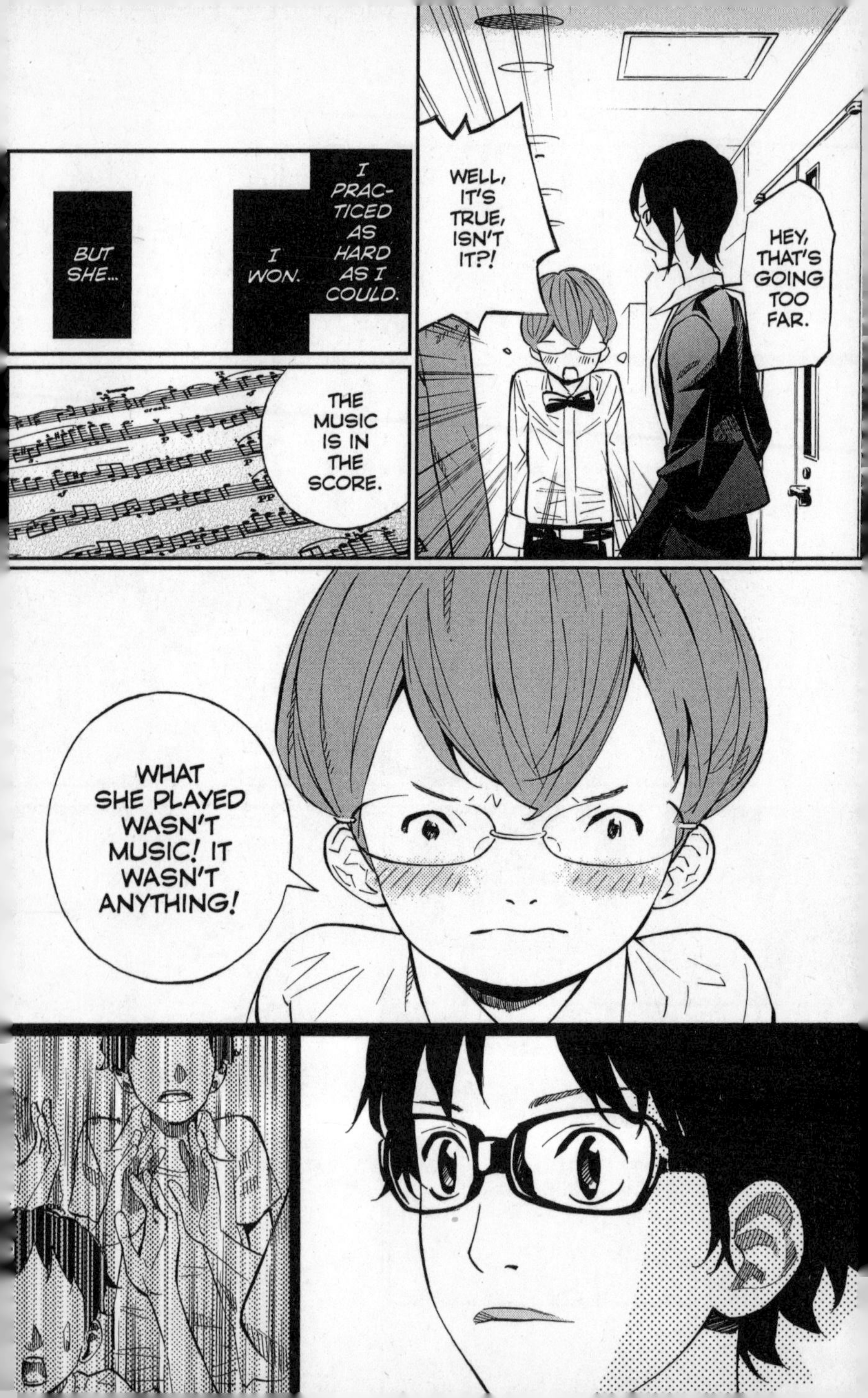
HEY, THAT'S GOING TOO FAR.
WELL, IT'S TRUE, ISN'T IT?!
I PRACTICED AS HARD AS I COULD.
I WON.
BUT SHE...
THE MUSIC IS IN THE SCORE.
WHAT SHE PLAYED WASN'T MUSIC! IT WASN'T ANYTHING!

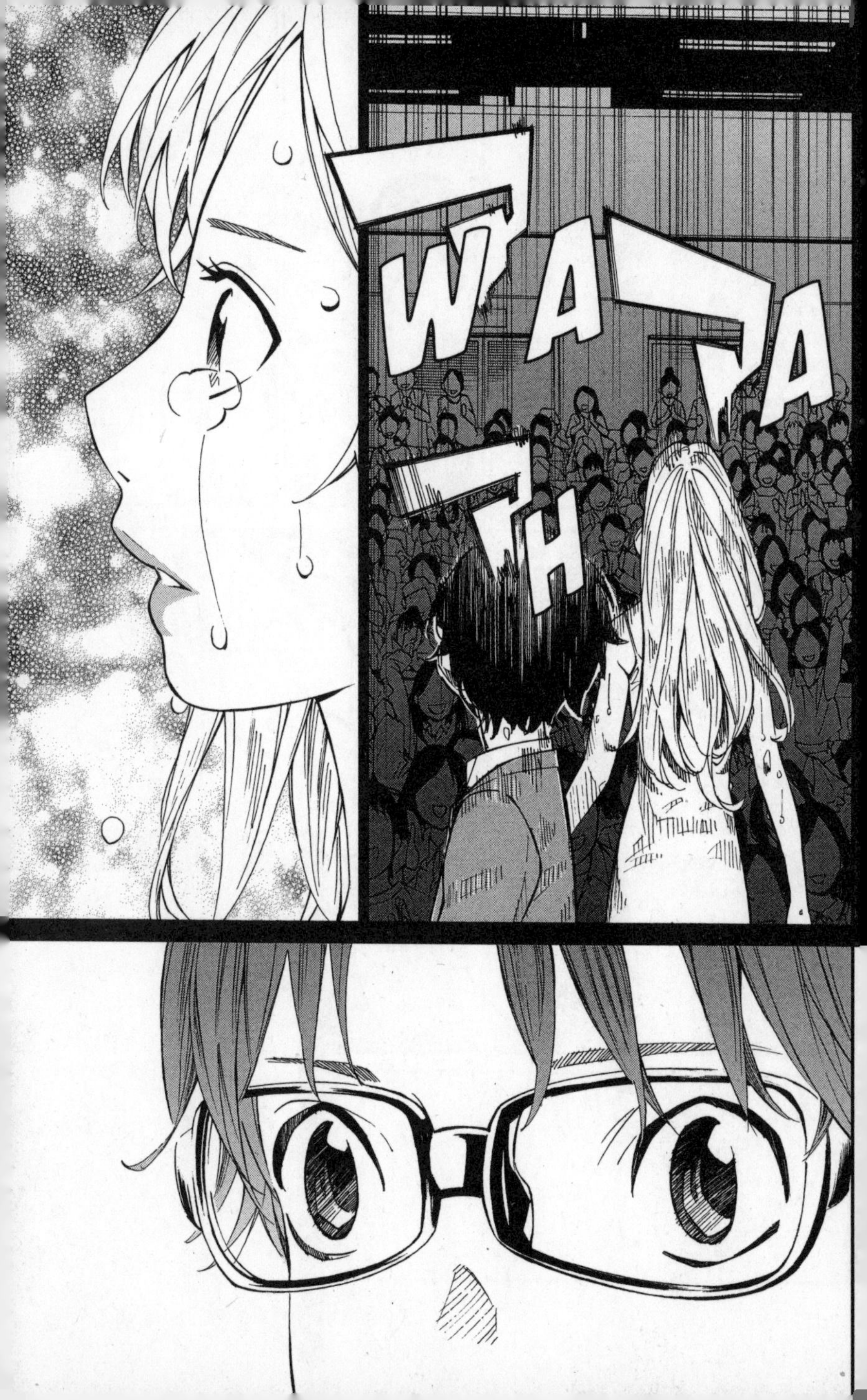
WAAH

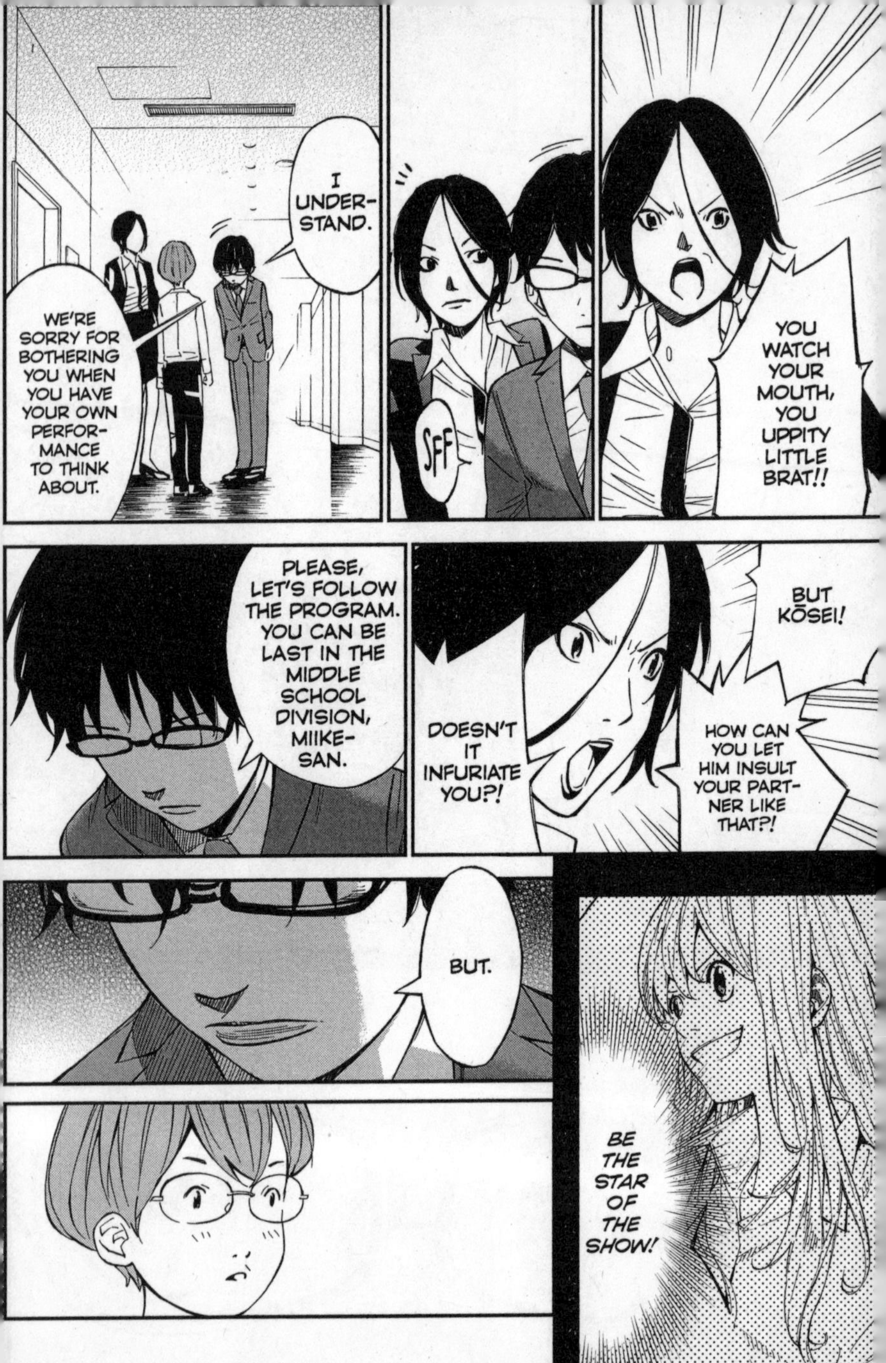
YOU WATCH YOUR MOUTH, YOU UPPITY LITTLE BRAT!!
SFF
I UNDER-STAND.
WE'RE SORRY FOR BOTHERING YOU WHEN YOU HAVE YOUR OWN PERFOR-MANCE TO THINK ABOUT.
BUT KŌSEI!
HOW CAN YOU LET HIM INSULT YOUR PART-NER LIKE THAT?!
DOESN'T IT INFURIATE YOU?!
PLEASE, LET'S FOLLOW THE PROGRAM. YOU CAN BE LAST IN THE MIDDLE SCHOOL DIVISION, MIIKE-SAN.
BE THE STAR OF THE SHOW!
BUT.

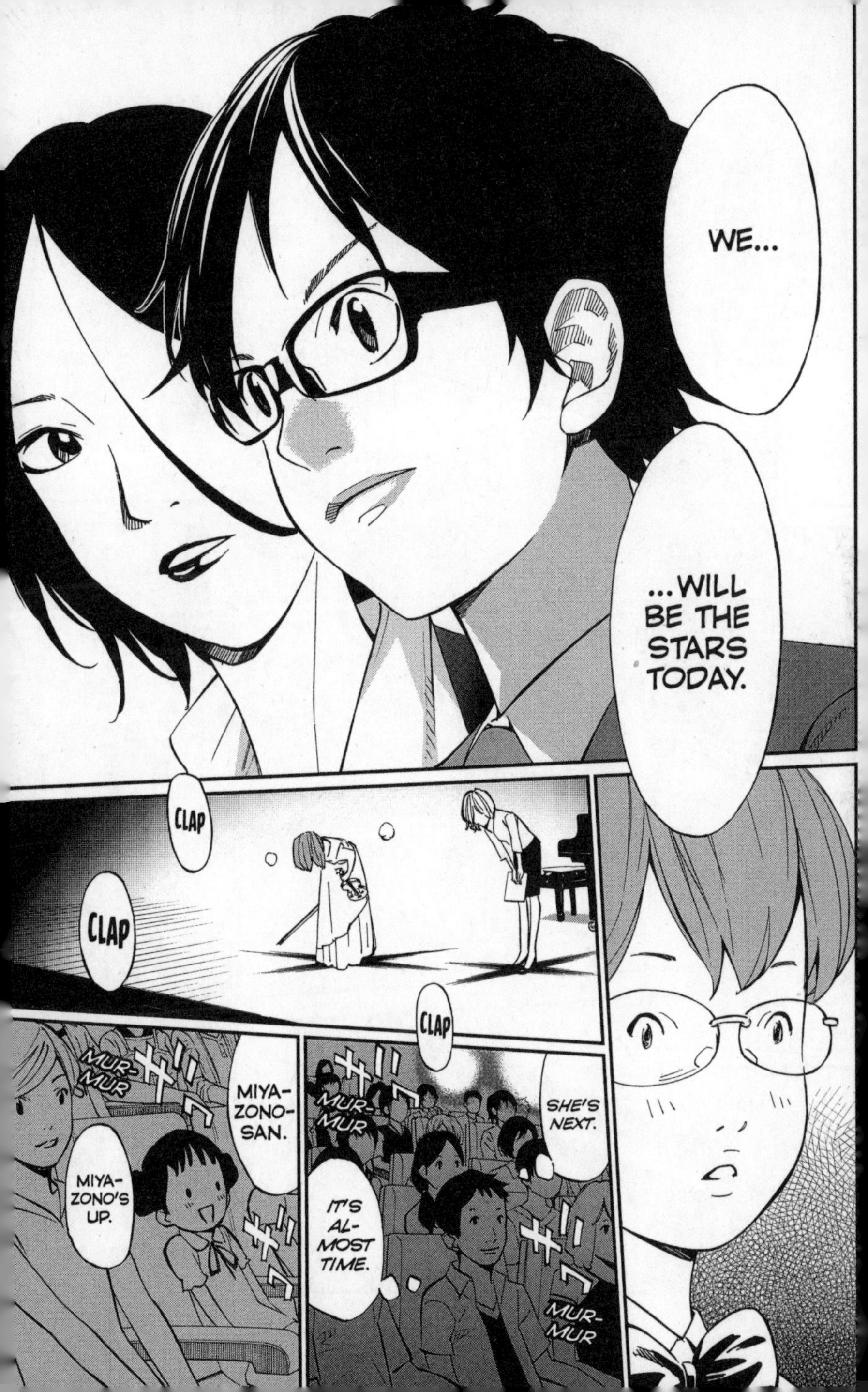
WE...
...WILL BE THE STARS TODAY.
SHE'S NEXT.
CLAP
CLAP
CLAP
MUR-MUR
IT'S AL-MOST TIME.
MUR-MUR
MUR-MUR
MIYA-ZONO-SAN.
MIYA-ZONO'S UP.

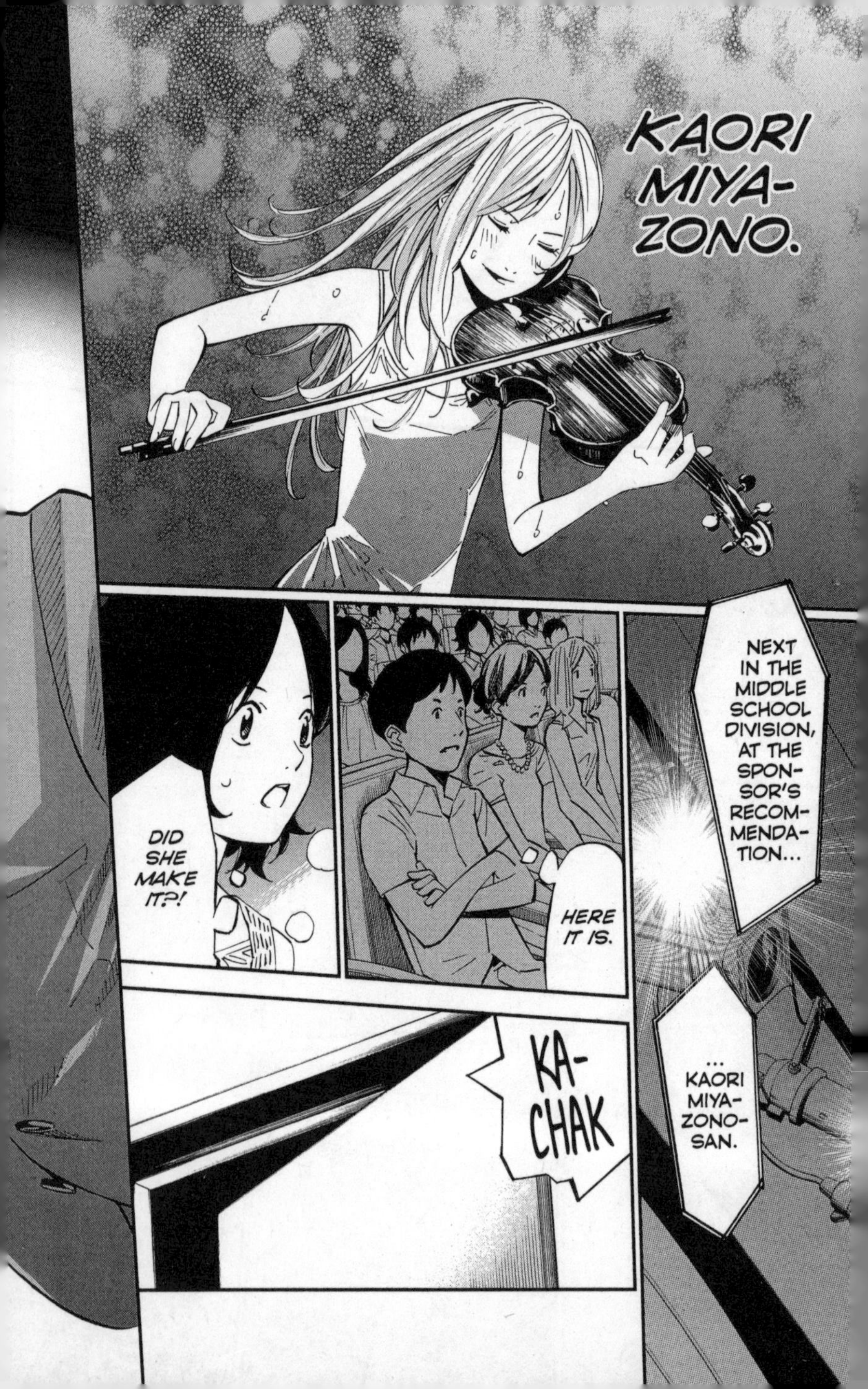
KAORI MIYA-ZONO.
NEXT IN THE MIDDLE SCHOOL DIVISION, AT THE SPON-SOR'S RECOMMENDA-TION...
...KAORI MIYA-ZONO-SAN.
HERE IT IS.
DID SHE MAKE IT?!
KA-CHAK

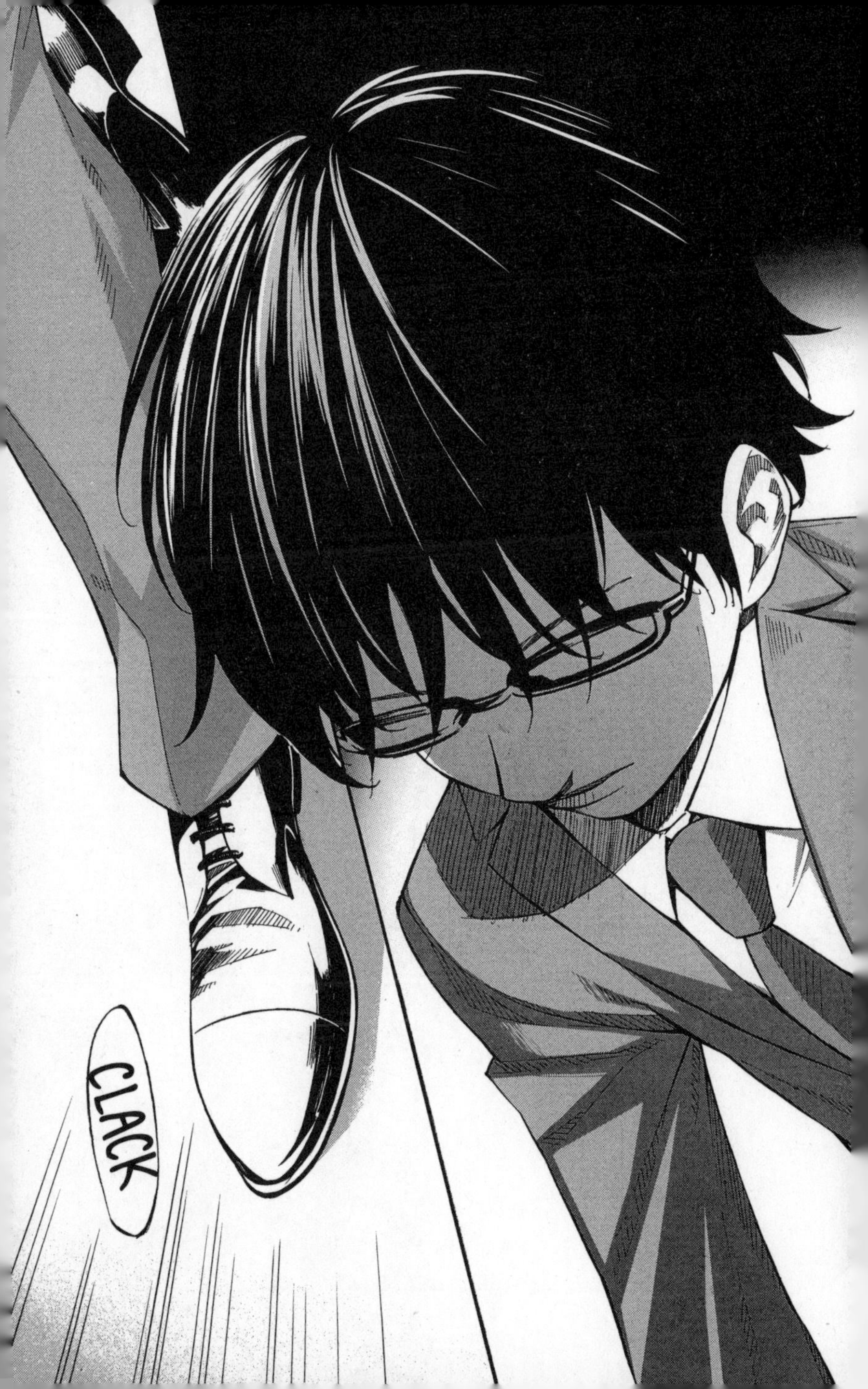
CLACK

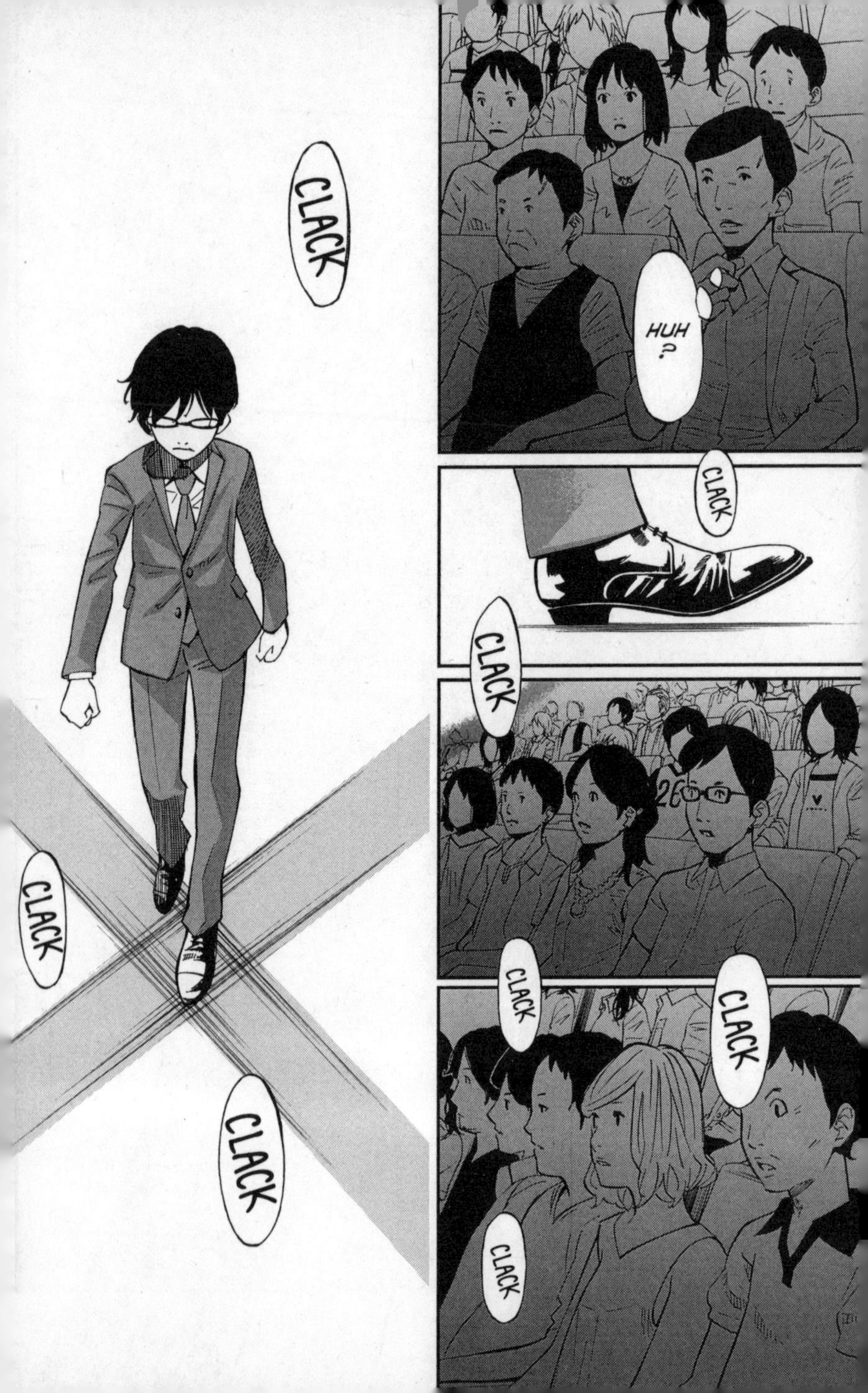
HUH?
CLACK
CLACK
CLACK
CLACK
CLACK
CLACK
CLACK
CLACK
CLACK

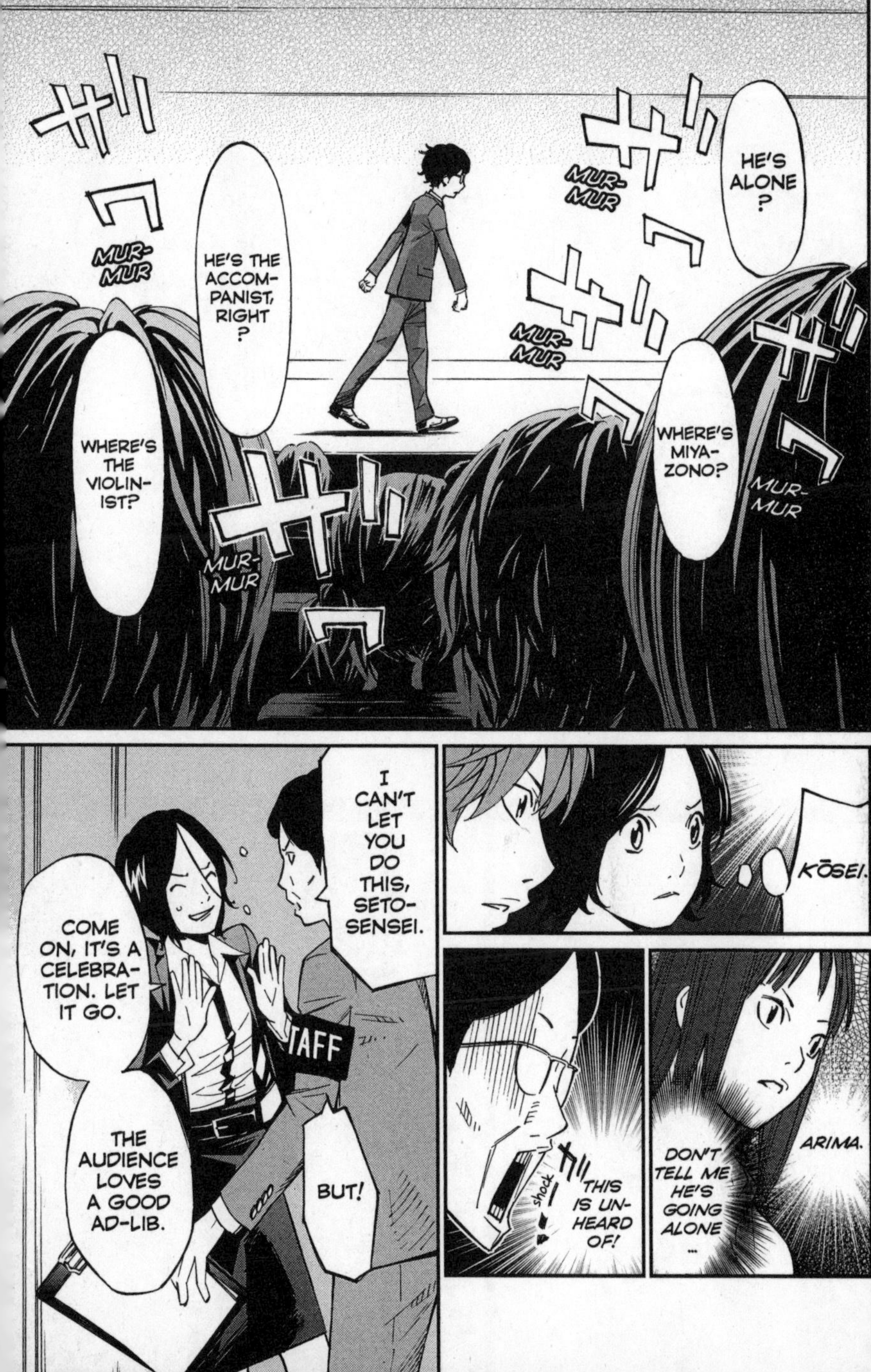
HE'S ALONE?
MUR-MUR
MUR-MUR
WHERE'S MIYA-ZONO?
MUR-MUR
HE'S THE ACCOM-PANIST, RIGHT?
MUR-MUR
WHERE'S THE VIOLIN-IST?
MUR-MUR
KŌSEI.
ARIMA.
DON'T TELL ME HE'S GOING ALONE...
THIS IS UN-HEARD OF!
shock
I CAN'T LET YOU DO THIS, SETO-SENSEI.
COME ON, IT'S A CELEBRA-TION. LET IT GO.
TAFF
BUT!
THE AUDIENCE LOVES A GOOD AD-LIB.

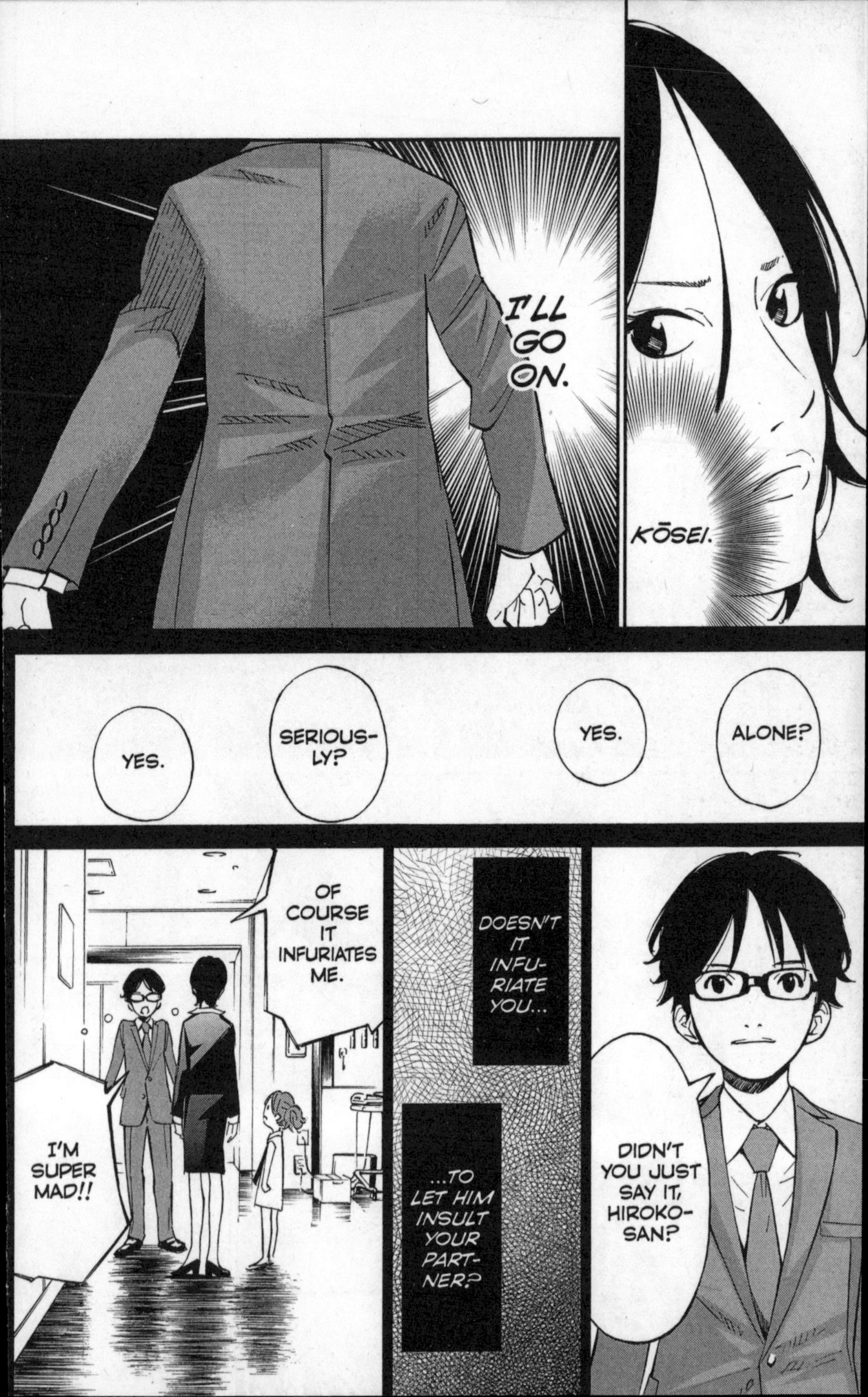
KŌSEI.
I'LL GO ON.
ALONE?
YES.
SERIOUS-LY?
YES.
DIDN'T YOU JUST SAY IT, HIROKO-SAN?
DOESN'T IT INFURIATE YOU...
...TO LET HIM INSULT YOUR PARTNER?
OF COURSE IT INFURIATES ME.
I'M SUPER MAD!!

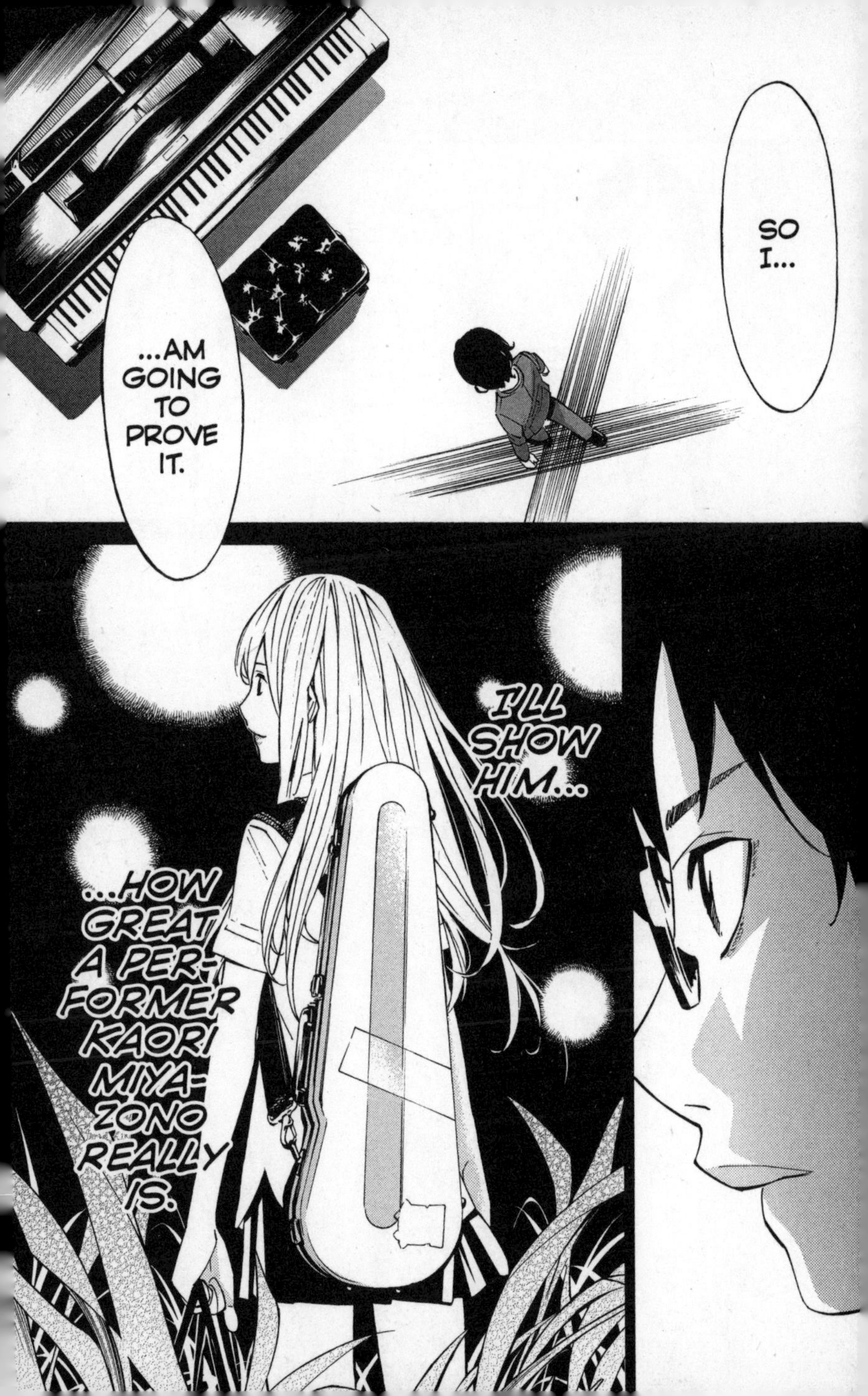
SO I...
...AM GOING TO PROVE IT.
I'LL SHOW HIM...
...HOW GREAT A PER-FORMER KAORI MIYA-ZONO REALLY IS.

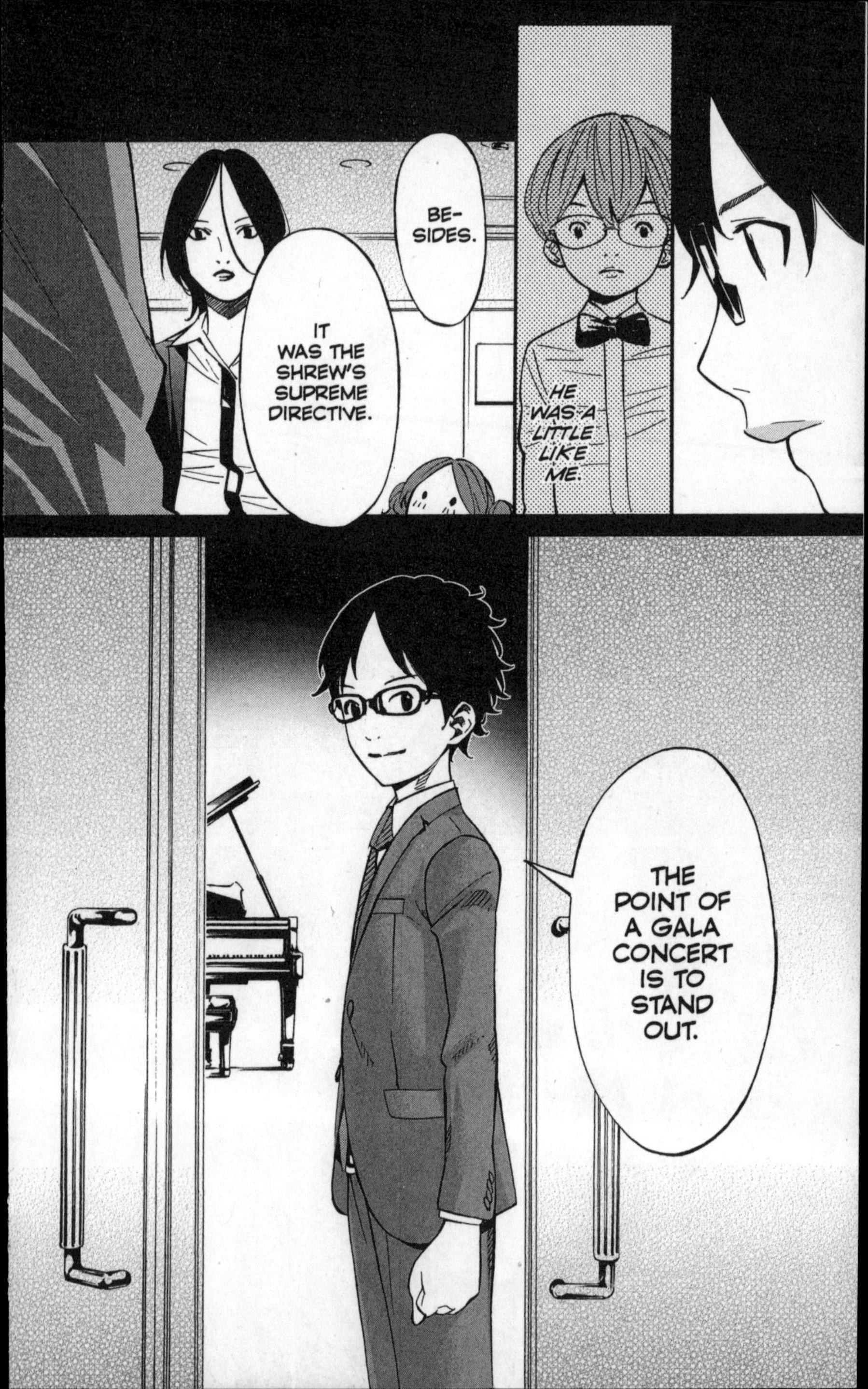
HE WAS A LITTLE LIKE ME.
BE-SIDES.
IT WAS THE SHREW'S SUPREME DIRECTIVE.
THE POINT OF A GALA CONCERT IS TO STAND OUT.

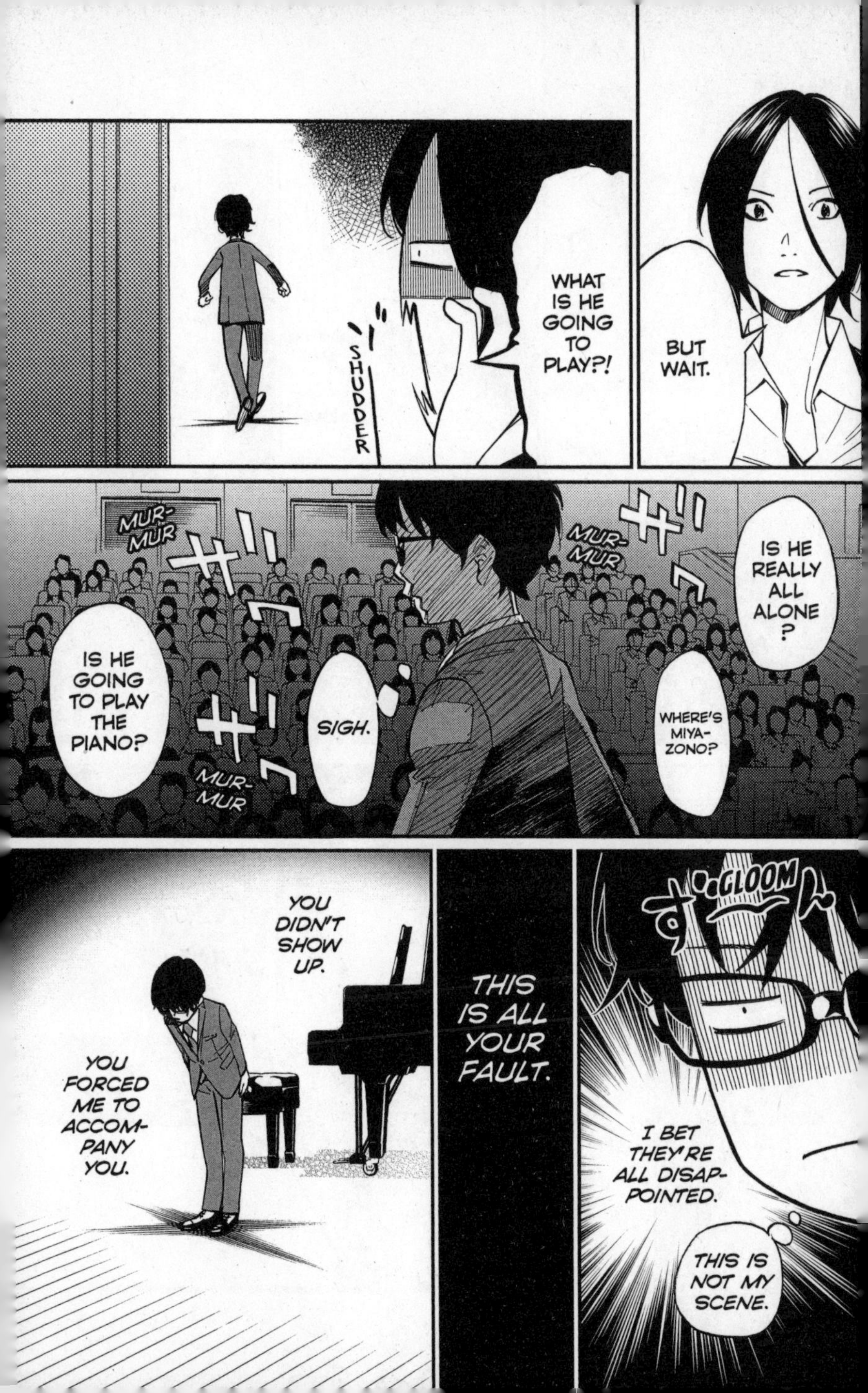
BUT WAIT.
WHAT IS HE GOING TO PLAY?!
SHUDDER
IS HE REALLY ALL ALONE?
MUR-MUR
WHERE'S MIYA-ZONO?
SIGH.
MUR-MUR
IS HE GOING TO PLAY THE PIANO?
MUR-MUR
GLOOM
I BET THEY'RE ALL DISAP-POINTED.
THIS IS NOT MY SCENE.
THIS IS ALL YOUR FAULT.
YOU DIDN'T SHOW UP.
YOU FORCED ME TO ACCOM-PANY YOU.

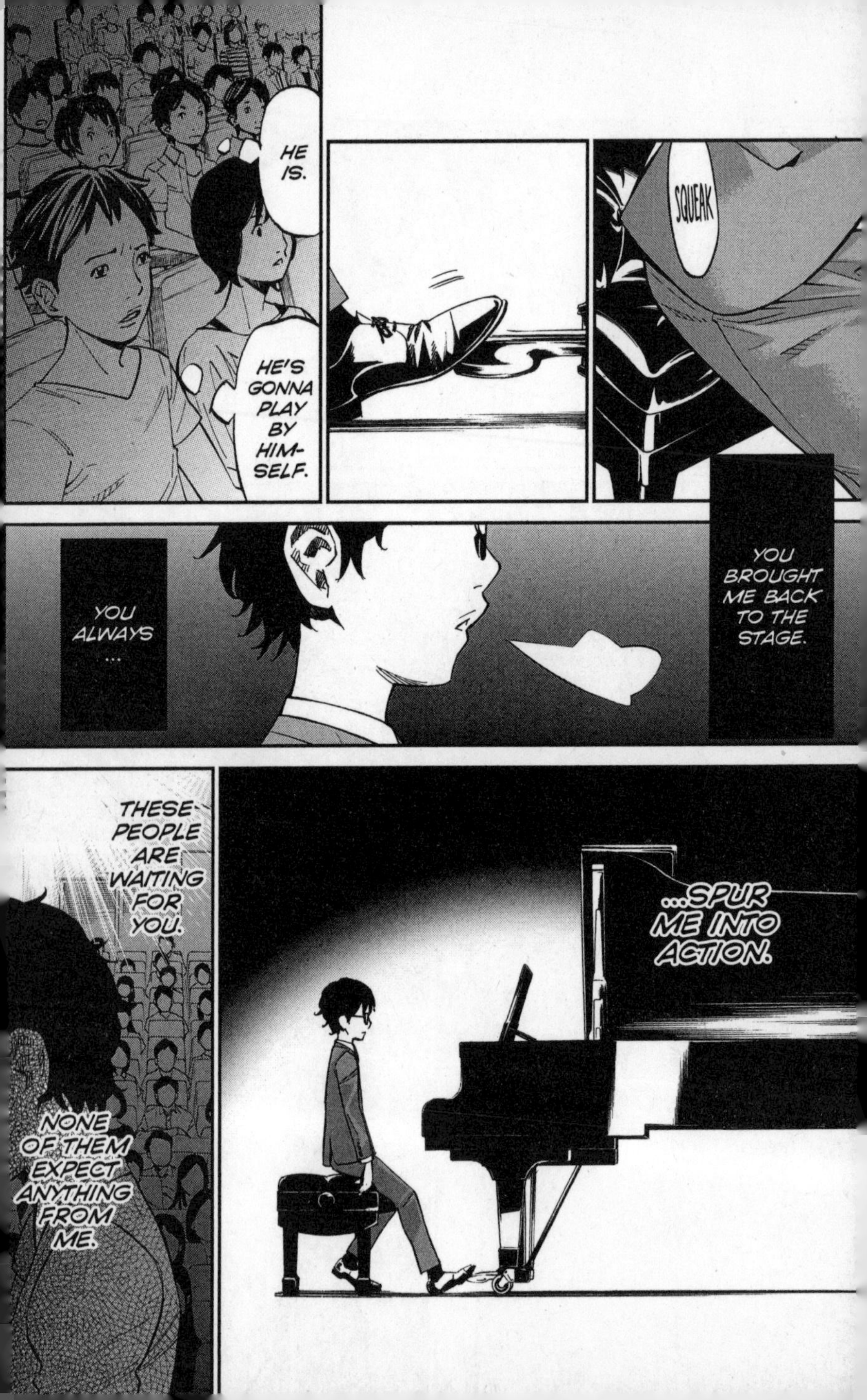
SQUEAK
HE IS.
HE'S GONNA PLAY BY HIMSELF.
YOU BROUGHT ME BACK TO THE STAGE.
YOU ALWAYS ...
...SPUR ME INTO ACTION.
THESE PEOPLE ARE WAITING FOR YOU.
NONE OF THEM EXPECT ANYTHING FROM ME.

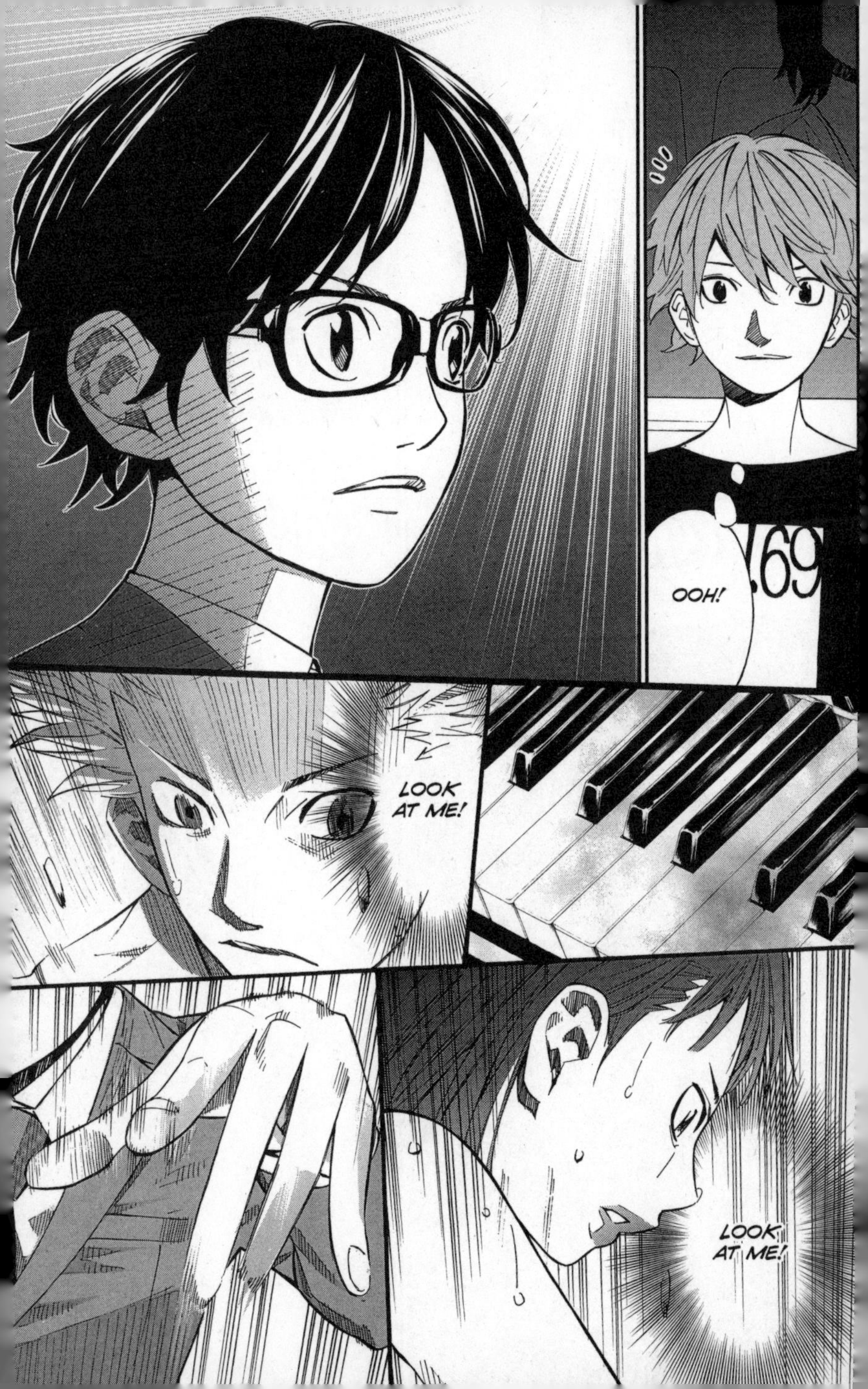
169
OOH!
LOOK AT ME!
LOOK AT ME!

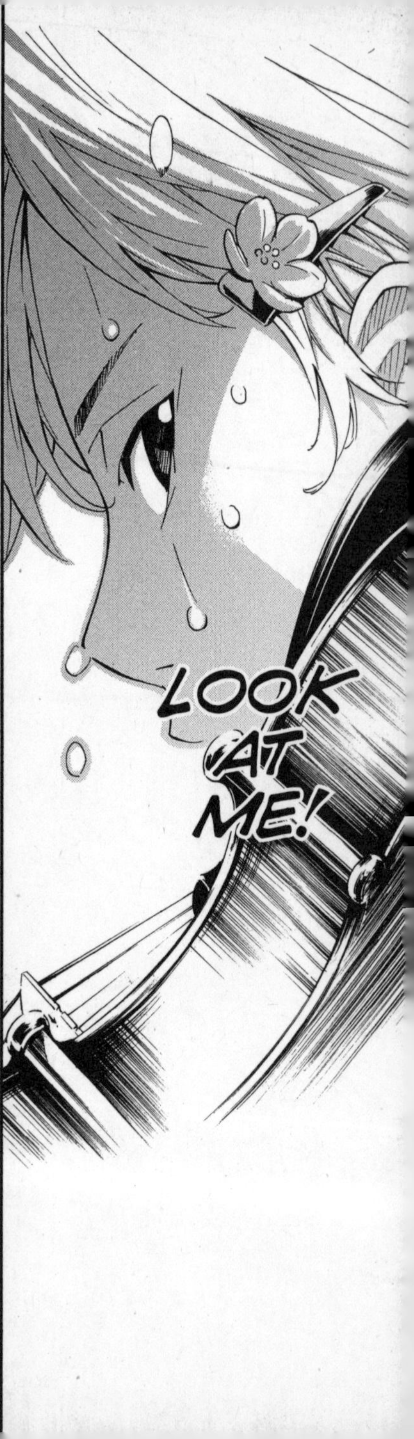
LOOK AT ME!
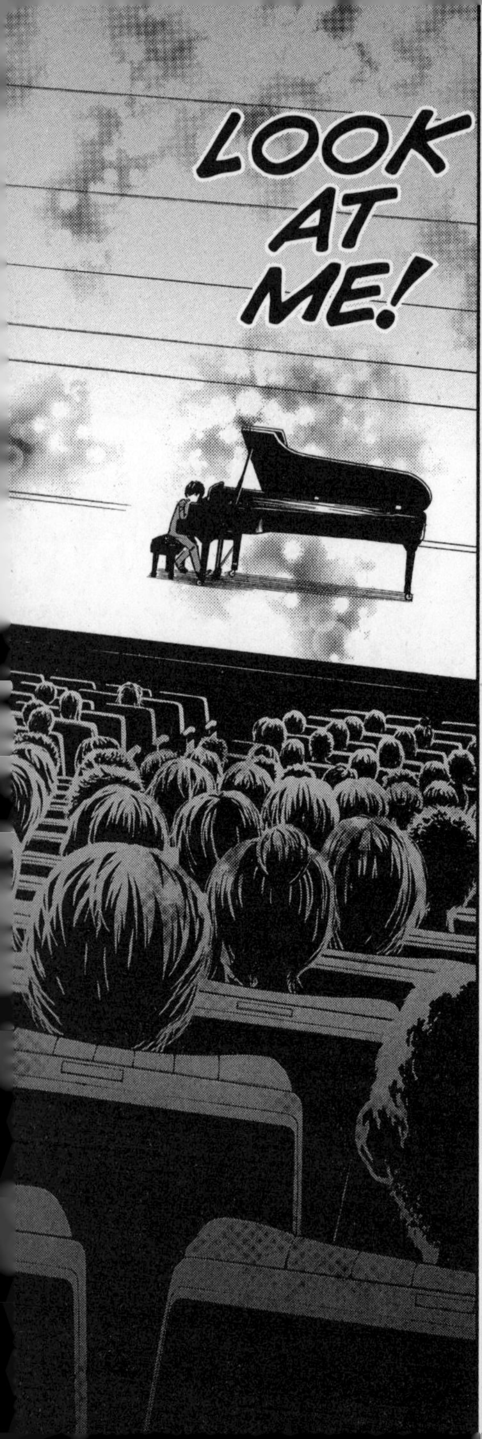
LOOK AT ME!

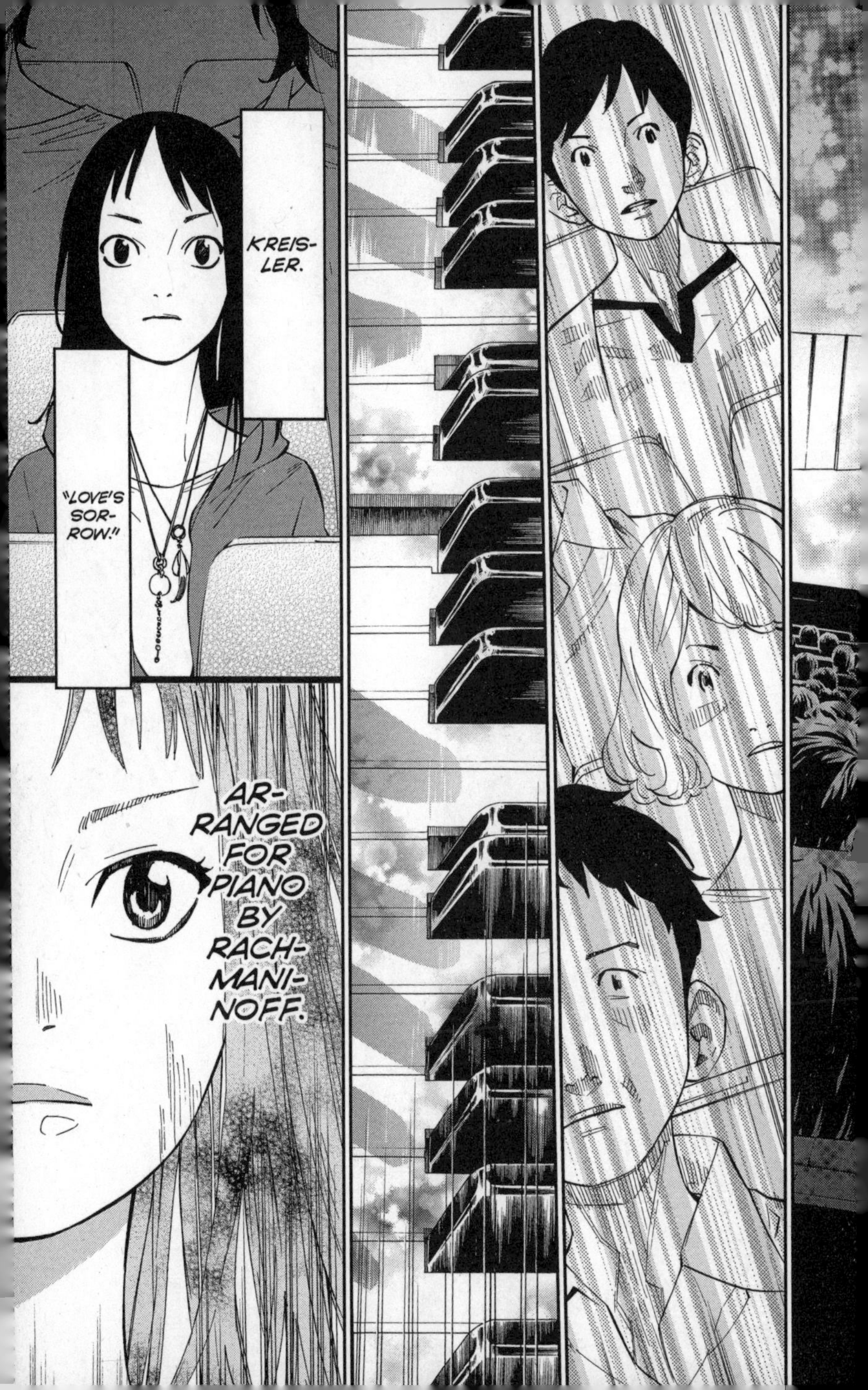
KREIS-LER.
"LOVE'S SOR-ROW."
AR-RANGED FOR PIANO BY RACH-MANI-NOFF.

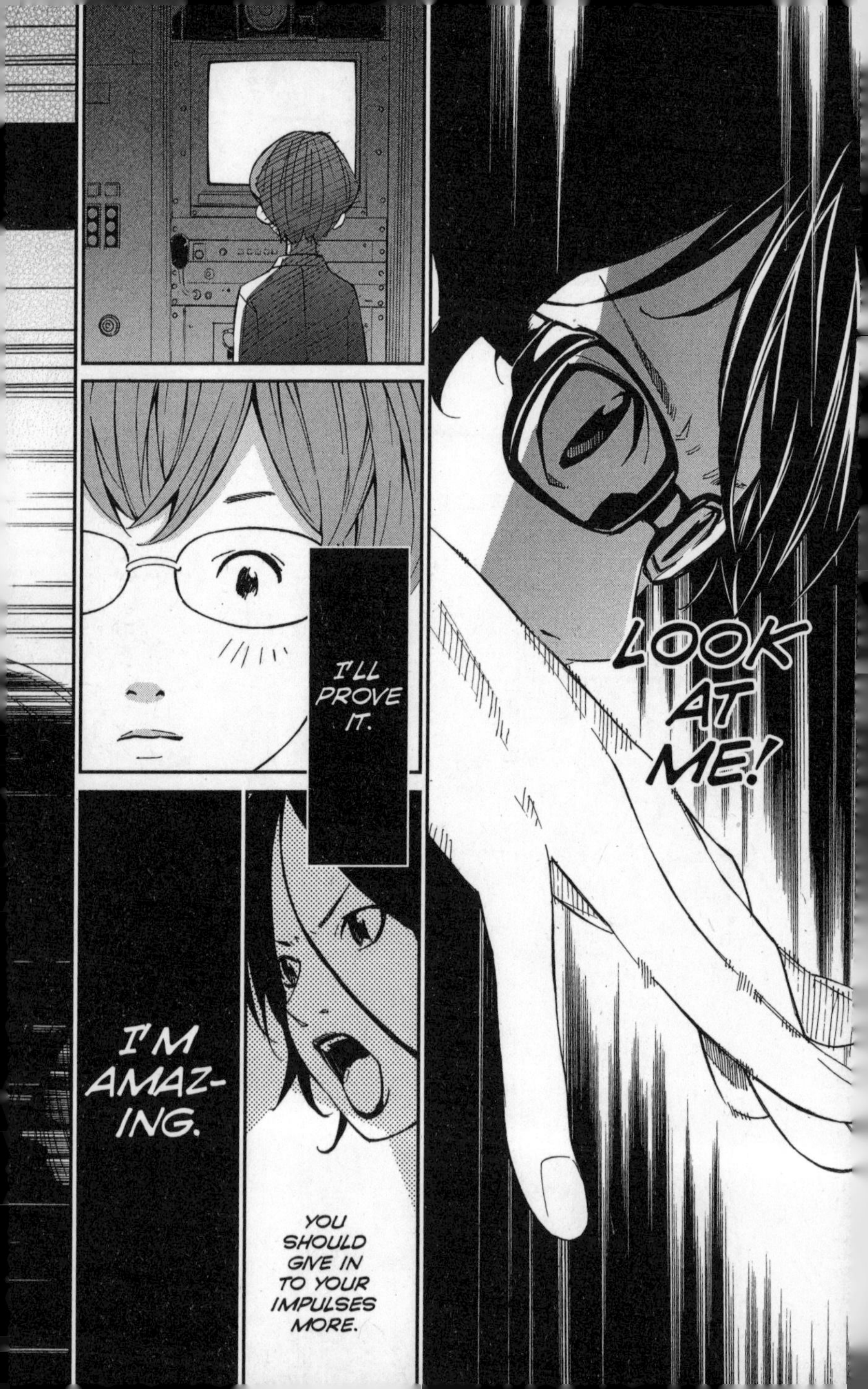
LOOK AT ME!
I'LL PROVE IT.
YOU SHOULD GIVE IN TO YOUR IMPULSES MORE.
I'M AMAZ-ING.

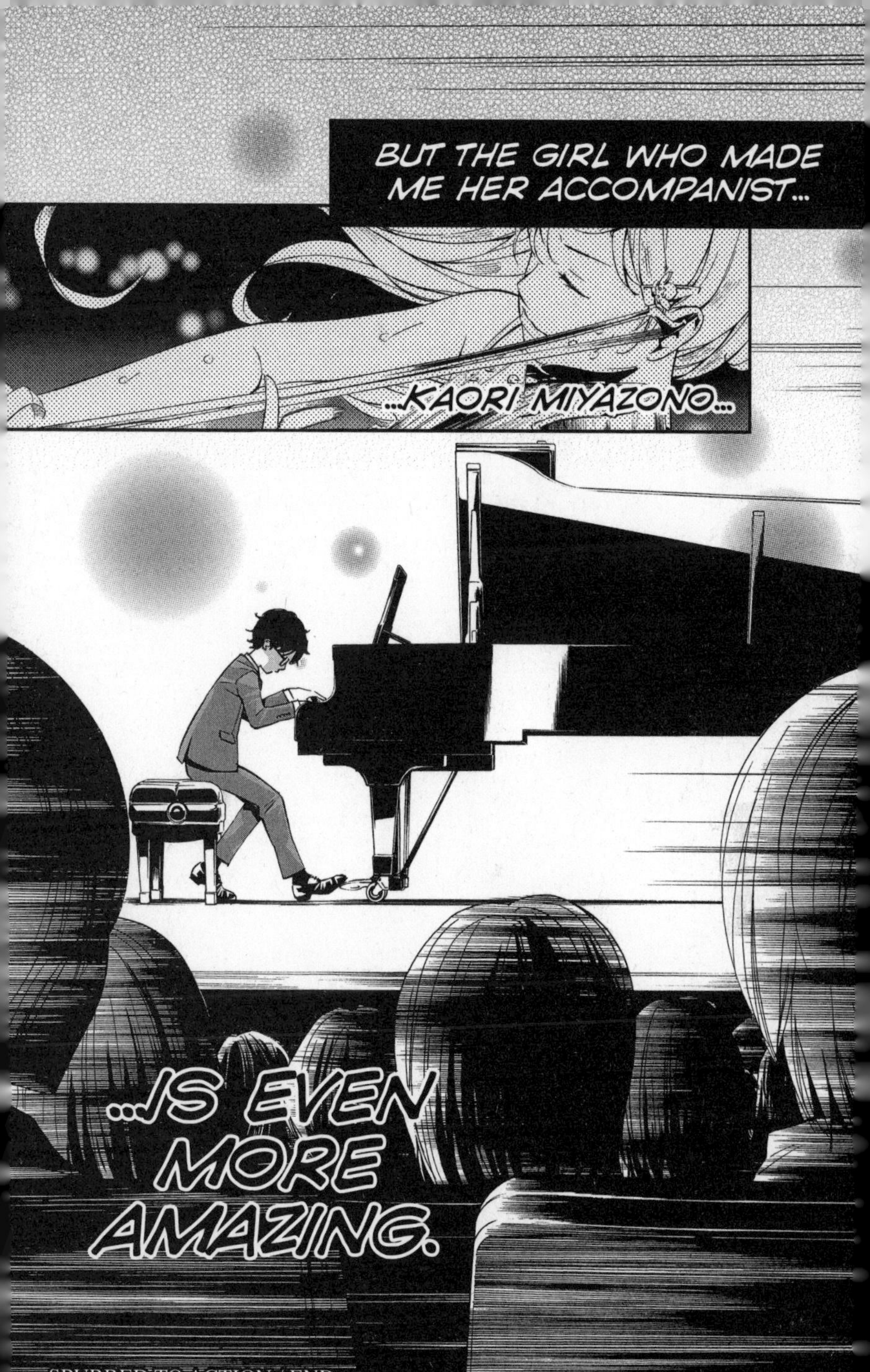
BUT THE GIRL WHO MADE ME HER ACCOMPANIST...
...KAORI MIYAZONO...
...IS EVEN MORE AMAZING.

SPURRED TO ACTION / END

YOUR LIE IN APRIL FEATURED MUSIC

SERGEI RACHMANINOFF'S ARRANGEMENT OF FRITZ KREISLER'S *LIEBESLEID*

Fritz Kreisler and Sergei Rachmaninoff were both very active in the late 19th and early 20th centuries as brilliant masters of the violin and piano, respectively.

Kreisler would perform countless pieces of his own composition, claiming they were arrangements of manuscripts composed by "the old masters." (Twenty-five years after they were published, it was revealed he had written them himself.)

Of those pieces, the three pieces that make up the *Alt-Wiener Tanzweisen* (*Old Viennese Melodies*)—*Liebesfreud* (*Love's Joy*), *Liebesleid* (*Love's Sorrow*), and *Schön Rosmarin* (*Lovely Rosemary*)—are especially famous and beloved for reminding the listener of the golden age of 19th-century Vienna.

Rachmaninoff, Kreisler's contemporary, arranged the beautiful melancholy emotions of *Love's Sorrow* into a piano solo.

With its nimble, quick technique and deep harmonies covering a broad range of the keyboard, the great scale of the arrangement, which only could have been accomplished by Rachmaninoff, reflects the virtuosity of the late romantic period and adds a new charm to Kreisler's work. In this masterpiece, we can feel the pain that exists even within the happiest of loves.

(Pianist Masanori Sugano, lecturer at Tokyo University of the Arts and Musashino Academia Musicae)

Watch it on YouTube (Search "Monthly Shonen Magazine Your Lie in April Featured Music")

Special Thanks:

AKINORI ŌSAWA

MASANORI SUGANO

RIEKO IKEDA

KAORI YAMAZAKI

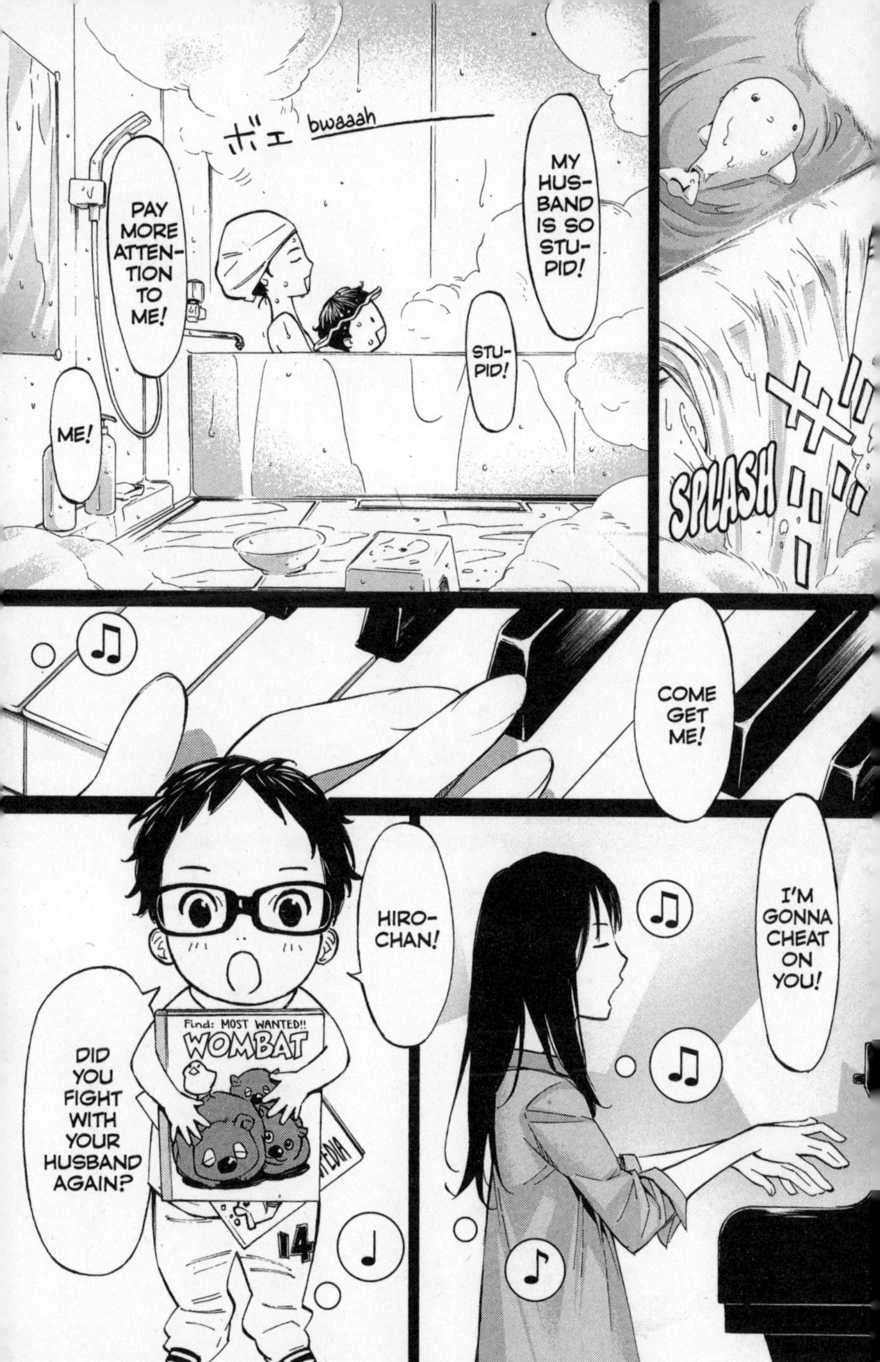
SPLASH
MY HUSBAND IS SO STUPID!
STUPID!
ボエ bwaaah
PAY MORE ATTENTION TO ME!
ME!
COME GET ME!
I'M GONNA CHEAT ON YOU!
HIRO-CHAN!
DID YOU FIGHT WITH YOUR HUSBAND AGAIN?
Find: MOST WANTED!! WOMBAT

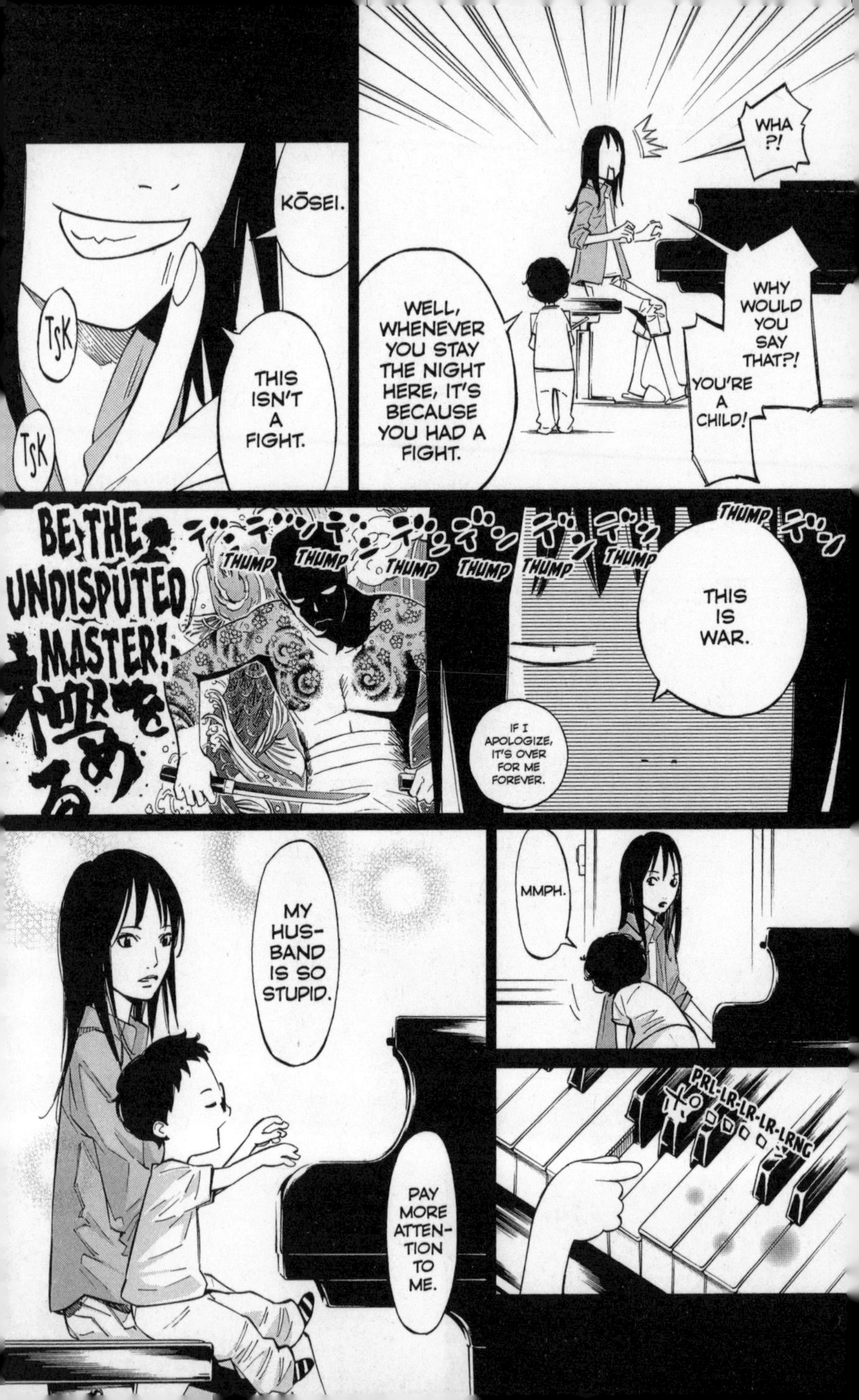
WHA ?!
WHY WOULD YOU SAY THAT?!
YOU'RE A CHILD!
WELL, WHENEVER YOU STAY THE NIGHT HERE, IT'S BECAUSE YOU HAD A FIGHT.
KŌSEI.
TSK
TSK
THIS ISN'T A FIGHT.
THIS IS WAR.
IF I APOLOGIZE, IT'S OVER FOR ME FOREVER.
THUMP THUMP THUMP THUMP THUMP THUMP THUMP
BE THE UNDISPUTED MASTER!
MMPH.
PRL-LR-LR-LR-LRNG
MY HUS-BAND IS SO STUPID.
PAY MORE ATTEN-TION TO ME.

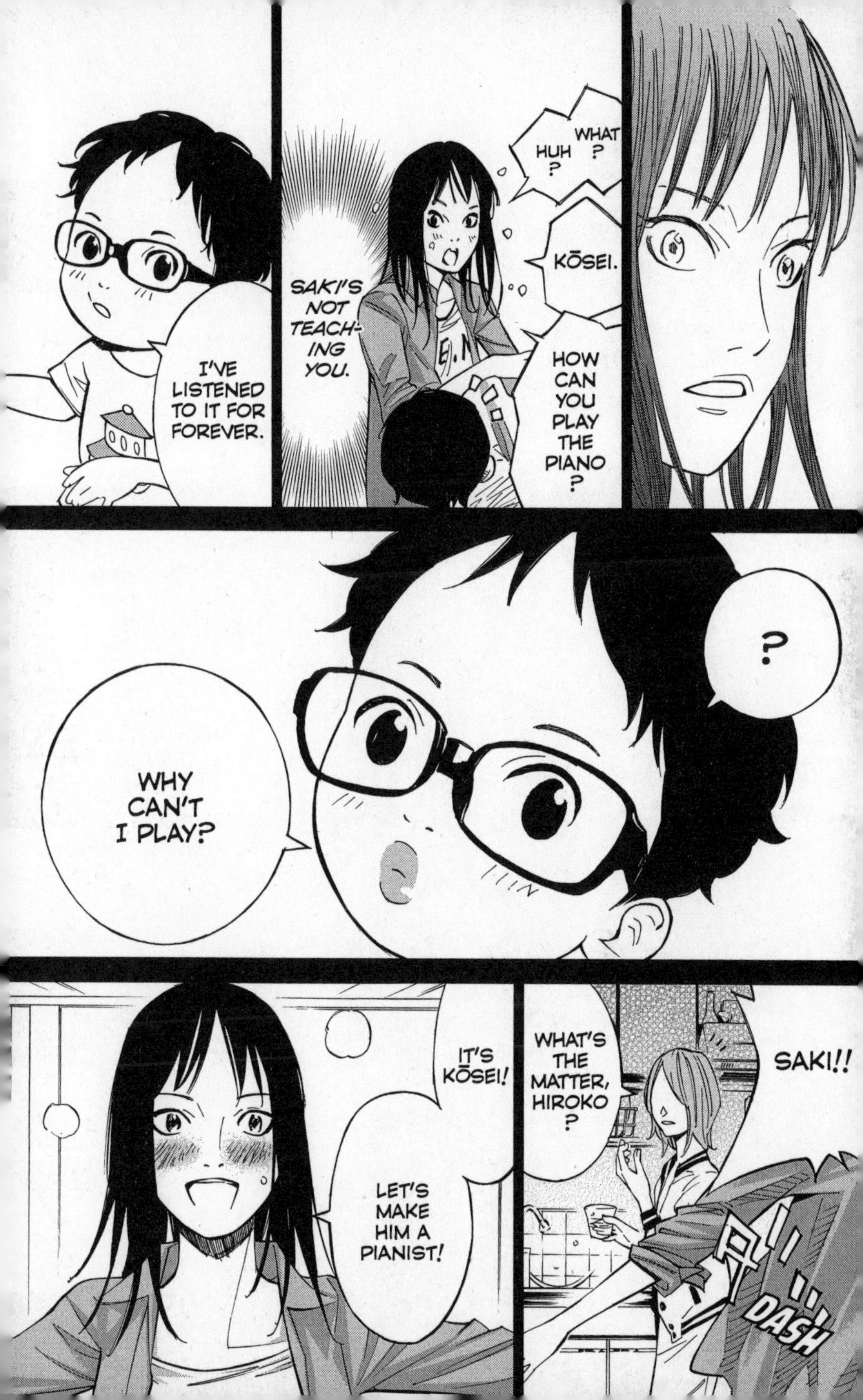
HUH? WHAT?
KŌSEI.
HOW CAN YOU PLAY THE PIANO?
SAKI'S NOT TEACHING YOU.
I'VE LISTENED TO IT FOR FOREVER.
?
WHY CAN'T I PLAY?
SAKI!!
WHAT'S THE MATTER, HIROKO?
DASH
IT'S KŌSEI!
LET'S MAKE HIM A PIANIST!

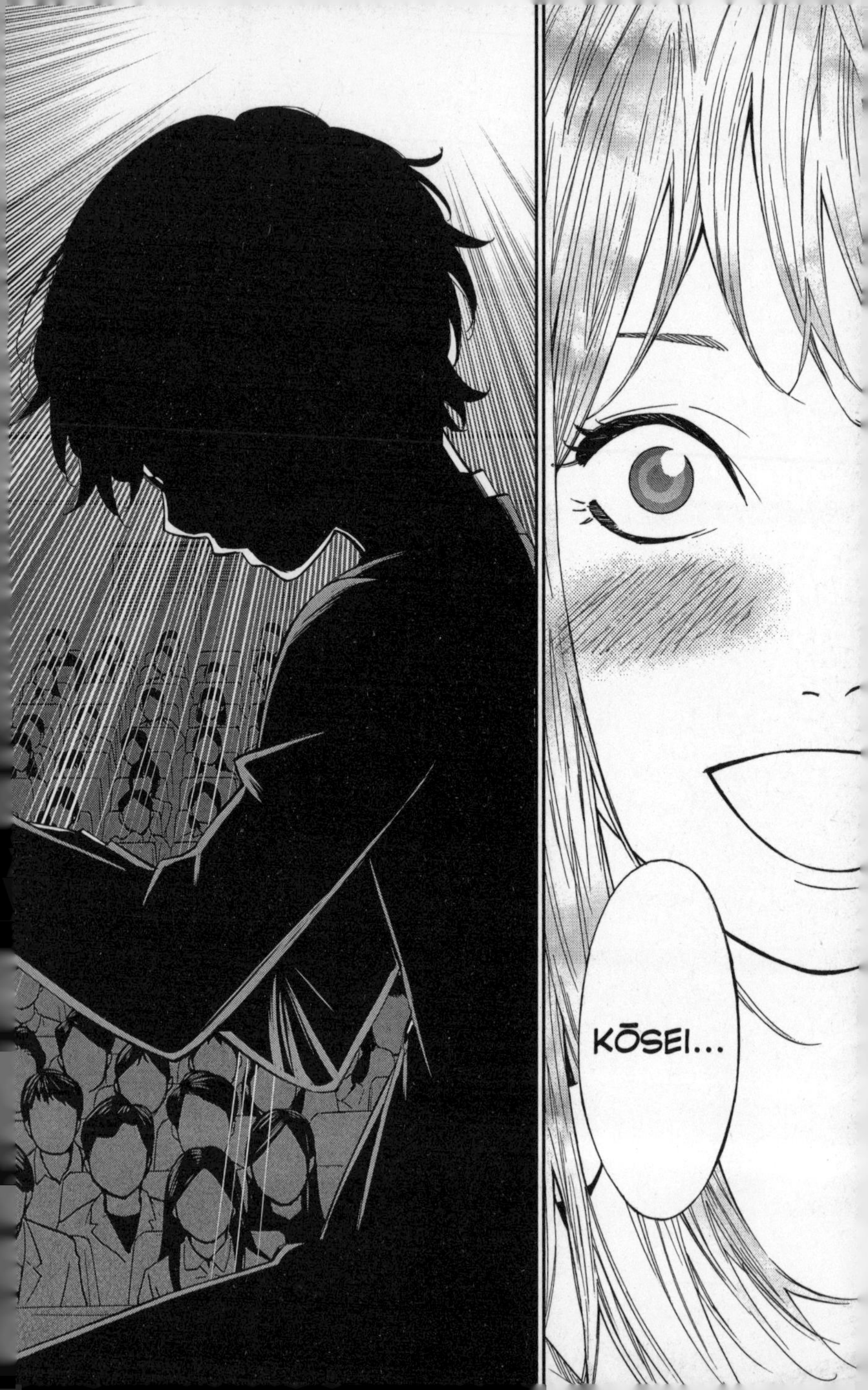
KŌSEI...

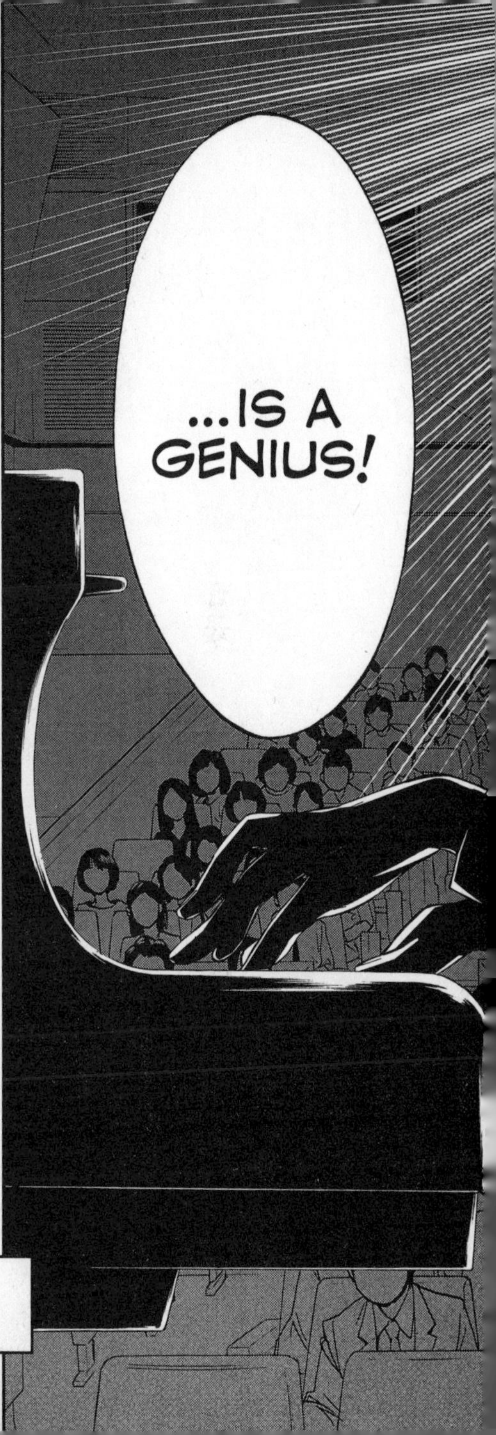
...IS A GENIUS!

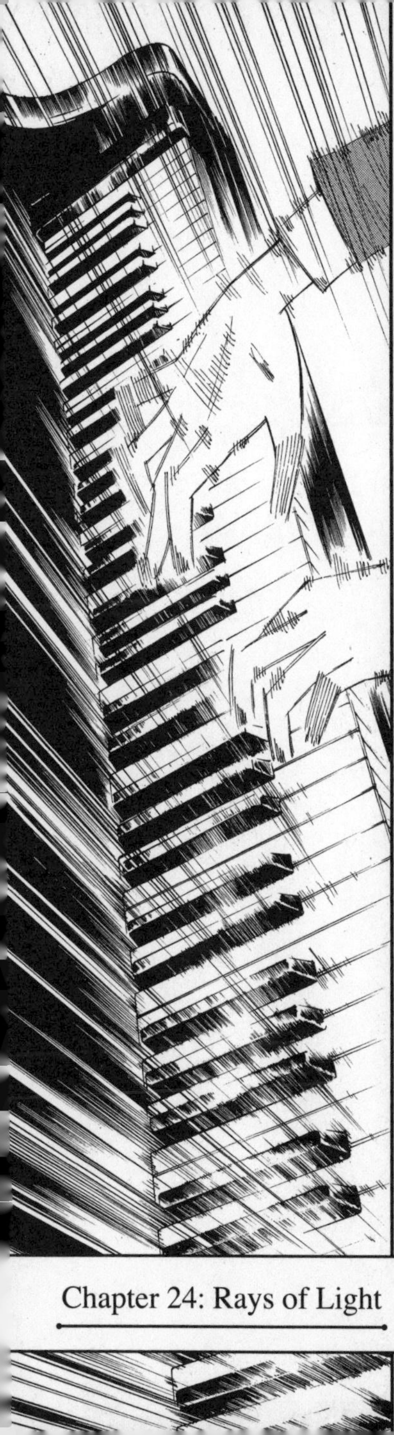

Chapter 24: Rays of Light

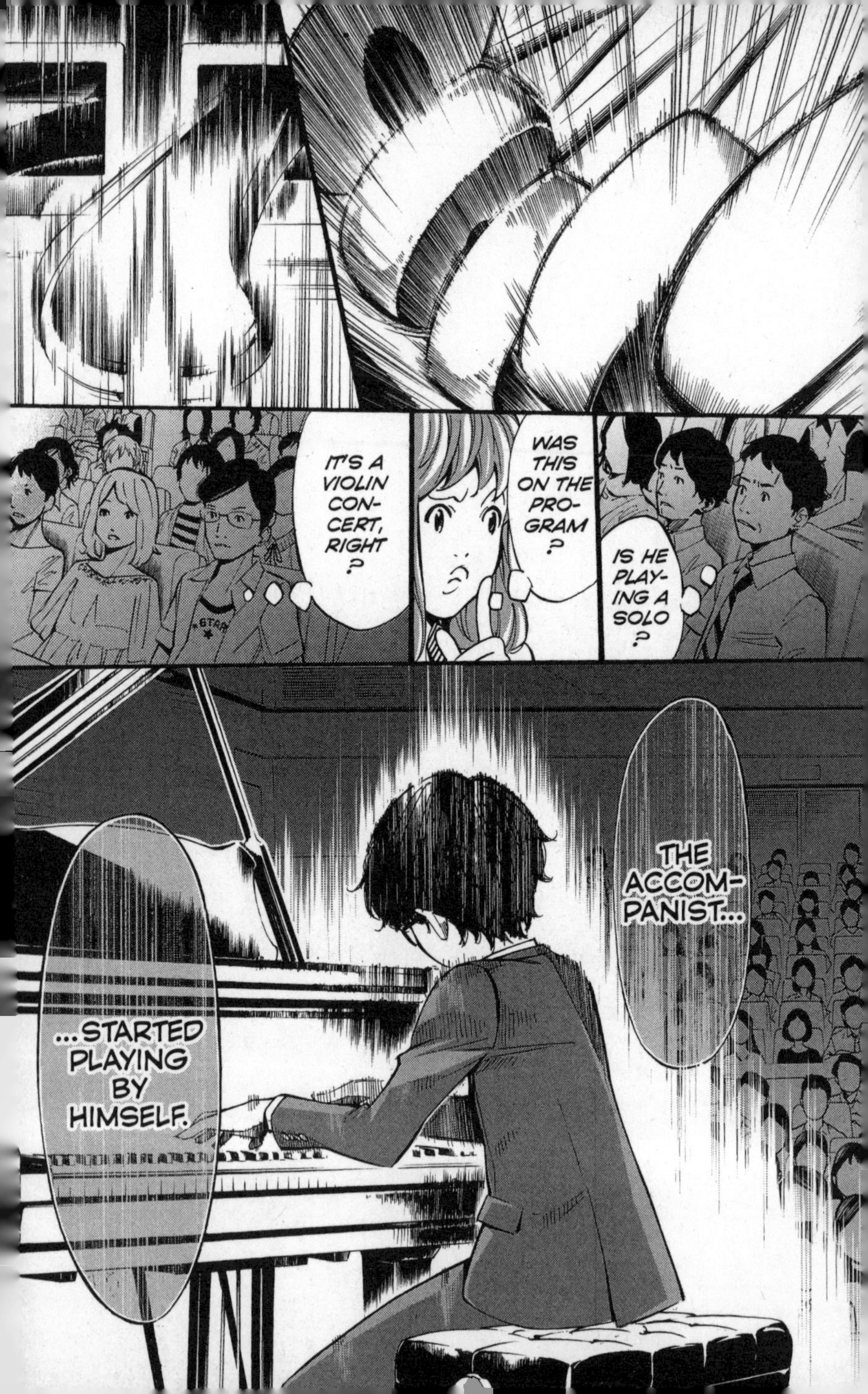
IS HE PLAYING A SOLO?
WAS THIS ON THE PROGRAM?
IT'S A VIOLIN CONCERT, RIGHT?
THE ACCOMPANIST...
...STARTED PLAYING BY HIMSELF.

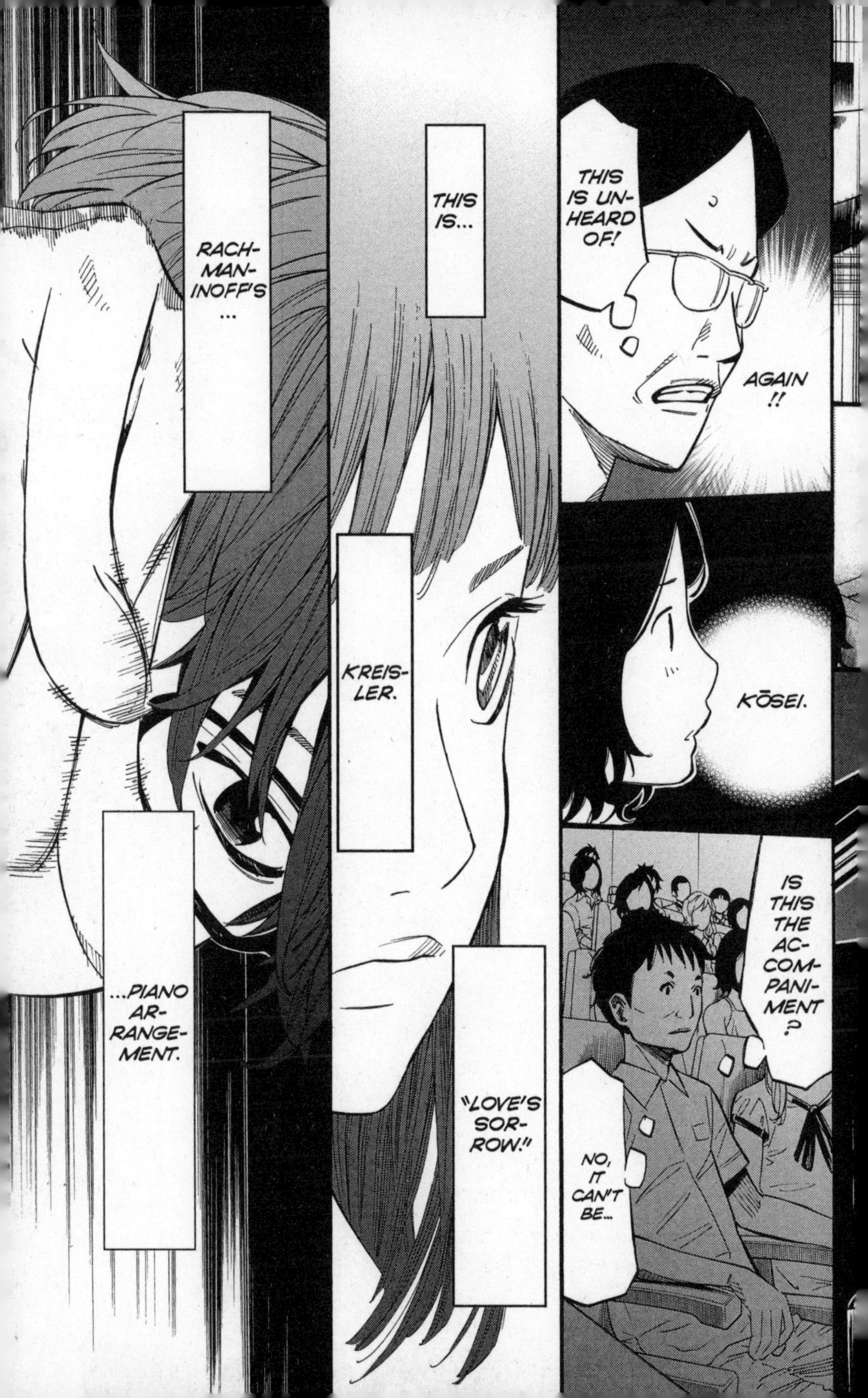
THIS IS UNHEARD OF!
AGAIN!!
KŌSEI.
IS THIS THE ACCOMPANIMENT?
NO, IT CAN'T BE...
THIS IS...
KREISLER.
"LOVE'S SORROW."
RACHMANINOFF'S...
...PIANO ARRANGEMENT.

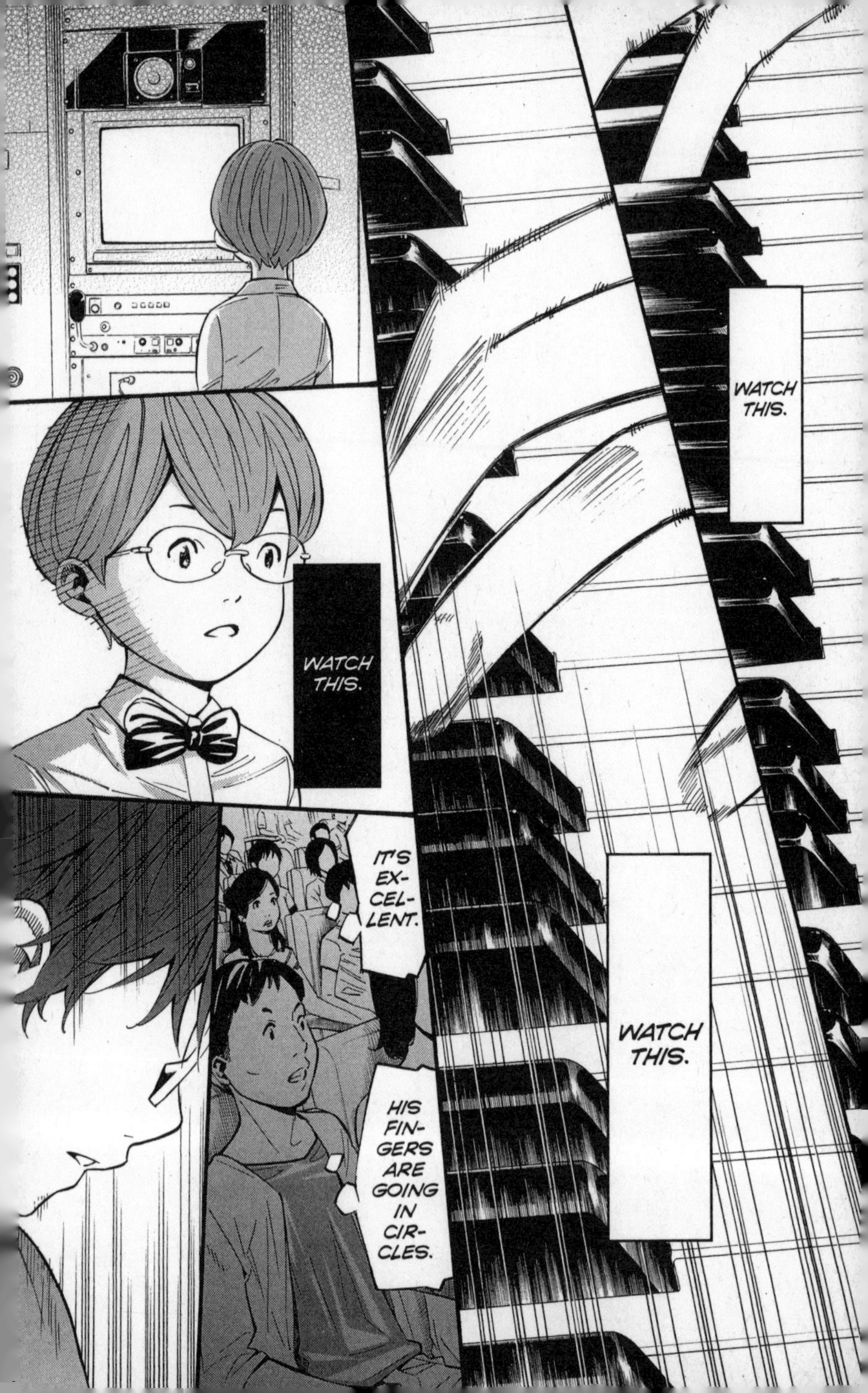
WATCH THIS.
WATCH THIS.
WATCH THIS.
IT'S EXCELLENT.
HIS FINGERS ARE GOING IN CIRCLES.

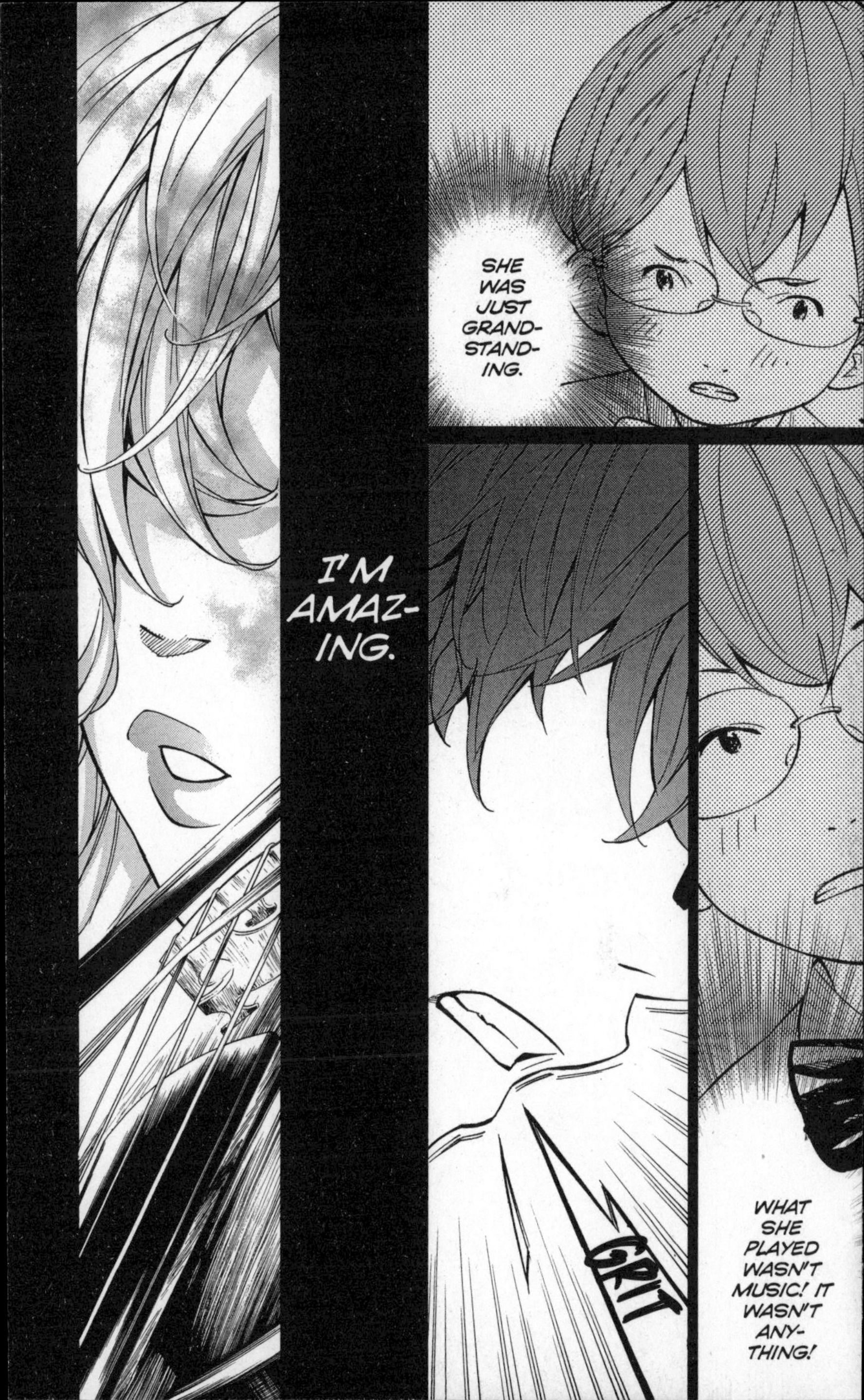
SHE WAS JUST GRANDSTANDING.
WHAT SHE PLAYED WASN'T MUSIC! IT WASN'T ANYTHING!
GRIT
I'M AMAZING.

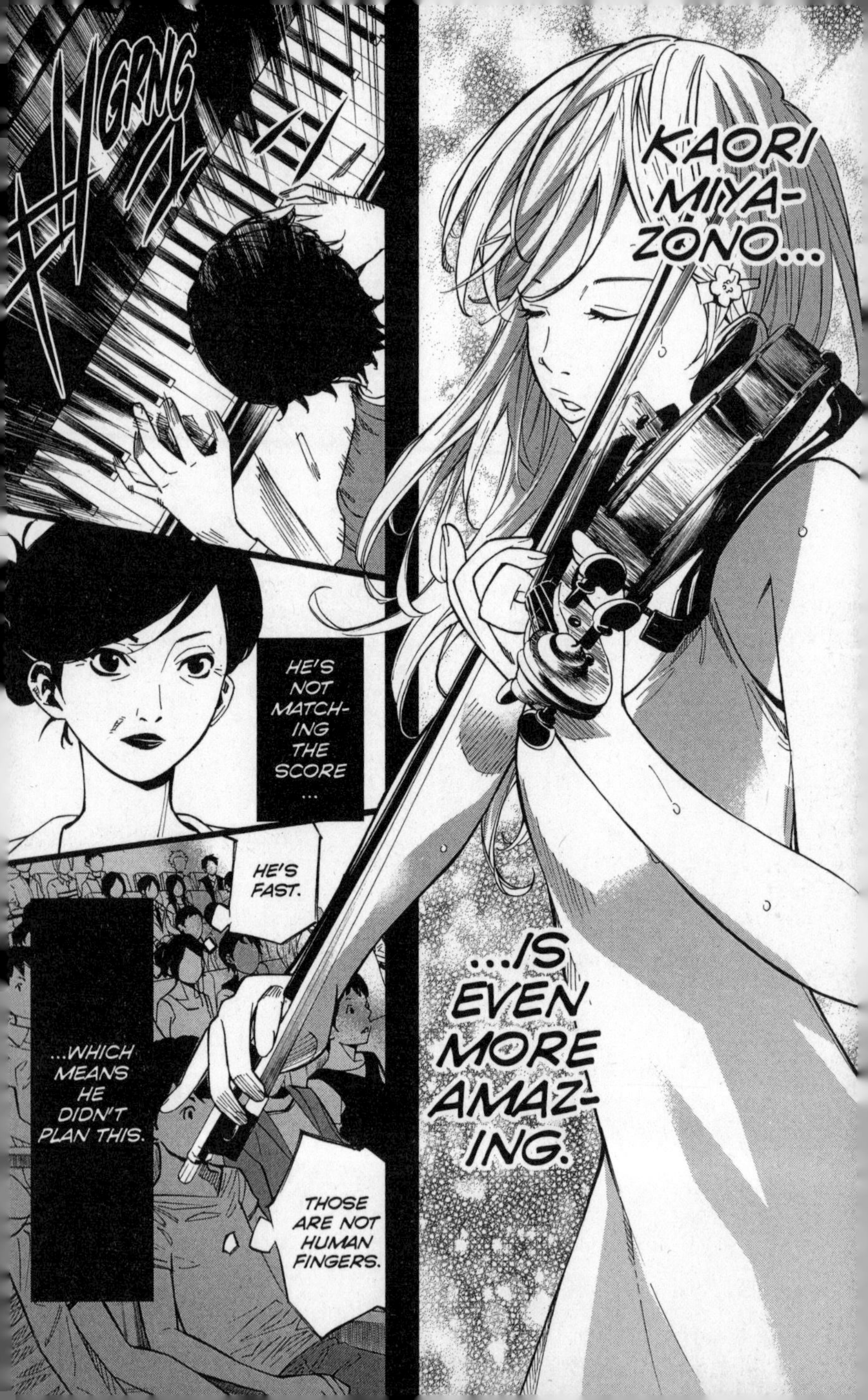

KAORI MIYA-ZONO...
...IS EVEN MORE AMAZ-ING.
HGRNG
HE'S NOT MATCH-ING THE SCORE ...
HE'S FAST.
...WHICH MEANS HE DIDN'T PLAN THIS.
THOSE ARE NOT HUMAN FINGERS.

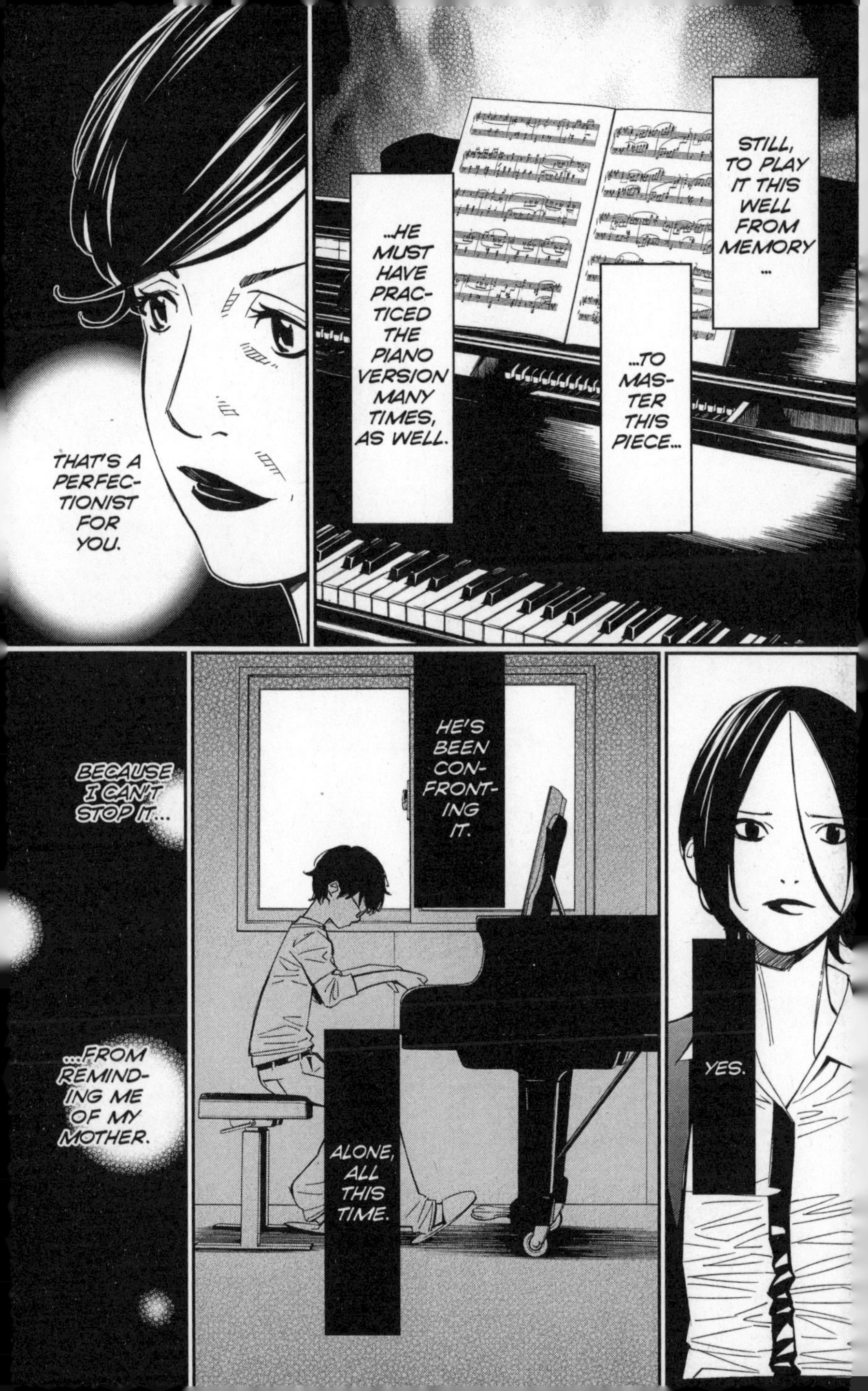
STILL, TO PLAY IT THIS WELL FROM MEMORY...
...TO MASTER THIS PIECE...
...HE MUST HAVE PRACTICED THE PIANO VERSION MANY TIMES, AS WELL.
THAT'S A PERFECTIONIST FOR YOU.
YES.
HE'S BEEN CONFRONTING IT.
ALONE, ALL THIS TIME.
BECAUSE I CAN'T STOP IT...
...FROM REMINDING ME OF MY MOTHER.

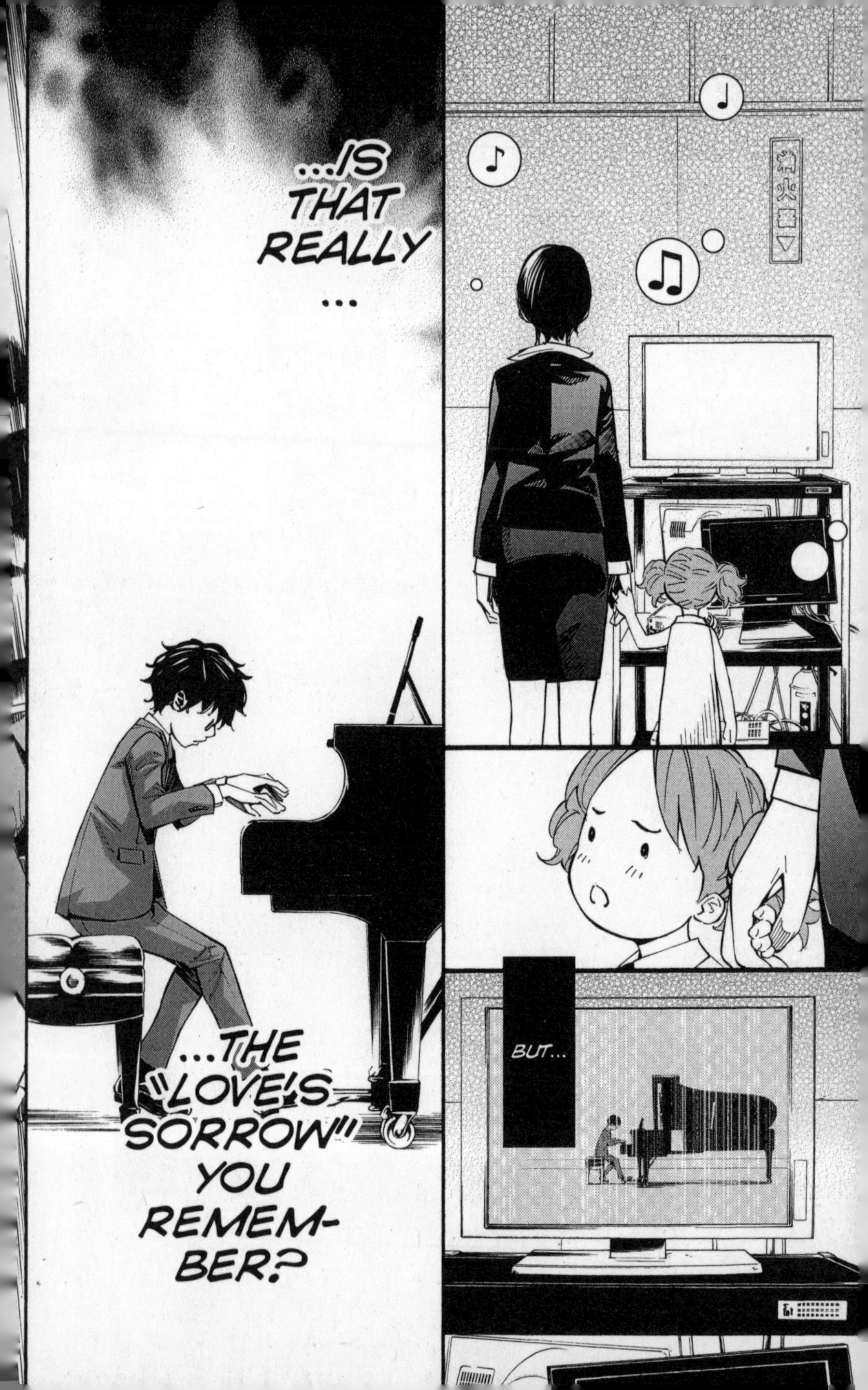
BUT...
...IS THAT REALLY ...
...THE "LOVE'S SORROW" YOU REMEMBER?

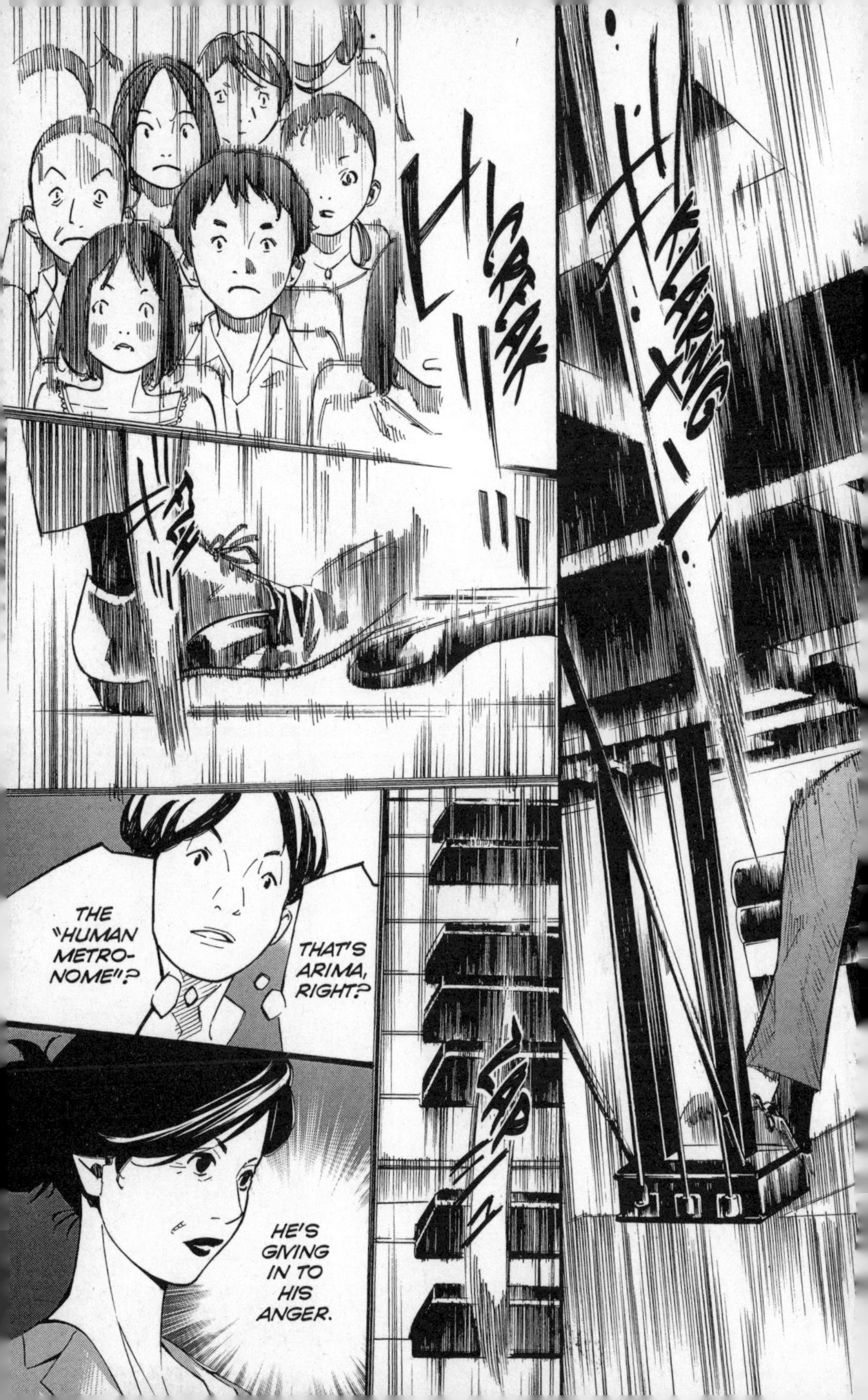
KLARNG
CREAK
THAT'S ARIMA, RIGHT?
THE "HUMAN METRO-NOME"?
HE'S GIVING IN TO HIS ANGER.

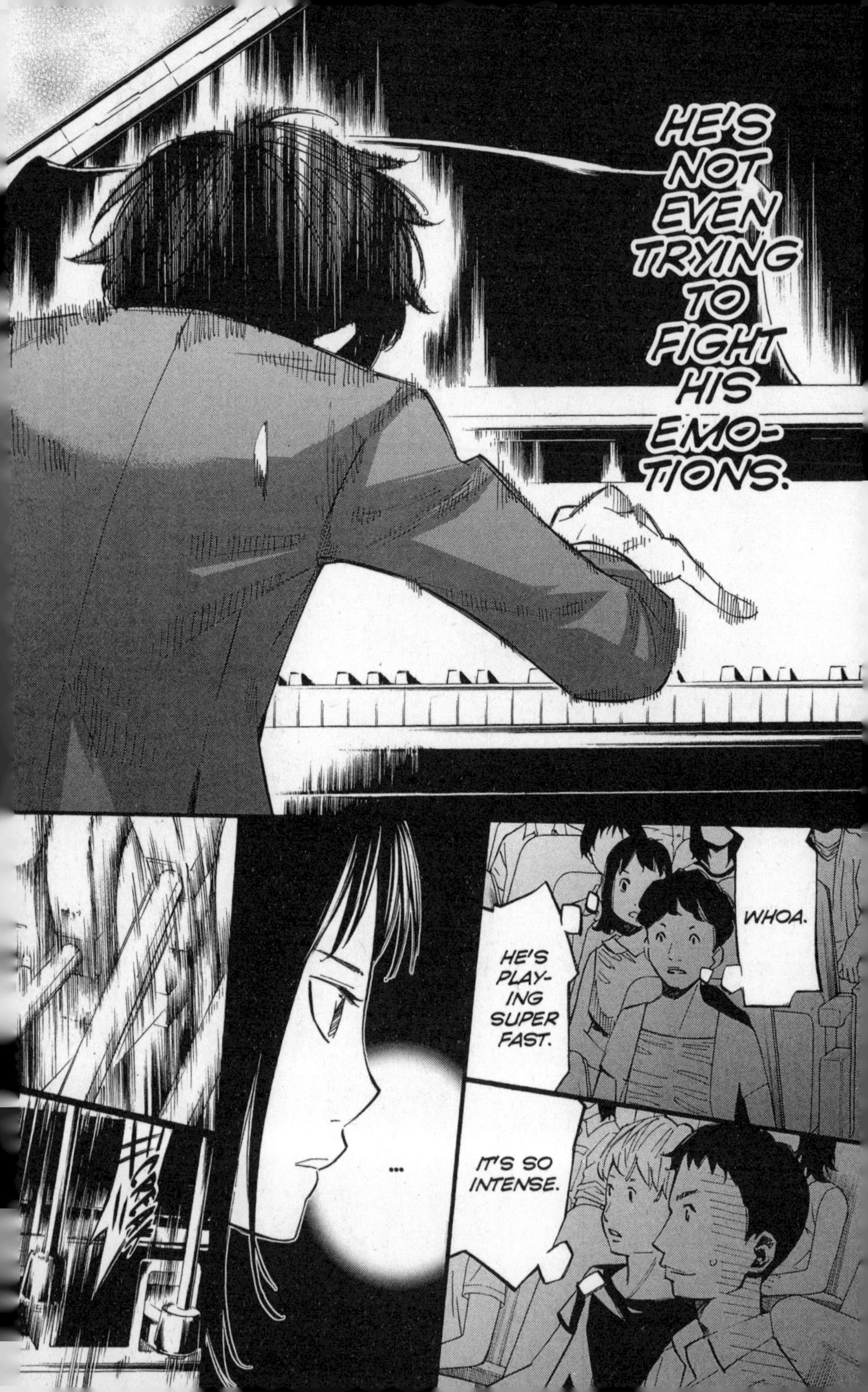
HE'S NOT EVEN TRYING TO FIGHT HIS EMO-TIONS.
WHOA.
HE'S PLAY-ING SUPER FAST.
IT'S SO INTENSE.
...

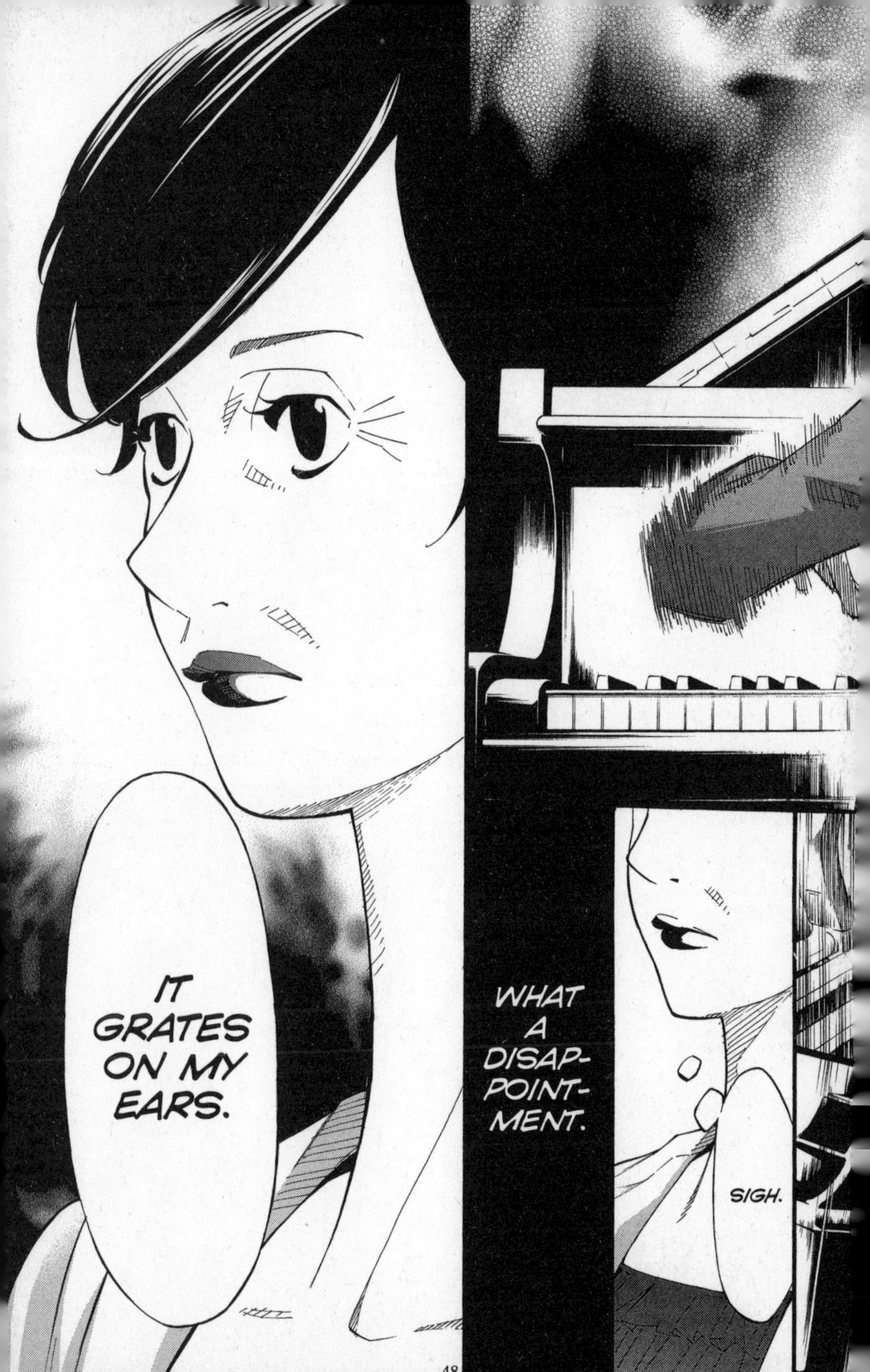
SIGH.
WHAT A DISAPPOINTMENT.
IT GRATES ON MY EARS.

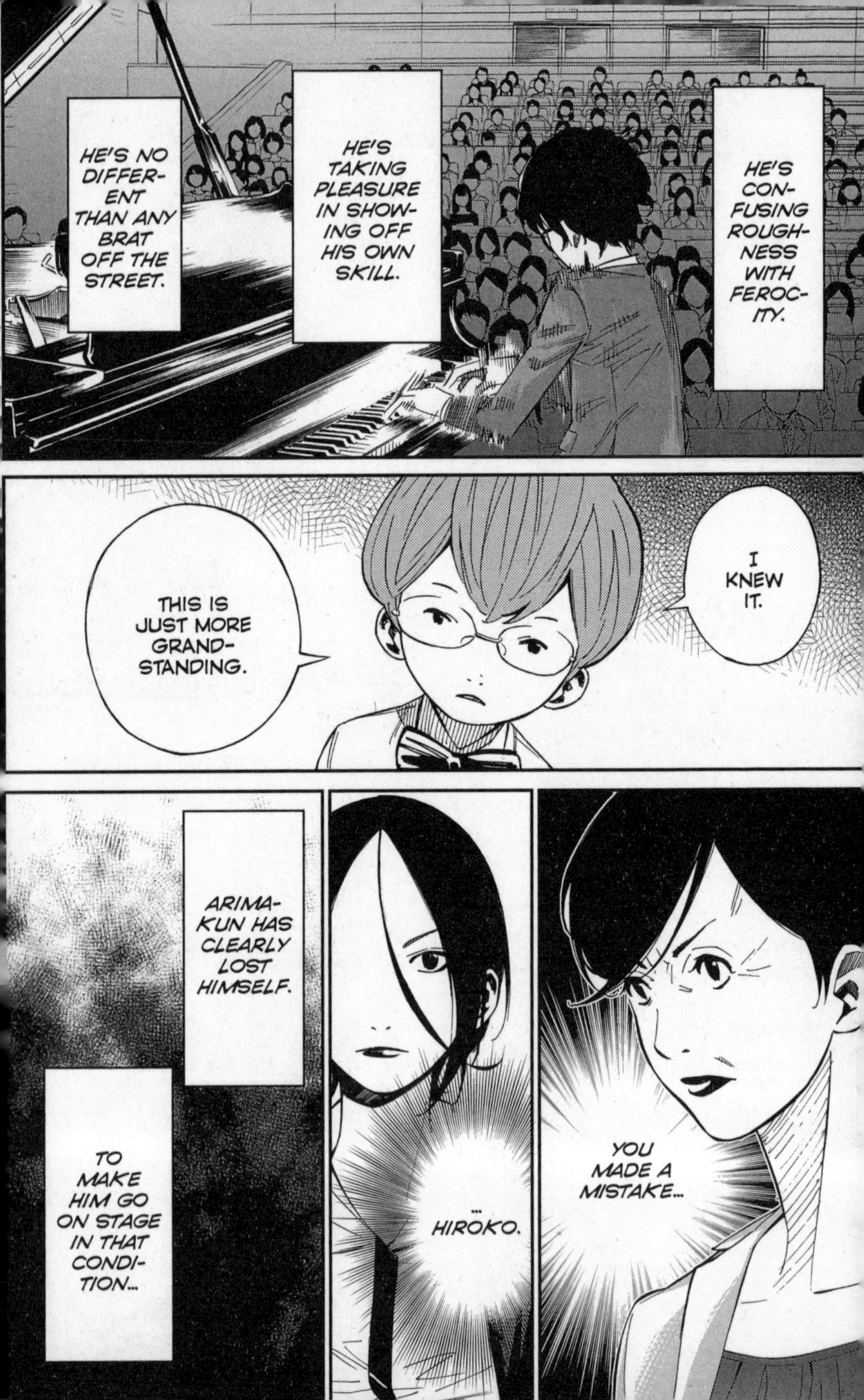
HE'S CONFUSING ROUGHNESS WITH FEROCITY.
HE'S TAKING PLEASURE IN SHOWING OFF HIS OWN SKILL.
HE'S NO DIFFERENT THAN ANY BRAT OFF THE STREET.
I KNEW IT.
THIS IS JUST MORE GRANDSTANDING.
YOU MADE A MISTAKE...
... HIROKO.
ARIMA-KUN HAS CLEARLY LOST HIMSELF.
TO MAKE HIM GO ON STAGE IN THAT CONDITION...

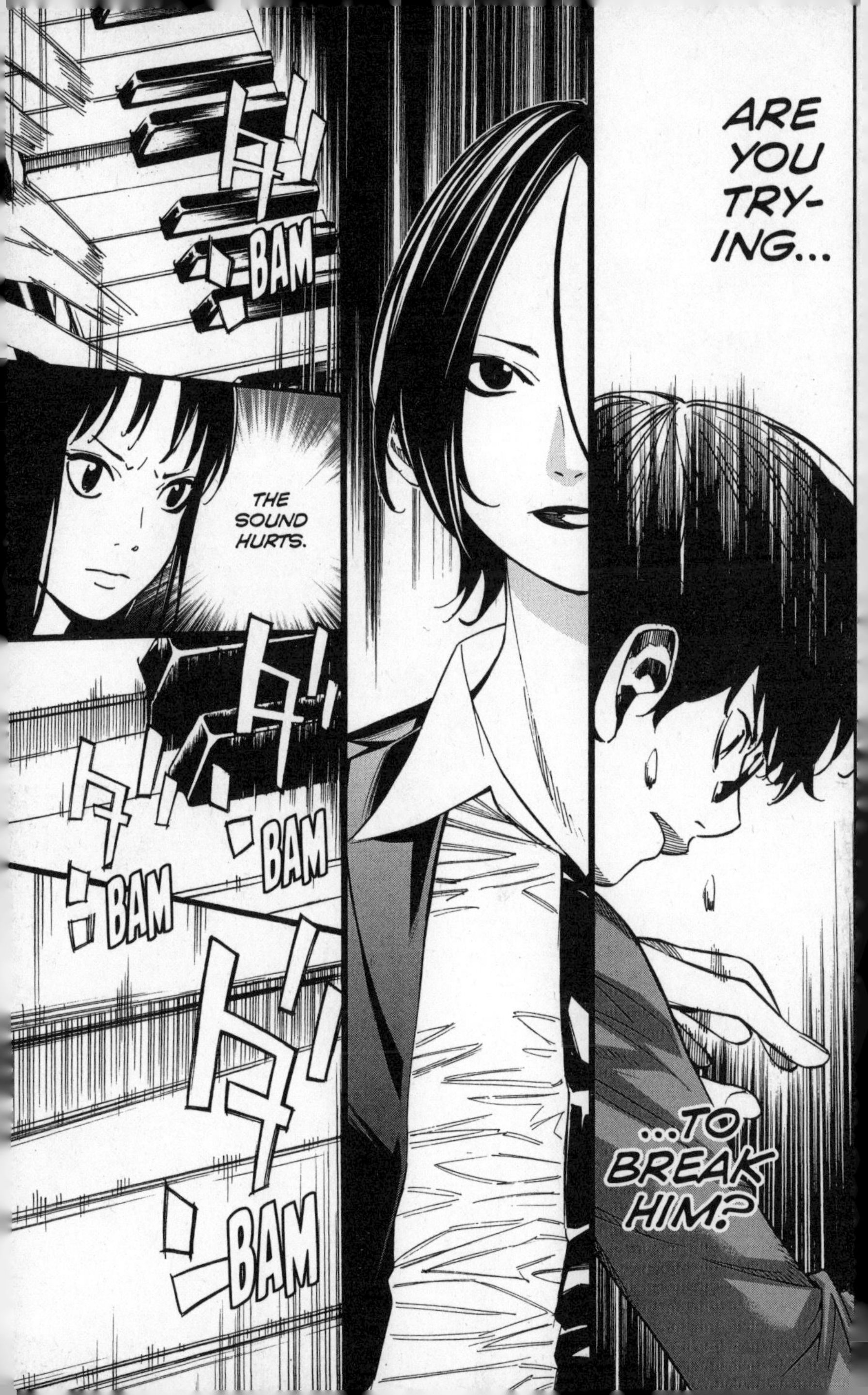
ARE YOU TRY-ING...
...TO BREAK HIM?
BAM
THE SOUND HURTS.
BAM
BAM
BAM

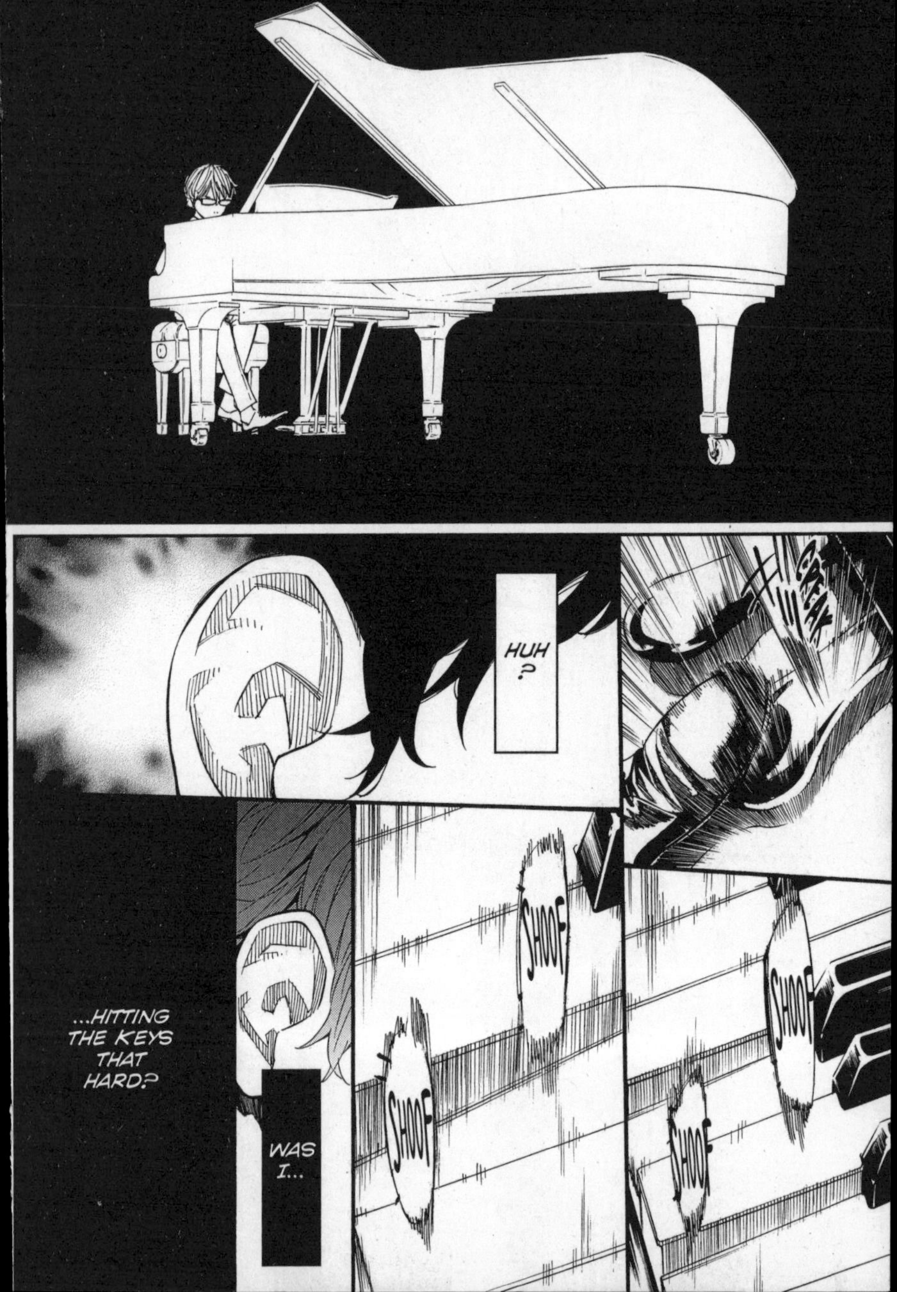
CREAK
HUH?
SHOOF
SHOOF
SHOOF
SHOOF
WAS I...
...HITTING THE KEYS THAT HARD?

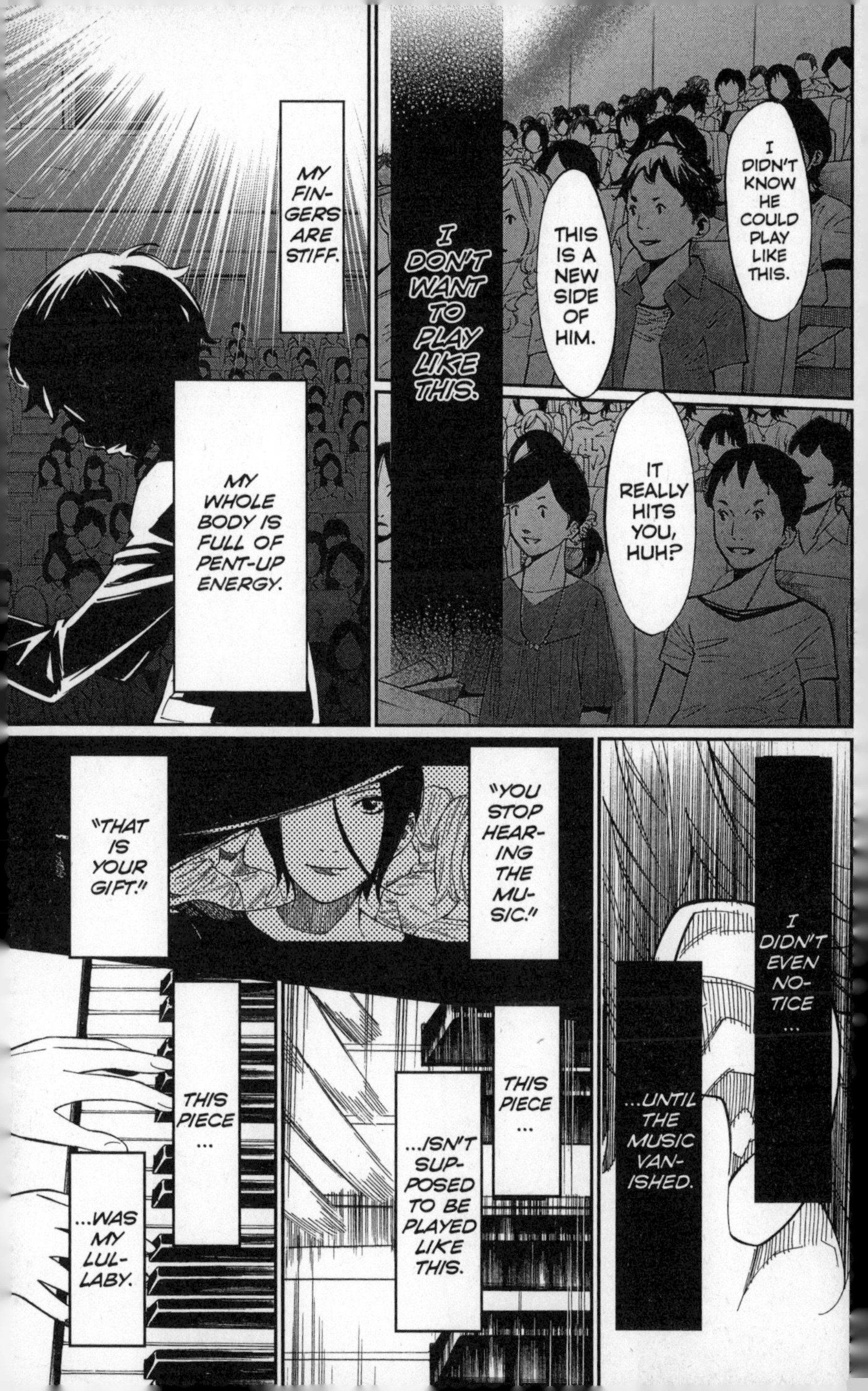
I DIDN'T KNOW HE COULD PLAY LIKE THIS.
THIS IS A NEW SIDE OF HIM.
IT REALLY HITS YOU, HUH?
I DON'T WANT TO PLAY LIKE THIS.
MY FINGERS ARE STIFF.
MY WHOLE BODY IS FULL OF PENT-UP ENERGY.
I DIDN'T EVEN NOTICE...
...UNTIL THE MUSIC VANISHED.
"YOU STOP HEARING THE MUSIC."
"THAT IS YOUR GIFT."
THIS PIECE...
...ISN'T SUPPOSED TO BE PLAYED LIKE THIS.
THIS PIECE...
...WAS MY LULLABY.

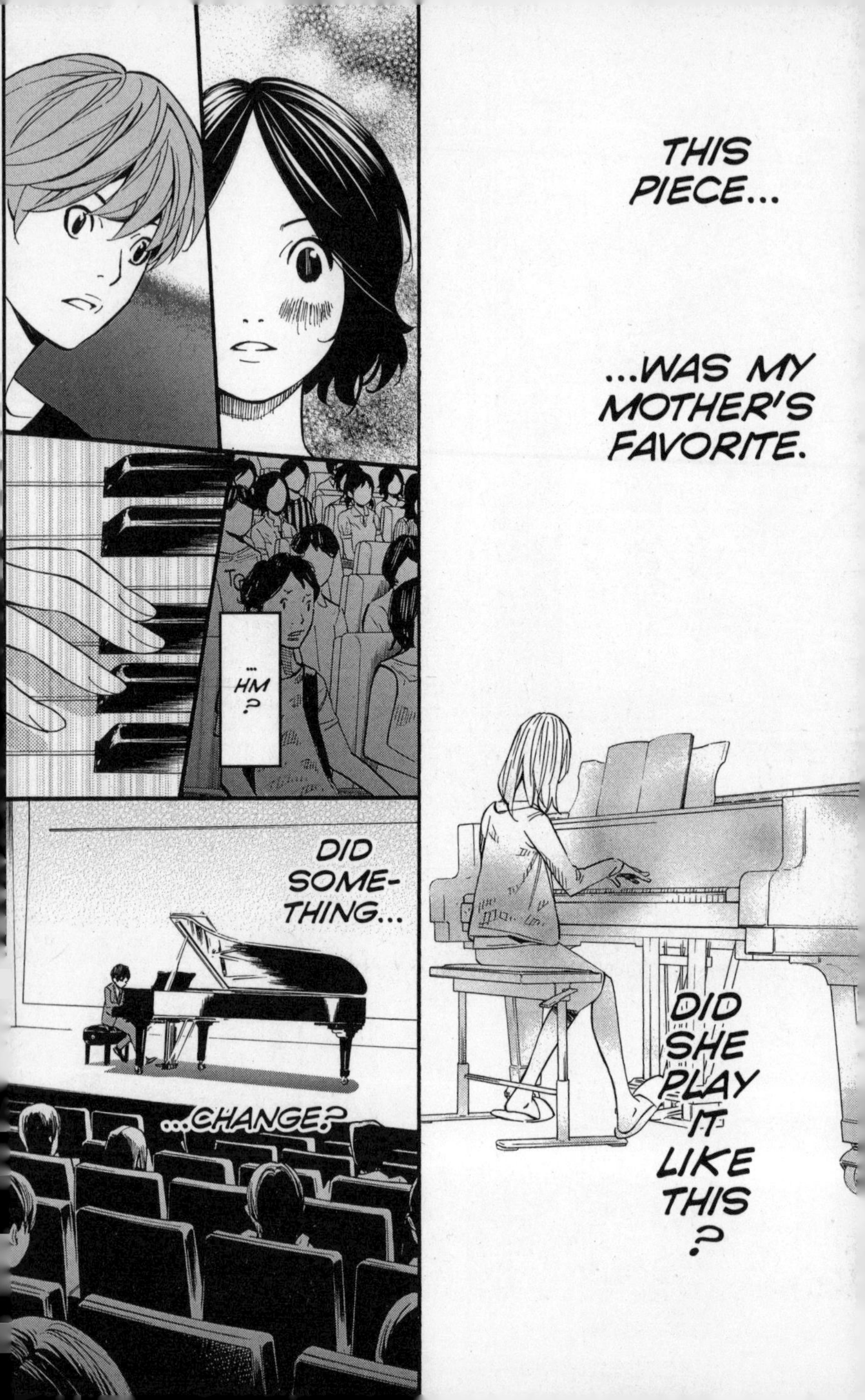
THIS PIECE...
...WAS MY MOTHER'S FAVORITE.
DID SHE PLAY IT LIKE THIS?
...HM?
DID SOME-THING...
...CHANGE?

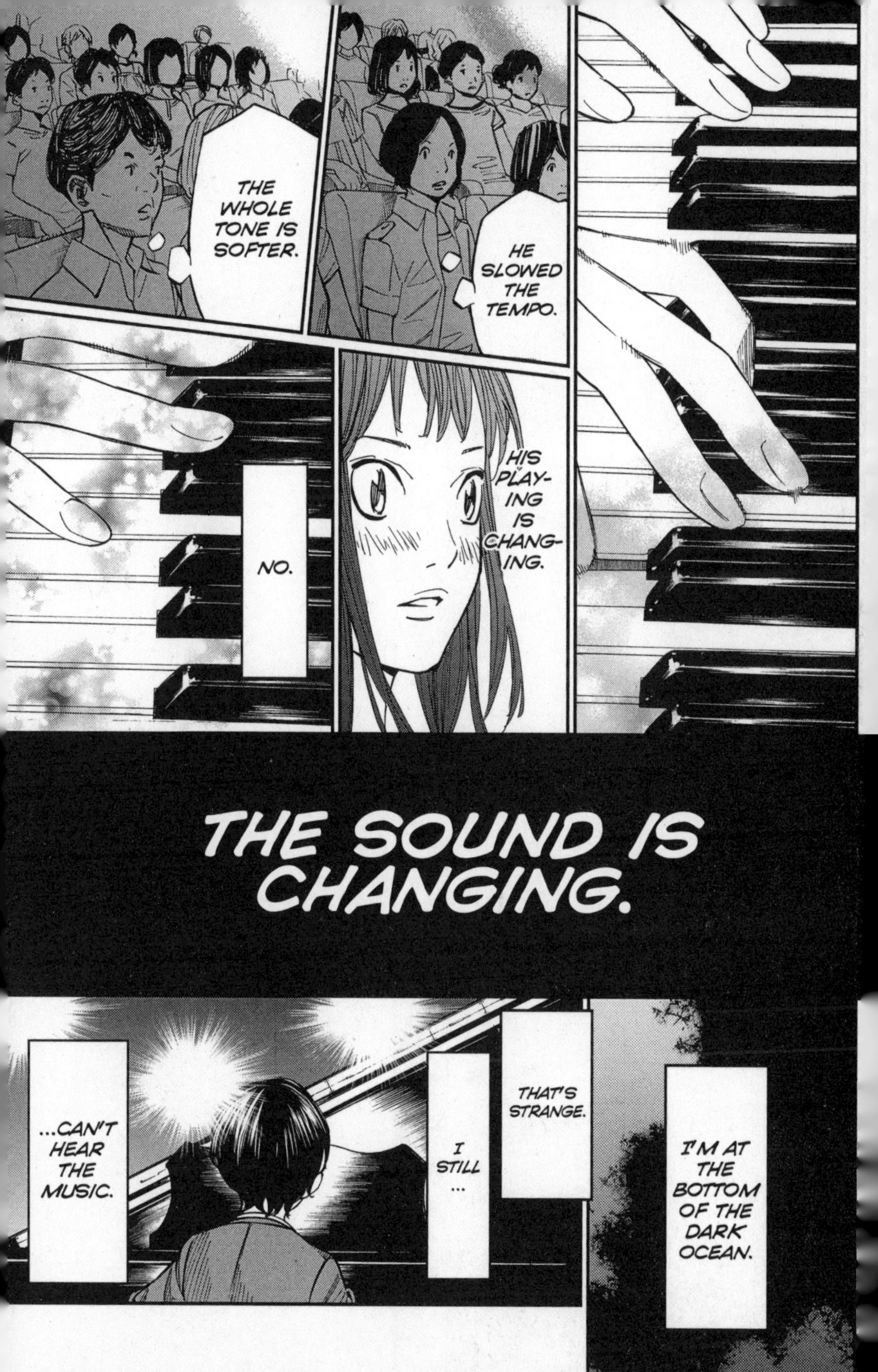
HE SLOWED THE TEMPO.
THE WHOLE TONE IS SOFTER.
HIS PLAY-ING IS CHANG-ING.
NO.
THE SOUND IS CHANGING.
I'M AT THE BOTTOM OF THE DARK OCEAN.
THAT'S STRANGE.
I STILL ...
...CAN'T HEAR THE MUSIC.

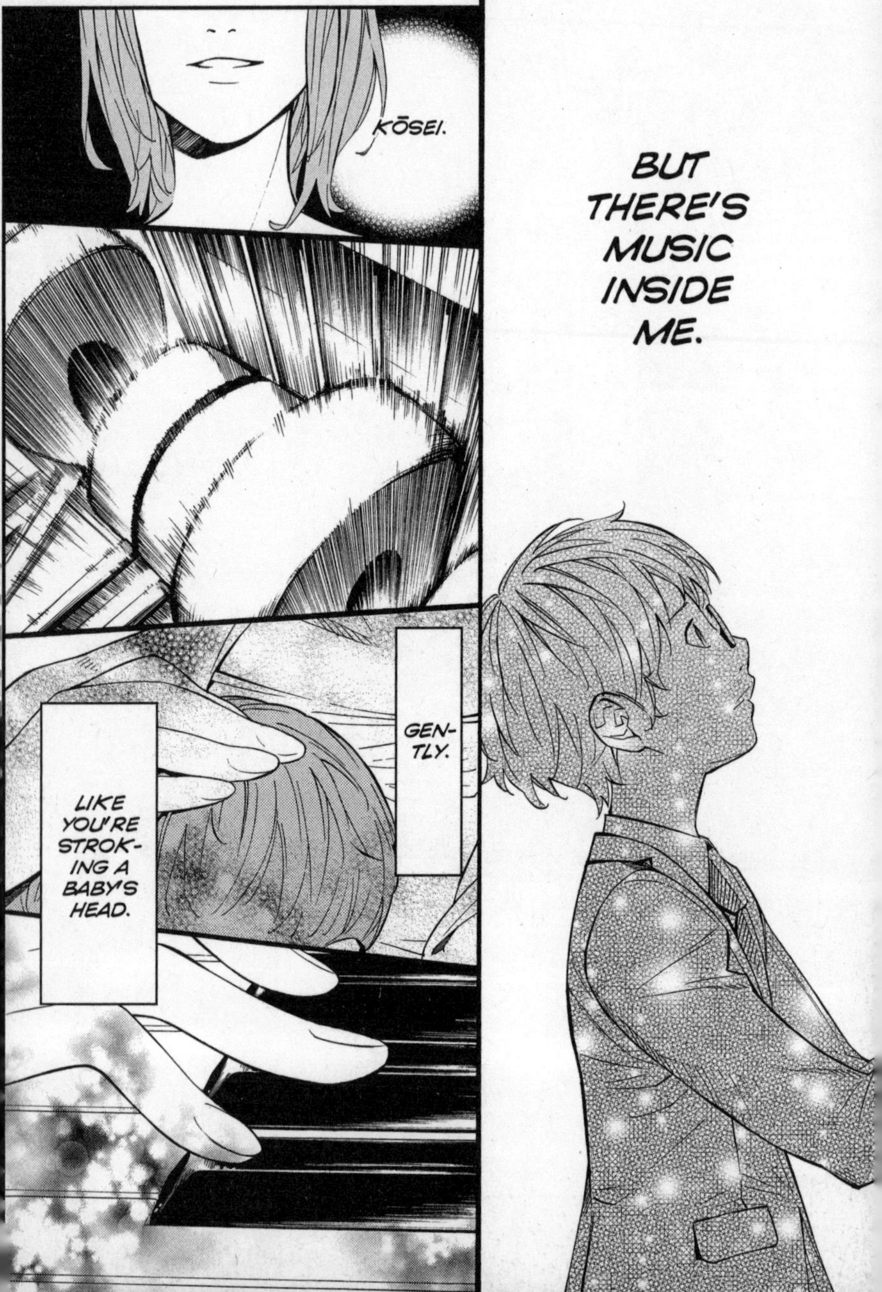
BUT THERE'S MUSIC INSIDE ME.
KŌSEI.
GEN-TLY.
LIKE YOU'RE STROK-ING A BABY'S HEAD.

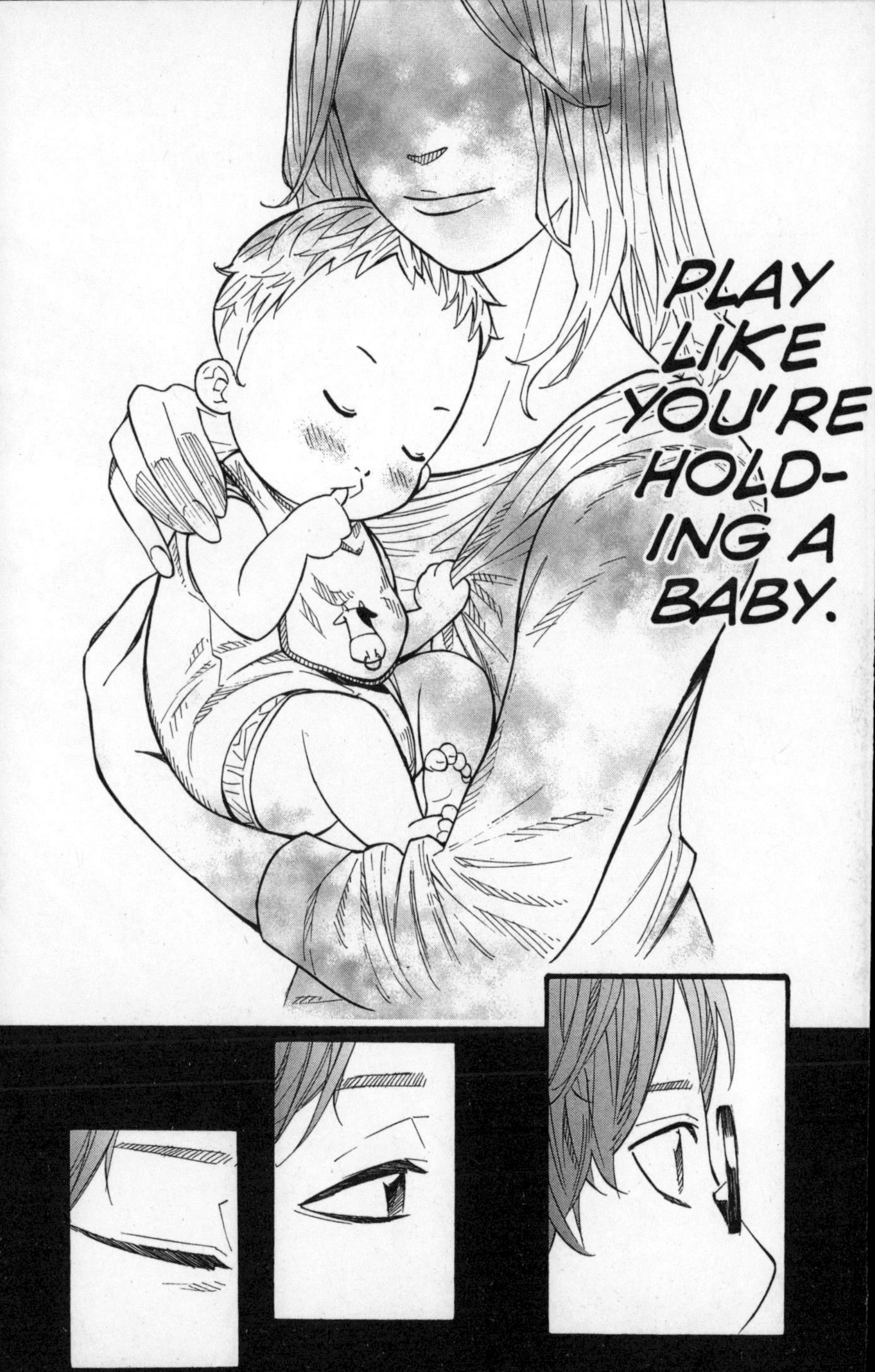
PLAY LIKE YOU'RE HOLD-ING A BABY.

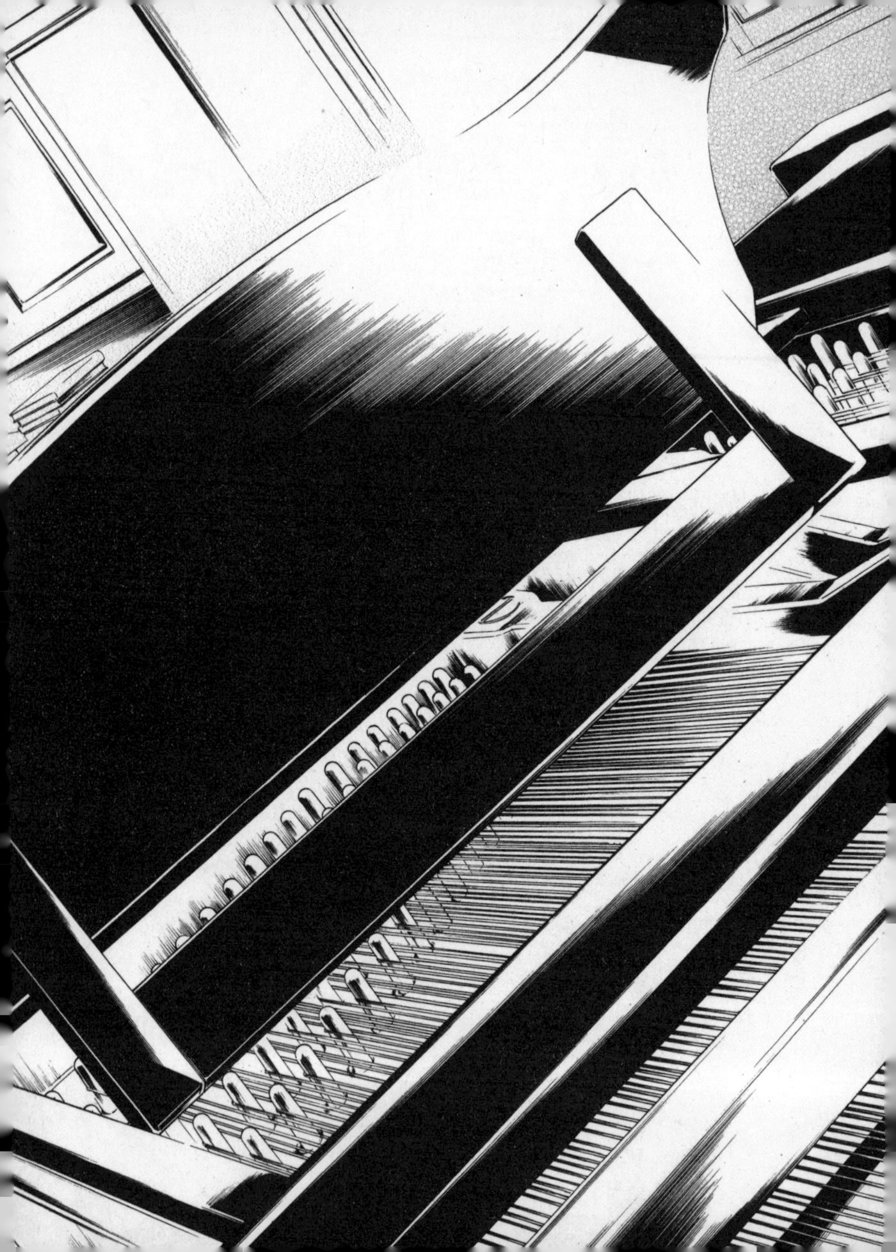

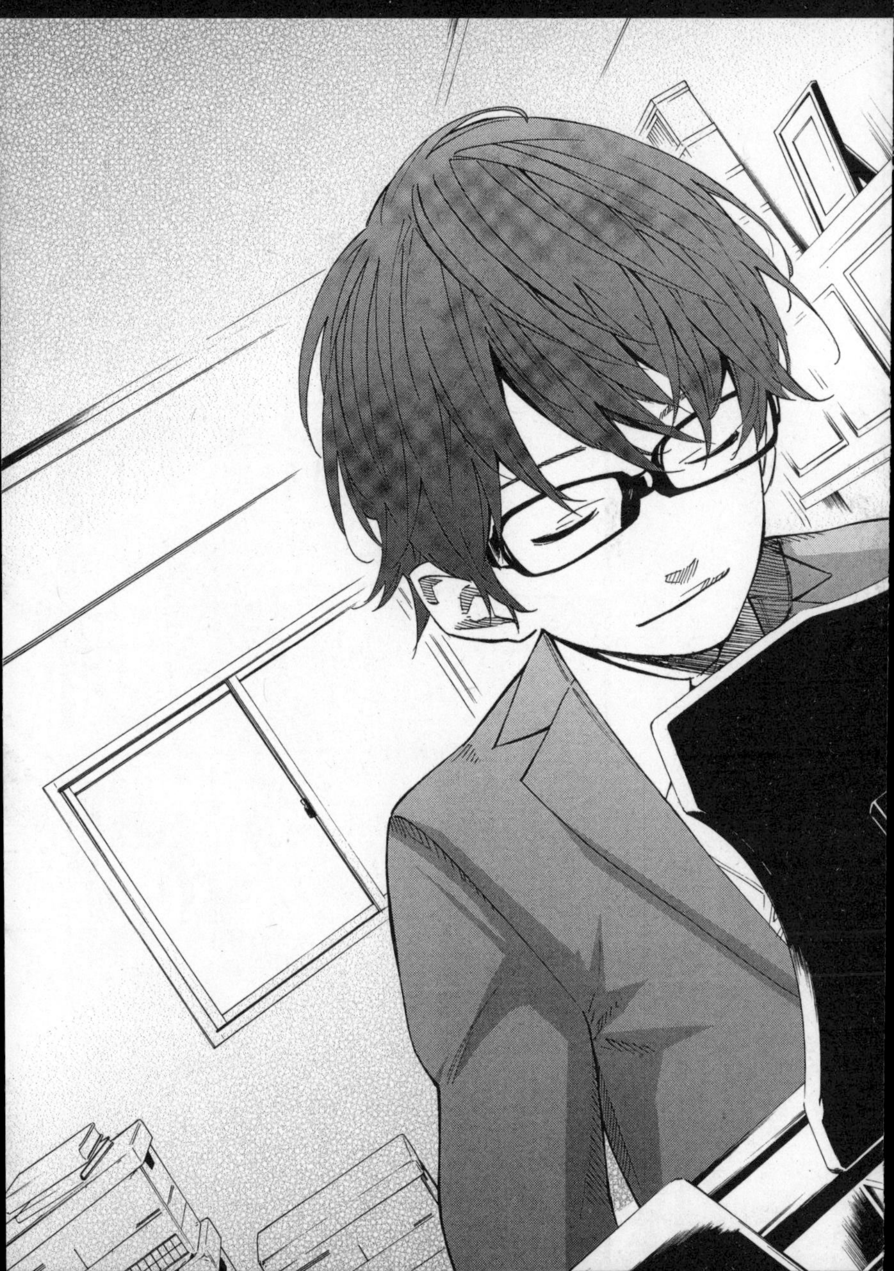

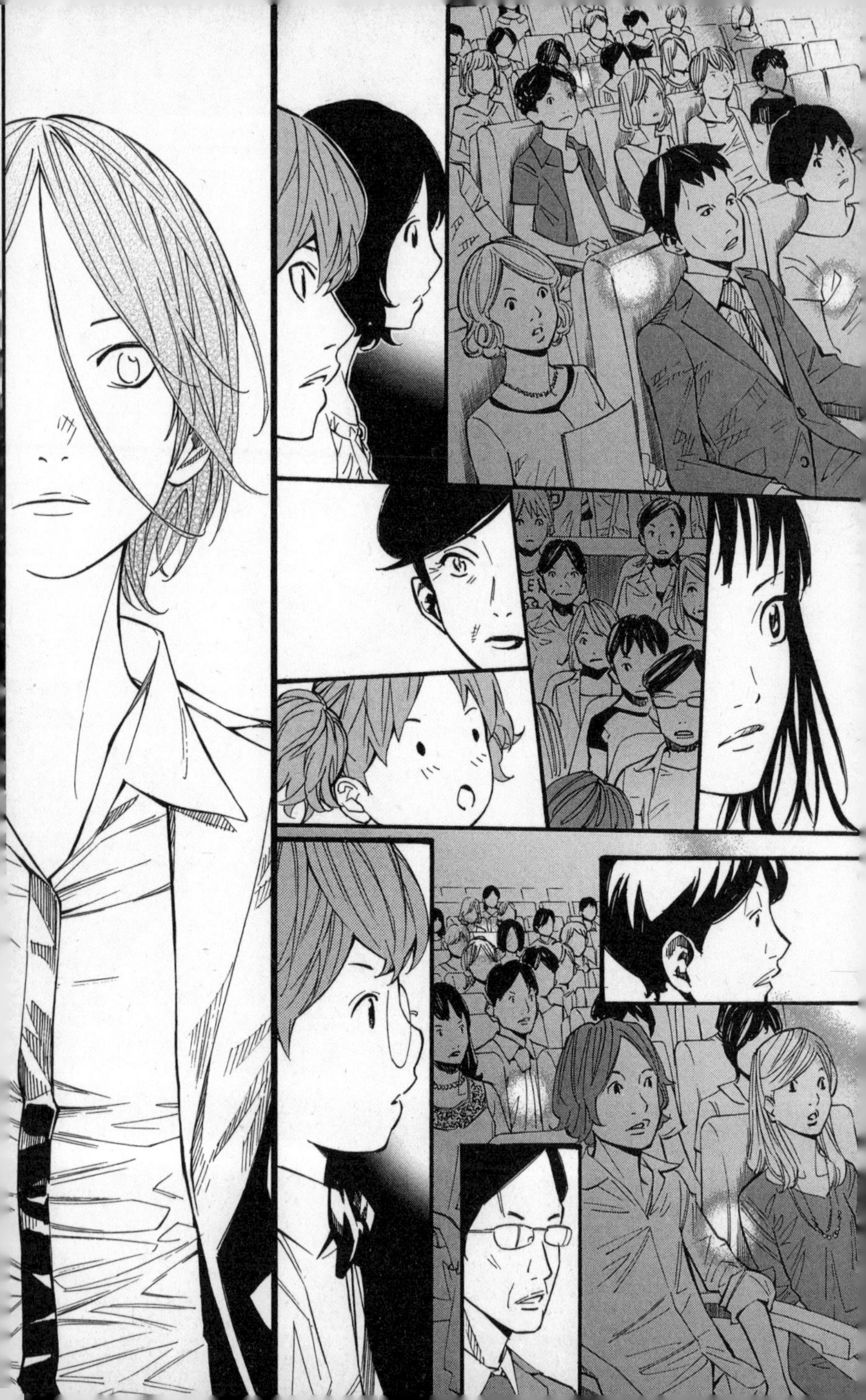

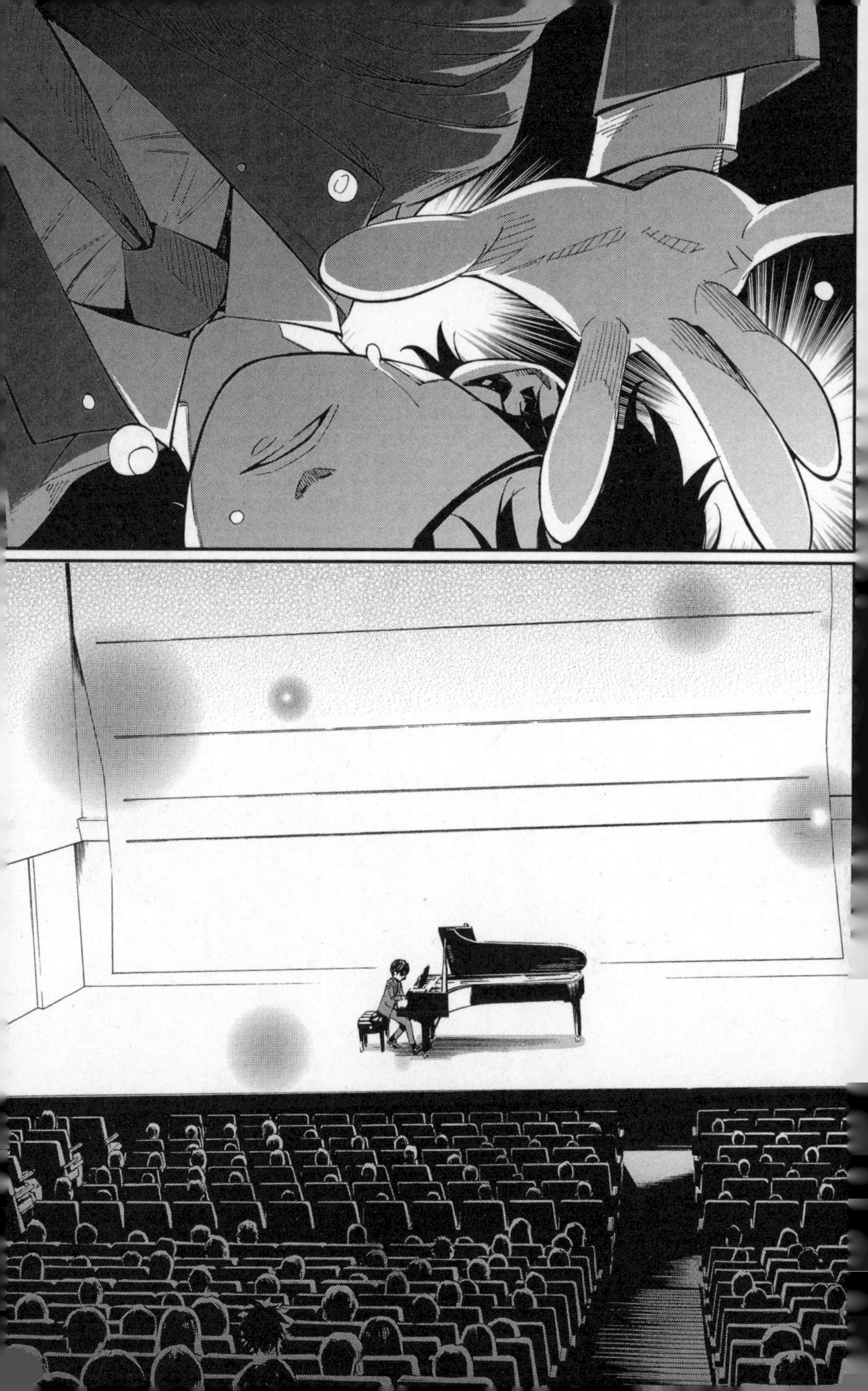

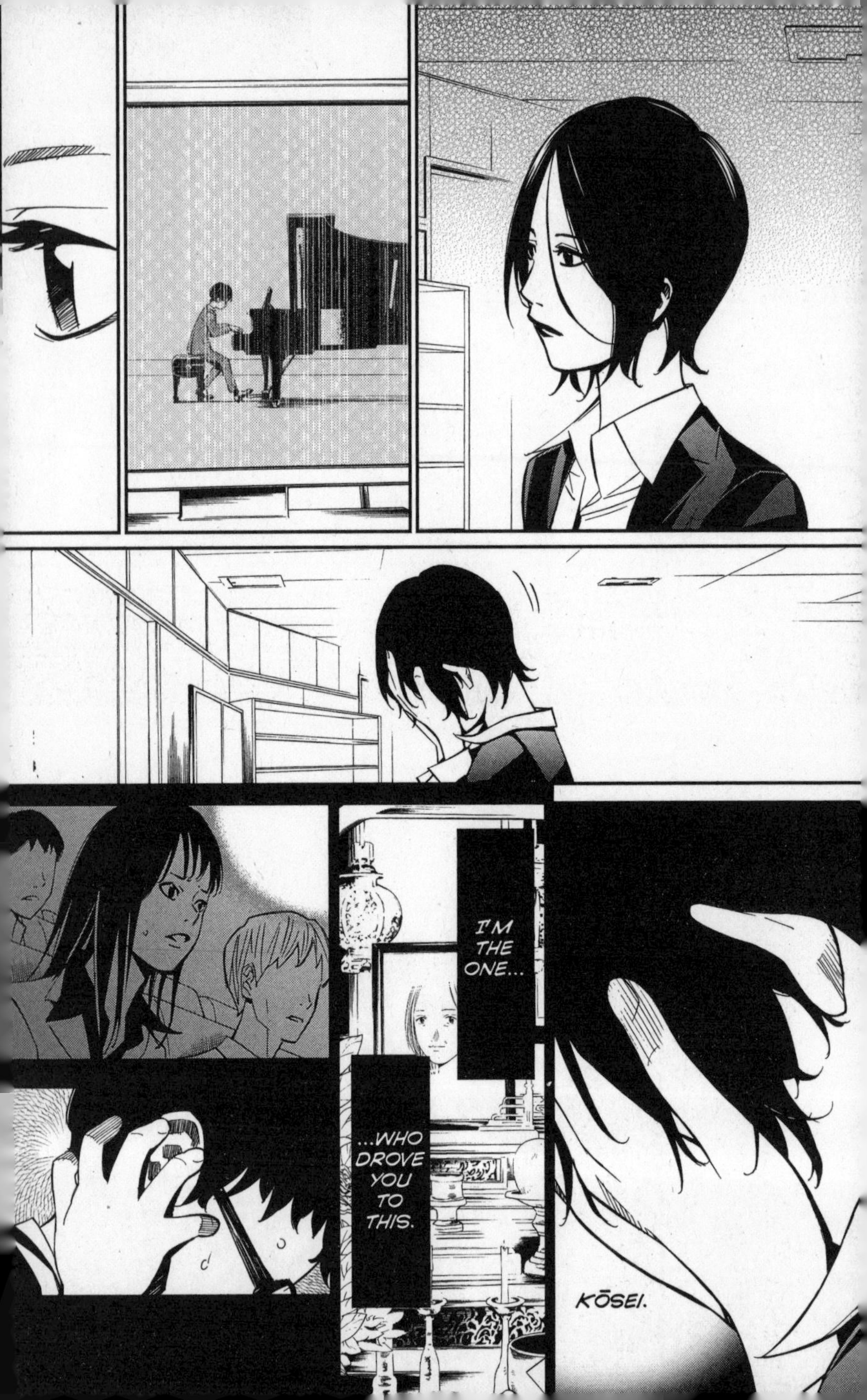
KŌSEI.
I'M THE ONE...
...WHO DROVE YOU TO THIS.

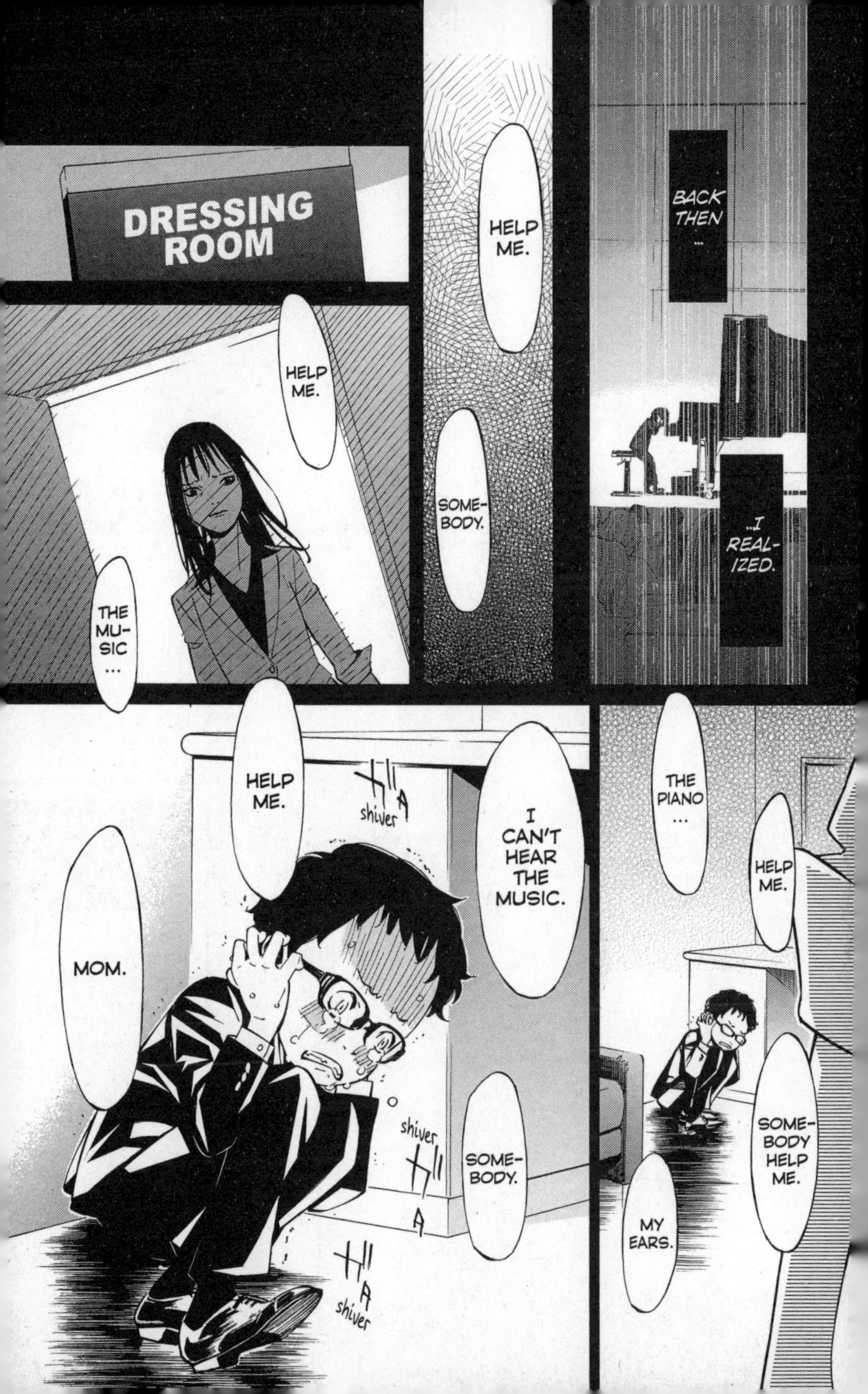

BACK THEN ...
...I REALIZED.
HELP ME.
SOME-BODY.
DRESSING ROOM
HELP ME.
THE MU-SIC ...
THE PIANO ...
HELP ME.
SOME-BODY HELP ME.
MY EARS.
I CAN'T HEAR THE MUSIC.
HELP ME.
shiver
MOM.
SOME-BODY.
shiver
shiver

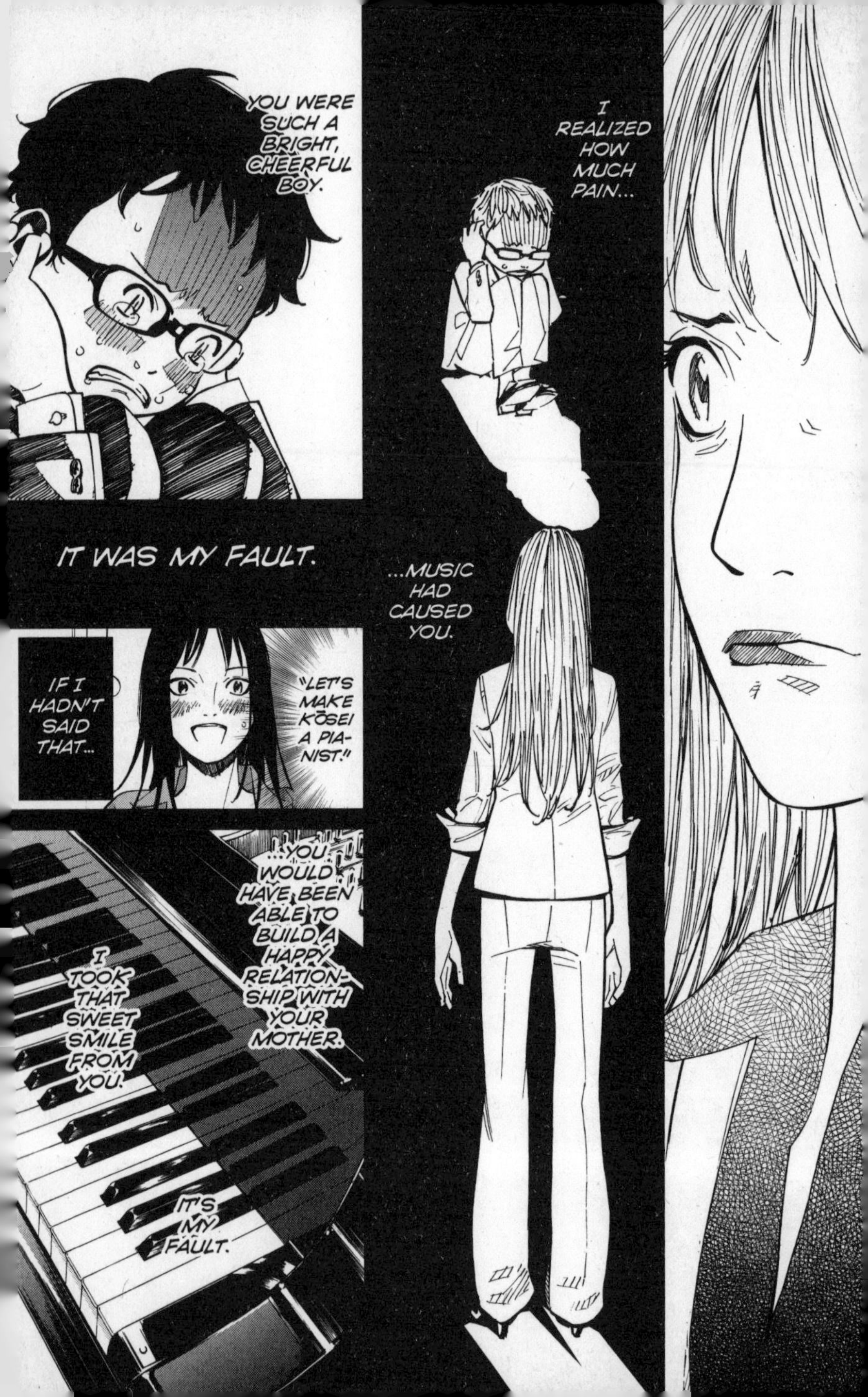
I REALIZED HOW MUCH PAIN...
...MUSIC HAD CAUSED YOU.
YOU WERE SUCH A BRIGHT, CHEERFUL BOY.
IT WAS MY FAULT.
"LET'S MAKE KŌSEI A PIANIST."
IF I HADN'T SAID THAT...
...YOU WOULD HAVE BEEN ABLE TO BUILD A HAPPY RELATIONSHIP WITH YOUR MOTHER.
I TOOK THAT SWEET SMILE FROM YOU.
IT'S MY FAULT.

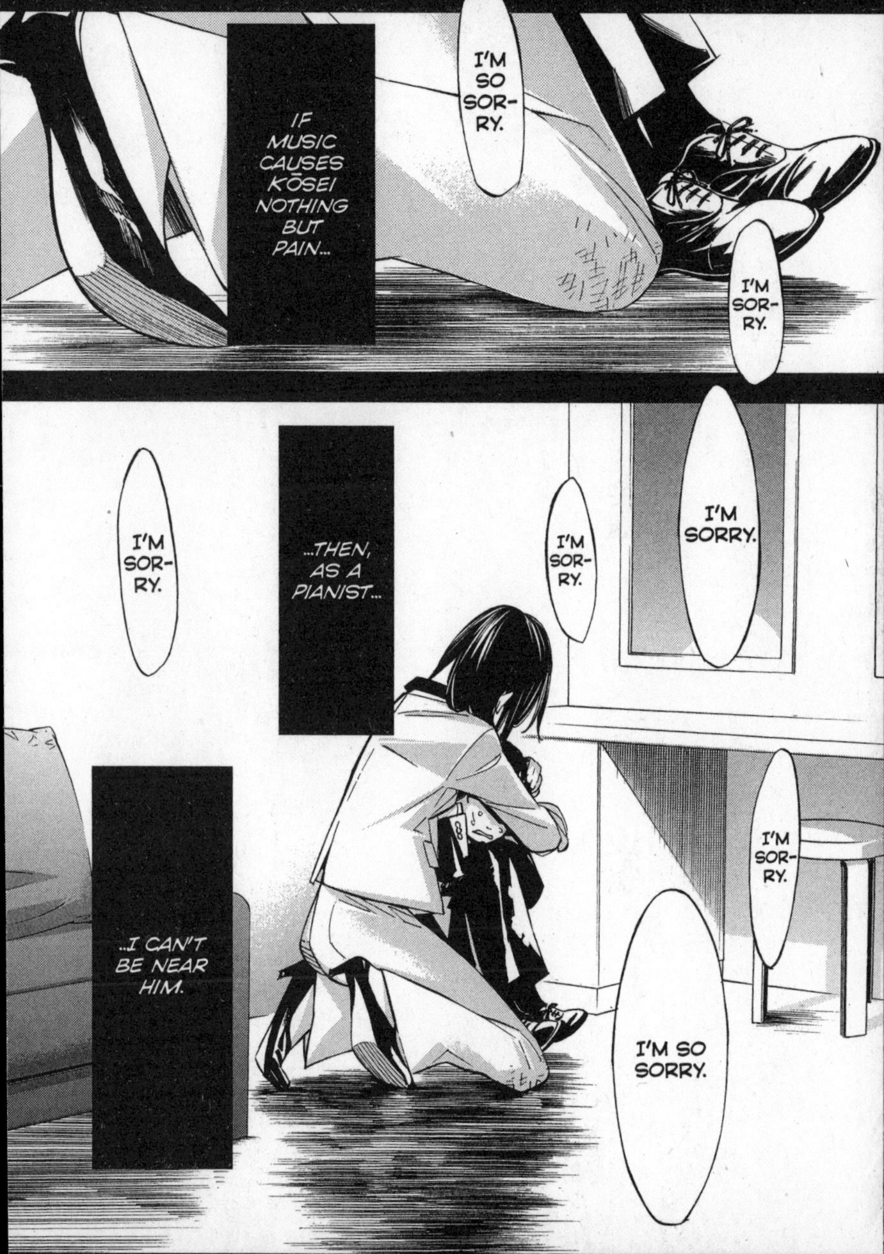
I'M SORRY.
I'M SO SORRY.
IF MUSIC CAUSES KŌSEI NOTHING BUT PAIN...
I'M SORRY.
I'M SORRY.
...THEN, AS A PIANIST...
I'M SORRY.
I'M SORRY.
I'M SO SORRY.
...I CAN'T BE NEAR HIM.

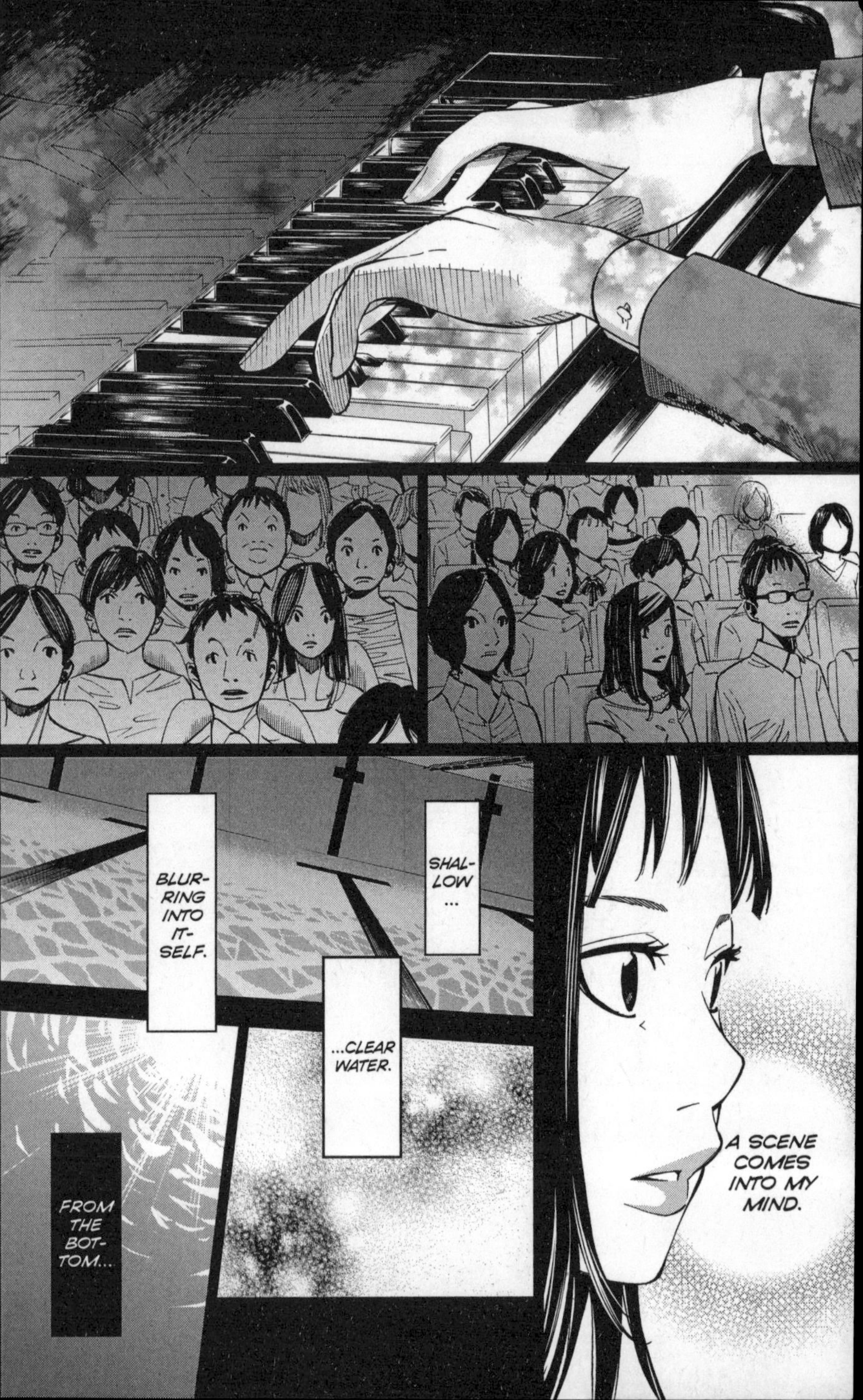
A SCENE COMES INTO MY MIND.
SHAL-LOW...
BLUR-RING INTO IT-SELF.
...CLEAR WATER.
FROM THE BOT-TOM...

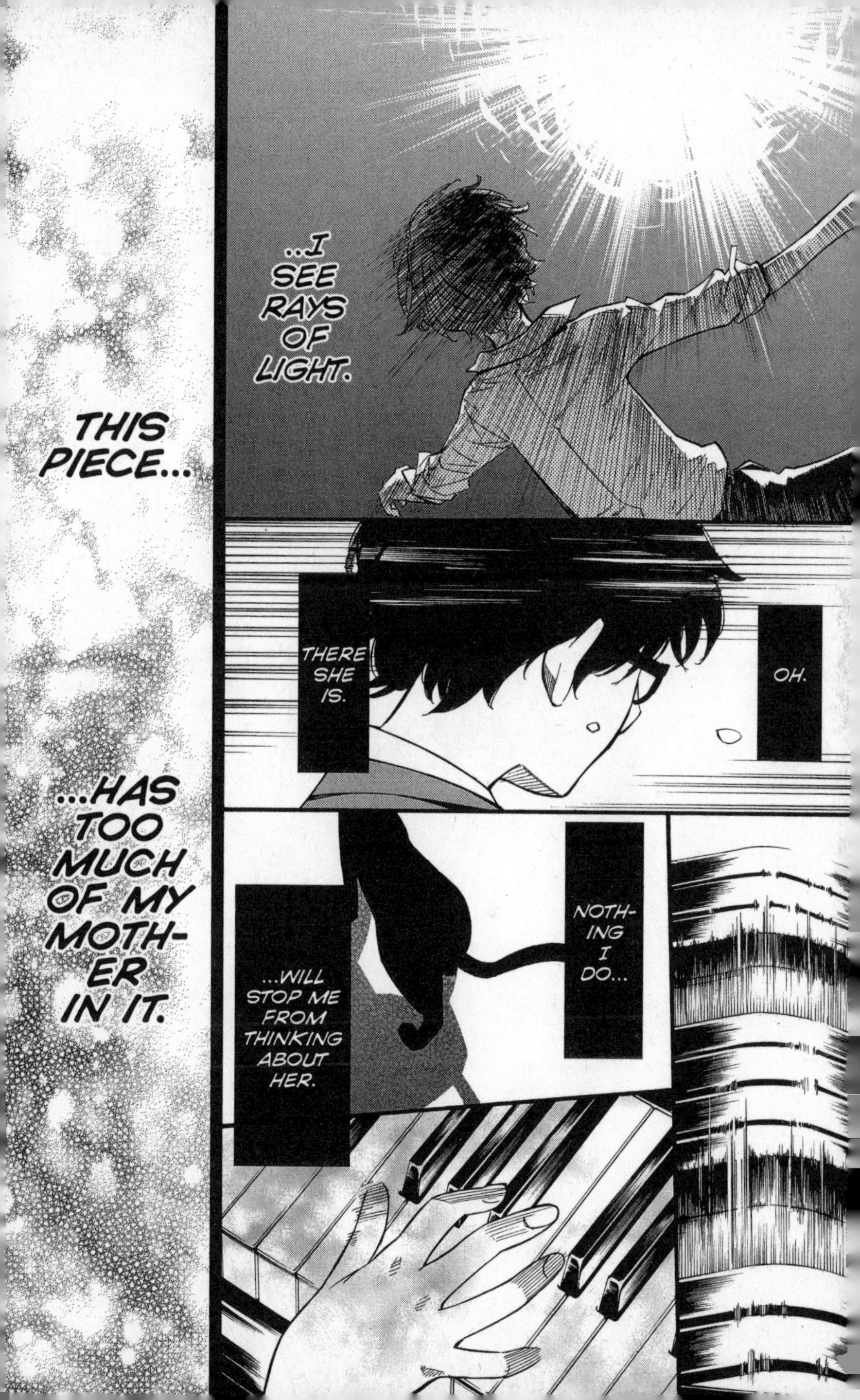
...I SEE RAYS OF LIGHT.
OH.
THERE SHE IS.
NOTHING I DO...
...WILL STOP ME FROM THINKING ABOUT HER.
THIS PIECE...
...HAS TOO MUCH OF MY MOTHER IN IT.

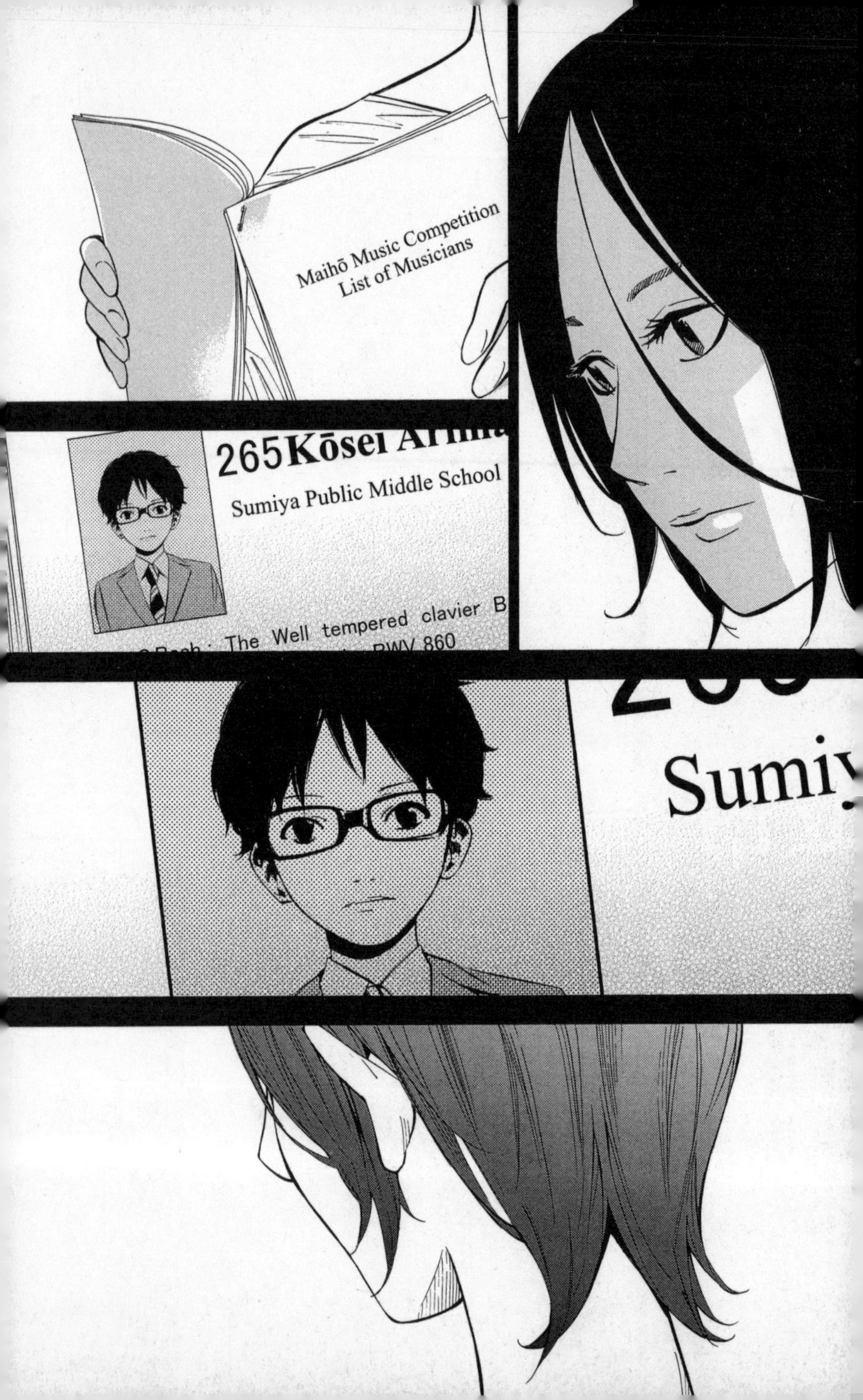
Maihō Music Competition
List of Musicians
265Kōsei
Sumiya Public Middle School
The Well tempered clavier B

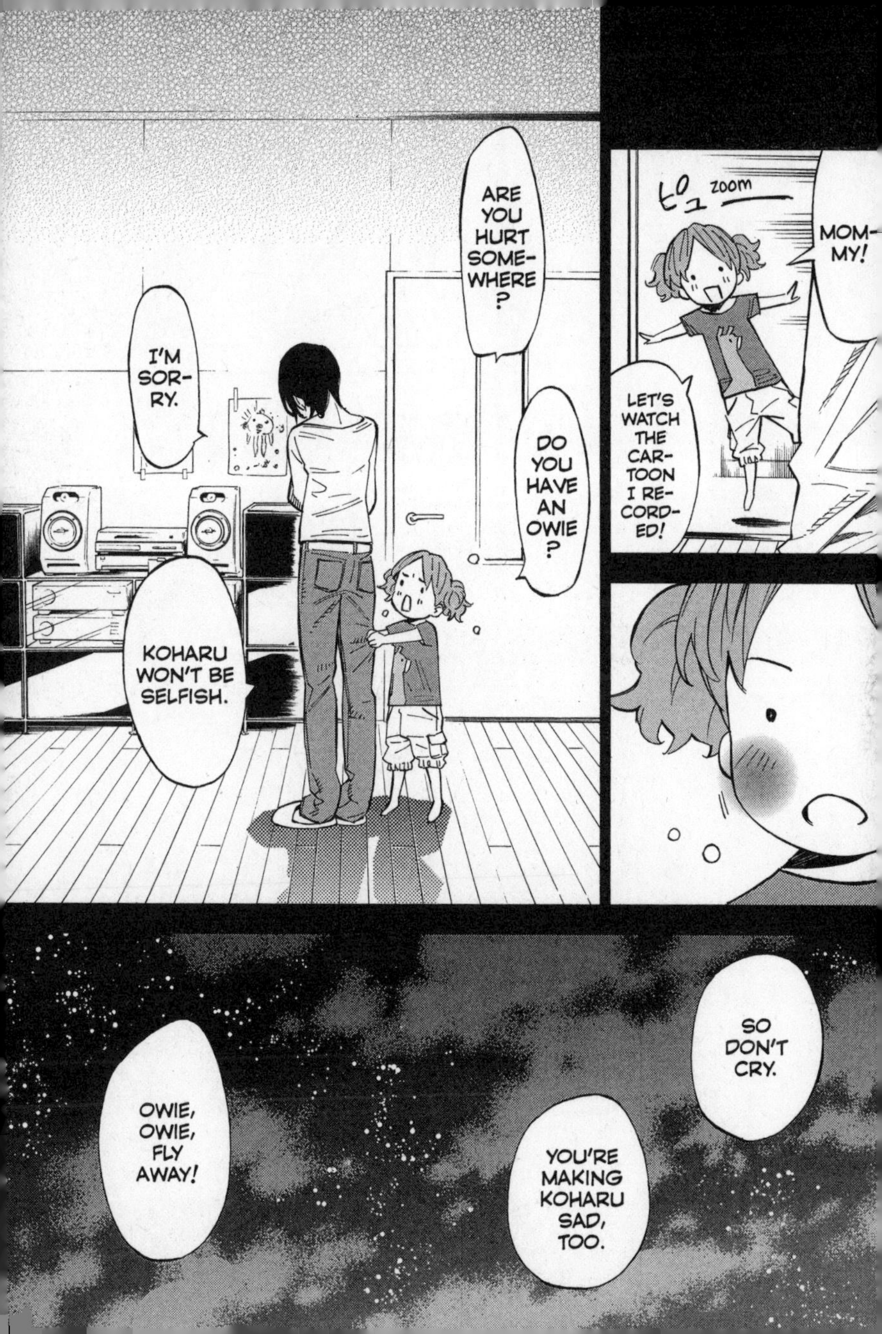
ピュ ZOOM
MOMMY!
LET'S WATCH THE CARTOON I RECORDED!
ARE YOU HURT SOMEWHERE?
DO YOU HAVE AN OWIE?
I'M SORRY.
KOHARU WON'T BE SELFISH.
SO DON'T CRY.
YOU'RE MAKING KOHARU SAD, TOO.
OWIE, OWIE, FLY AWAY!

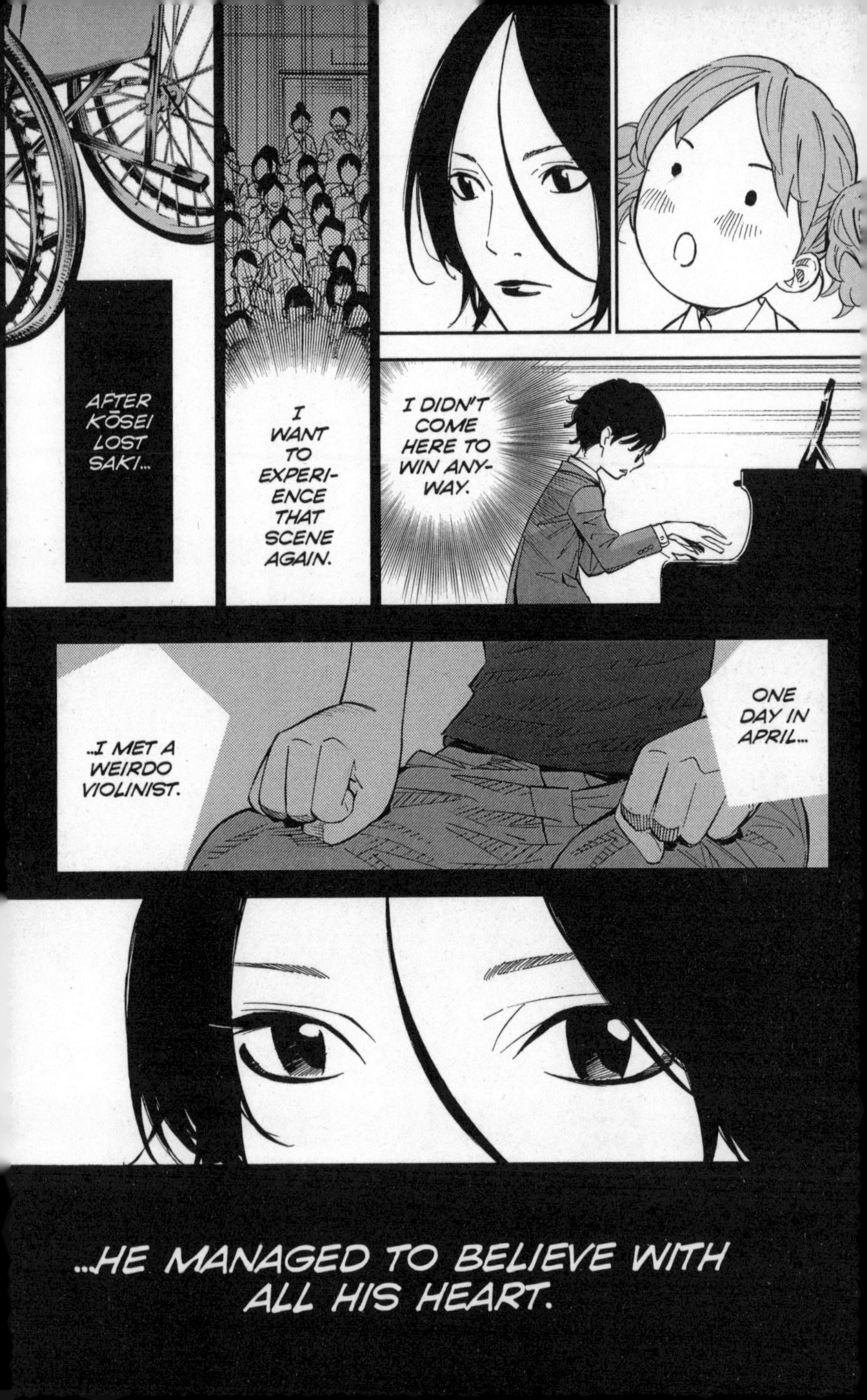
I DIDN'T COME HERE TO WIN ANY-WAY.
I WANT TO EXPERIENCE THAT SCENE AGAIN.
AFTER KŌSEI LOST SAKI...
ONE DAY IN APRIL...
...I MET A WEIRDO VIOLINIST.
...HE MANAGED TO BELIEVE WITH ALL HIS HEART.

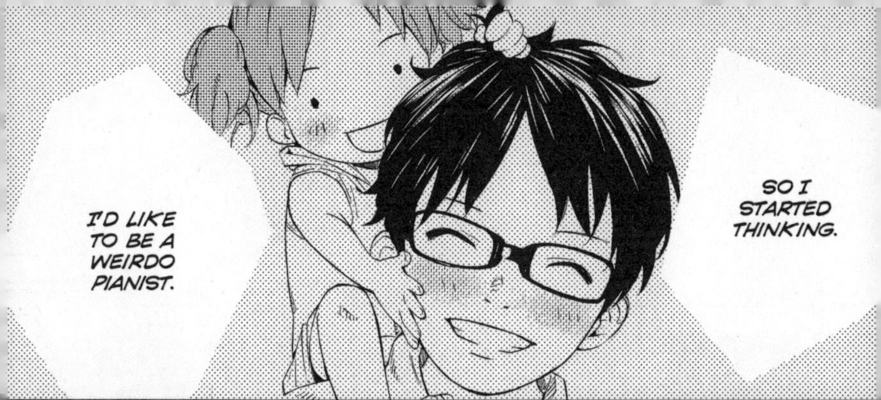
SO I STARTED THINKING.
I'D LIKE TO BE A WEIRDO PIANIST.
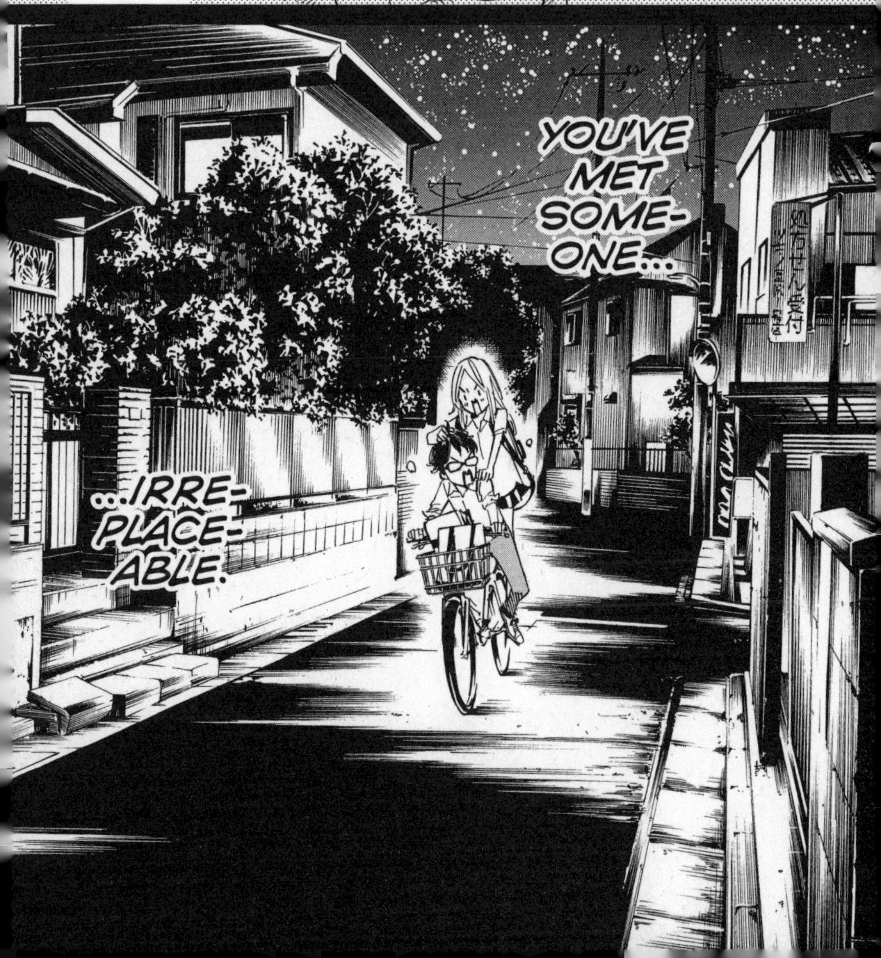
YOU'VE MET SOME-ONE...
...IRRE-PLACE-ABLE.

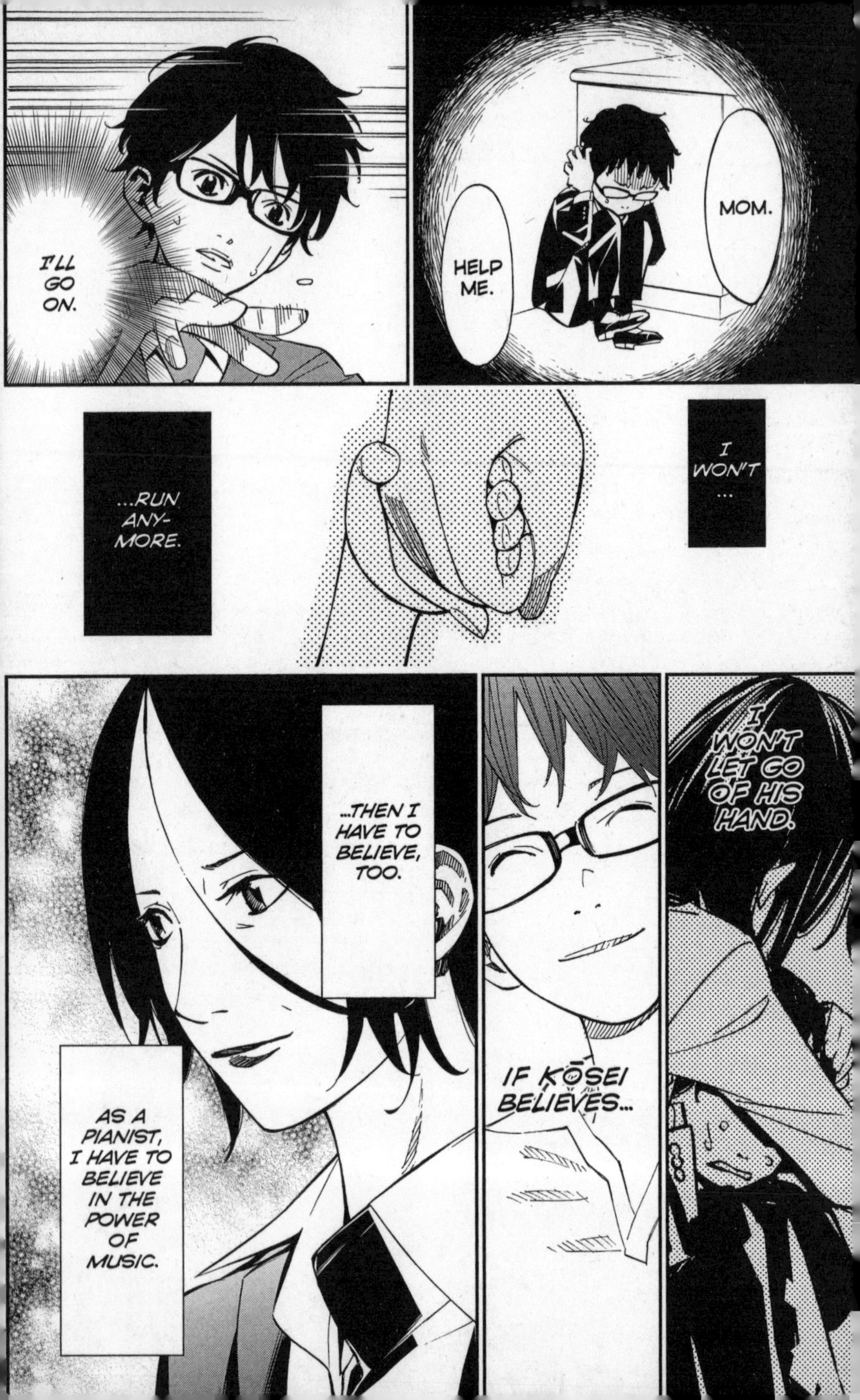
MOM.
HELP ME.
I'LL GO ON.
I WON'T...
...RUN ANYMORE.
I WON'T LET GO OF HIS HAND.
IF KŌSEI BELIEVES...
...THEN I HAVE TO BELIEVE, TOO.
AS A PIANIST, I HAVE TO BELIEVE IN THE POWER OF MUSIC.

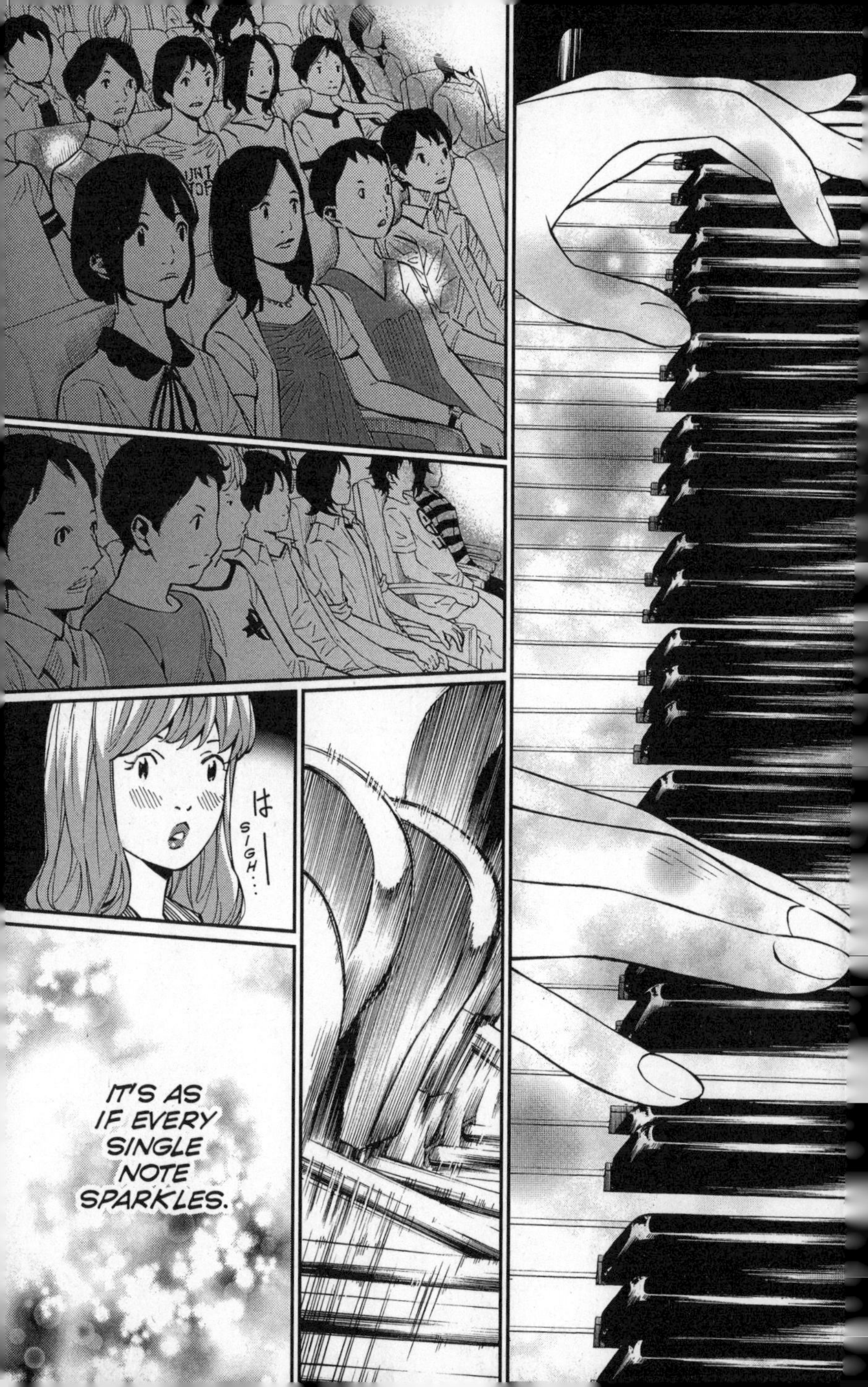

はー SIGH...
IT'S AS IF EVERY SINGLE NOTE SPARKLES.

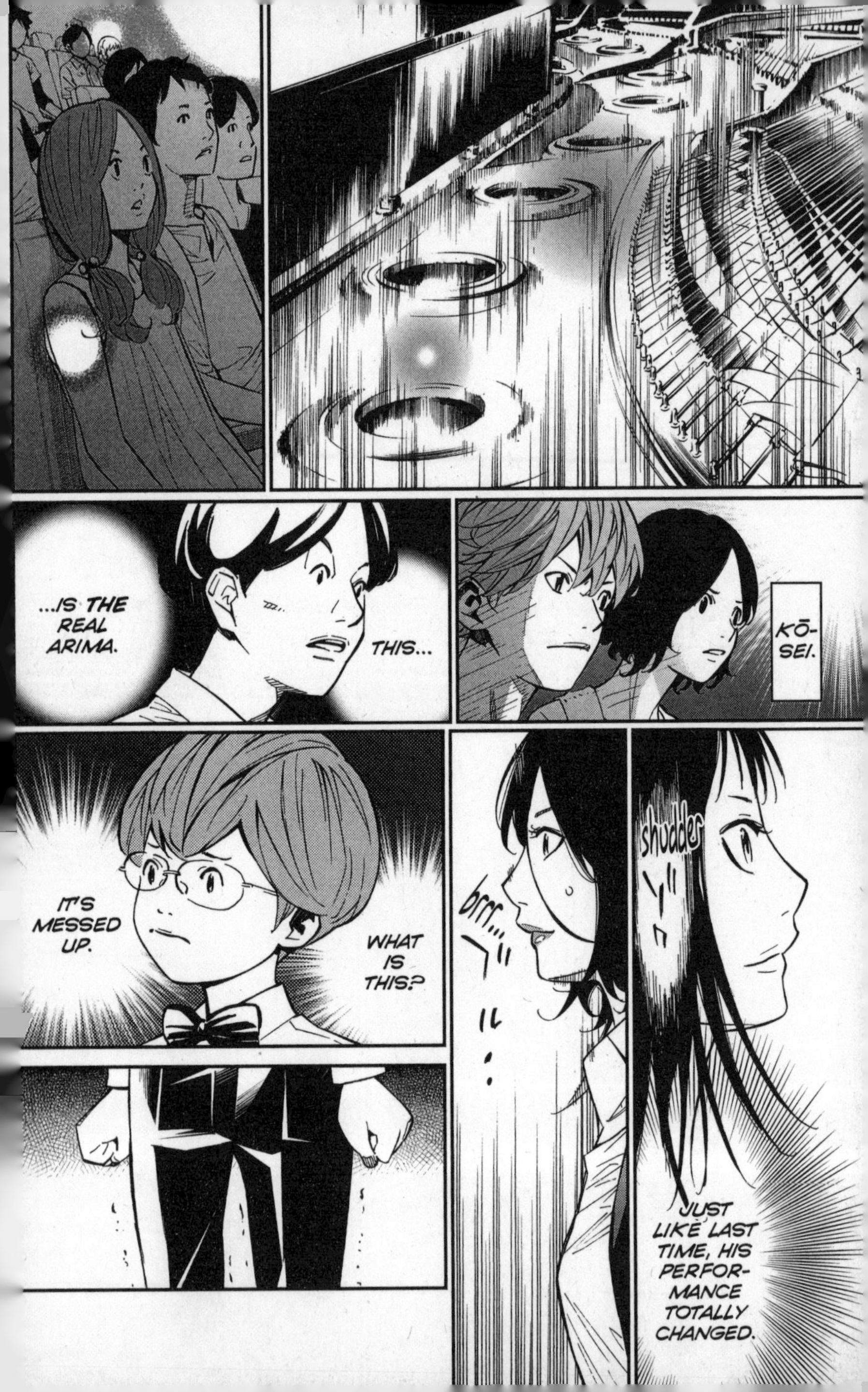
KŌ-
SEI.
THIS...
...IS THE REAL ARIMA.
shudder
JUST LIKE LAST TIME, HIS PERFORMANCE TOTALLY CHANGED.
brrr...
WHAT IS THIS?
IT'S MESSED UP.

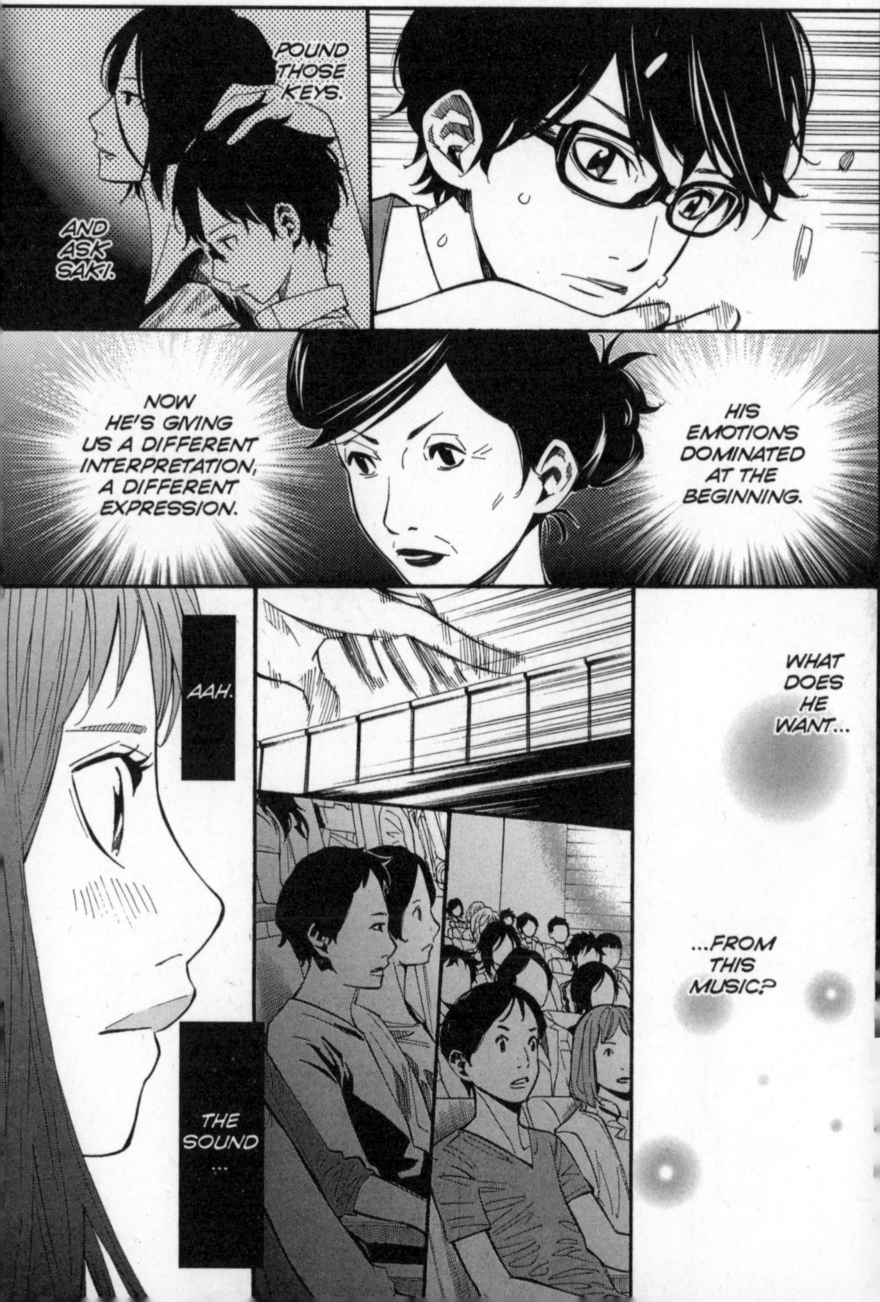
POUND THOSE KEYS.
AND ASK SAKI.
HIS EMOTIONS DOMINATED AT THE BEGINNING.
NOW HE'S GIVING US A DIFFERENT INTERPRETATION, A DIFFERENT EXPRESSION.
WHAT DOES HE WANT...
...FROM THIS MUSIC?
AAH.
THE SOUND...

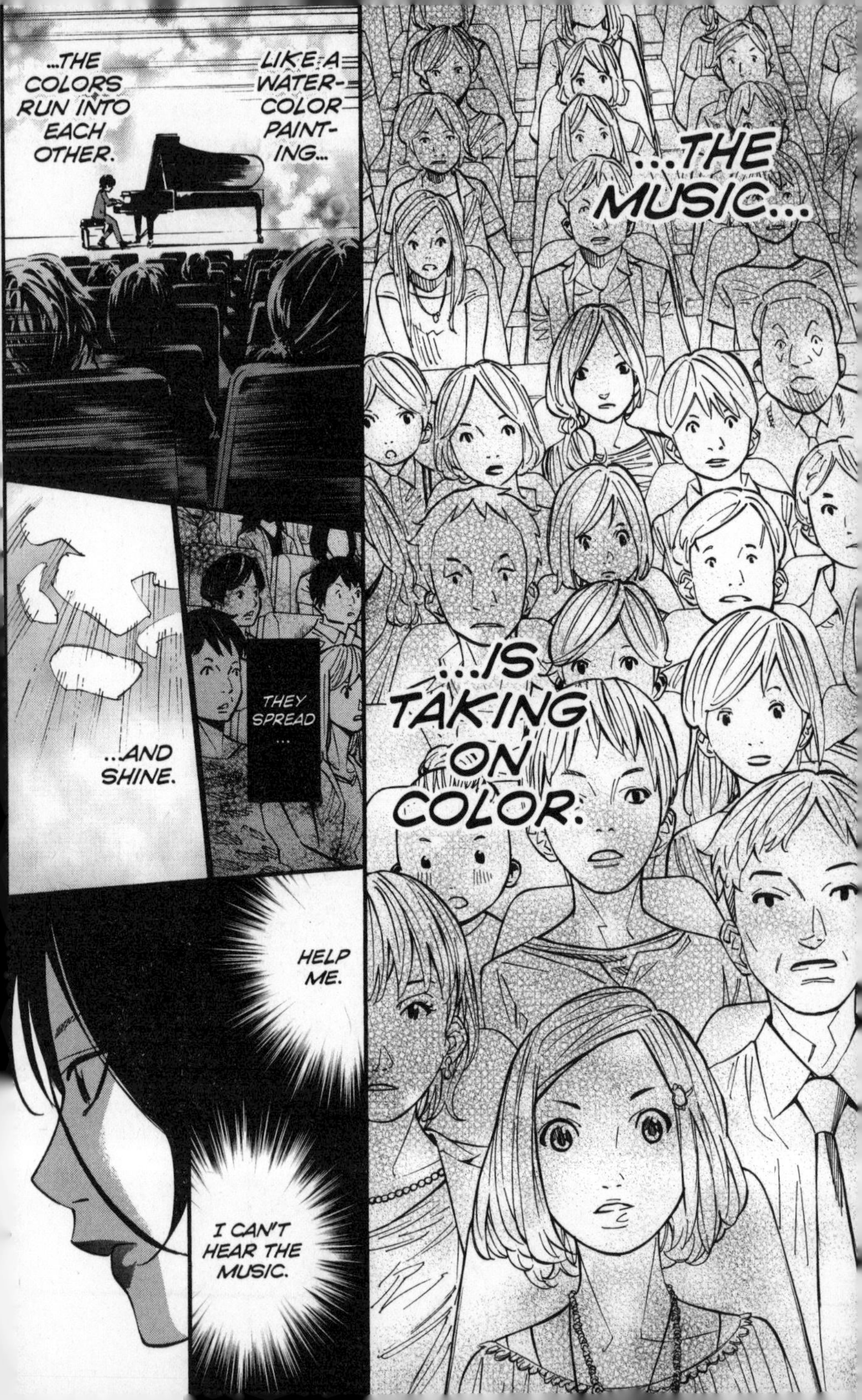
...THE MUSIC...
...IS TAKING ON COLOR.
LIKE A WATER-COLOR PAINT-ING...
...THE COLORS RUN INTO EACH OTHER.
THEY SPREAD ...
...AND SHINE.
HELP ME.
I CAN'T HEAR THE MUSIC.

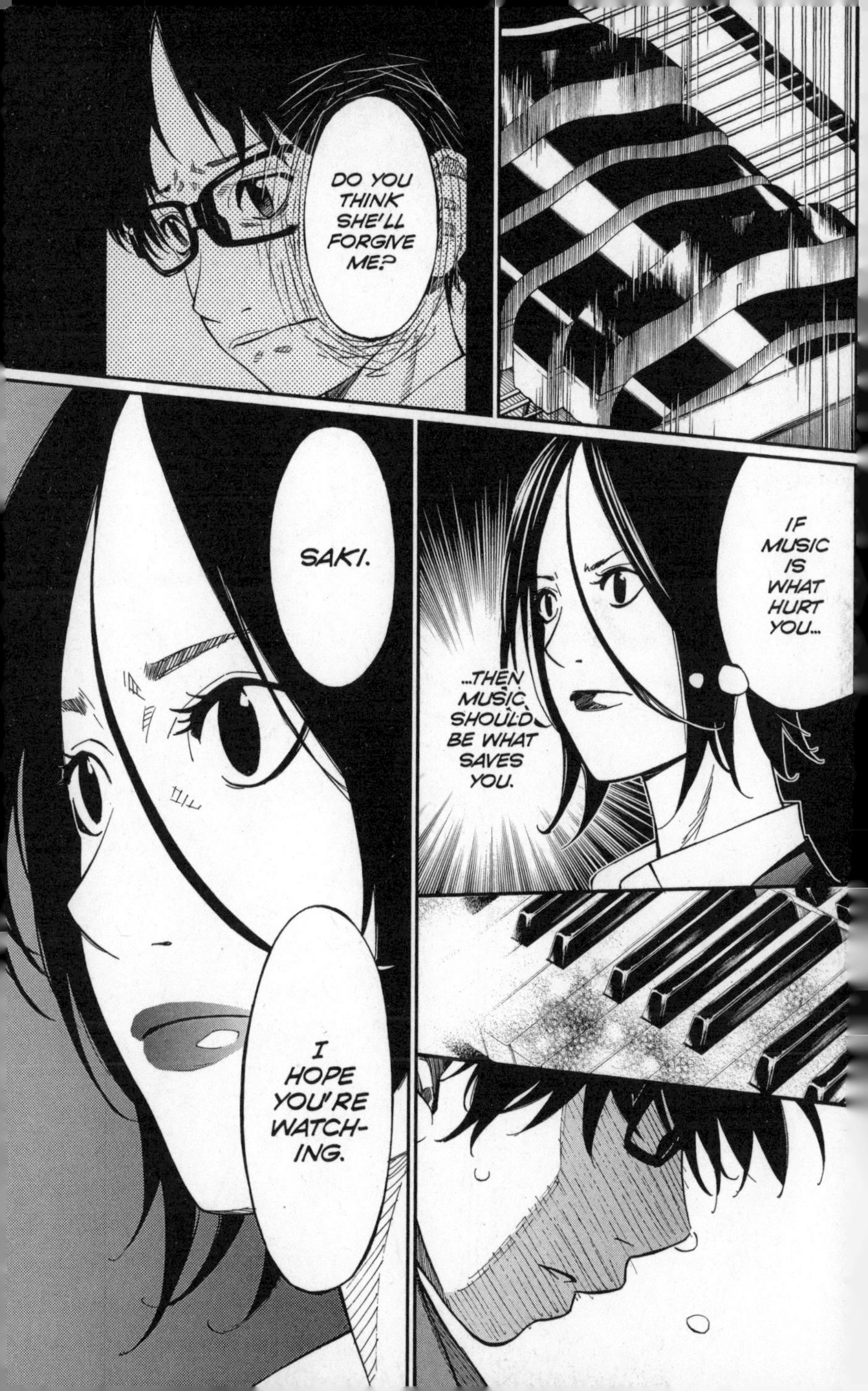
DO YOU THINK SHE'LL FORGIVE ME?
IF MUSIC IS WHAT HURT YOU...
...THEN MUSIC SHOULD BE WHAT SAVES YOU.
SAKI.
I HOPE YOU'RE WATCH-ING.

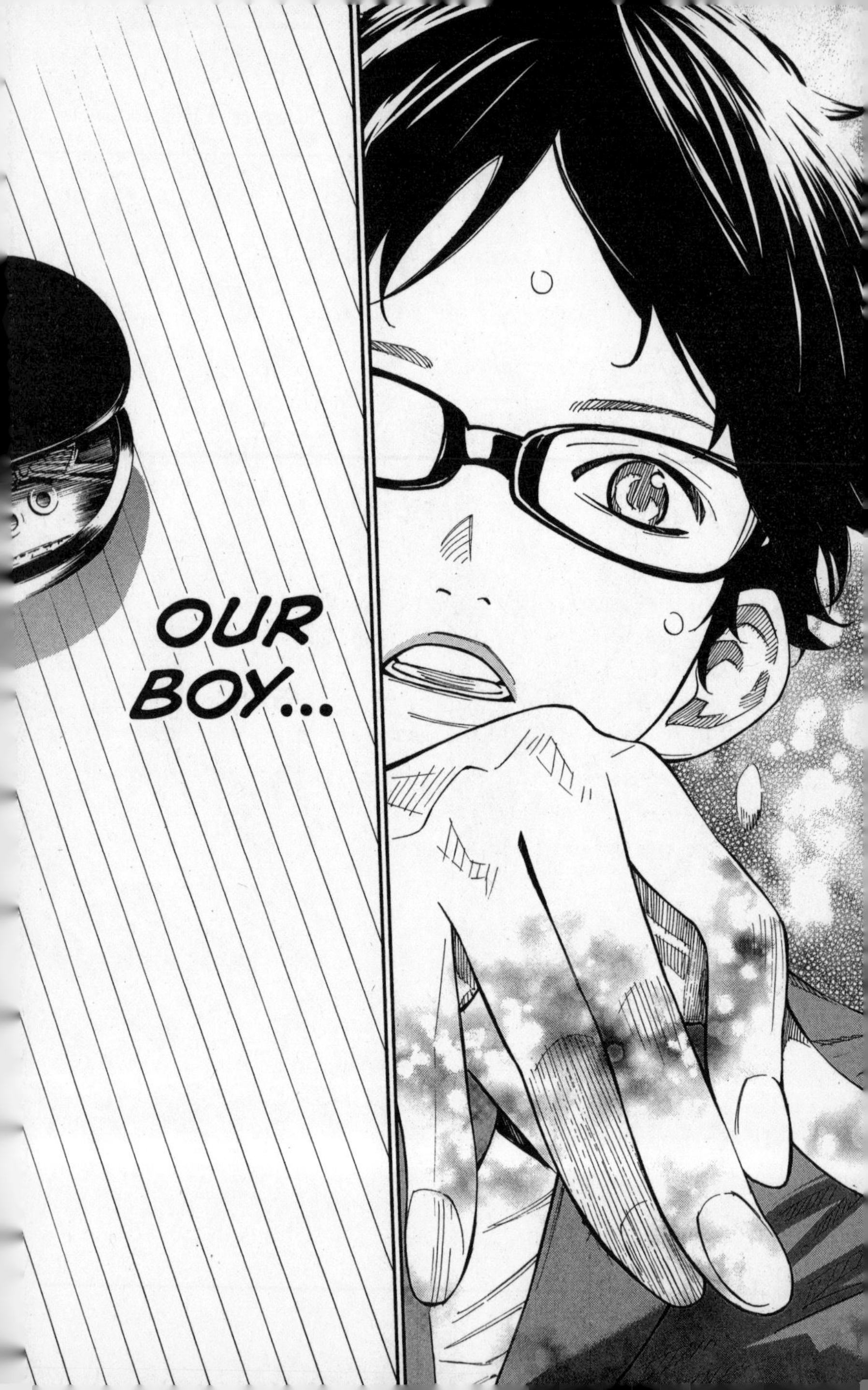
OUR BOY...

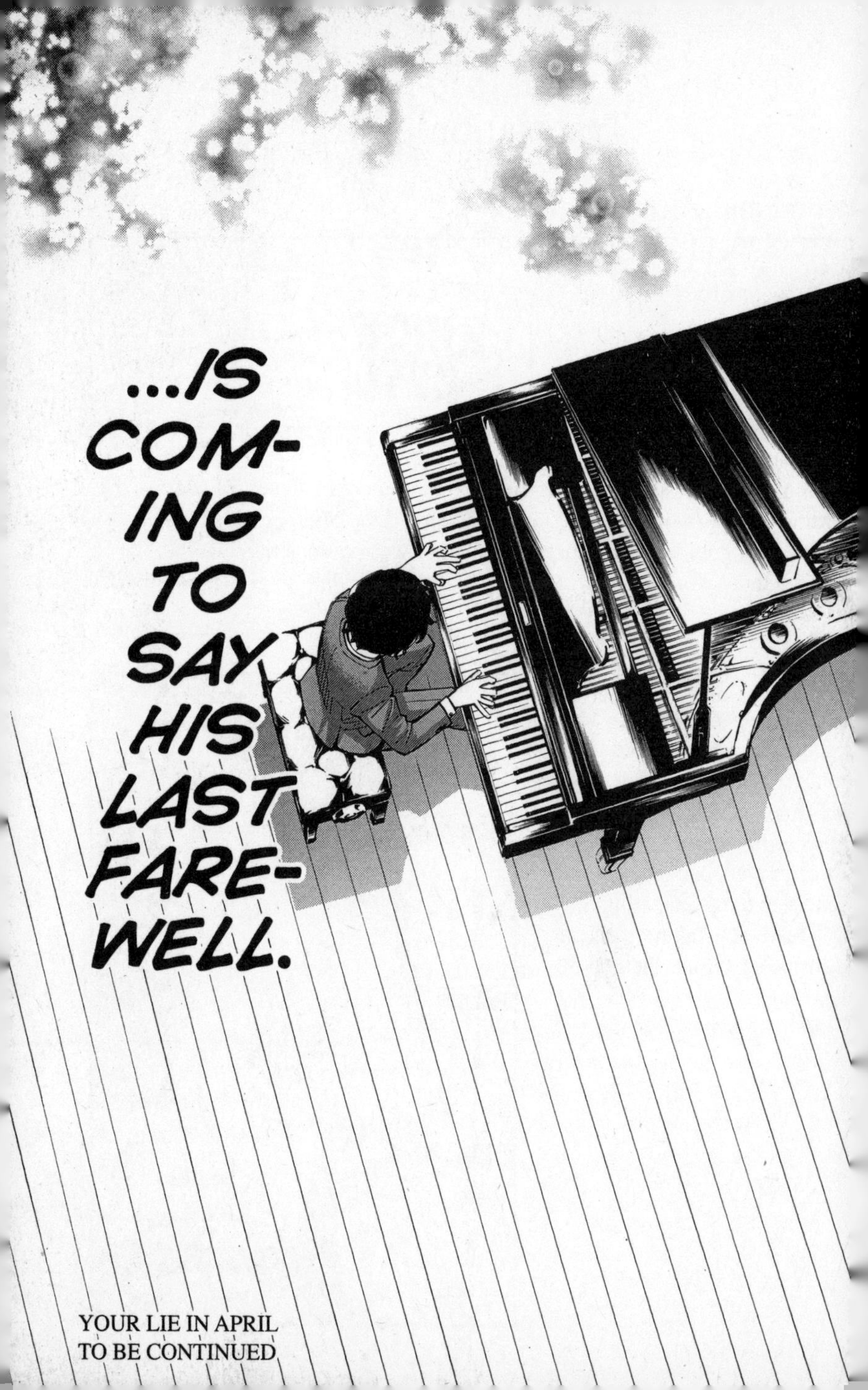
...IS COMING TO SAY HIS LAST FAREWELL.

YOUR LIE IN APRIL
TO BE CONTINUED

Translation Notes

Good audience, page 11

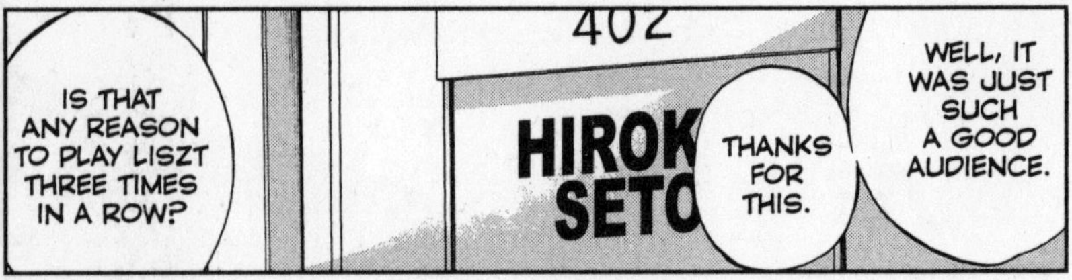
WELL, IT WAS JUST SUCH A GOOD AUDIENCE.
THANKS FOR THIS.
IS THAT ANY REASON TO PLAY LISZT THREE TIMES IN A ROW?

More specifically, Hiroko describes her audience as *nosejōzu*, which is a slightly more positive way of saying “manipulative”—they’re good at getting people on board with what they want. This often involves making people feel good about themselves. In other words, since they like her enough to ask for an encore, she was more than willing to give it to them... five times.

Prayer plaques, page 44

The plaques shown here are called *ema* and are used to write wishes or prayers that are then offered to the god or gods of the shrine. Many of these prayers concern passing school exams, indicating that this festival is taking place at a shrine of Tenjin, the god of learning.

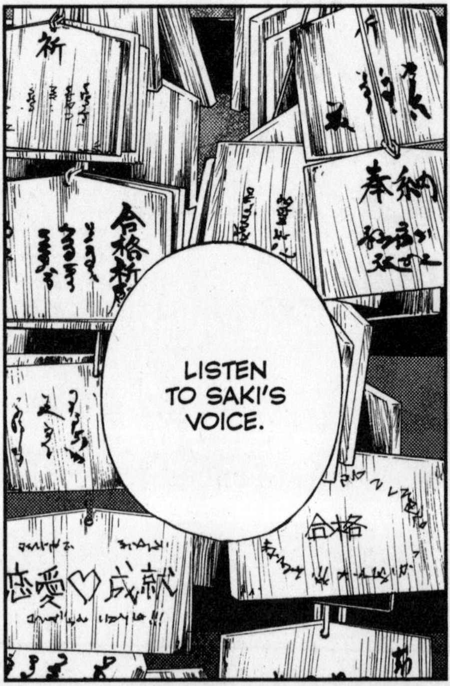
LISTEN TO SAKI'S VOICE.

Uji kintoki, page 57

Uji kintoki is a flavor of shaved ice that's actually a combination of two flavors, kind of like the Japanese version of Neapolitan. The flavors used are matcha green tea and azuki red bean.

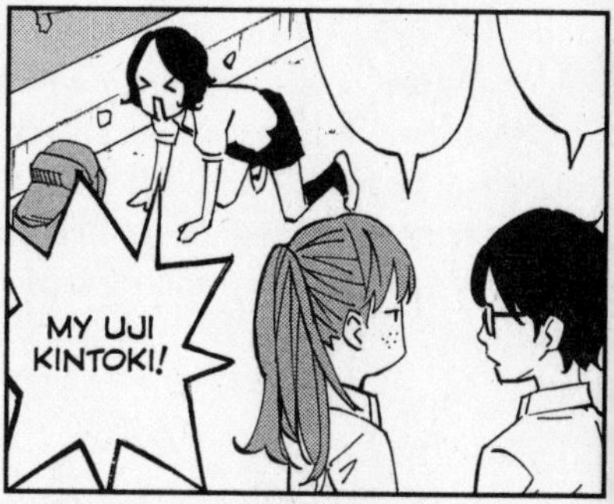
MY UJI KINTOKI!

Plebeian old hags, page 111

The word this young musician uses for "plebeian" is *miihaa*, which refers to someone who is easily swayed by the latest fads. In other words, he thinks they only like Kaori's music because it's the current "cool" thing to do and not because they know anything about quality violin music.

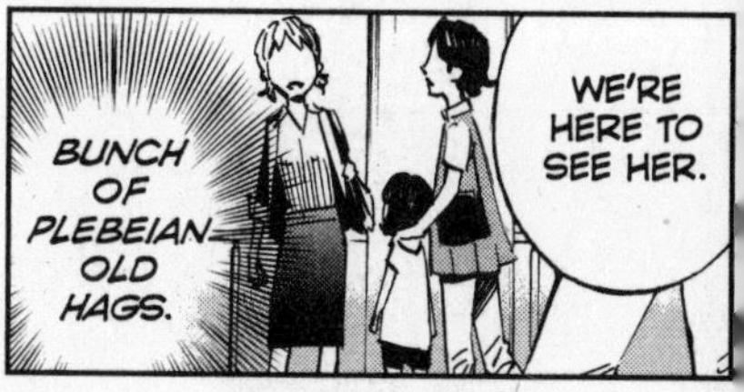
WE'RE HERE TO SEE HER.
BUNCH OF PLEBEIAN OLD HAGS.

Tsundere, page 114

A "tsundere" is someone who is usually prickly (*tsuntsun* in Japanese) but, under special conditions near that special someone, may show their tender (*deredere*) side.

Michelangeli and Pogorelić, page 119

Both of these people are famous pianists; apparently Kōsei doesn't know many violinists. Arturo Benedetti Michelangeli is considered one of the greatest pianists

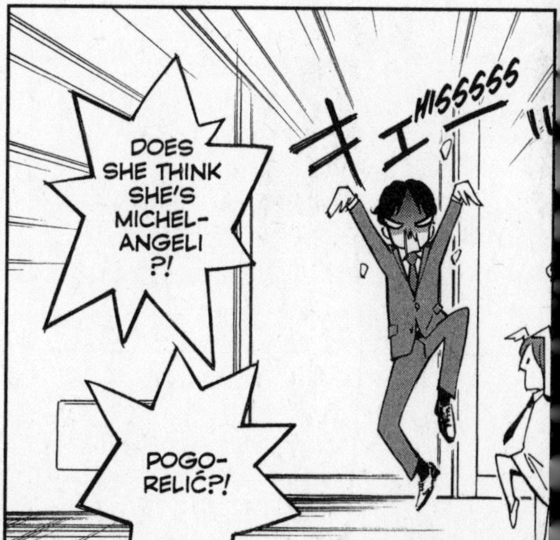
HISSSSS
DOES SHE THINK SHE'S MICHEL-ANGELI ?!
POGO-RELIĆ?!

famously did not like giving concerts. He was also known for playing pieces as perfectly as humanly possible, like the real-life version of Kōsei. Ivo Pogorelić was known for his eccentric and controversial interpretations of music; he made himself famous by losing the Chopin Piano Competition, causing one of the judges (another famous pianist, Martha Argerich) to resign from the jury in protest of what she thought was a mistake in judging.

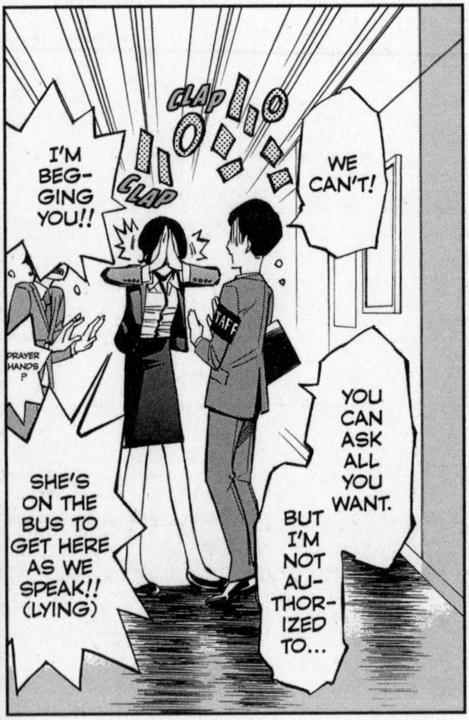
WE CAN'T!
CLAP
CLAP
I'M BEG- GING YOU!!
PRAYER HANDS?
YOU CAN ASK ALL YOU WANT.
BUT I'M NOT AU- THOR- IZED TO...
SHE'S ON THE BUS TO GET HERE AS WE SPEAK!! (LYING)

Prayer hands, page 124

Hiroko is clapping her hands in a way very similar to the clapping done at Shinto shrines to honor the gods there and request favors from them. In other words, she's treating this staff member with the same respect she would a god—or is at least making a show of such respect.

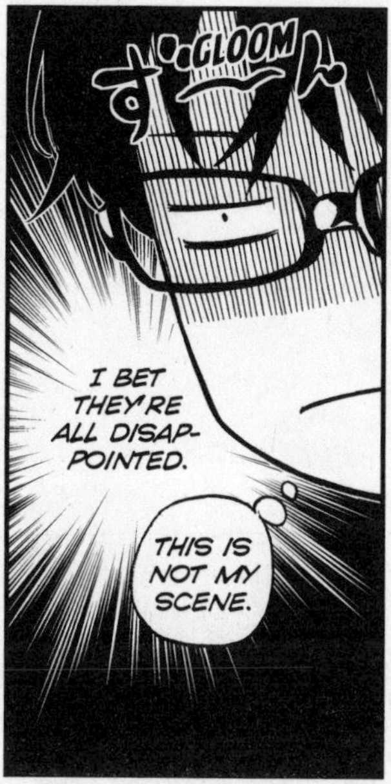
GLOOM
I BET THEY'RE ALL DISAPPOINTED.
THIS IS NOT MY SCENE.

Not my scene, page 139

What Kōsei says here is a play on words: *gara ja nai* usually means "this is not my style," but in this case the phrase has a double meaning—he's at the gala (*gara*) concert, so it's not his gala in addition to not being his style. It is the translators' hope that, while their rendering of the line doesn't have quite the same meaning as "not my style," it still reflects Kōsei's feelings of insecurity, knowing the audience hasn't come to listen to him.

Owie, owie, fly away, page 181

To make someone feel better when they have a boo-boo, it's common to put one's hands over the injury and make a gesture to indicate tossing the pain away. This is a placebo much like "kissing it better."

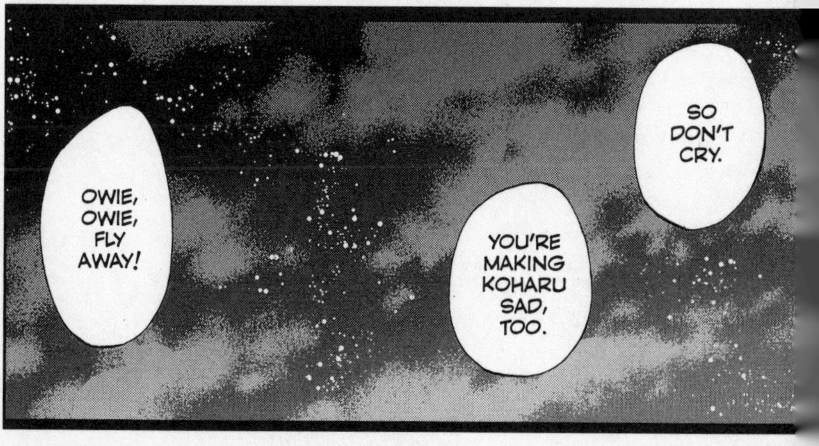
SO DON'T CRY.
YOU'RE MAKING KOHARU SAD, TOO.
OWIE, OWIE, FLY AWAY!

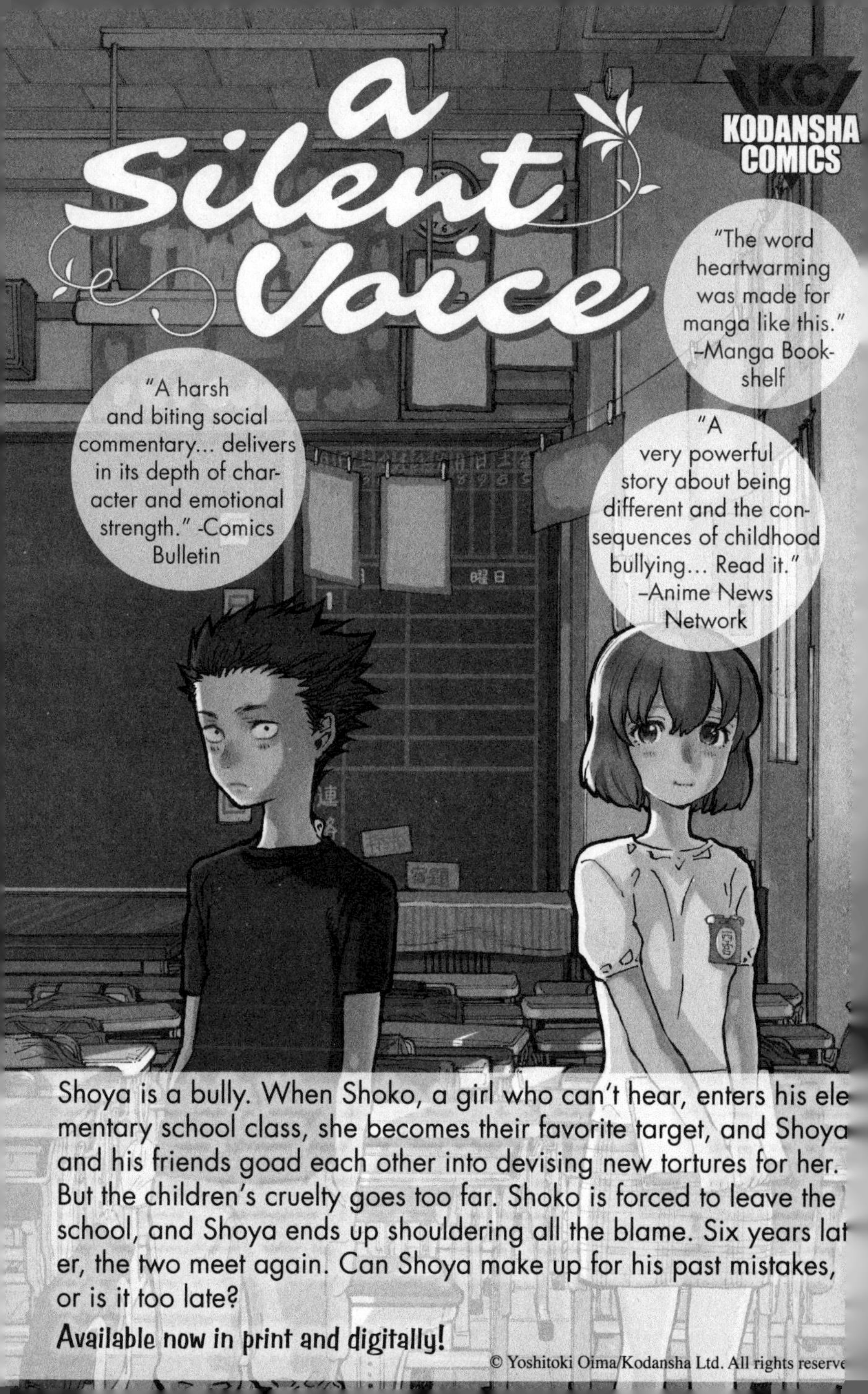
a Silent Voice
KODANSHA COMICS
"The word heartwarming was made for manga like this." –Manga Bookshelf
"A harsh and biting social commentary... delivers in its depth of character and emotional strength." -Comics Bulletin
"A very powerful story about being different and the consequences of childhood bullying… Read it." –Anime News Network
Shoya is a bully. When Shoko, a girl who can't hear, enters his ele
mentary school class, she becomes their favorite target, and Shoya
and his friends goad each other into devising new tortures for her.
But the children's cruelty goes too far. Shoko is forced to leave the
school, and Shoya ends up shouldering all the blame. Six years lat
er, the two meet again. Can Shoya make up for his past mistakes,
or is it too late?
Available now in print and digitally!
© Yoshitoki Oima/Kodansha Ltd. All rights reserve

FINALLY, A LOWER-COST OMNIBUS EDITION OF FAIRY TAIL! CONTAINS VOLUMES 1-5. ONLY $39.99!

-NEARLY 1,000 PAGES!
-EXTRA LARGE 7"x10.5" TRIM SIZE!
-HIGH-QUALITY PAPER!

KC
KODANSHA
COMICS

Fairy Tail takes place in a world filled with magic. 17-year-old Lucy is a wizard-in-training who wants to join a magic guild so that she can become a full-fledged wizard. She dreams of joining the most famous guild, known as Fairy Tail. One day she meets Natsu, a boy raised by a dragon which vanished when he was young. Natsu has devoted his life to finding his dragon father. When Natsu helps Lucy out of a tricky situation, she discovers that he is a member of Fairy Tail, and our heroes' adventure together begins.

FAIRY TAIL

MASTER'S EDITION

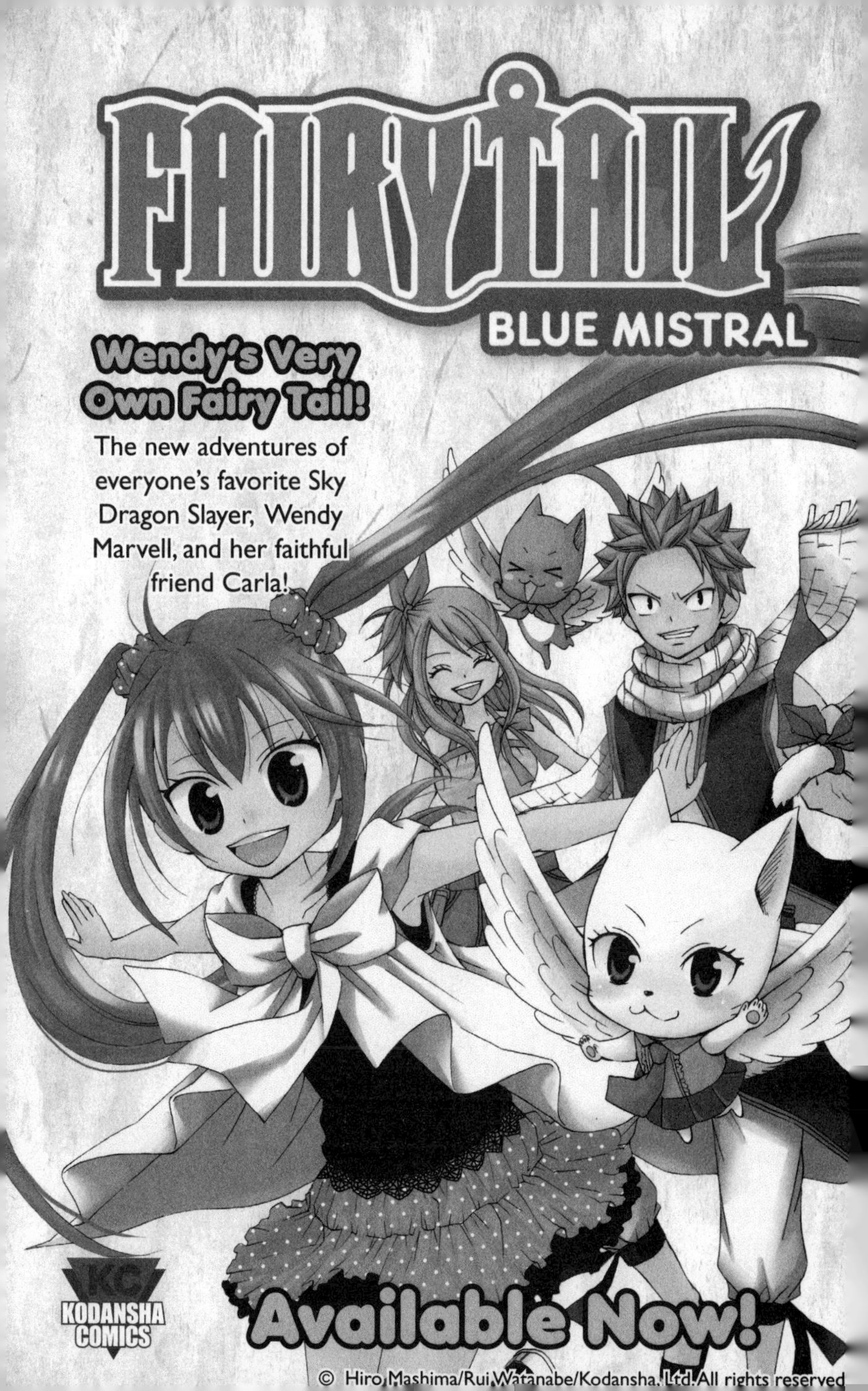

FAIRY TAIL
BLUE MISTRAL

Wendy's Very Own Fairy Tail!

The new adventures of everyone's favorite Sky Dragon Slayer, Wendy Marvell, and her faithful friend Carla!

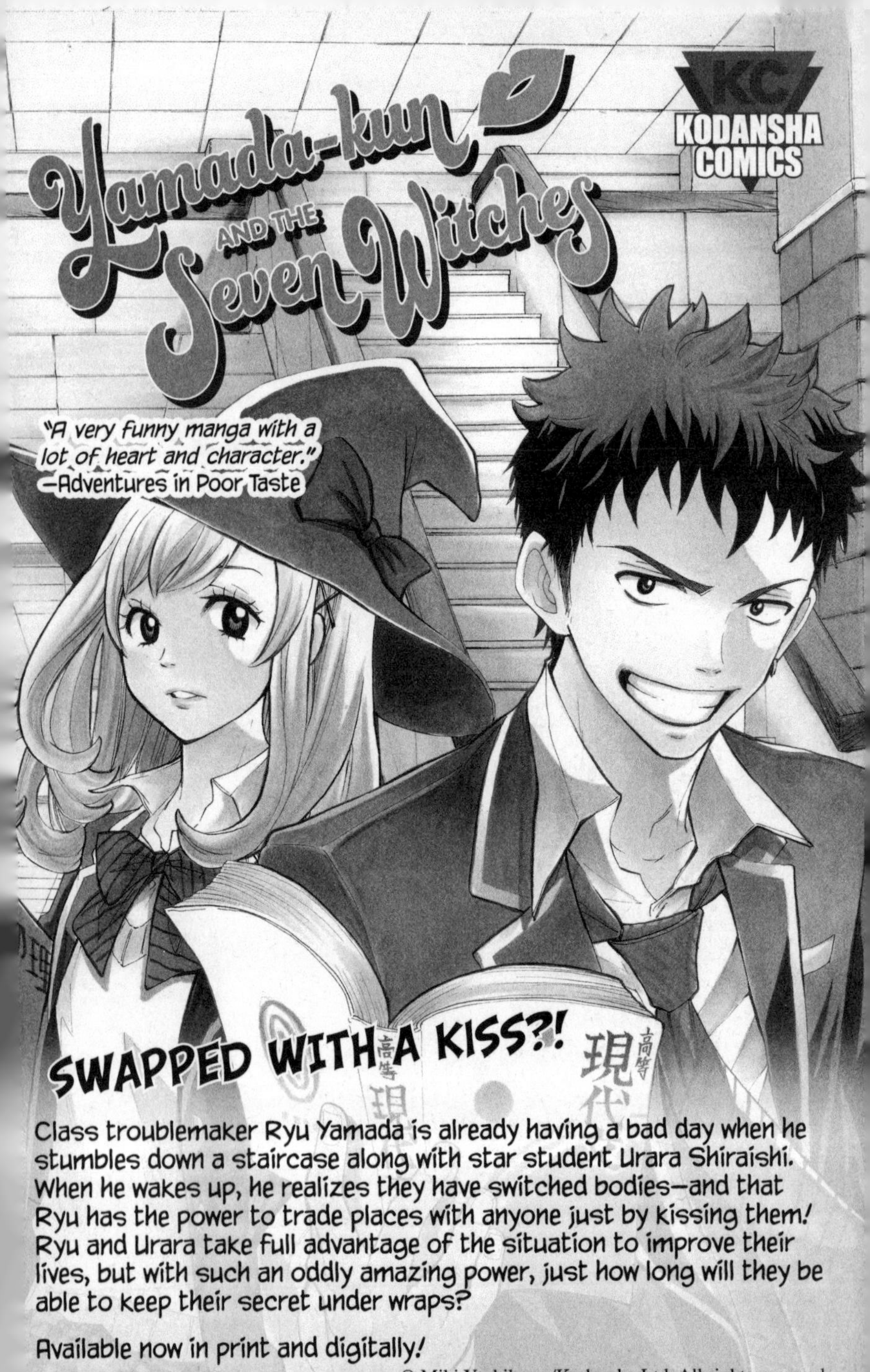
KC KODANSHA COMICS
Yamada-kun AND THE Seven Witches
"A very funny manga with a lot of heart and character."
—Adventures in Poor Taste
SWAPPED WITH A KISS?!
Class troublemaker Ryu Yamada is already having a bad day when he stumbles down a staircase along with star student Urara Shiraishi. When he wakes up, he realizes they have switched bodies—and that Ryu has the power to trade places with anyone just by kissing them! Ryu and Urara take full advantage of the situation to improve their lives, but with such an oddly amazing power, just how long will they be able to keep their secret under wraps?
Available now in print and digitally!

Say I Love You.

Mei Tachibana has no friends — and says she doesn't need them!
But everything changes when she accidentally roundhouse kicks the most popular boy in school! However, Yamato Kurosawa isn't angry in the slightest—in fact, he thinks his ordinary life could use an unusual girl like Mei. But winning Mei's trust will be a tough task. How long will she refuse to say, "I love you"?

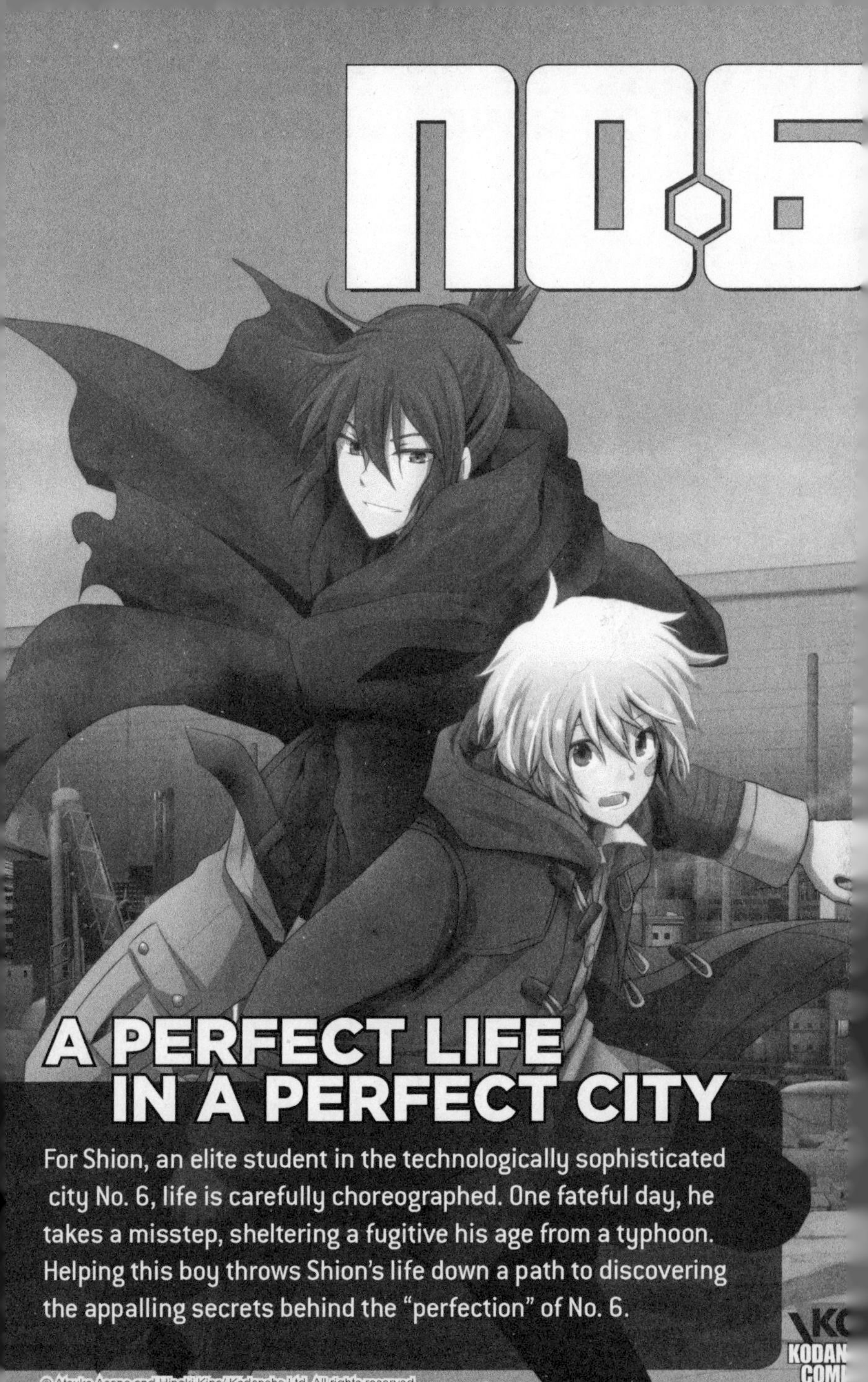
NO.6
A PERFECT LIFE IN A PERFECT CITY
For Shion, an elite student in the technologically sophisticated city No. 6, life is carefully choreographed. One fateful day, he takes a misstep, sheltering a fugitive his age from a typhoon. Helping this boy throws Shion's life down a path to discovering the appalling secrets behind the "perfection" of No. 6.

KODANSHA
COMICS

DEVIL SURVIVOR

AFTER DEMONS BREAK THROUGH INTO THE HUMAN WORLD, TOKYO MUST BE QUARANTINED. WITHOUT POWER AND STUCK IN A SUPERNATURAL WARZONE, 17-YEAR-OLD KAZUYA HAS ONLY ONE HOPE: HE MUST USE THE *"COMP,"* A DEVICE CREATED BY HIS COUSIN NAOYA CAPABLE OF SUMMONING AND SUBDUING DEMONS, TO DEFEAT THE INVADERS AND TAKE BACK THE CITY.

BASED ON THE POPULAR VIDEO GAME FRANCHISE B' *ATLUS!*

INUYASHIKI

A superhero like none you've ever seen, from the creator of "Gantz"!

Ichiro Inuyashiki is down on his luck. He looks much older than his 58 years, his children despise him, and his wife thinks he's a useless coward. So when he's diagnosed with stomach cancer and given three months to live, it seems the only one who'll miss him is his dog.

Then a blinding light fills the sky, and the old man is killed... only to wake up later in a body he almost recognizes as his own. Can it be that Ichiro Inuyashiki is no longer human?

Comes in extra-large editions with color pages!

KC KODANSHA COMICS

A Kodansha Comics Trade Paperback Original

Your Lie in April volume 6 copyright © 2013 Naoshi Arakawa
English translation copyright © 2016 Naoshi Arakawa

Published in the United States by Kodansha Comics, an imprint of Kodansha USA Publishing, LLC, New York.

Publication rights for this English edition arranged through Kodansha Ltd, Tokyo.

ISBN 978-1-63236-176-9

Special thanks:
Akinori Osawa, Rieko Ikeda, and Kaori Yamazaki

Printed in the United States of America.

www.kodanshacomics.com

9 8 7 6 5 4 3 2 1
Translation: Alethea and Athena Nibley
Lettering: Scott Brown
Editing: Abigail Blackman
Kodansha Comics edition cover design by Phil Balsman

TOMARE!

STOP

You're going the wrong way!

Manga is a completely different type of reading experience.

To start at the beginning, Go to the end!

That's right! Authentic manga is read the traditional Japanese way—from right to left, exactly the opposite of how American books are read. It's easy to follow: Just go to the other end of the book and read each page—and each panel—from right side to left side, starting at the top right. Now you're experiencing manga as it was meant to be!